THE EASY LATIN FAKE BOOK

Melody, Lyrics and Simplifie

100 Songs in THE Key of "C"

THE EASY LATIN FAKE BOOK

ISBN 978-1-4234-6371-9

HAL•LEONARD® CORPORATION

7777 W. BLUEMOUND RD. P.O. BOX 13819 MILWAUKEE, WI 53213

For all works contained herein:
Unauthorized copying, arranging, adapting, recording, Internet posting, public performance,
or other distribution of the printed music in this publication is an infringement of copyright.
Infringers are liable under the law.

Visit Hal Leonard Online at
www.halleonard.com

THE EASY LATIN FAKE BOOK

CONTENTS

4	INTRODUCTION	56	Feelings (¿Dime?)
6	Adiós	60	A Felicidade
5	Água De Beber (Water to Drink)	59	Flamingo
8	Always in My Heart (Siempre En Mi Corazón)	62	The Fool on the Hill
10	Amapola (Pretty Little Poppy)	64	Frenesí
12	Amor (Amor, Amor, Amor)	66	A Gay Ranchero
14	Anema E Core (With All My Heart)	68	The Gift! (Recado Bossa Nova)
16	Aquellos Ojos Verdes (Green Eyes)	70	The Girl from Ipanema (Garôta De Ipanema)
18	Bésame Mucho (Kiss Me Much)	72	Gitanerias
20	Blame It on the Bossa Nova	74	Granada
22	Brazil	78	Guadalajara
11	The Breeze and I	81	Guantanamera
24	Call Me	84	How Insensitive (Insensatez)
26	Carioca	82	I Get Ideas
28	Chega De Saudade (No More Blues)	86	It's Impossible (Somos Novios)
34	Cherry Pink and Apple Blossom White	88	Kiss of Fire
36	The Constant Rain (Chove Chuva)	83	La Cucaracha
31	Cuanto Le Gusta	92	Lisbon Antigua (In Old Lisbon)
38	Cumaná	91	Little Boat (O Barquinho)
40	A Day in the Life of a Fool (Manhã De Carnaval)	96	The Look of Love
44	Dindi	98	Love Me with All Your Heart (Cuando Calienta El Sol)
41	Don't Cry for Me Argentina	100	Malagueña
46	Don't Ever Go Away (Por Causa De Voce)	104	Mama Inez
48	El Choclo	106	Mambo Jambo (Que Rico El Mambo)
50	El Cumbanchero	95	Mambo #5
52	The End of a Love Affair	108	A Man and a Woman (Un Homme Et Une Femme)
54	Estate	103	Mañana

Page	Title
112	Maria Elena
114	Mas Que Nada
116	Meditation (Meditacāo)
111	Mi Vida
118	Miami Beach Rumba
120	More (Ti Guarderò Nel Cuore)
122	My Shawl
124	Negra Consentida (My Pet Brunette)
126	Never on Sunday
128	Noche Azul (Blue Night)
130	Noche De Ronda (Be Mine Tonight)
132	Once I Loved (Amor Em Paz) (Love in Peace)
134	One Note Samba (Samba De Uma Nota So)
136	Only Trust Your Heart
138	Our Language of Love
140	Perfidia
142	Poinciana (Song of the Tree)
144	Quiet Nights of Quiet Stars (Corcovado)
146	Quizás, Quizás, Quizás (Perhaps, Perhaps, Perhaps)
148	Retrato Em Branco E Preto
113	St. Thomas
150	Samba De Orfeu
152	Say "Sí, Sí"
154	She's a Carioca
156	Similau (See-me-lo)
158	Slightly Out of Tune (Desafinado)
160	Só Danco Samba (Jazz 'n' Samba)
162	So Nice (Summer Samba)
164	Someone to Light Up My Life (Se Todos Fossem Iguais A Voce)
166	Song of the Jet (Samba Do Avião)
168	South of the Border (Down Mexico Way)
170	Spanish Eyes
172	Speak Low
174	Sway (Quien Será)
176	Tango of Roses
178	Telephone Song
180	Tico Tico (Tico Tico No Fuba)
182	Time Was
184	Triste
186	Vaya Con Dios (May God Be with You)
188	Vivo Sonhando (Dreamer)
190	Watch What Happens
192	Wave
139	What a Diff'rence a Day Made
194	Yellow Days
196	You Belong to My Heart (Solamente Una Vez)
157	Yours (Cuando Se Quiere De Veras)
198	CHORD SPELLER

INTRODUCTION

What Is a Fake Book?

A fake book has one-line music notation consisting of melody, lyrics and chord symbols.

This lead sheet format is a "musical shorthand" which is an invaluable resource for all musicians—hobbyists to professionals.

Here's how *The Easy Latin Fake Book* differs from most standard fake books:

- All songs are in the key of C.

- Many of the melodies have been simplified.

- Only five basic chord types are used—major, minor, seventh, diminished and augmented.

- The music notation is larger for ease of reading.

In the event that you haven't used chord symbols to create accompaniment, or your experience is limited, a chord speller chart is included at the back of the book to help you get started.

Have fun!

ÁGUA DE BEBER
(Water to Drink)

Copyright © 1961, 1970 by EDIZIONI CAMPIDOGLIO - Roma Via D. Montverde, 11, Italy
English Lyrics Copyright © 1965 BEXHILL MUSIC CORP. and NORMAN GIMBEL for the World
Copyright Renewed
All Rights Administered by GIMBEL MUSIC GROUP, INC. (P.O. Box 15221, Beverly Hills, CA 90209 USA),
CORCOVADO MUSIC CORP., New York, NY and VM ENTERPRISES, INC., New York, NY
All Rights Reserved   Used by Permission

English Words by NORMAN GIMBEL
Portuguese Words by VINICIUS DE MORAES
Music by ANTONION CARLOS JOBIM

Moderately

Your love is rain, my heart the flow-er.
on dis-tant de-serts.

I need your love or I will die.
The rain can fall up-on the sea.

My ver-y life is in your pow-er.
The rain can fall up-on the flow-er.

Will I with-er and fade or bloom to
Since the rain has to fall let it fall

the sky? Ág-ua de be-ber, give the flow-er wa-
on me. Ág-ua de be-ber, Ág-ua de be-ber

-ter to drink. Ág-ua de be-ber, give the flow-er wa-
ca-ma-rá. Ág-ua de be-ber, Ág-ua de be-ber

1. -ter to drink.
2. The rain can fall ca-ma-rá.

ADIÓS

English Words by EDDIE WOODS
Spanish Translation and Music by ENRIC MADRIGUERA

Copyright © 1931 by Peer International Corporation
Copyright Renewed
International Copyright Secured   All Rights Reserved

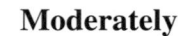

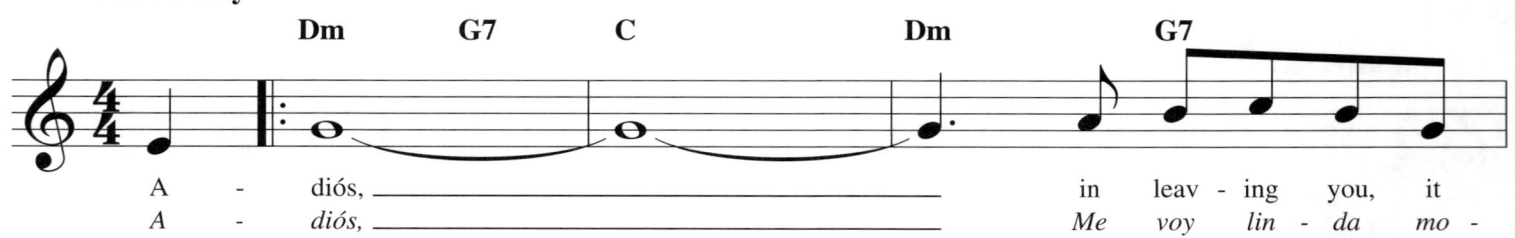

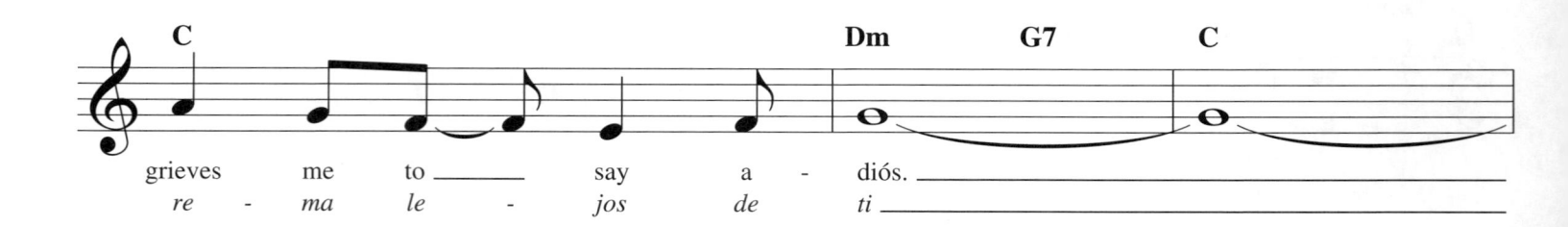

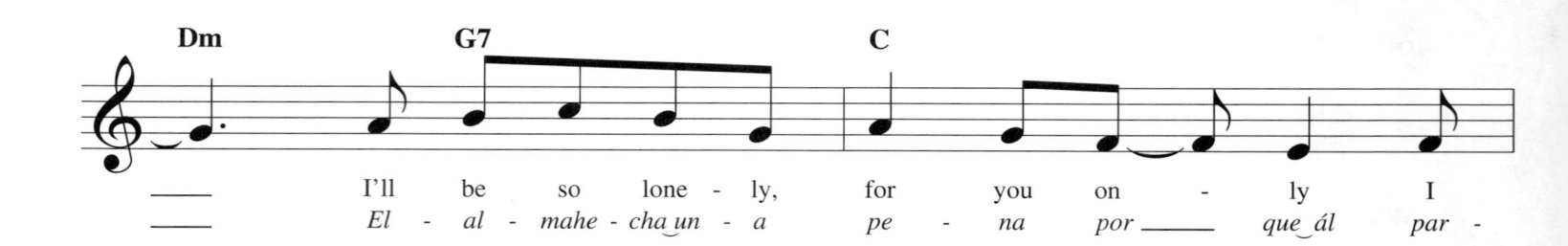

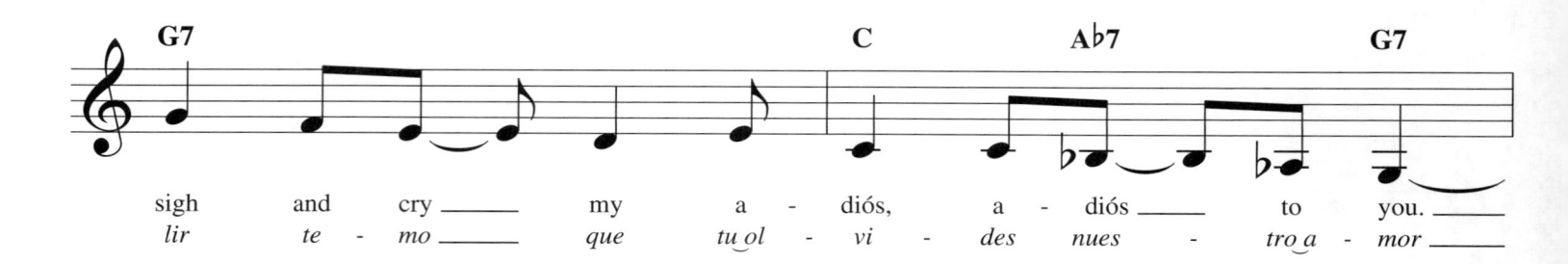

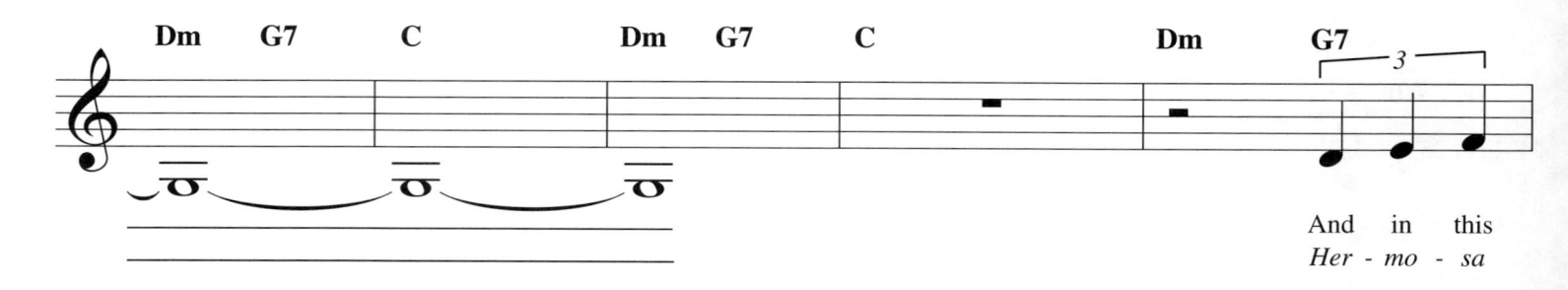

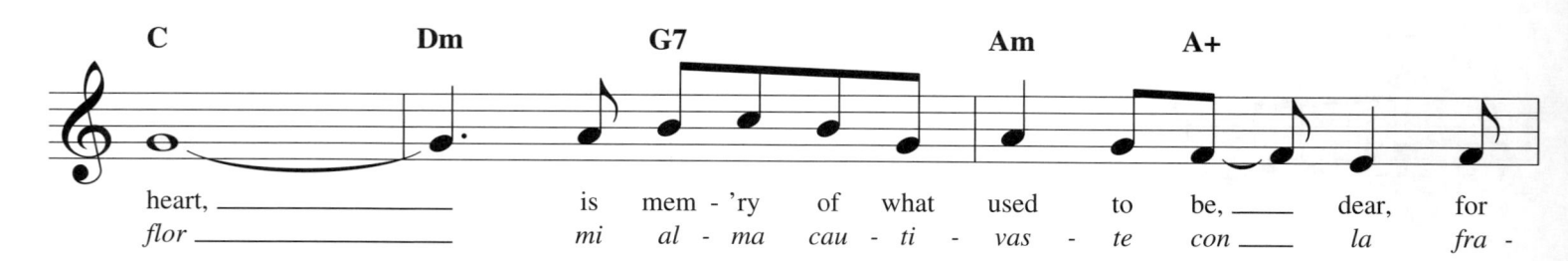

Moderately

A - diós, _____ in leav-ing you, it grieves me to _____ say a - diós. _____ I'll be so lone - ly, for you on - ly I sigh and cry _____ my a - diós, a - diós _____ to you. _____ And in this heart, _____ is mem - 'ry of what used to be, _____ dear, for

A - diós, _____ Me voy lin - da mo - re - ma le - jos de ti _____ El al - ma he cha un - a pe - na por _____ que al par - tir te mo _____ que tu ol - vi - des nues - tro a - mor _____ Her - mo - sa flor _____ mi al - ma cau - ti - vas - te con _____ la fra -

you and me ___ set a - part. ___ Moon
gan - cia de to can - dor ___ Tu

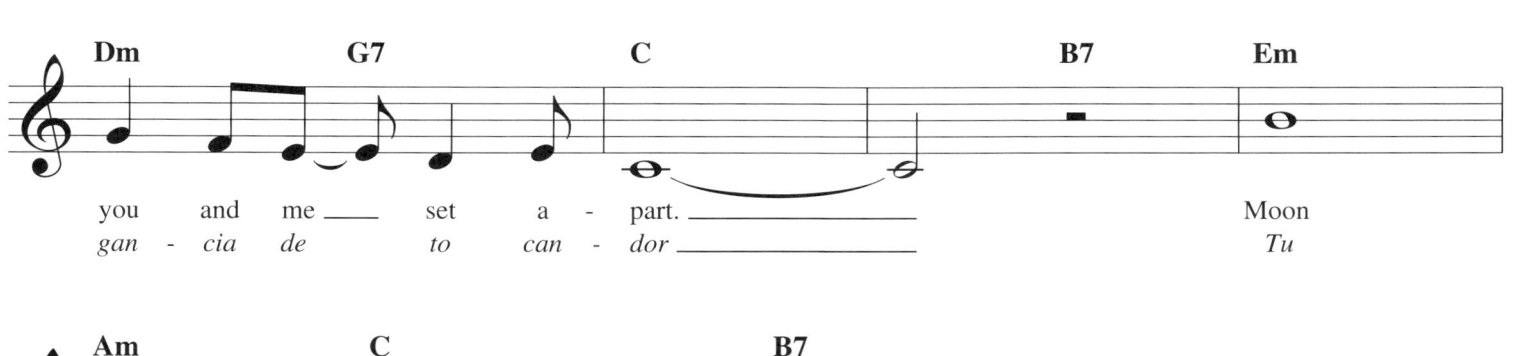

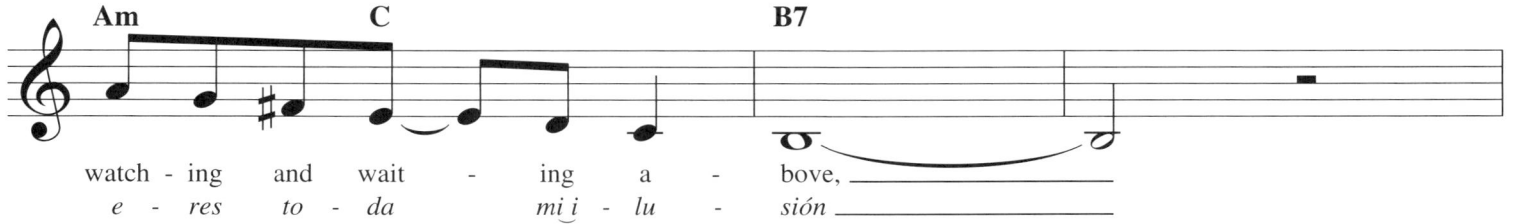

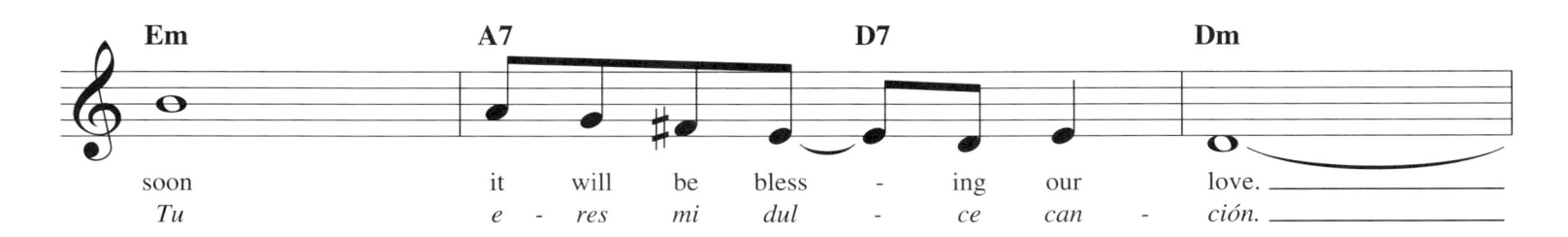

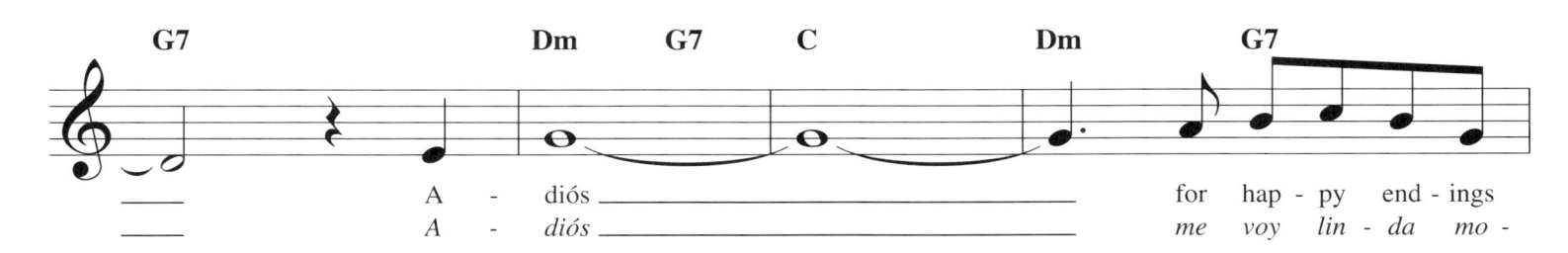

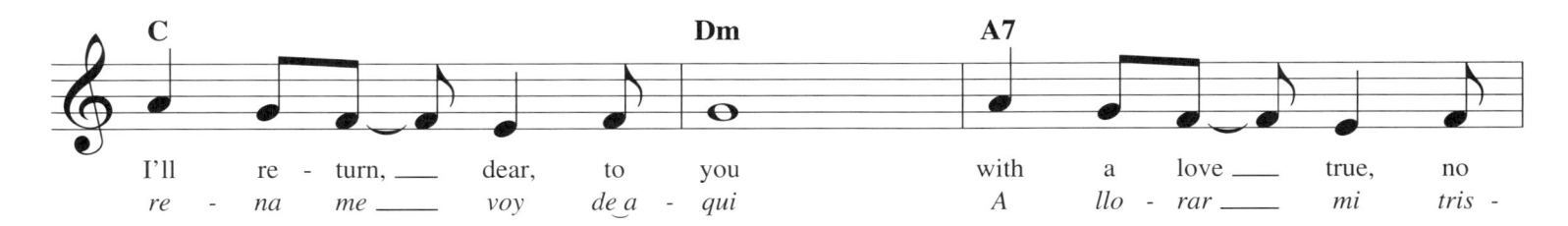

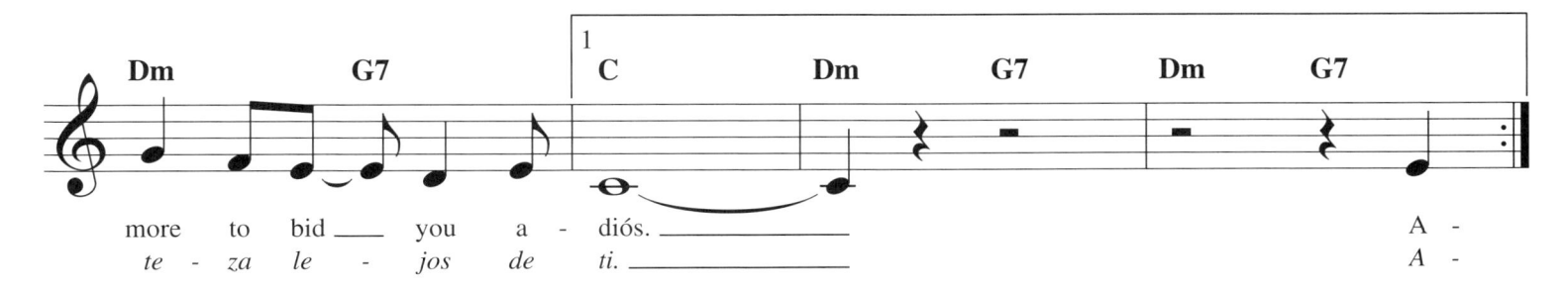

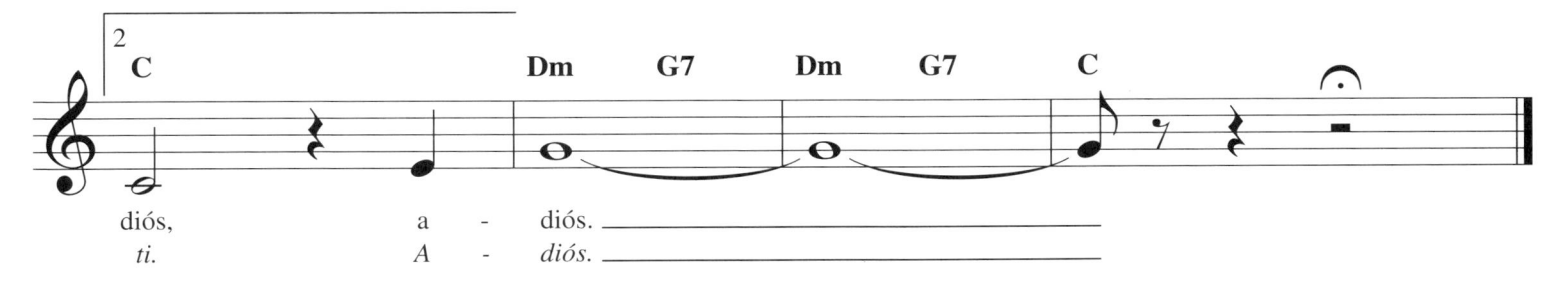

watch - ing and wait - ing a - bove, ___
e - res to - da mi i - lu - sión ___

soon it will be bless - ing our love. ___
Tu e - res mi dul - ce can - ción. ___

A - diós ___ for hap - py end - ings
A - diós ___ me voy lin - da mo -

I'll re - turn, ___ dear, to you with a love ___ true, no
re - na me ___ voy de a - qui A llo - rar ___ mi tris -

more to bid ___ you a - diós. ___ A -
te za le - jos de ti. ___ A -

diós, a - diós. ___
ti. A - diós. ___

ALWAYS IN MY HEART
(Siempre En Mi Corazón)
from ALWAYS IN MY HEART

Copyright © 1942 by Southern Music Pub. Co. Inc.
Copyright Renewed
International Copyright Secured   All Rights Reserved

Music and Spanish Words by ERNESTO LECUONA
English Words by KIM GANNON

Moderately

You are al-ways in my heart _____ e-ven though you're far a-
Siem-pre es-ta en mi co-ra-zón _____ el re-cuer-do de tu a-

way. _____ I can hear the mu-sic of _____ the song of
mor, _____ que al i-gual que tu can-ción _____ qui-tó de

love I sang with you. _____ You are al-ways in my
mi a-ma su do-lor. _____ Siem-pre es-ta en mi co-ra-

heart, _____ and when skies a-bove are grey, _____
zón _____ la nos-tal-gia de tu ser _____

_____ I re-mem-ber that you care _____ and then and
_____ ya ho-ra pue-do com-pren-der _____ qué dul-ce ha

there the sun breaks through. _____ Just be-fore I go to
si-do tu per-dón. _____ Ta vi-sión de mi so-

sleep there's a ren - dez - vous I keep,
ñar me hi - zo ver con e - mo - ción,
Gm
A7
and the dreams I al - ways meet help me for - get we're far a -
que fue tu al - ma ins - pi - ra - ción don - de a - pla - qué mi sed de a -
Dm
Fm
part. I don't know ex - act - ly when, dear,
mar. Hoy tan só - lo es pe - ro ver - te
C
C/E
E♭dim
but I'm sure we'll meet a - gain, dear, and my dar - ling, till we
y ya nun - ca más per - der - te, mien - tras tan - to que tu a -
G7
1
C
do you are al - ways in my heart.
mor, siem - pre es - ta én mi co - ra - zón.
2
C
You are al - ways in my heart.
Siem - pre es - ta én mi co - ra - zón.

AMAPOLA
(Pretty Little Poppy)

By JOSEPH M. LACALLE
New English Words by ALBERT GAMSE

Copyright © 1924 by Edward B. Marks Music Company
Copyright Renewed
International Copyright Secured All Rights Reserved
Used by Permission

Moderately

A-ma-po-la my pret-ty lit-tle pop-py you're like that love-ly flow'r so sweet and heav-en-ly. Since I found you, my heart is wrapped a-round you and lov-ing you, it seems to beat a rhap-so-dy. A-ma-po-la, the pret-ty lit-tle pop-py must cop-y its en-dear-ing charm from you. A-ma-po-la, a-ma-po-la, how I long to hear you say "I love you."

THE BREEZE AND I

Words by AL STILLMAN
Music by ERNESTO LECUONA

AMOR
(Amor, Amor, Amor)

Copyright © 1941, 1943, 1963, 1964 by Promotora Hispano Americana de Musica, S.A.
Copyrights Renewed
All Rights Administered by Peer International Corporation for the World
excluding Mexico and Central America
International Copyright Secured   All Rights Reserved

Music by GABRIEL RUIZ
Spanish Words by RICARDO LOPEZ MENDEZ
English Words by NORMAN NEWELL

Beguine

A - mor, A - mor, A - mor Na - cio de ti, Na - cio de mi de la es - pe - ran - za. A - mor, A - mor, A - mor Na - cio de Dios, pa - ra los dos, Na - cio del al - ma. Sen - tir que tus be - sos a - ni - da - ron en mi, I - gual que pa - lo - mas men - sa - je - ras de luz. Sa -

A - mor, A - mor, A - this word so sweet that I re - peat means I a - dore you. A - mor, my love, would you de - ny this heart that I have placed be - fore you. I can't find an - oth - er word with mean - ing so clear, my lips try to whis - per sweet - er things in your ear. But

G Abdim Am D7
ber que mis be - sos se que - da - ron en ti, ha - cien - do en tus la - bios la se -
some - how or oth - er, noth - ing sounds quite so dear as this soft ca - ress - ing word I
G7 C
nal de la cruz. A - mor, A - mor, A -
know. A - mor, A - mor, my
mor na - cio de ti, na - cio de
love, when you're a - way, there is no
G7
mi, de la es - pe - ran - za. A -
day, and nights are lone - ly. A -
Dm
mor, A - mor, A - mor Na - cio de
mor, A - mor, my love, make life di -
G7 1 C Dm G7
Dios, pa - ra los dos, Na - cio del al - ma. A -
vine, say you'll be mine and love me on - ly. A -
2 C
dos, Na - cio del al - ma.
mine and love me on - ly.

ANEMA E CORE
(With All My Heart)

Copyright © 1954 by B & G AKST PUBLISHING CO.
Copyright Renewed
All Rights for the U.S. Administered by THE SONGWRITERS GUILD OF AMERICA
All Rights for Canada and Japan Controlled and Administered by SONGS OF UNIVERSAL, INC.
International Copyright Secured   All Rights Reserved

English Lyric by MANN CURTIS and HARRY AKST
Italian Lyric by TITO MANLIO
Music by SALVE d'ESPOSITO

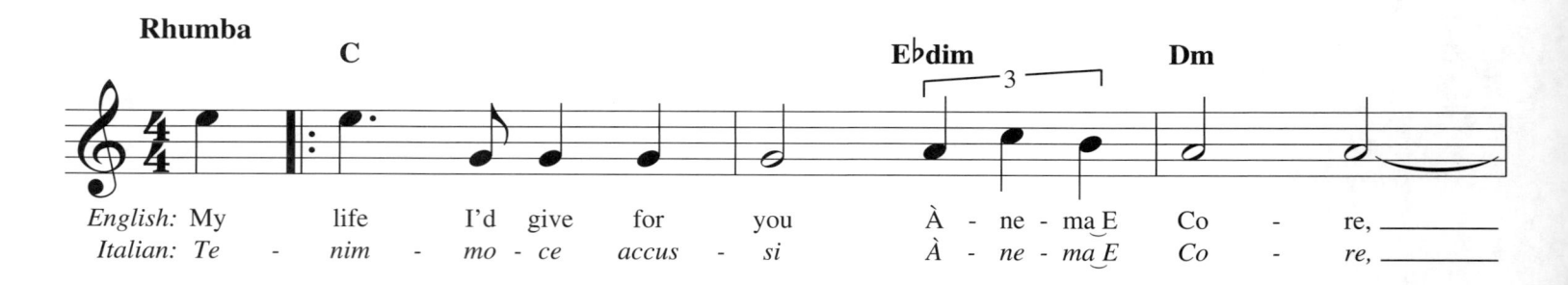

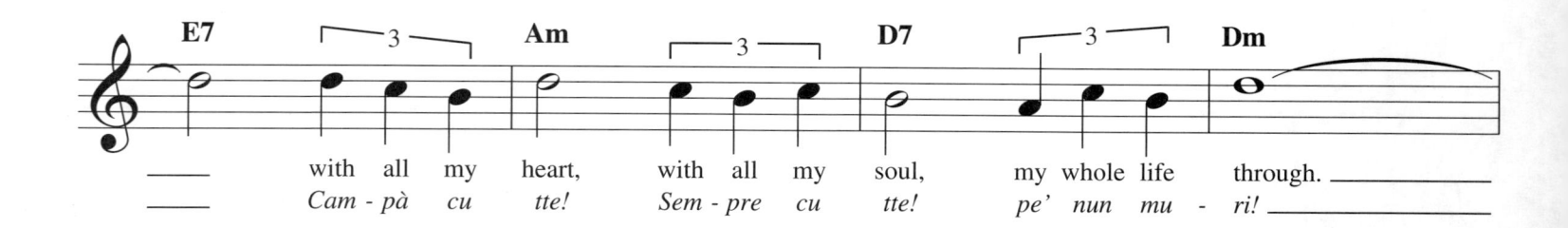

Rhumba

English: My life I'd give for you À - ne - ma E Co - re,
Italian: Te - nim - mo ce accus - si À - ne - ma E Co - re,

I on - ly live for you, À - ne - ma E Co - re.
Nun - ce las sam - mo cchiú, man - co pe' n'o - ra

I have but one de - sire and it's to love you,
Stu de - si - de - rio'e te, me fà pa - u - ra,

with all my heart, with all my soul, my whole life through.
Cam - pà cu tte! Sem - pre cu tte! pe' nun mu - ri!

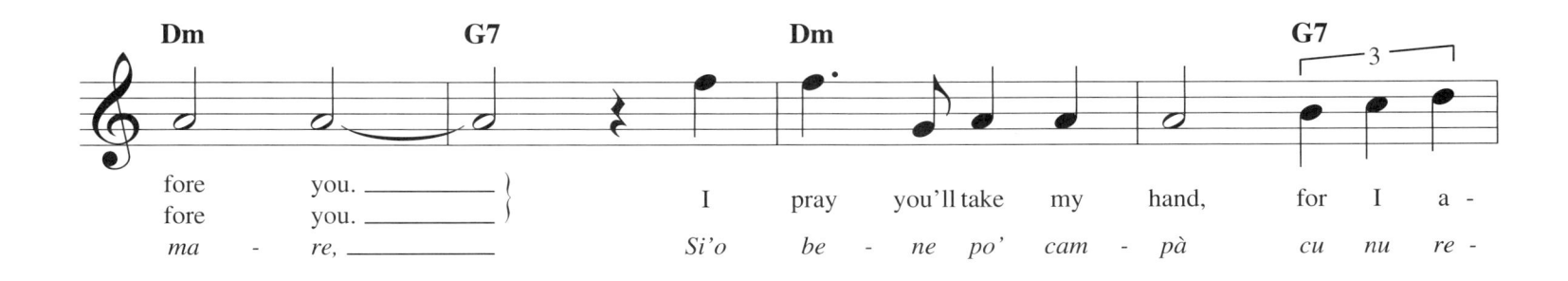

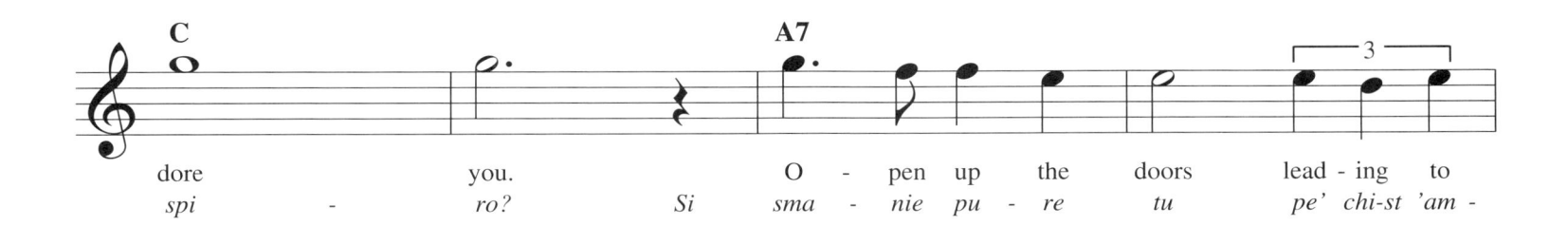

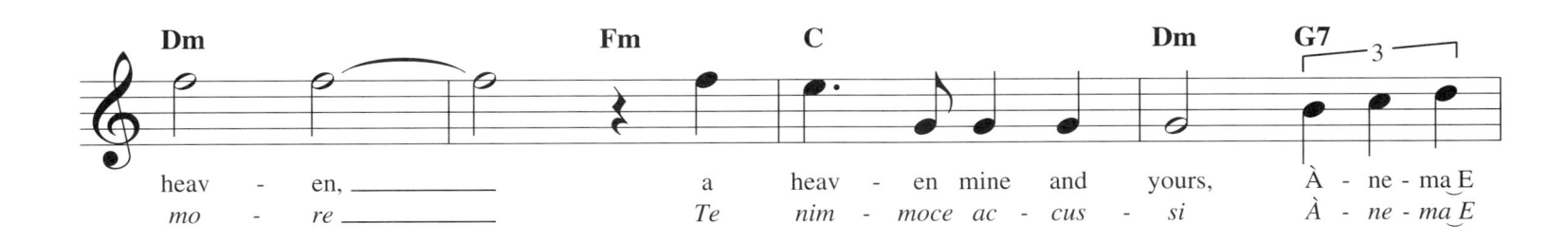

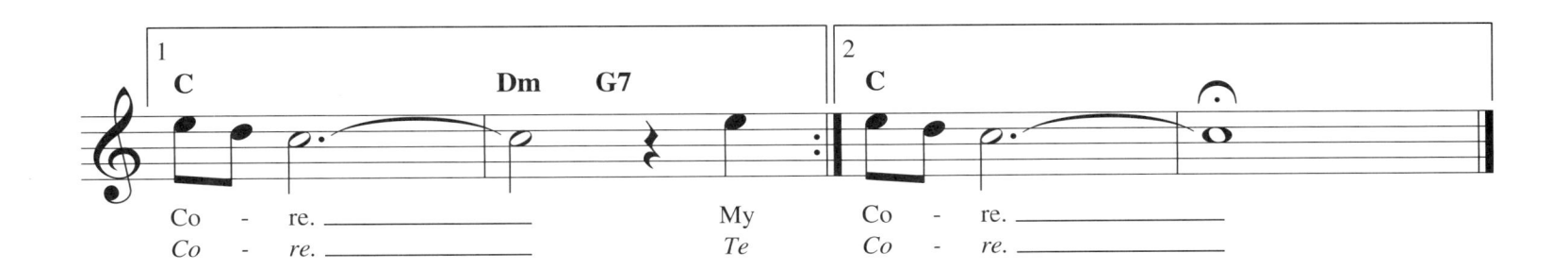

From stars I'll make your crown and kneel be-
In ev-'ry dream I stand breath-less be-
Che ce di-cim-mo a-ffà pa-ro-le a-

fore you. I pray you'll take my hand, for I a-
fore you.
ma - re, Si 'o be - ne po' cam-pà cu nu re-

dore you. O-pen up the doors lead-ing to
spi - ro? Si sma-nie pu - re tu pe' chi-st 'am-

heav - en, a heav-en mine and yours, À - ne-ma E
mo - re Te nim - moce ac-cus - si À - ne-ma E

1. Co - re. My Co - re.
Co - re. Te Co - re.

2. Co - re.

AQUELLOS OJOS VERDES
(Green Eyes)

Music by NILO MENENDEZ
Spanish Words by ADOLFO UTRERA
English Words by E. RIVERA and E. WOODS

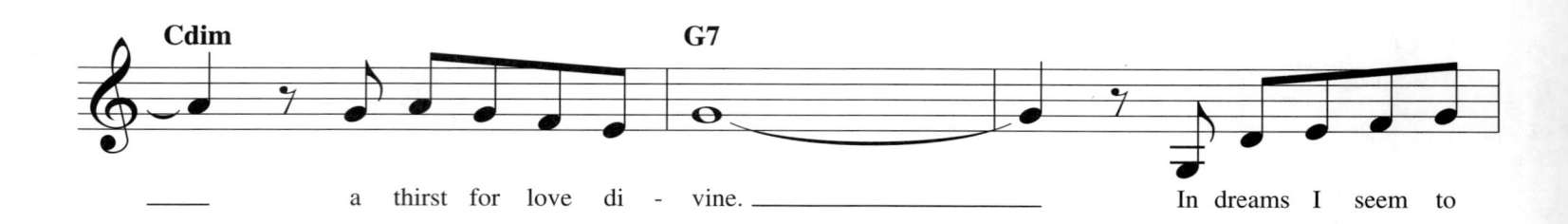

Copyright © 1929, 1931 by Peer International Corporation
Copyrights Renewed
International Copyright Secured All Rights Reserved

Moderately

Your green eyes with their soft lights, your eyes that promise sweet nights bring to my soul a longing a thirst for love divine. In dreams I seem to hold you to find you and enfold you our lips meet, and our hearts too, with a thrill so sublime.

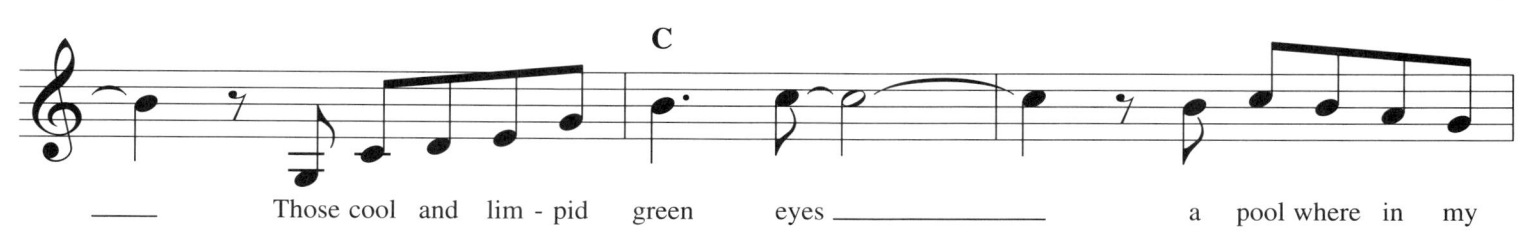

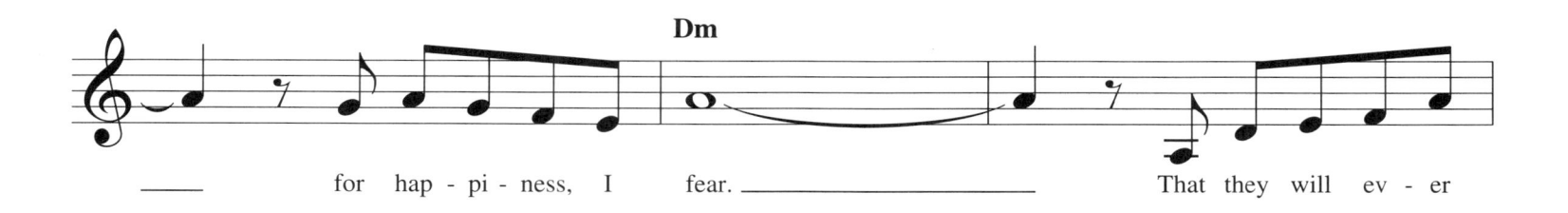

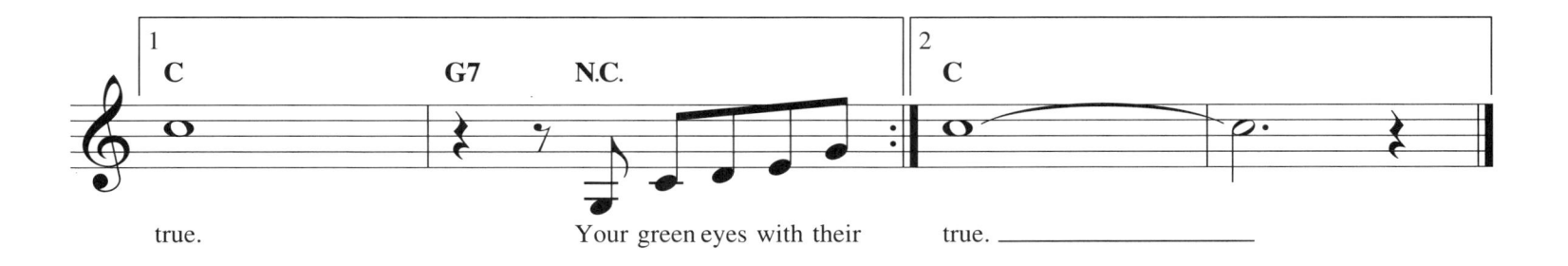

Those cool and lim-pid green eyes, a pool where in my love lies so deep, that in my search-ing for hap-pi-ness, I fear. That they will ev-er haunt me all through my life they'll taunt me, but will they ev-er want me? Green eyes, make my dreams come true.

Your green eyes with their true.

BÉSAME MUCHO
(Kiss Me Much)

Copyright © 1941, 1943 by Promotora Hispano Americana de Musica, S.A.
Copyrights Renewed
All Rights Administered by Peer International Corporation
International Copyright Secured   All Rights Reserved

Music and Spanish Words by CONSUELO VELAZQUEZ
English Words by SUNNY SKYLAR

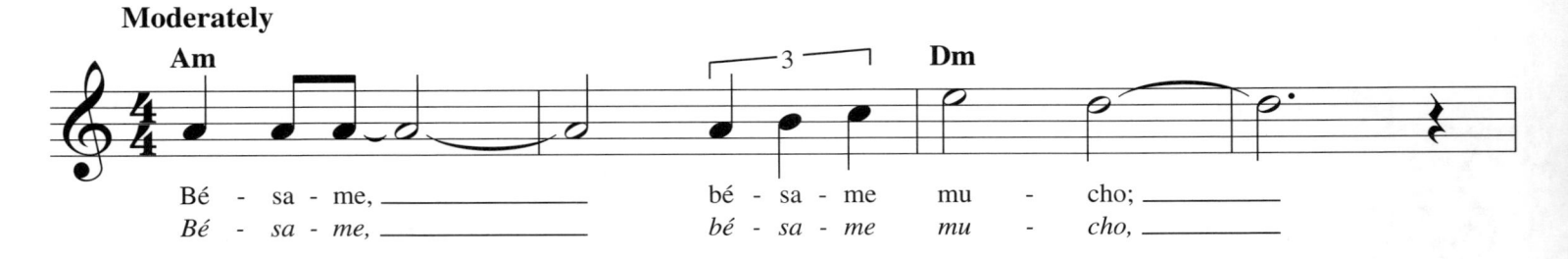

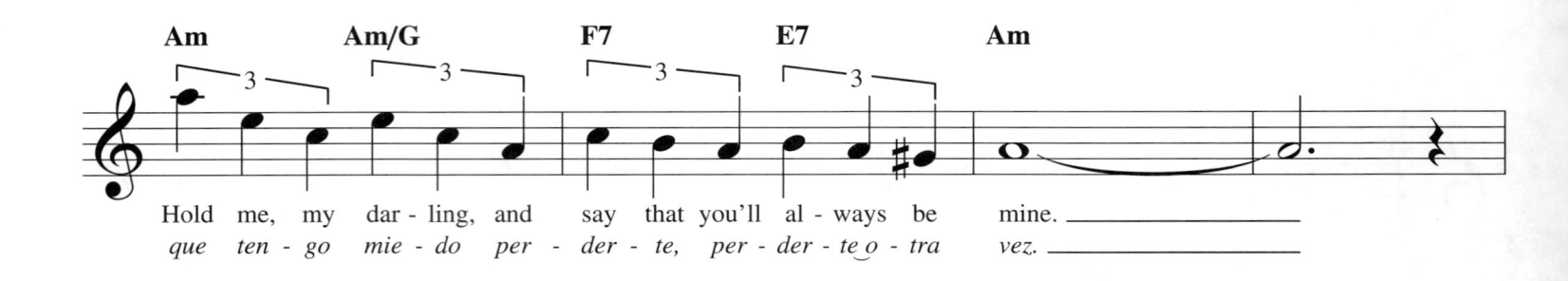

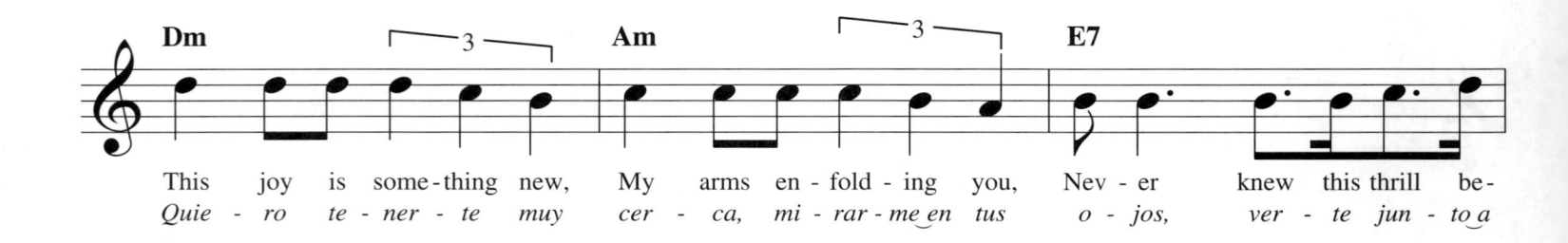

Moderately

Bé - sa - me, bé - sa - me mu - cho;
Bé - sa - me, bé - sa - me mu - cho,

Each time I cling to your kiss I hear mu - sic di - vine;
co - mo si fue - ra es - ta no - che la úl - ti - ma vez;

bé - sa - me mu - cho,
bé - sa - me mu - cho,

Hold me, my dar - ling, and say that you'll al - ways be mine.
que ten - go mie - do per - der - te, per - der - te o - tra vez.

This joy is some - thing new, My arms en - fold - ing you, Nev - er knew this thrill be -
Quie - ro te - ner - te muy cer - ca, mi - rar - me en tus o - jos, ver - te jun - to a

Am Dm Am
fore; Who ev - er thought I'd be hold - ing you close to me,
mí, pien - sa que tal vez ma - ña - na yo ya es - ta - ré
B7 F7 E7 Am
Whisp'ring "It's you I a - dore;" Dear - est one, if you should
le - jos, muy le - jos de ti. Bé - sa - me, bé - sa - me
Dm C♯dim Dm E7
leave me, Each lit - tle dream would take wing and my life would be
mu - cho, co - mo si fue - ra es - ta no - che la úl - ti - ma
Am A7 Dm
through; bé - sa - me mu - cho;
vez; bé - sa - me mu - cho,
Am Am/G F7 E7
Love me for - ev - er and make all my dreams come
que ten - go mie - do per - der - te, per - der - te des -
1 Am F7 E7 2 Am
true. true.
pués. pués.

BLAME IT ON THE BOSSA NOVA

Words and Music by BARRY MANN
and CYNTHIA WEIL

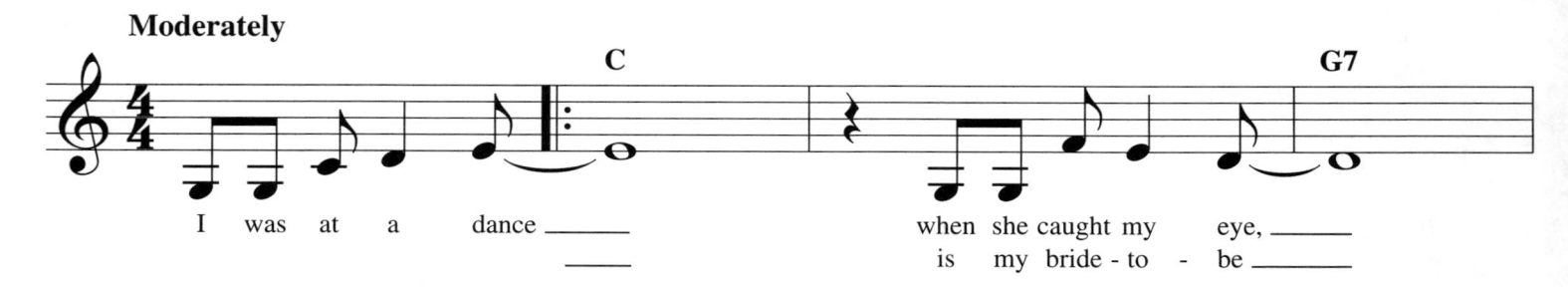

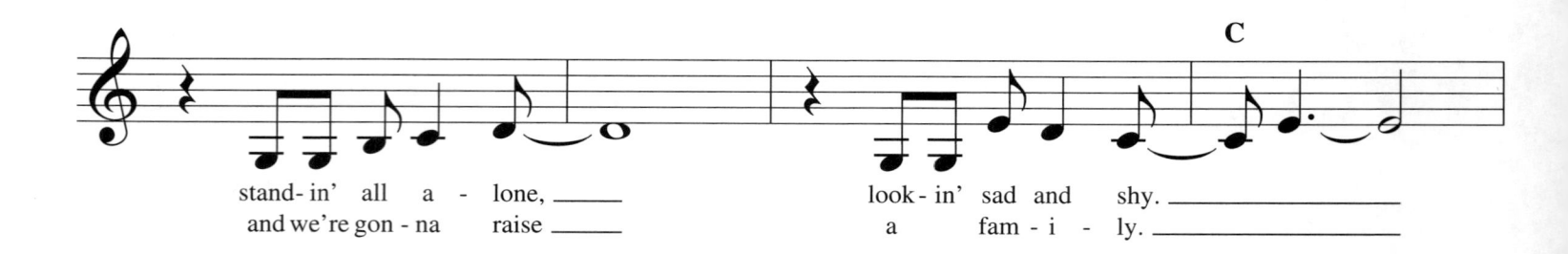

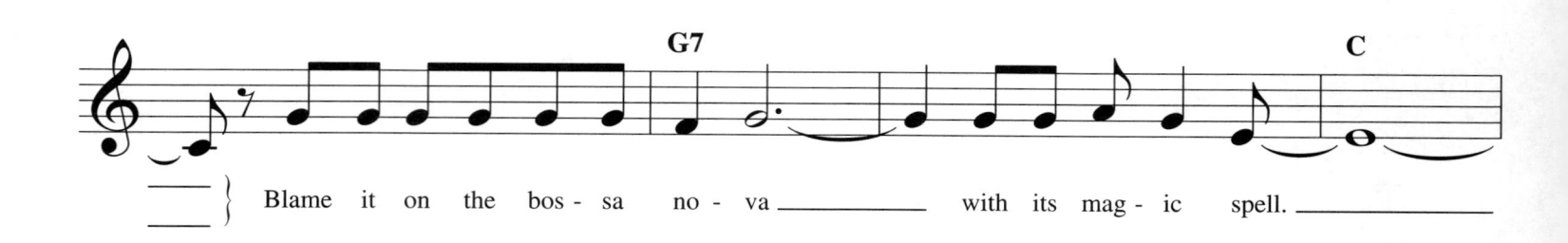

© 1962 (Renewed 1990) SCREEN GEMS-EMI MUSIC INC.
All Rights Reserved   International Copyright Secured   Used by Permission

Moderately

I was at a dance when she caught my eye,
___ is my bride-to-be

stand-in' all a-lone, look-in' sad and shy.
and we're gon-na raise a fam-i-ly.

We be-gan to dance, sway-in' to and fro
And when our kids ask how it came a-bout,

and soon I knew I'd nev-er let her go.
I'm gon-na say to them with-out a doubt:

Blame it on the bos-sa no-va with its mag-ic spell.

Blame it on the bos-sa no-va that she did so well.

F
Oh, it all be - gan with just one lit - tle dance, but soon it end - ed
C G7
up a big ro - mance. Blame it on the bos - sa no - va,
C
the dance of love. Now was it the moon
G7 C
or the stars a - bove?
G7
Now was it the tune the Bos - sa No - va
C F C
1 2
the dance of love? Now that lit - tle girl

BRAZIL

Original Words and Music by ARY BARROSO
English Lyrics by S.K. RUSSELL

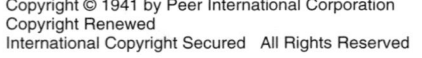

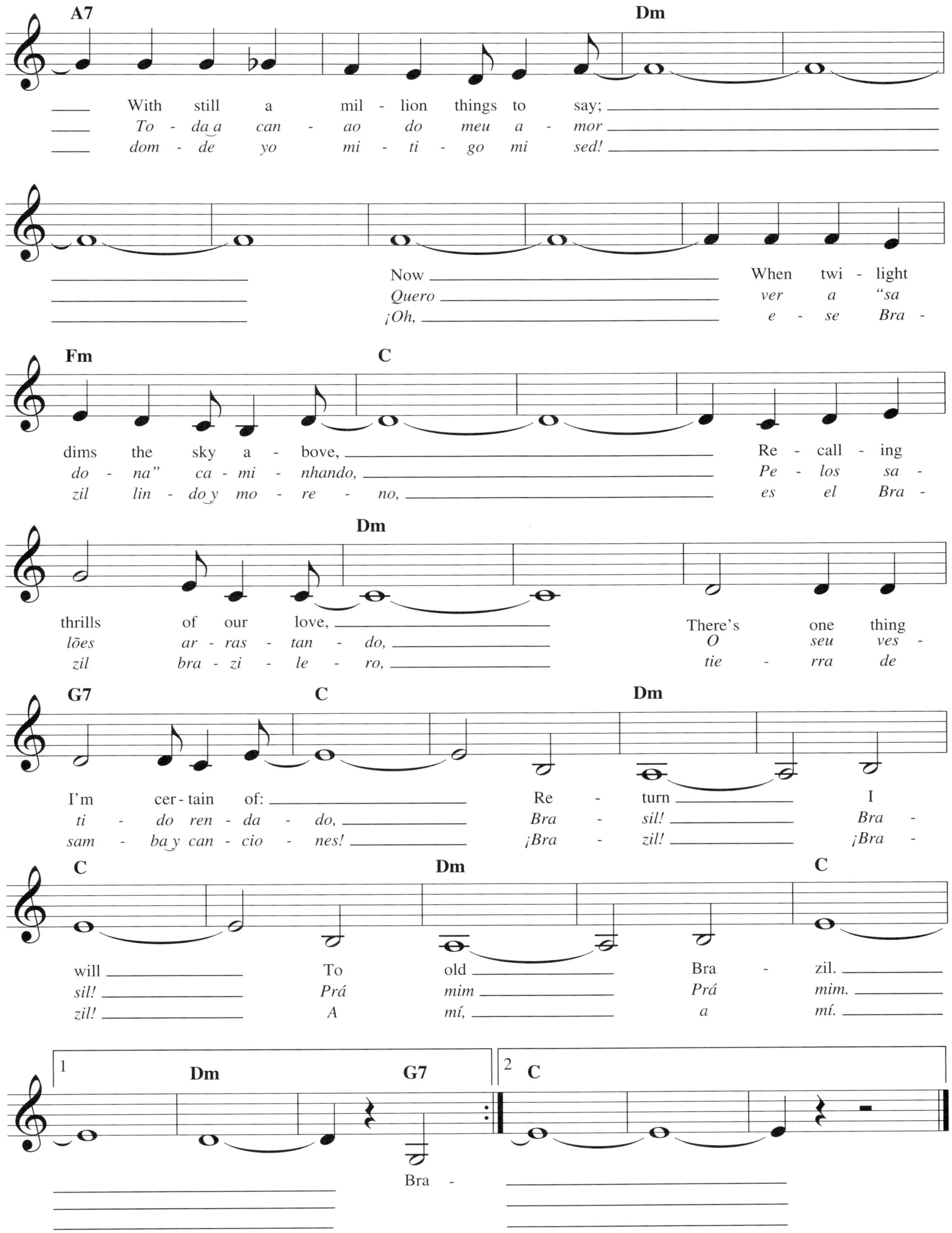
A7
Dm
With still a mil - lion things to say;
To - da a can - ao do meu a - mor
dom - de yo mi - ti - go mi sed!
Now When twi - light
Quero ver a "sa
¡Oh, e - se Bra -
Fm
C
dims the sky a - bove, Re - call - ing
do - na" ca - mi - nhando, Pe - los sa -
zil lin - do y mo - re - no, es el Bra -
Dm
thrills of our love, There's one thing
lões ar - ras - tan - do, O seu ves -
zil bra - zi - le - ro, tie - rra de
G7
C
Dm
I'm cer - tain of: Re - turn I
ti - do ren - da - do, Bra - sil! Bra -
sam - ba y can - cio - nes! ¡Bra - zil! ¡Bra -
C
Dm
C
will To old Bra - zil.
sil! Prá mim Prá mim.
zil! A mí, a mí.
1
Dm
G7
Bra -
2
C

CALL ME

Words and Music by
TONY HATCH

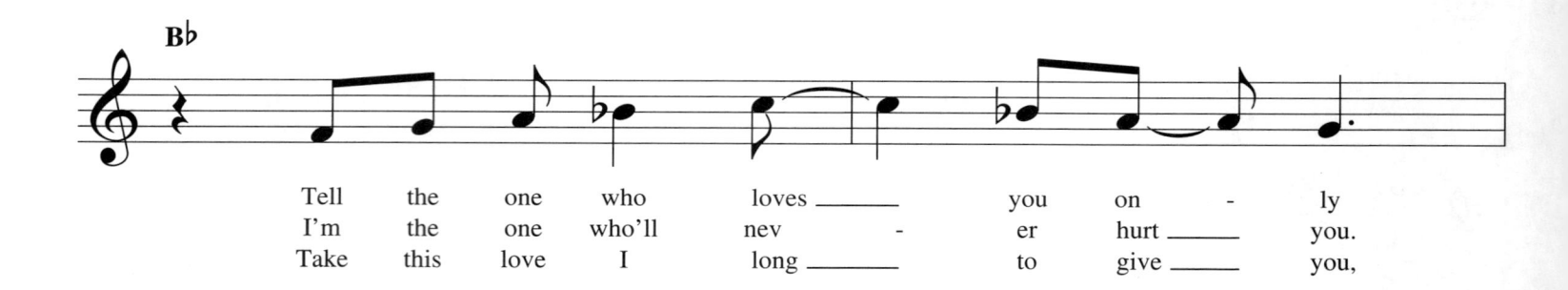

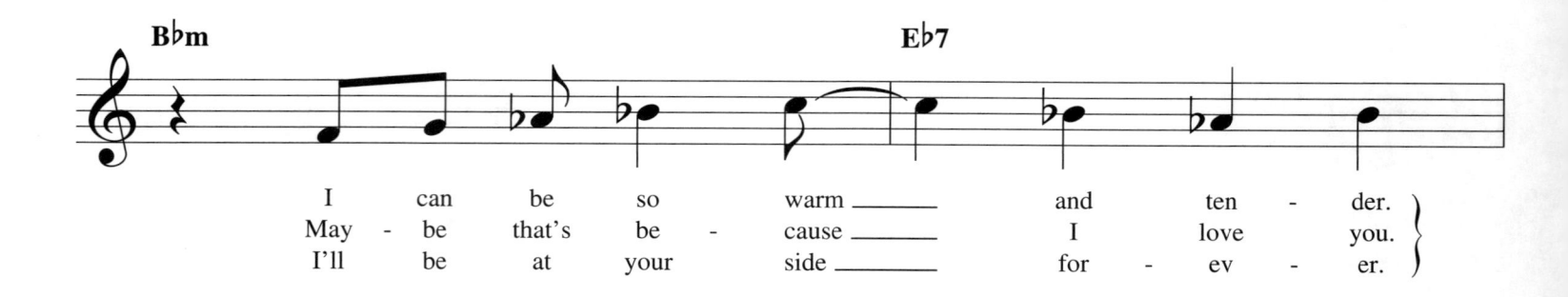

Moderately

If you're feeling sad and lonely,
When it seems your friends desert you,
If you call, I'll be right with you.

there's a service I can render.
there's somebody thinking of you.
You and I should be together.

Tell the one who loves you only
I'm the one who'll never hurt you.
Take this love I long to give you,

I can be so warm and tender.
Maybe that's because I love you.
I'll be at your side forever.

Call me! Don't be afraid; you can call me.

| Fm | Ab | To Coda / Fm |

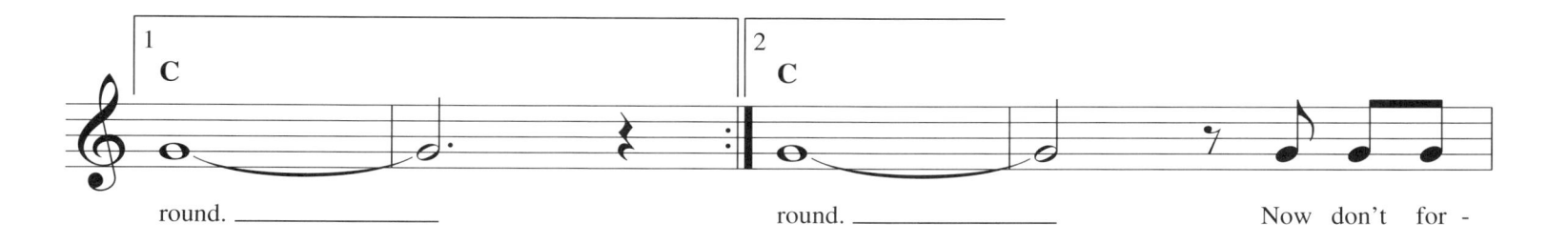

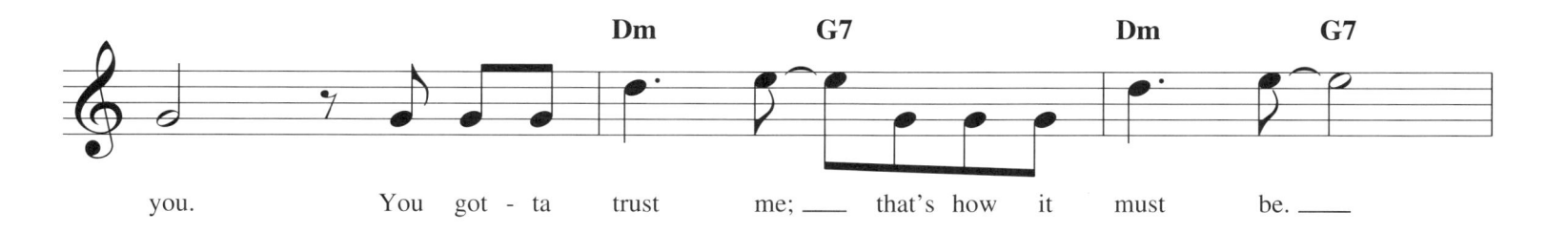

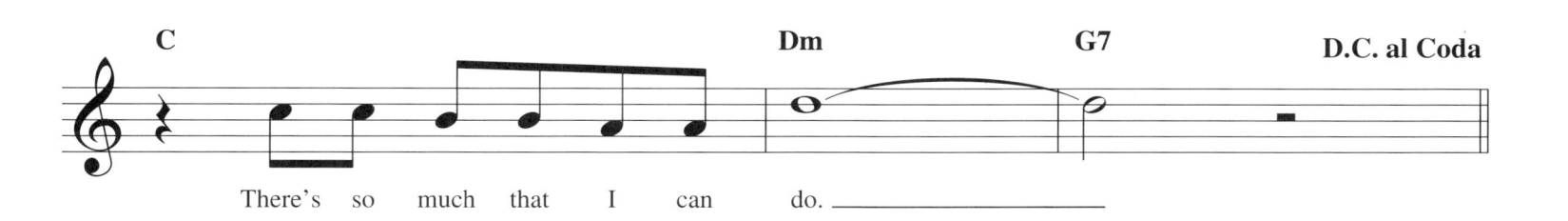

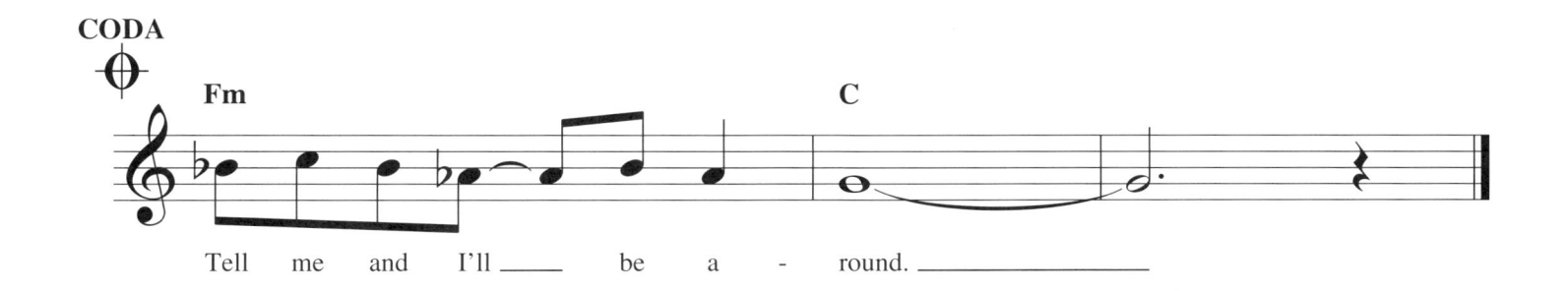

May-be it's late, __ but just call me. __ Tell me and I'll __ be a-

|1. C | 2. C |

round. _____ round. _____ Now don't for-

| Dm | G7 | Dm | G7 | C |

get me, __ 'cause if you let me, __ I will al-ways stay by

| | Dm | G7 | Dm | G7 |

you. You got-ta trust me; __ that's how it must be. __

| C | Dm | G7 | D.C. al Coda |

There's so much that I can do. _____

CODA

| Fm | C |

Tell me and I'll __ be a-round. _____

CARIOCA
from FLYING DOWN TO RIO

Words by GUS KAHN and EDWARD ELISCU
Music by VINCENT YOUMANS

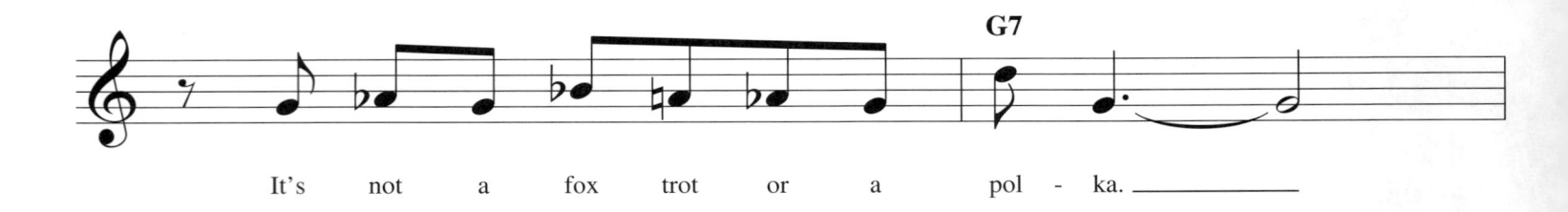

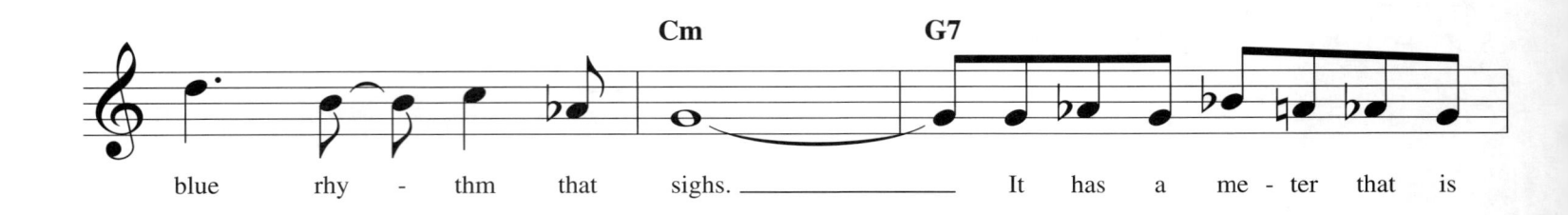

Moderate Latin beat

Say, have you seen that Ca - ri - o - ca? It's not a fox trot or a pol - ka. It has a lit - tle bit of new rhy - thm, a blue rhy - thm that sighs. It has a me - ter that is trick - y, a bit of wick - ed, wack - i - wick - y. But when you dance it with a new love, there'll be true love ___ in her eyes. ___ You'll dream ___ of the new Ca-ri-o-ca. ___ Its theme ___ is a kiss and a sigh. ___ You'll dream ___ of the new Ca-ri-o-ca, ___ when mu-sic and lights are gone ___ and we're say-ing good-bye. ___

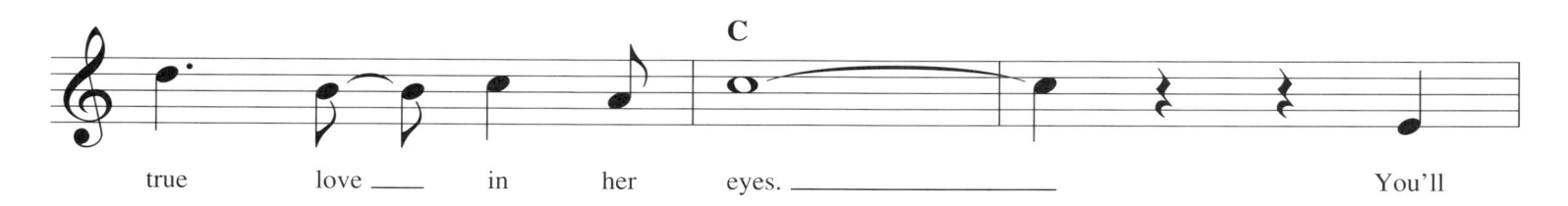

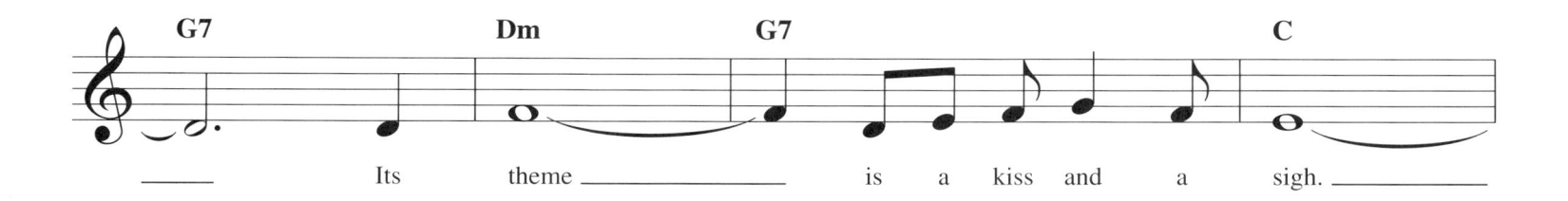

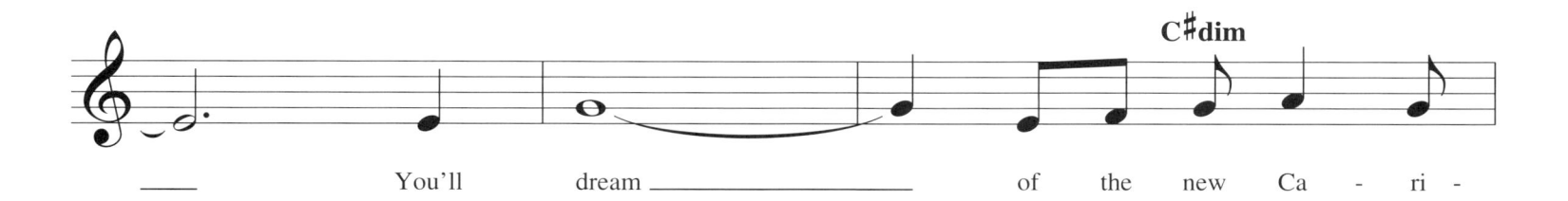

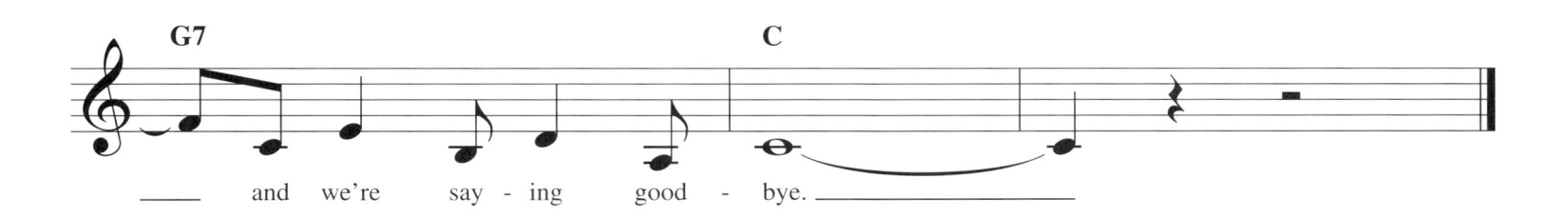

CHEGA DE SAUDADE
(No More Blues)

Copyright © 1962 and 1967 Editora Musical Arapua, Sao Paulo, Brazil
Copyrights Renewed
Corcovado Music Corp., New York, NY and VM Enterprises, New York, NY control all publication rights for the U.S.A.
Bendig Music Corp. controls all publication rights for Canada
International Copyright Secured   All Rights Reserved

English Lyric by JON HENDRICKS
and JESSIE CAVANAUGH
Original Text by VINICIUS DE MORAES
Music by ANTONIO CARLOS JOBIM

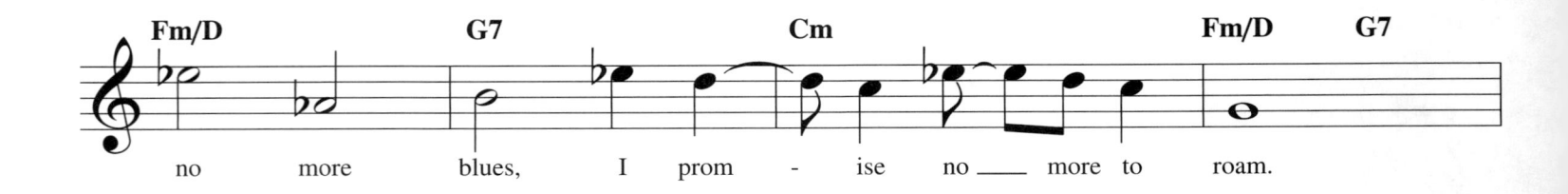

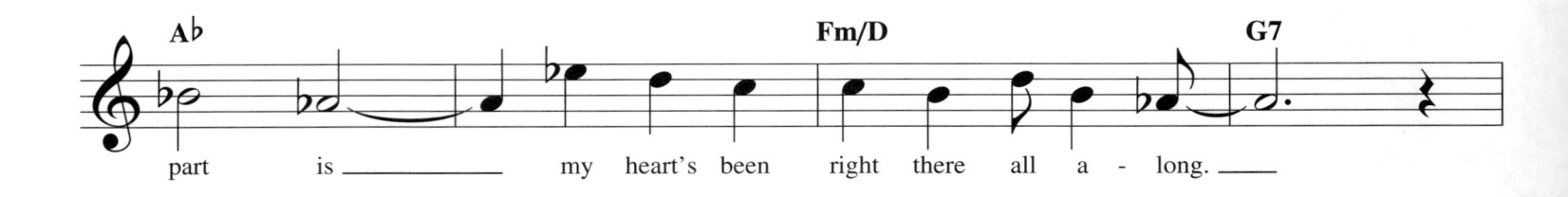

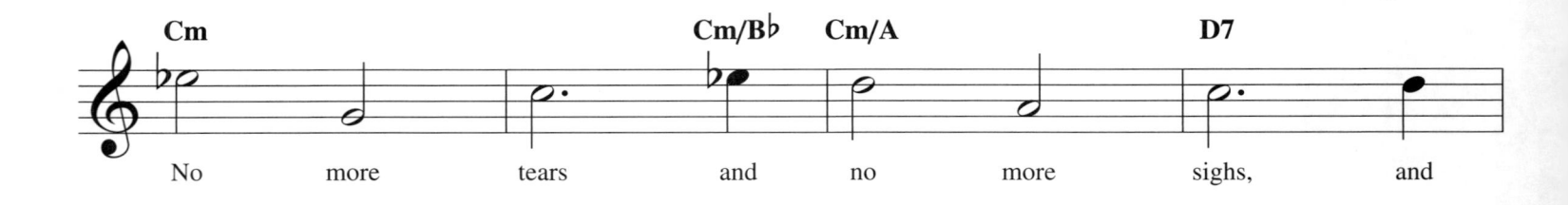

Bossa Nova

No more blues, I'm goin' back home. No, no more blues, I promise no more to roam. Home is where the heart is, the funny part is my heart's been right there all along. No more tears and no more sighs, and no more fears, I'll say no more good-byes.

If trav-el beck-ons me I swear I'm gon-na re-fuse, I'm gon-na set-tle down and there'll be no more blues. Ev-'ry day while I am far a-way my thoughts turn home-ward, for-ev-er home-ward. I trav-elled 'round the world in search of hap-pi-ness, but all my hap-pi-ness I found was in my home-town.

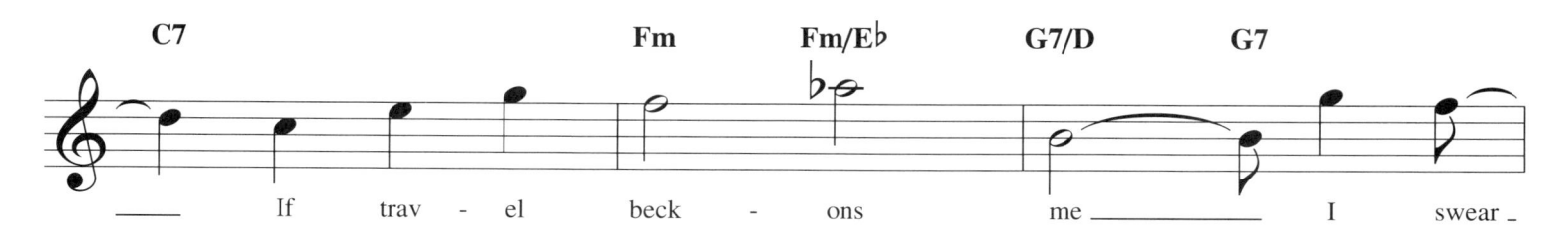

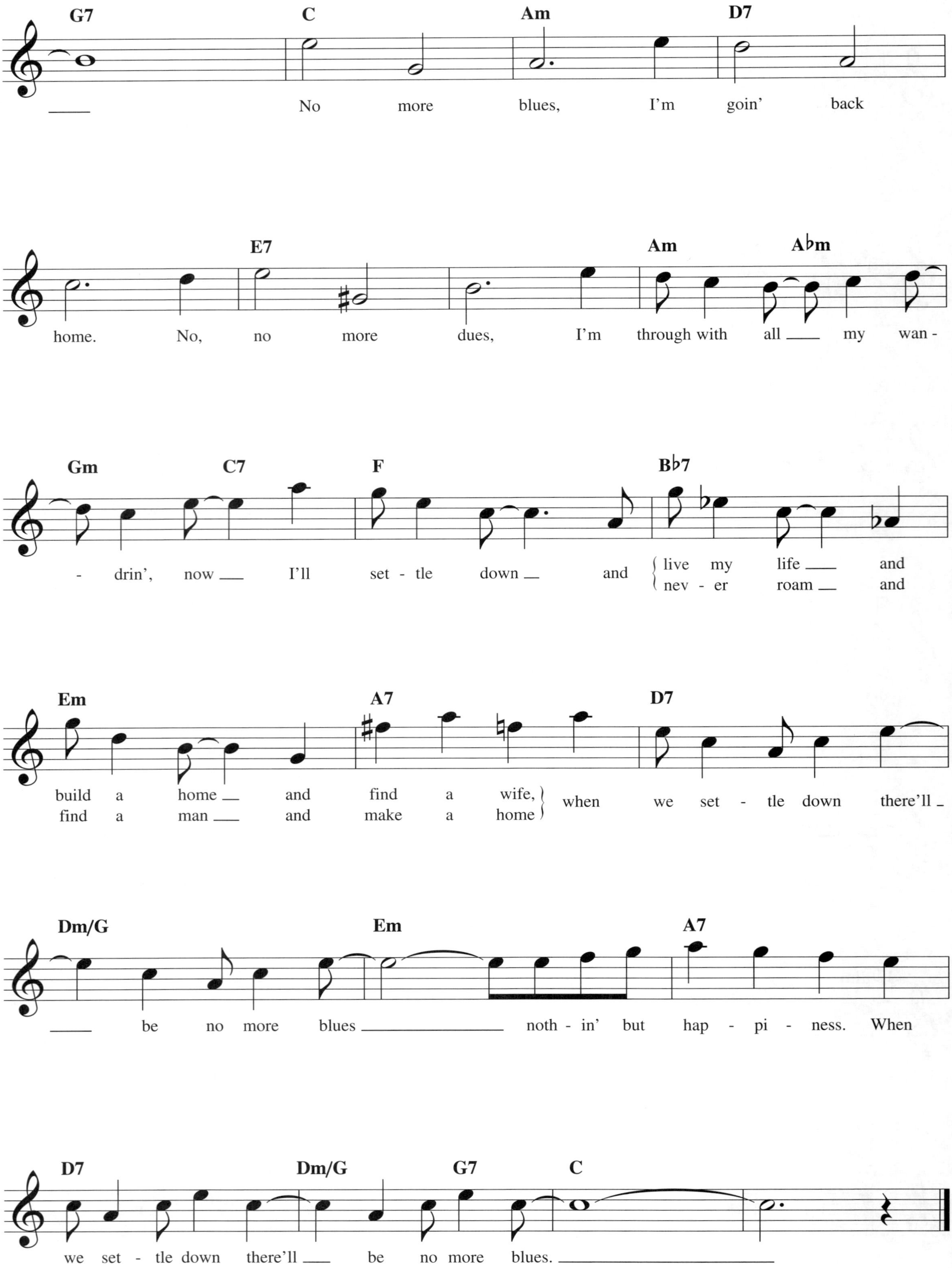
G7 C Am D7
No more blues, I'm goin' back
E7 Am A♭m
home. No, no more dues, I'm through with all my wan-
Gm C7 F B♭7
-drin', now I'll set-tle down and live my life and
nev-er roam and
Em A7 D7
build a home and find a wife,
find a man and make a home
when we set-tle down there'll
Dm/G Em A7
be no more blues nothin' but hap-pi-ness. When
D7 Dm/G G7 C
we set-tle down there'll be no more blues.

CUANTO LE GUSTA

Copyright © 1948 by Peer International Corporation
Copyright Renewed
International Copyright Secured   All Rights Reserved

Original Words and Music by GABRIEL RUIZ
English Words by RAY GILBERT

Bright tempo

Cuan-to le gus-ta, le gus-ta, le gus-ta, le gus-ta, le gus-ta, le gus-ta, le gus-ta, cuan-to le gus-ta, le gus-ta, le gus-ta, le gus-ta, le gus-ta, le gus-ta. We got-ta get go-in', where we go-in'? And what-a we gon-na do? We're on our way to "some-where," the three of us and you. What-'ll we see there, who will be there, what-'ll be the big sur-

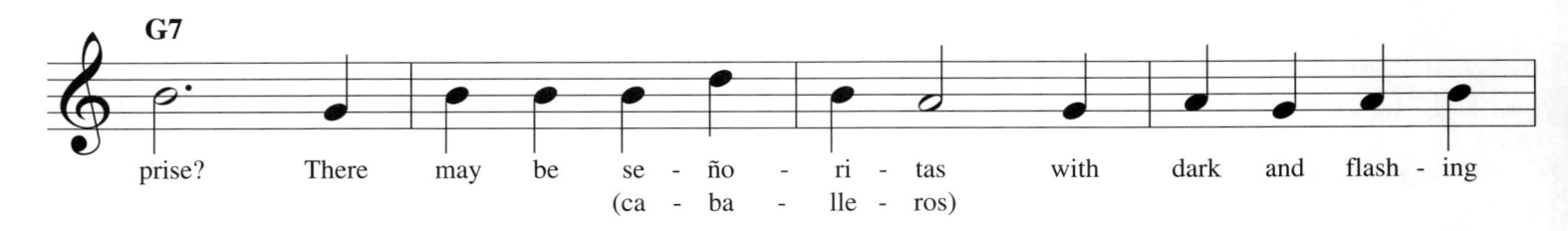

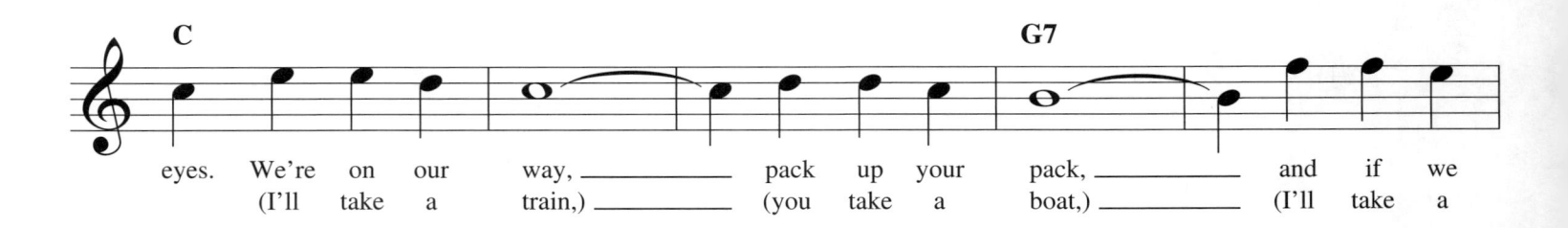

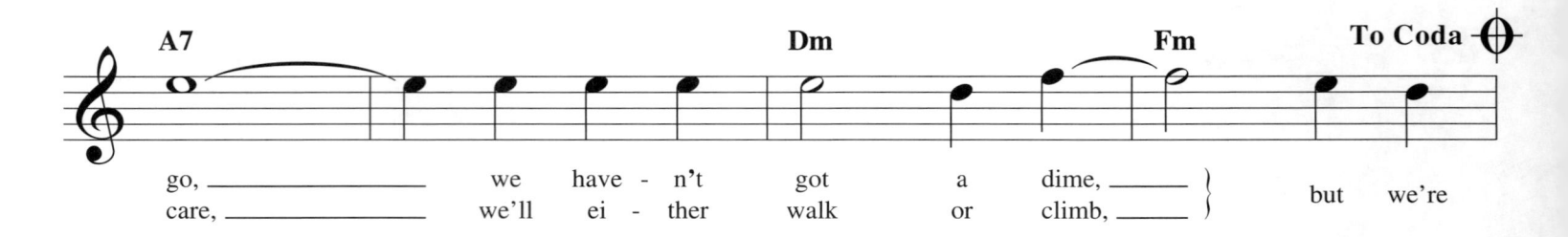

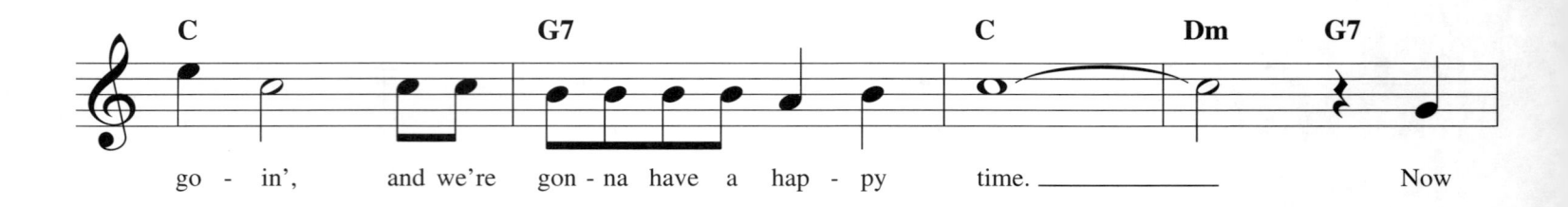

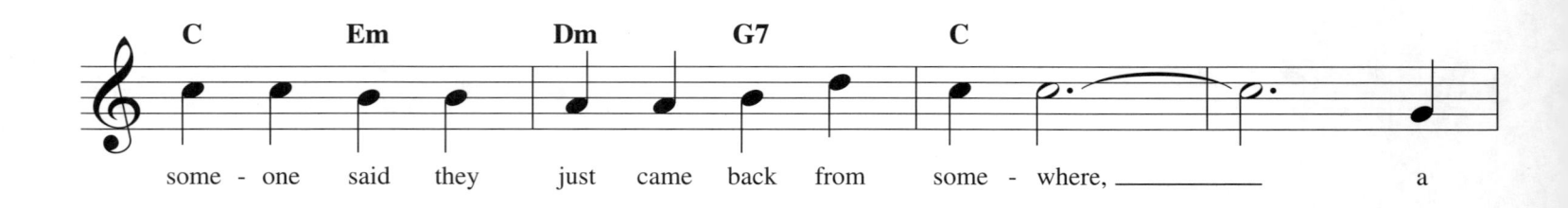

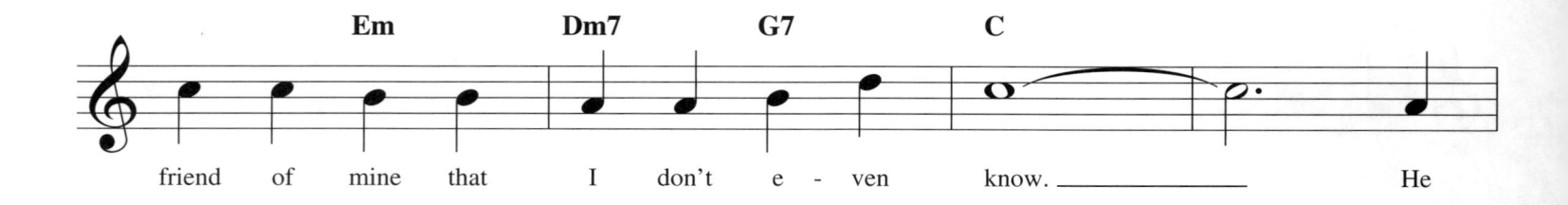

G7 prise? There may be se - ño - ri - tas with dark and flash - ing
(ca - ba - lle - ros)

C **G7** eyes. We're on our way, _____ pack up your pack, _____ and if we
(I'll take a train,) _____ (you take a boat,) _____ (I'll take a

C stay, _____ we won't come back. _____ How can we
plane,) _____ (you ride the goat.) _____ Oh, we don't

A7 **Dm** **Fm** *To Coda* go, _____ we have - n't got a dime, _____ but we're
care, _____ we'll ei - ther walk or climb, _____

C **G7** **C** **Dm** **G7** go - in', and we're gon - na have a hap - py time. _____ Now

C **Em** **Dm** **G7** **C** some - one said they just came back from some - where, _____ a

Em **Dm7** **G7** **C** friend of mine that I don't e - ven know. _____ He said there's lots of fun if we can get there; _____ if that's the case, _____ that's the place, _____ the place we want to go. _____ We

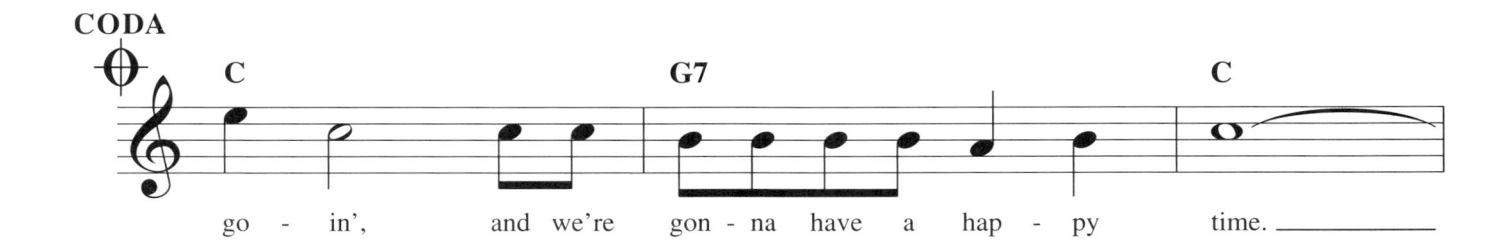

CODA
goin', and we're gonna have a happy time. _____ Cuan-to le gus-ta, le gus-ta, le gus-ta, le gus-ta, le gus-ta, le gus-ta, le gus-ta, cuan-to le gus-ta, le gus-ta, le gus-ta, le gus-ta, le gus-ta, le gus-ta.

CHERRY PINK AND APPLE BLOSSOM WHITE
from UNDERWATER

French Words by JACQUES LARUE
English Words by MACK DAVID
Music by MARCEL LOUIGUY

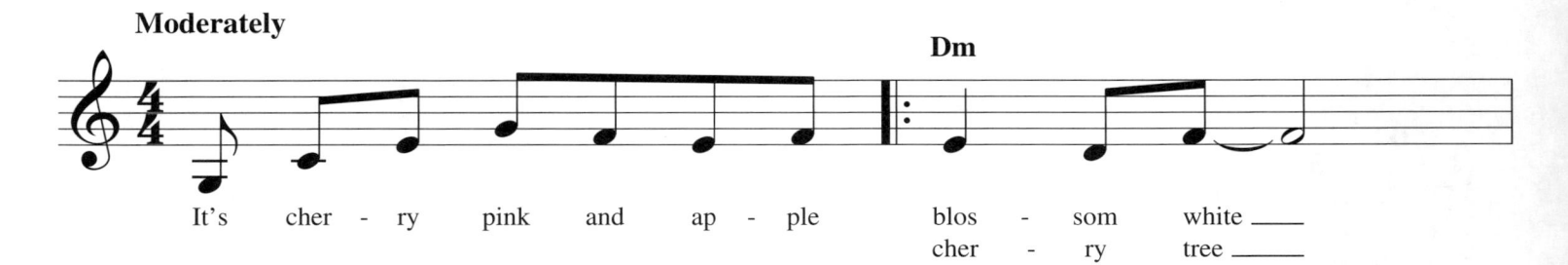

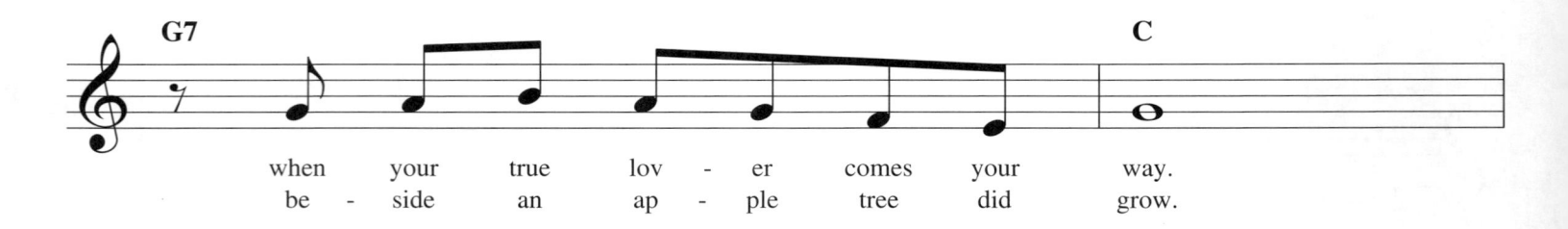

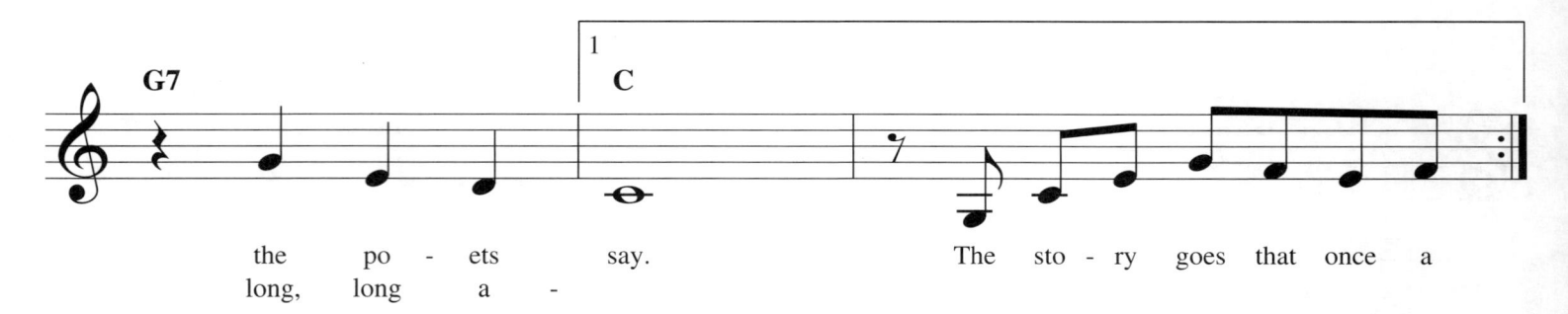

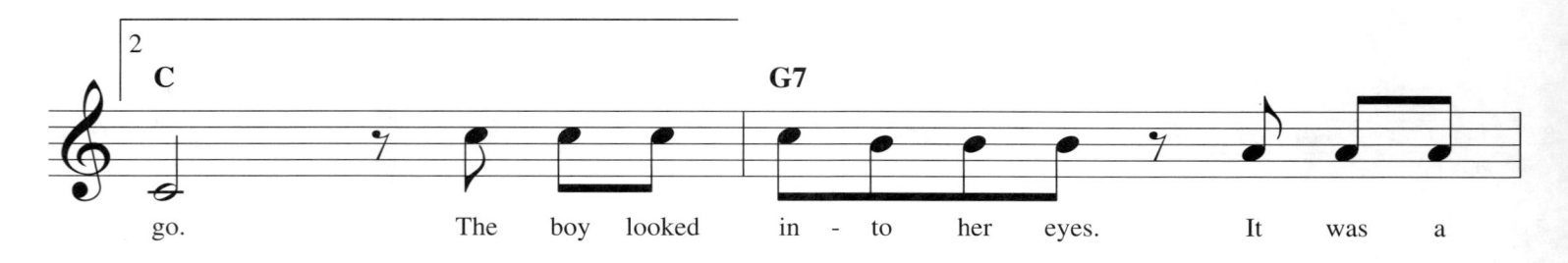

Copyright © 1950, 1951 by Editions Hortensia
Copyrights Renewed, Assigned to Chappell & Co. and
Universal – PolyGram International Publishing, Inc.
International Copyright Secured   All Rights Reserved

Moderately

It's cher-ry pink and ap-ple blos-som white
cher-ry tree

when your true lov-er comes your way.
be-side an ap-ple tree did grow.

It's cher-ry pink and ap-ple blos-som white
And there a boy once met his bride to be

1. the po-ets say. The sto-ry goes that once a
2. long, long a-

go. The boy looked in-to her eyes. It was a

sight to en-thrall, the breez-es joined in their sighs. The blos-soms start - ed to fall. And as they gen - tly ca - ressed, the lov - ers looked up to find the branch - es of the two trees were in - ter - twined. And that is why the po - ets al - ways write, if there's a new moon bright a - bove, it's cher - ry pink and ap - ple blos - som white when you're in love.

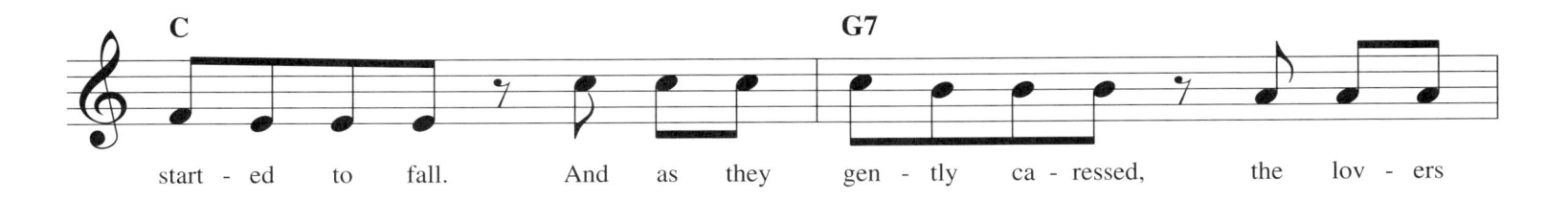

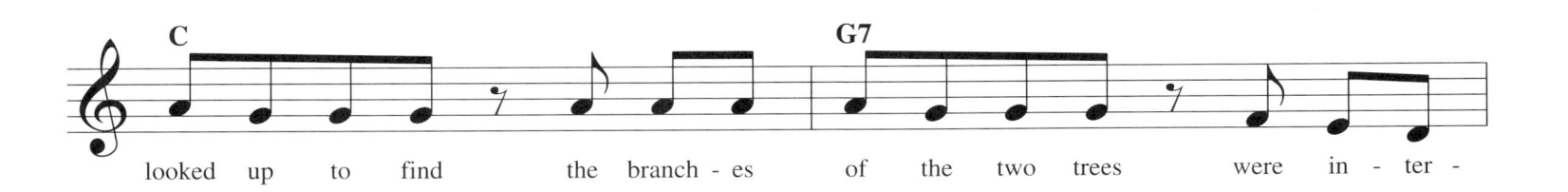

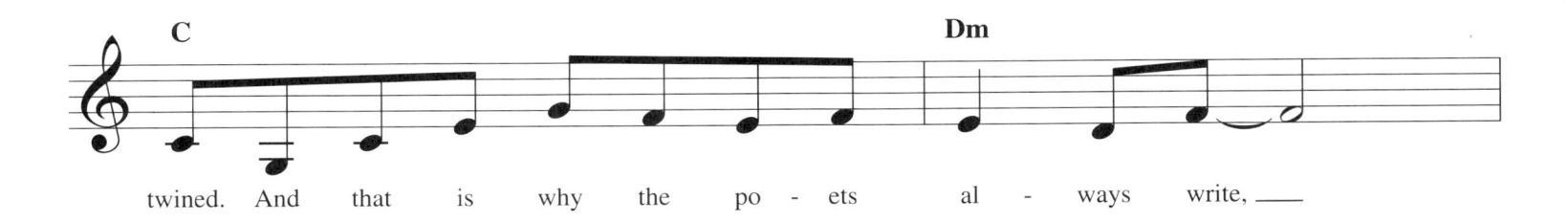

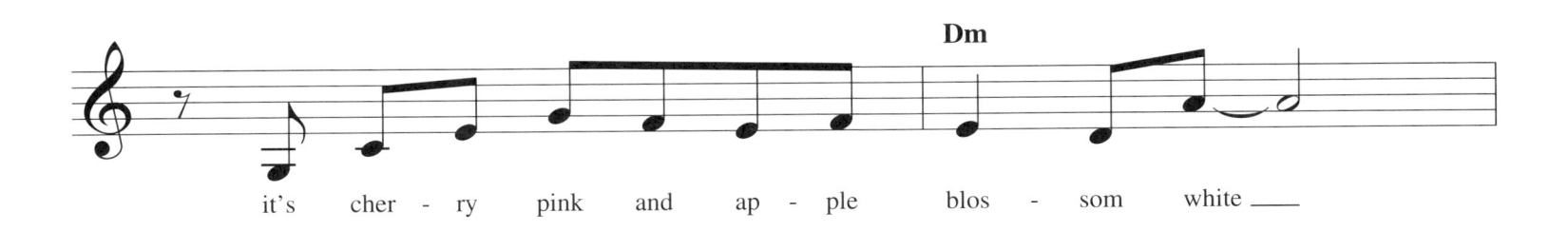

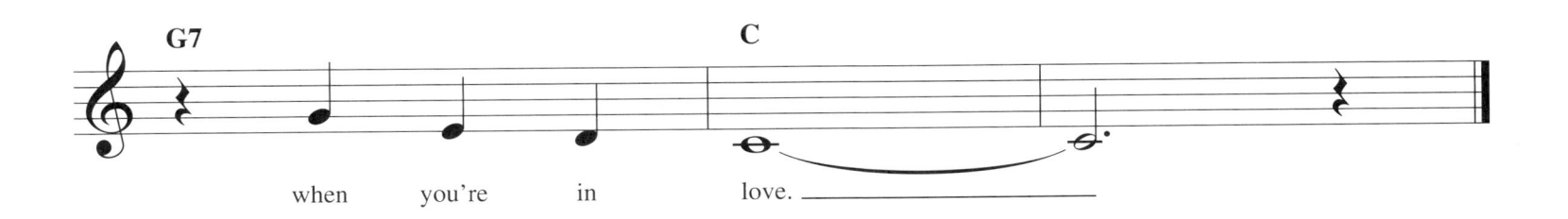

THE CONSTANT RAIN
(Chove Chuva)

Copyright © 1963 by Peermusic Do Brasil Edicoes Musicais Ltda.
Copyright Renewed
All Rights Administered by Peer International Corporation
International Copyright Secured   All Rights Reserved

Original Words and Music by JORGE BEN
English Words by NORMAN GIMBEL

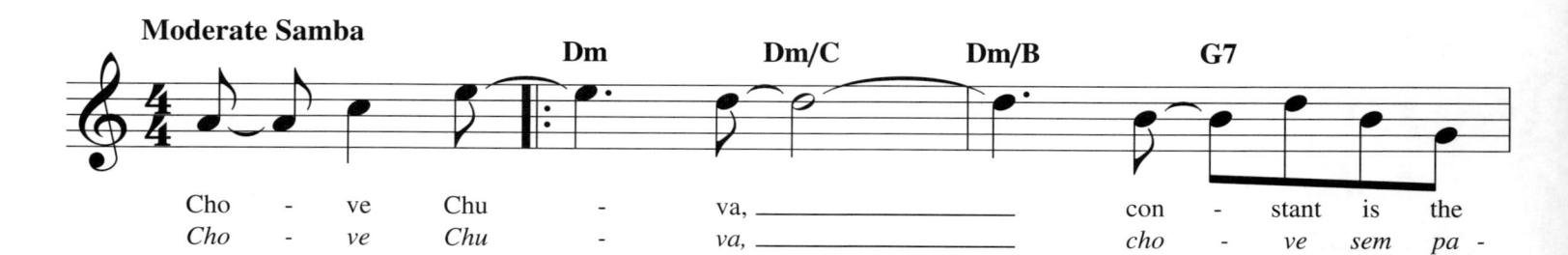

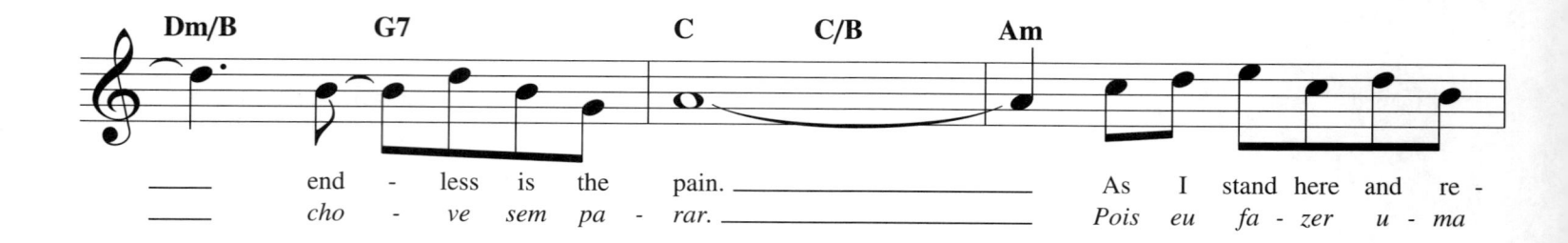

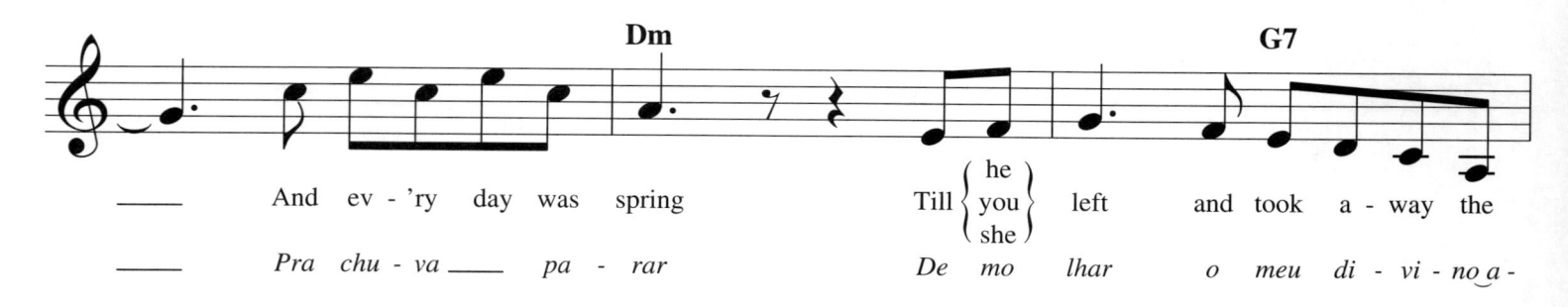

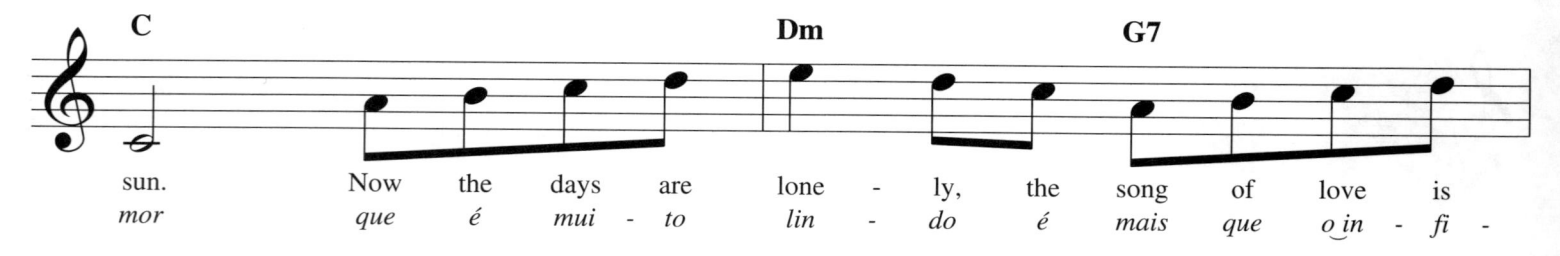

Moderate Samba

Cho - ve Chu - va, _____ con - stant is the rain. _____
Cho - ve Chu - va, _____ cho - ve sem pa - rar. _____

Cho - ve Chu - va, _____ _____ end - less is the pain. _____ As I stand here and re -
Cho - ve Chu - va, _____ _____ cho - ve sem pa - rar. _____ Pois eu fa - zer u - ma

mem - ber ____ that once, our ____ hearts were one. _____
pre - ce ____ Pra deus nos - sos Se - nhor _____

And ev - 'ry day was spring   Till { he / you / she } left and took a - way the
Pra chu - va ___ pa - rar   De mo lhar o meu di - vi - no a -

sun.   Now the days are lone - ly, the song of love is
mor   que é mui - to lin - do é mais que o in - fi -

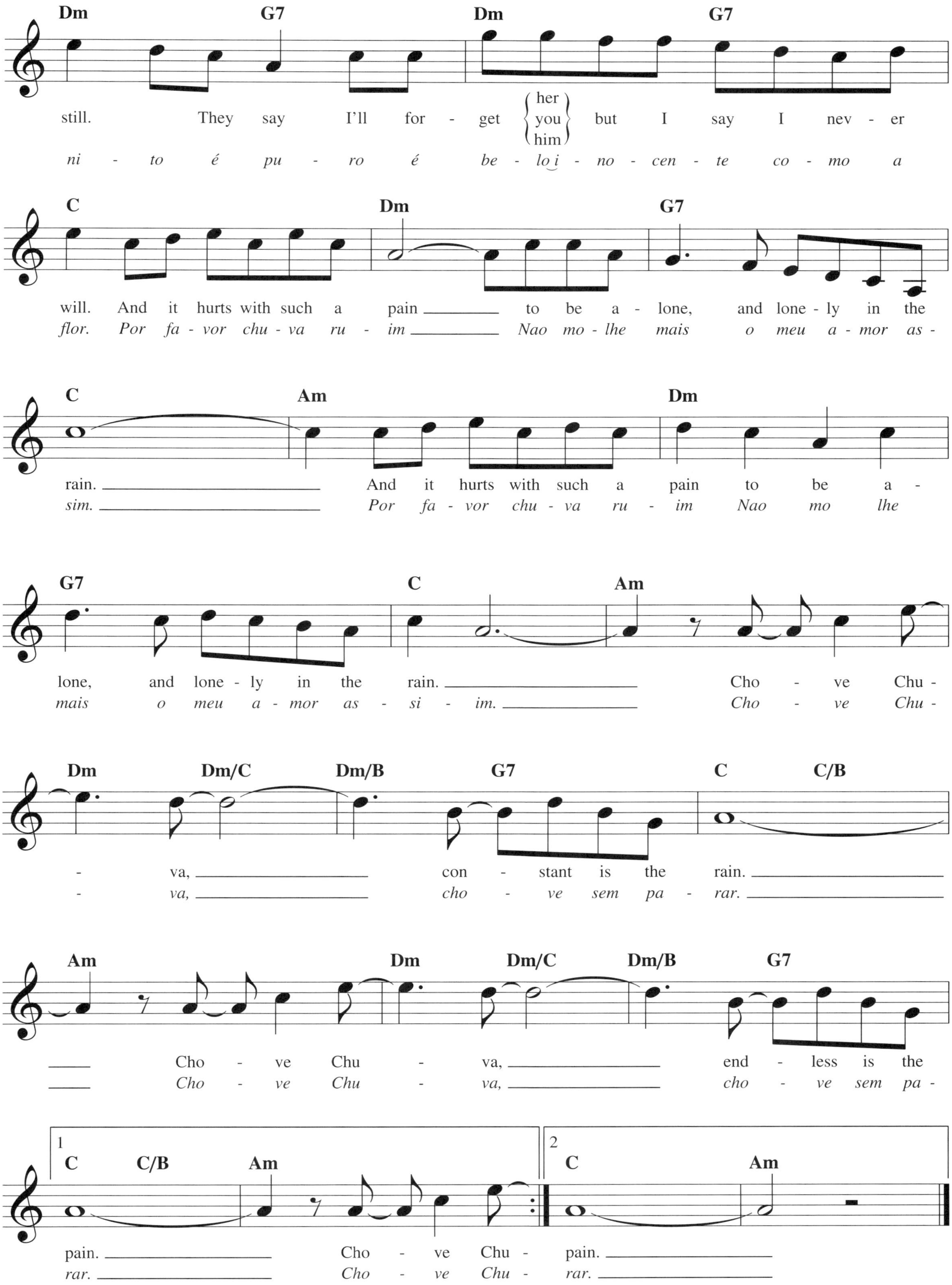
Dm G7 Dm G7
still. They say I'll for - get her / you / him but I say I nev - er
ni - to é pu - ro é be - lo i - no - cen - te co - mo a
C Dm G7
will. And it hurts with such a pain to be a - lone, and lone - ly in the
flor. Por fa - vor chu - va ru - im Nao mo - lhe mais o meu a - mor as -
C Am Dm
rain. And it hurts with such a pain to be a -
sim. Por fa - vor chu - va ru - im Nao mo lhe
G7 C Am
lone, and lone - ly in the rain. Cho - ve Chu -
mais o meu a - mor as - si - im. Cho - ve Chu -
Dm Dm/C Dm/B G7 C C/B
- va, con - stant is the rain.
- va, cho - ve sem pa - rar.
Am Dm Dm/C Dm/B G7
Cho - ve Chu - va, end - less is the
Cho - ve Chu - va, cho - ve sem pa -
1 C C/B Am 2 C Am
pain. Cho - ve Chu - pain.
rar. Cho - ve Chu - rar.

CUMANÁ

Copyright © 1947 Harold Spina, Assigned to Spina Music
Copyright Renewed
International Copyright Secured   All Rights Reserved

Words by HAROLD SPINA and ROC HILLMAN
Music by BARCLAY ALLEN

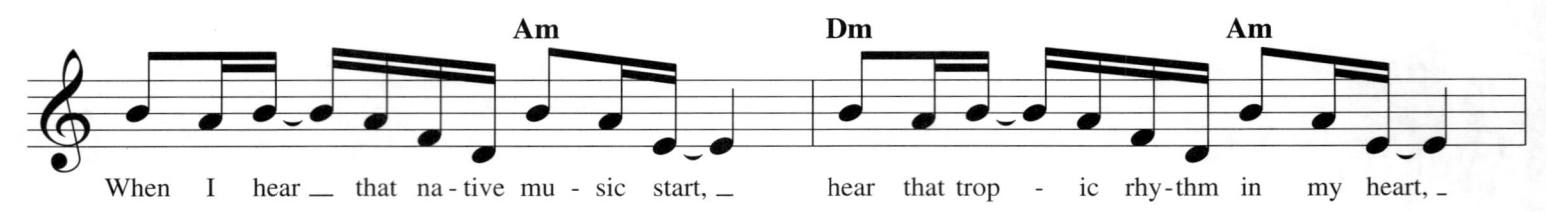

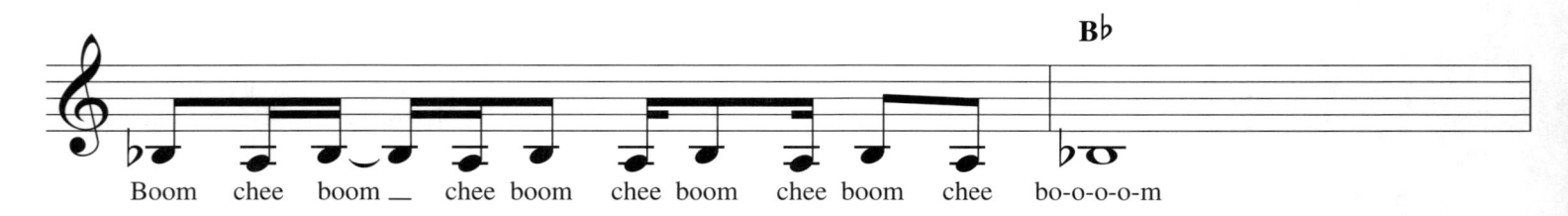

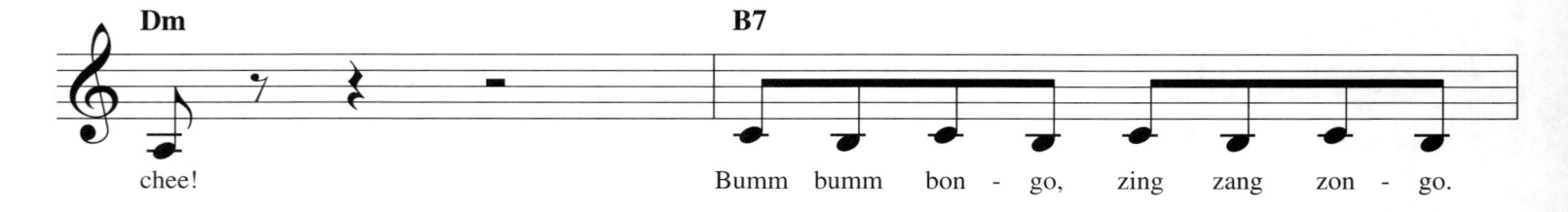

Cu-ma-ná, Cu-ma-ná, on the coast of Ven-e-zu-e-la. Cu-ma-ná, Cu-ma-ná, ev-'ry night ex-cit-ing and ga-la. Cu-ma-ná, Cu-ma-ná, bon-go drums keep pound-ing, re-sound-ing. When I hear that na-tive mu-sic start, hear that trop-ic rhy-thm in my heart, we can nev-er, nev-er, be a-part. I got-ta go to Cu-ma-ná. Bumm bumm bon-go, zing zang zon-go. Boom chee boom chee boom chee boom chee boom chee bo-o-o-om chee! Bumm bumm bon-go, zing zang zon-go.

E Dm
Boom chee boom chee boom chee boom chee boom chee boom! Chee!
E7 Am
Beat - ing, re - peat - ing and call - ing to me. Cu - ma - ná, Cu - ma - ná, on the
Dm E7
coast of Ven - e - zu - e - la. Cu - ma - ná, Cu - ma - ná, ev - 'ry
Am
night ex - cit - ing and ga - la. Cu - ma - ná, Cu - ma - ná, bon - go
Dm Am
drums keep pound - ing, re - sound - ing. When I hear that na - tive mu - sic start,
Dm Am Dm Am
hear that trop - ic rhy - thm in my heart, we can nev - er, nev - er, be a - part. I
E7 1 Am
got - ta go to Cu - ma - ná. Cu - ma -
2 Am E7 Am E F
ná. Got - ta go got - ta go got - ta go got - ta go got - ta
E F E Am E7 Am
go got - ta go got - ta go to Cu - ma - ná!

A DAY IN THE LIFE OF A FOOL
(Manhã De Carnaval)

Words by CARL SIGMAN
Music by LUIZ BONFA

Copyright © 1959 by Les Nouvelles Editions Meridian
English Lyric Copyright © 1966 by Music Sales Corporation
Copyrights Renewed
All Rights for Les Nouvelles Editions Meridian Administered by Chappell & Co.
International Copyright Secured   All Rights Reserved

Slow Bossa Nova

A day in the life of a fool, a sad and a long, lonely day. I walk the avenue and hope I'll run into the welcome sight of you coming my way. I stop just across from your door but you're never home anymore. So back to my room and there in the gloom I cry tears of goodbye. 'Til you come back to me, that's the way it will be ev'ry day in the life of a fool.

DON'T CRY FOR ME ARGENTINA
from EVITA

Copyright © 1976, 1977 EVITA MUSIC LTD.
Copyright Renewed
All Rights for the United States and Canada Controlled and Administered by
UNIVERSAL MUSIC CORP.
All Rights Reserved   Used by Permission

Words by TIM RICE
Music by ANDREW LLOYD WEBBER

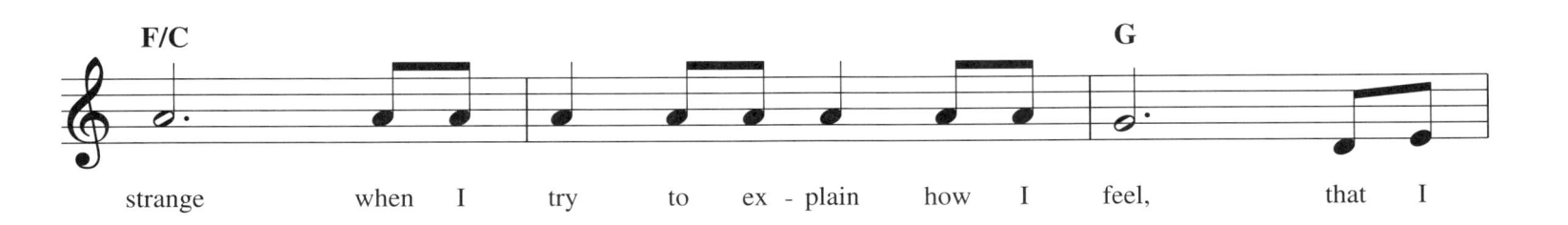

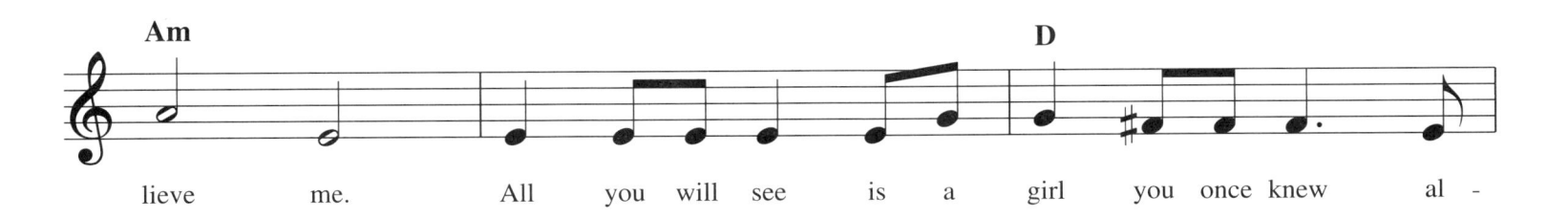

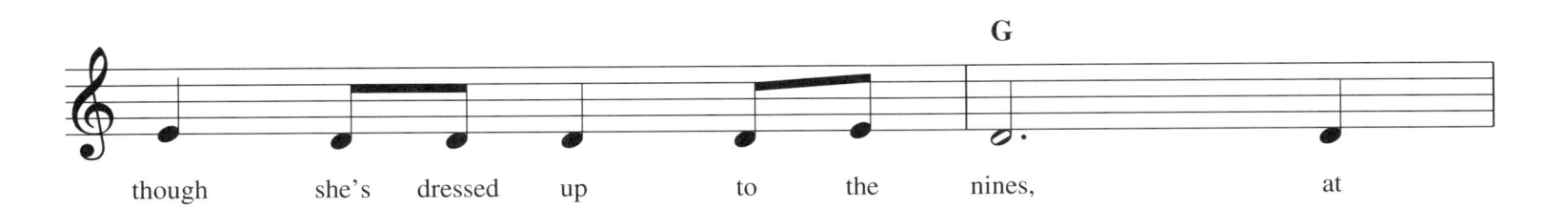

Moderately

It won't be eas-y. You'll think it strange when I try to ex-plain how I feel, that I still need your love af-ter all that I've done. You won't be-lieve me. All you will see is a girl you once knew al-though she's dressed up to the nines, at

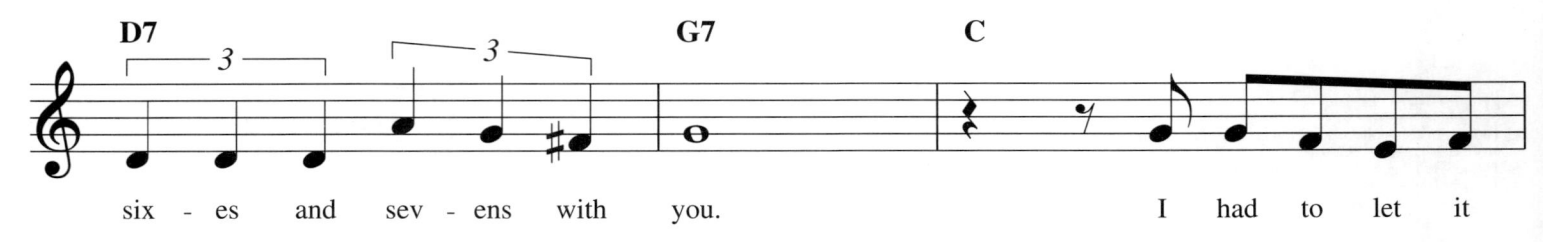

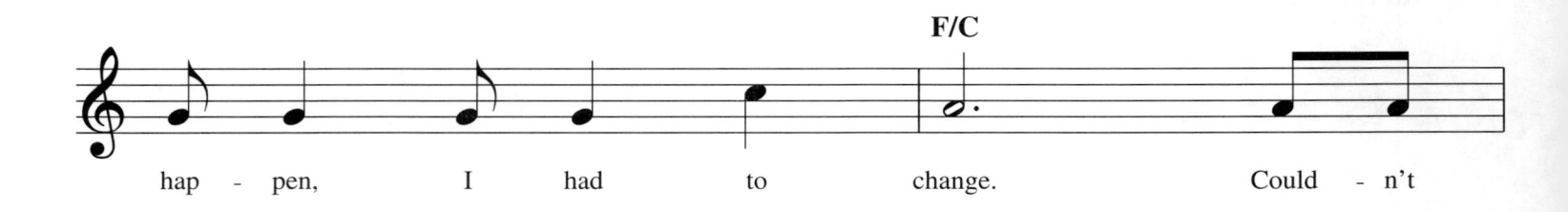

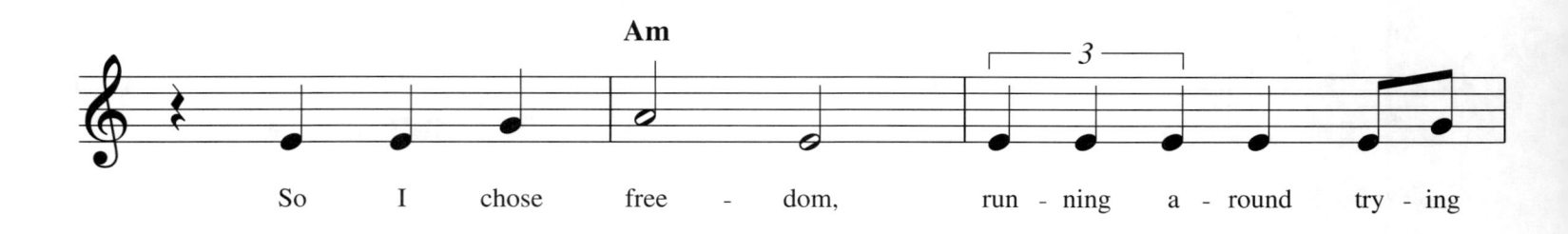

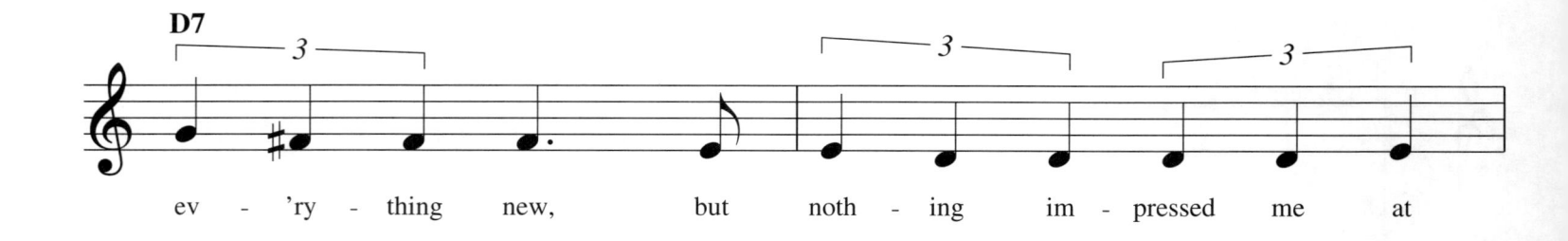

sixes and sevens with you. I had to let it happen, I had to change. Couldn't stay all my life down at heel looking out of the window, staying out of the sun. So I chose freedom, running around trying ev-'ry-thing new, but nothing impressed me at all. I never expected it to.

Don't cry for me Argentina. The truth is I never left you. All through my wild days, my mad existence, I kept my promise, don't keep your distance. Have I said too much? There's nothing more I can think of to say to you. But all you have to do is look at me to know that ev-'ry word is true.

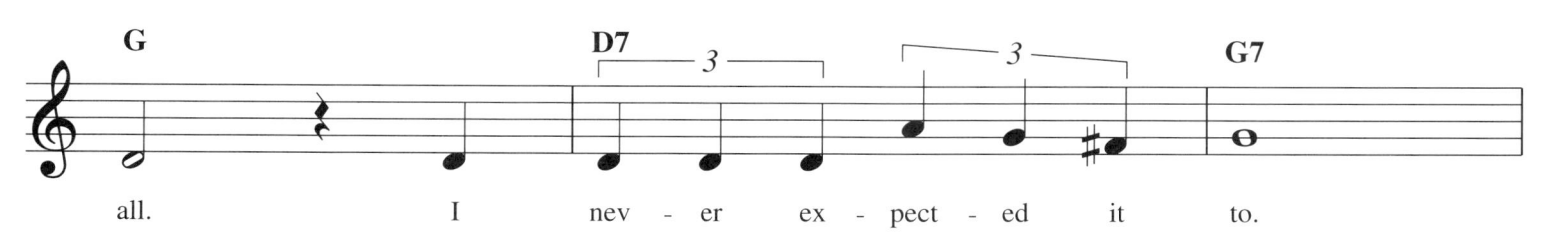

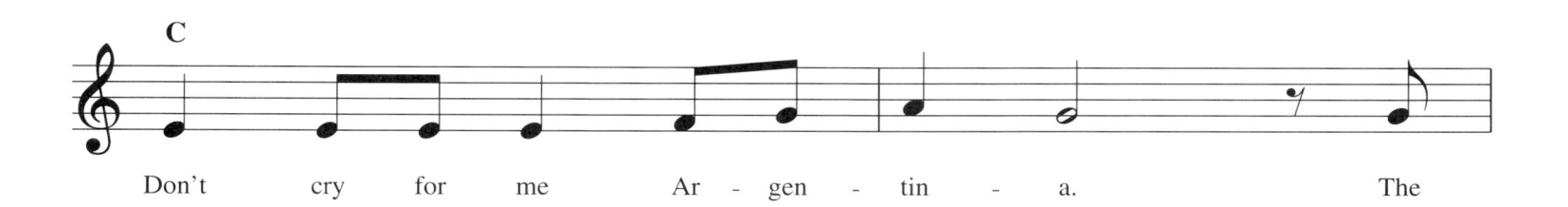

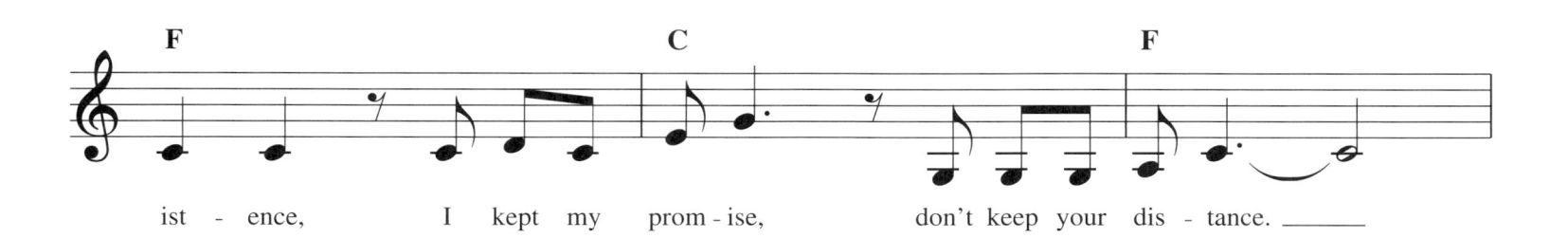

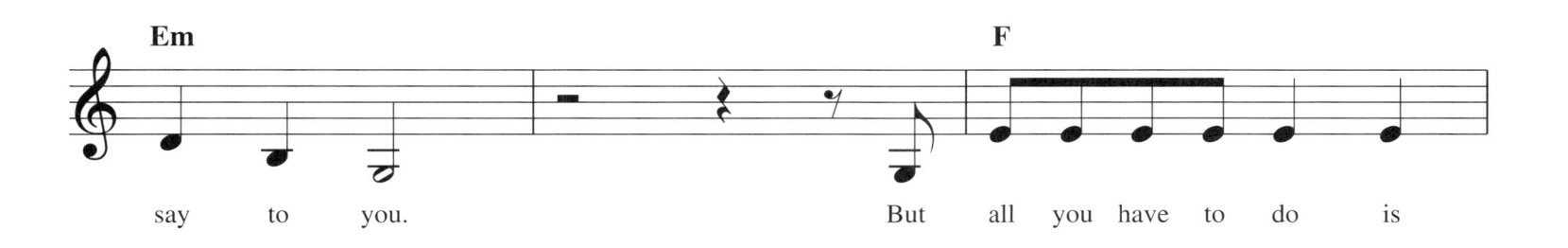

DINDI

Copyright © 1965 Antonio Carlos Jobim and Aloysio de Oliveira
Copyright Renewed, Assigned to Corcovado Music Corp. and Ipanema Music Corp.
International Copyright Secured   All Rights Reserved

Music by ANTONIO CARLOS JOBIM
Portuguese Lyrics by ALOYSIO DE OLIVEIRA
English Lyrics by RAY GILBERT

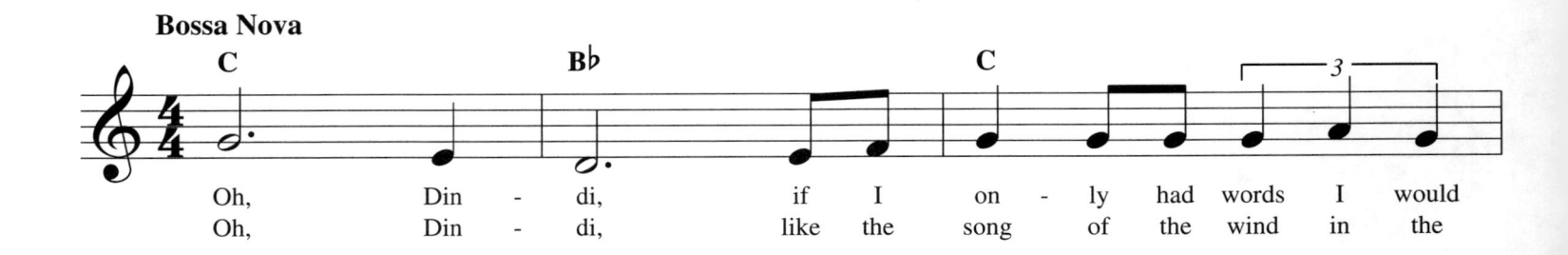

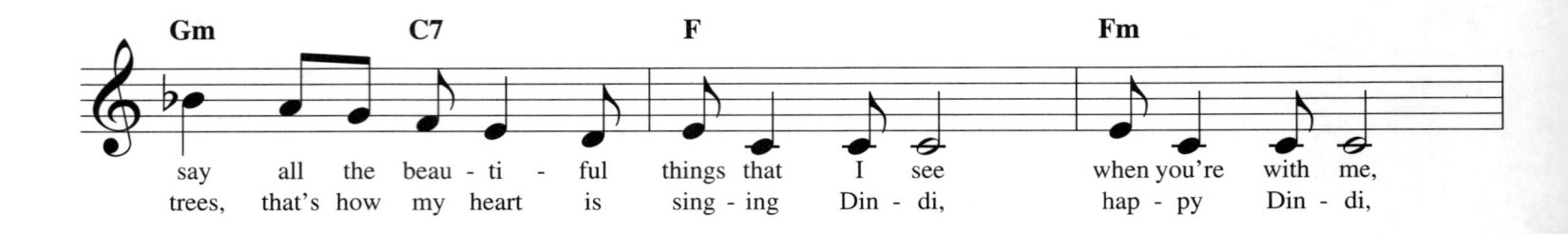

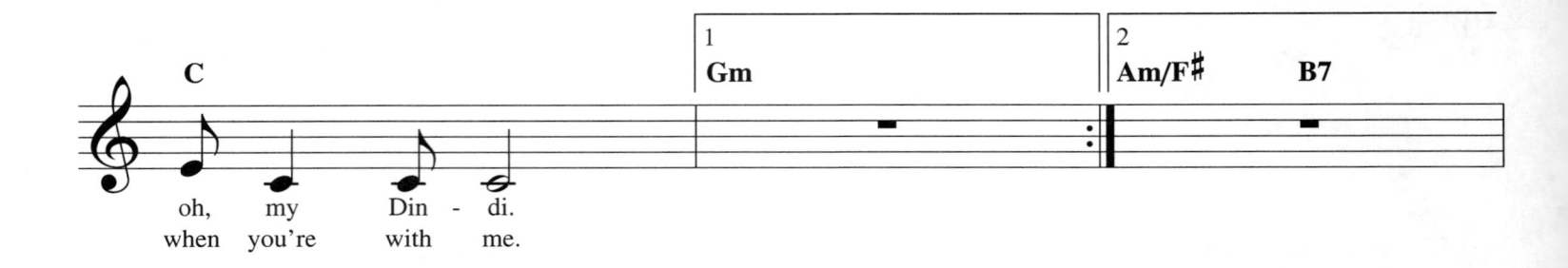

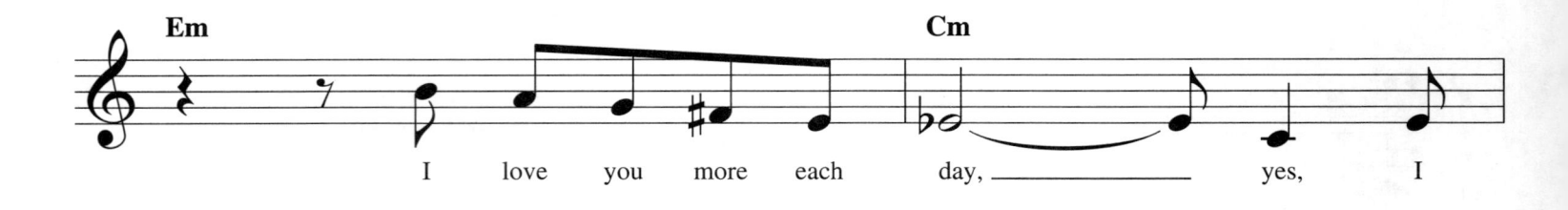

Bossa Nova

Oh, Din - di, if I on - ly had words I would
Oh, Din - di, like the song of the wind in the

say all the beau - ti - ful things that I see when you're with me,
trees, that's how my heart is sing - ing Din - di, hap - py Din - di,

oh, my Din - di.
when you're with me.

I love you more each day, yes, I

do, yes, I do.

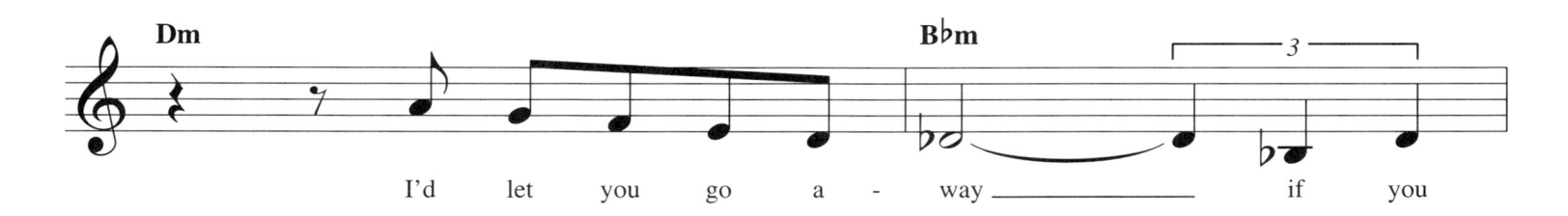

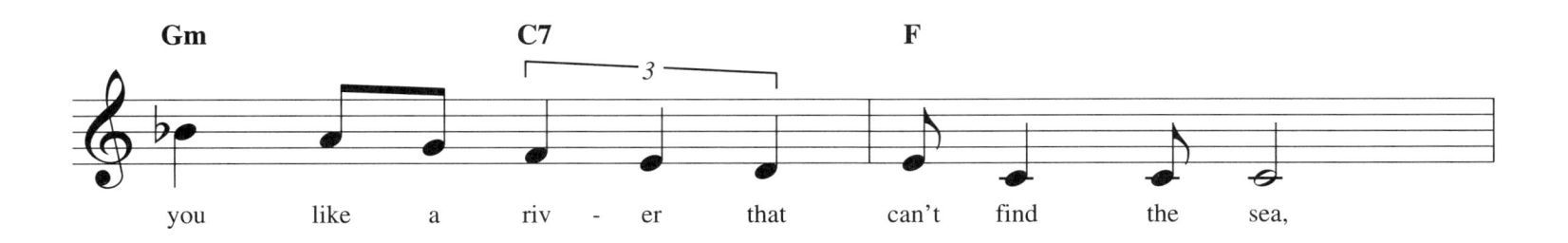

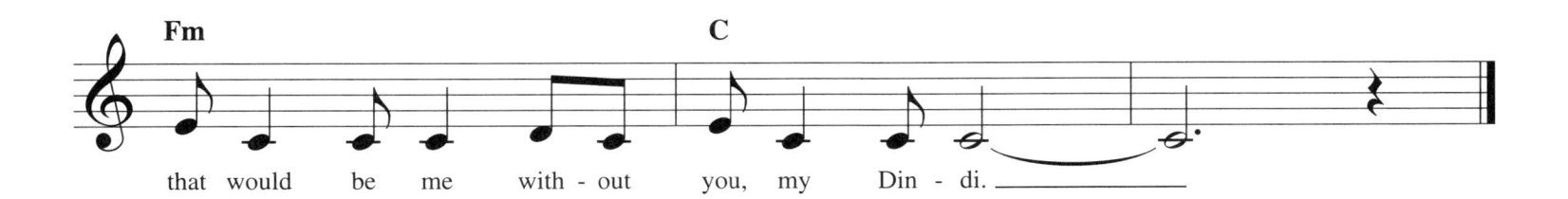

DON'T EVER GO AWAY
(Por Causa De Voce)

English Lyric by RAY GILBERT
Original Text by DOLORES DURAN
Music by ANTONIO CARLOS JOBIM

Em	Gm A7	Dm Dm/C

there. _____ Listen, my love, never
cê _____ *O - lha, meu bem, nun - ca*

Dm/B G7	Em	Gm A7

more, Don't ev - er go a - way. _____
mais Nos dei - xa por fa - vor _____

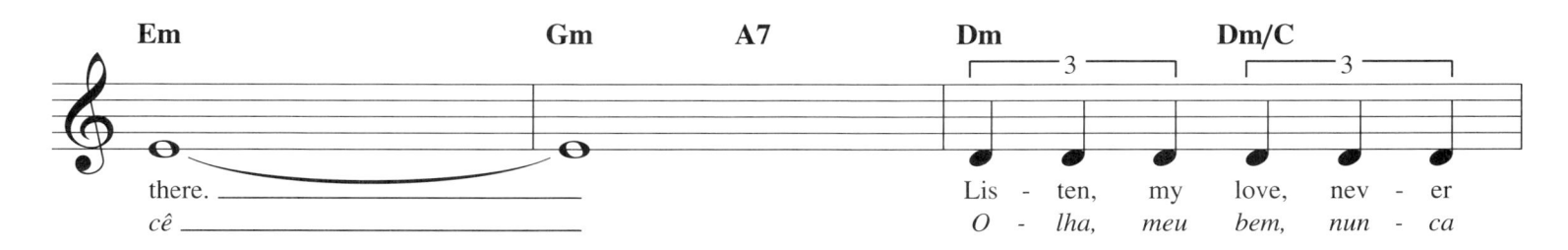

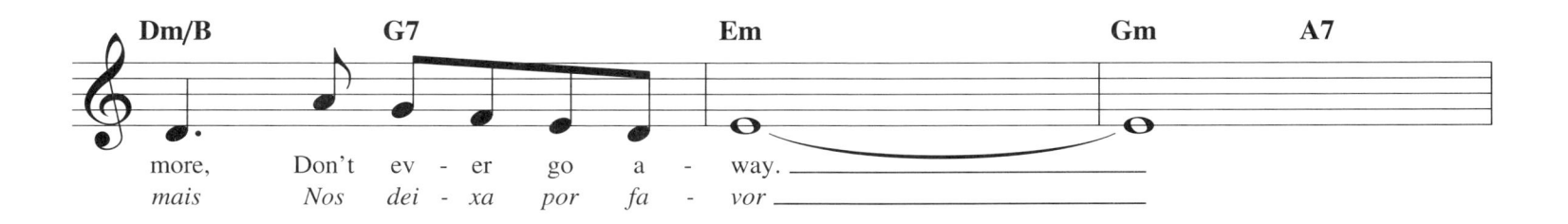

Dm G7	Gm/E

We are your life and your dream and we want you to stay. _____
So - mas a vi - da e o so - hno nos so - mos o a - mor. _____

A7	F	Am/F♯ Fm/D

_____ Come in, my love, come to me, _____ Don't let this heart - less
_____ *En - tre, meu bem, por fa - vôr* _____ *Não dei - xe o mun - do*

C E7/B	A7	Dm

world bring an - oth - er "good - bye," Em - brace me in a sim - ple way, don't speak, don't re -
mau lhe le - var ou - tra vez me a - bra - ce sim - ples - men - te não fa - le não

Fm/D	G7	C

mem - ber, And dar - ling, don't cry. _____
lem - bre, Não cho - re meu bem. _____

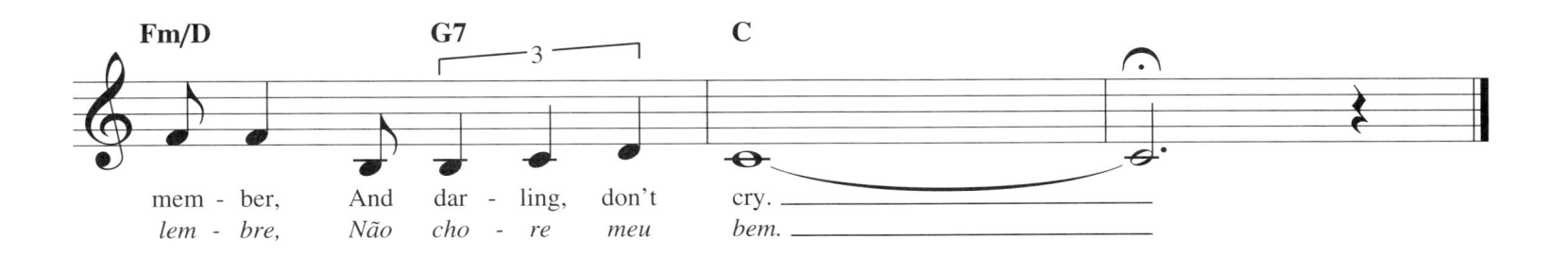

EL CHOCLO

B♭7 E♭ B♭7
E♭ G7 Cm
D7 G G7
C G7
C A7
Dm D7 G7
D7 G7 C
D.S. al Coda
CODA
Cm G7 Cm

EL CUMBANCHERO

Copyright © 1943 by Peer International Corporation
Copyright Renewed
International Copyright Secured   All Rights Reserved

Words and Music by
RAFAEL HERNANDEZ

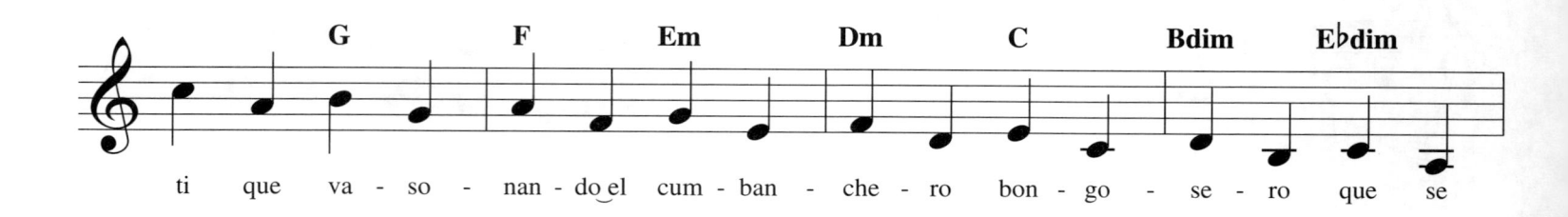

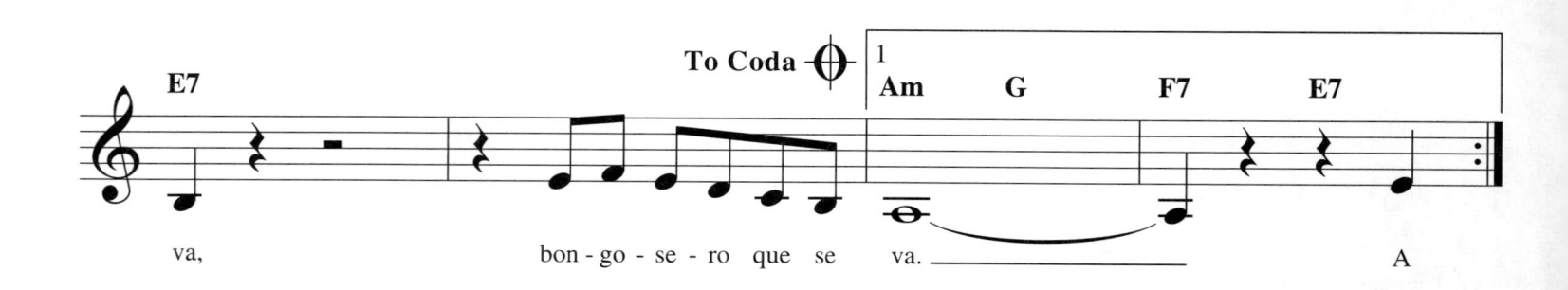

Lively

A cum - ba, cum - ba, cum - ba, cum - ban - che - ro. A bon - go, bon - go, bon - go, bon - go - se - ro. Pri - qui - ti que va so - nan - do el cum - ban - che - ro bon - go - se - ro que se va, bon - go - se - ro que se va. A

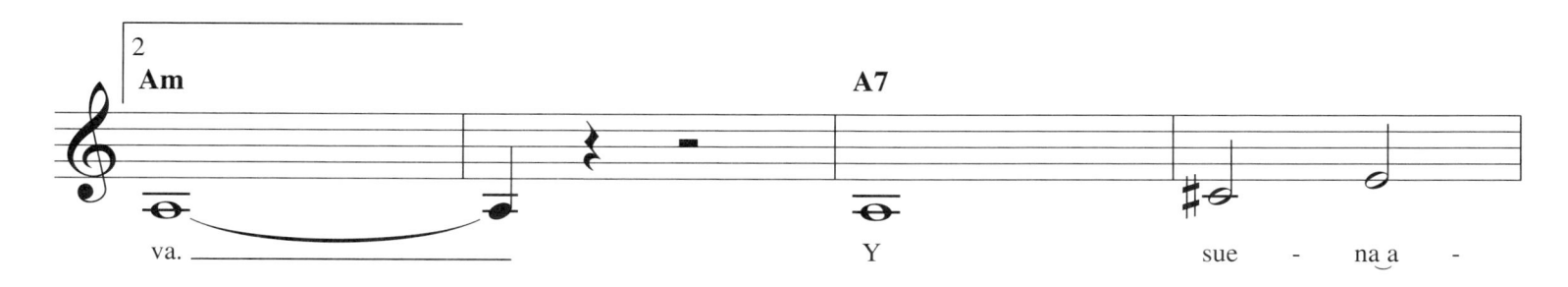

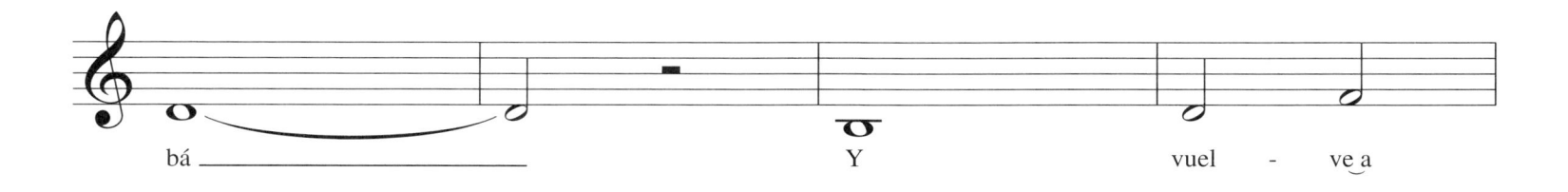

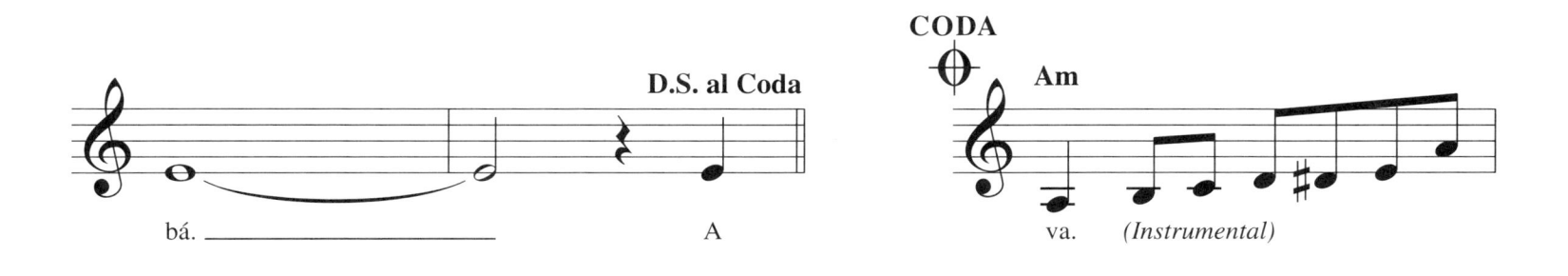

va. Y suena a-
si el tambor, biriquití bum-bum-
bá Y vuelve a
repicar, biriquití, bum-bum-
bá. A

CODA

va. *(Instrumental)*

THE END OF A LOVE AFFAIR

Copyright © 1950 UNIVERSAL MUSIC CORP.
Copyright Renewed
All Rights Reserved   Used by Permission

Words and Music by
EDWARD C. REDDING

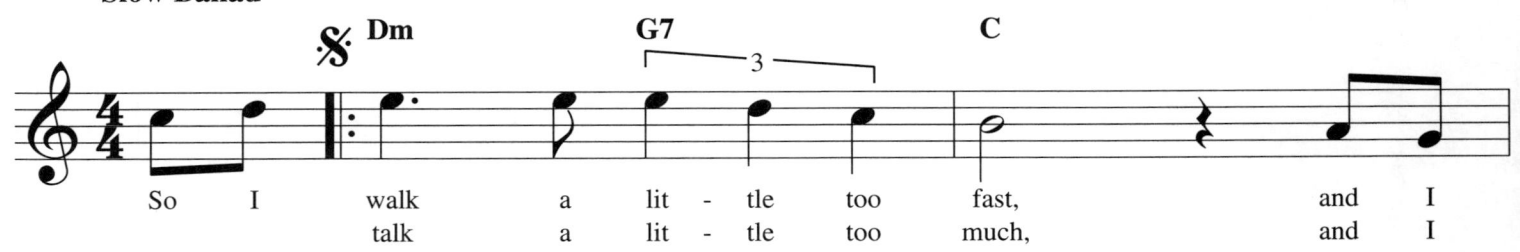

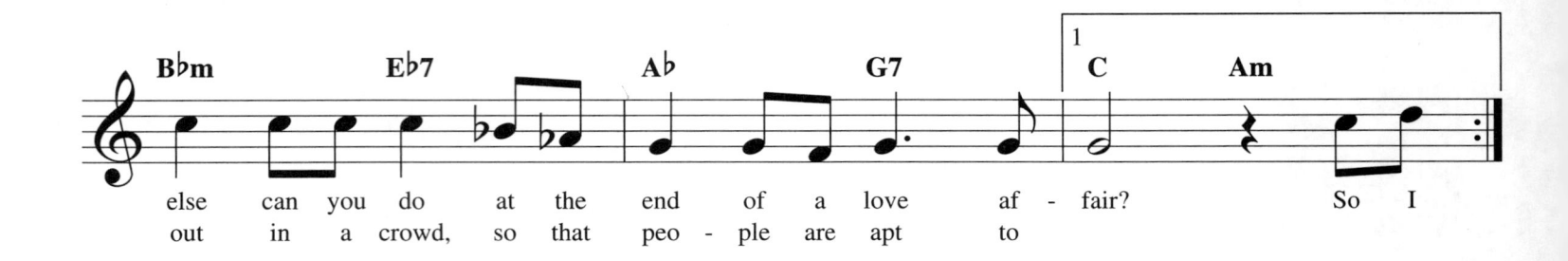

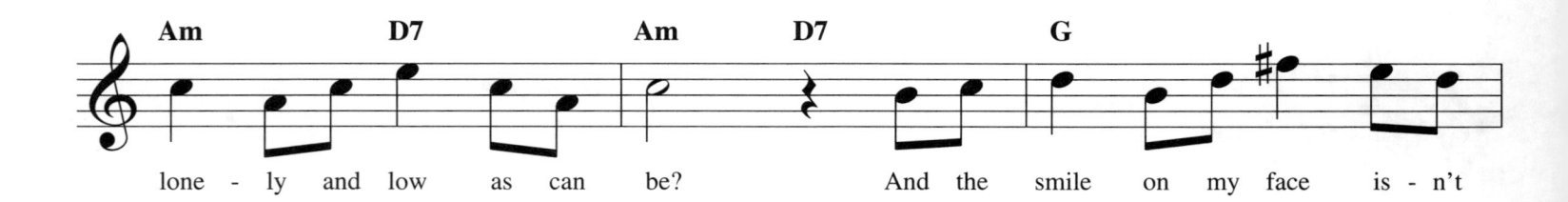

Slow Ballad

So I walk a lit - tle too fast, and I
talk a lit - tle too much, and I

drive a lit - tle too fast, and I'm reck - less, it's true, but what
laugh a lit - tle too much, and my voice is too loud when I'm

else can you do at the end of a love af - fair? So I
out in a crowd, so that peo - ple are apt to

stare. Do they know, do they care, that it's on - ly that I'm

lone - ly and low as can be? And the smile on my face is - n't

| Em | A7 | Am | D7 | Dm | G7 |

real - ly a smile at all! _____ So I

| Dm | G7 | C | Cm | F7 |

smoke a lit - tle too much, and I drink a lit - tle too

| B♭ | B♭m | E♭7 | B♭m | E♭7 |

much, and the tunes I re - quest are not al - ways the best, but the

| A♭ | G7 | Gm | C7 | F |

ones where the trum - pets blare! So I go at a mad - den - ing

| B♭7 | C | E♭dim |

pace, and I pre - tend that it's tak - ing { her / his } place. But what

| Dm | G7 | Dm | G7 | C | Am |

To Coda

else can you do at the end of a love af - fair?

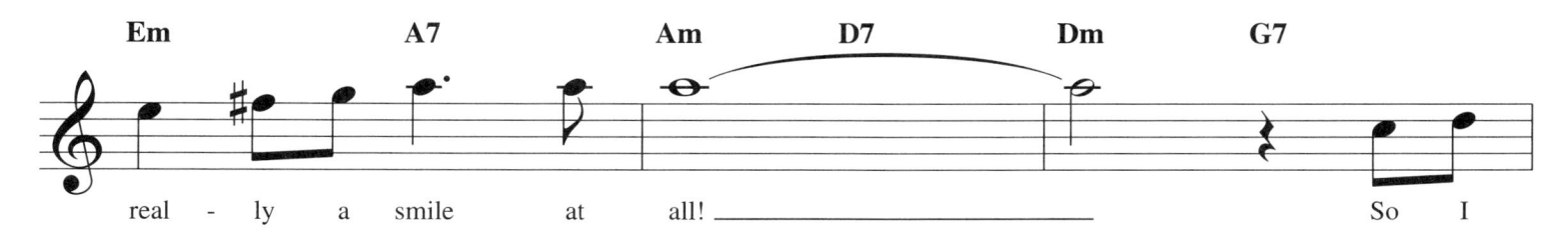

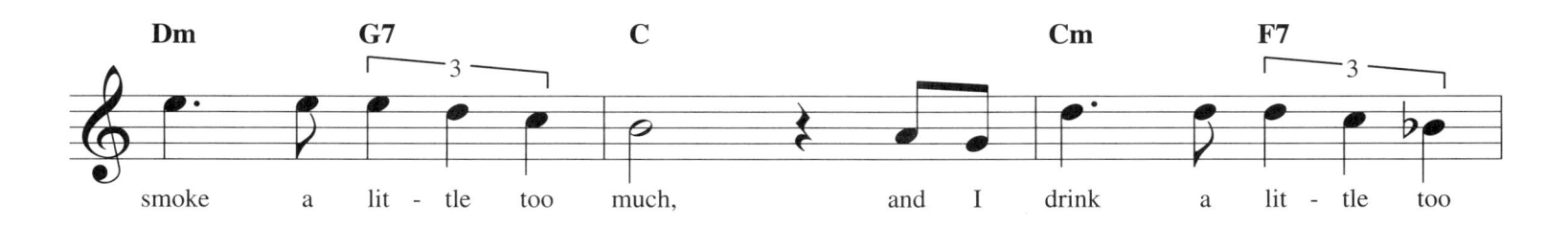

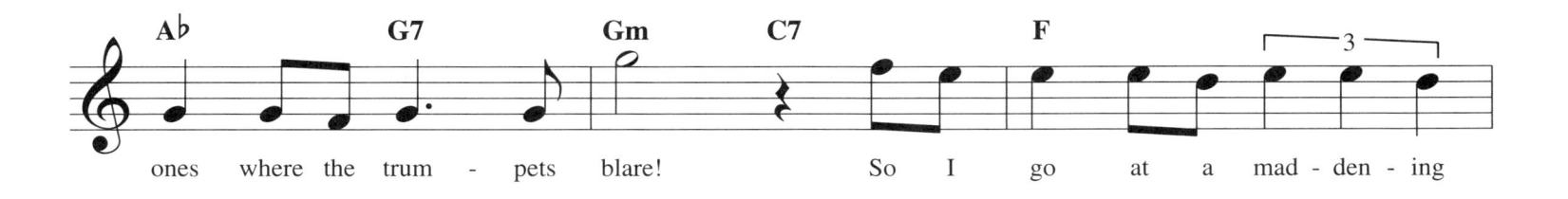

| Dm | G7 |

**D.S. al Coda
(with repeat)**

So I

CODA

| C |

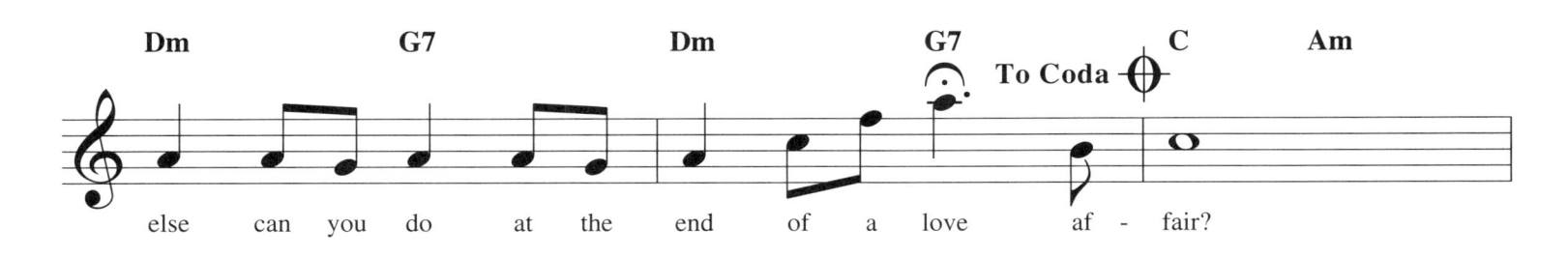

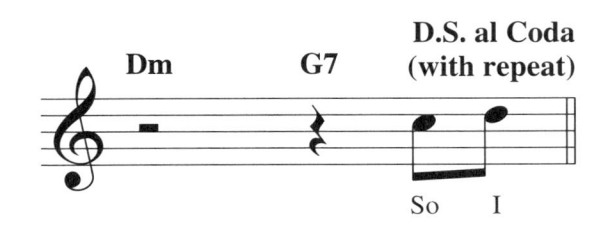

fair? _____

ESTATE

Music by BRUNO MARTINO
Lyrics by BRUNO BRIGHETTI

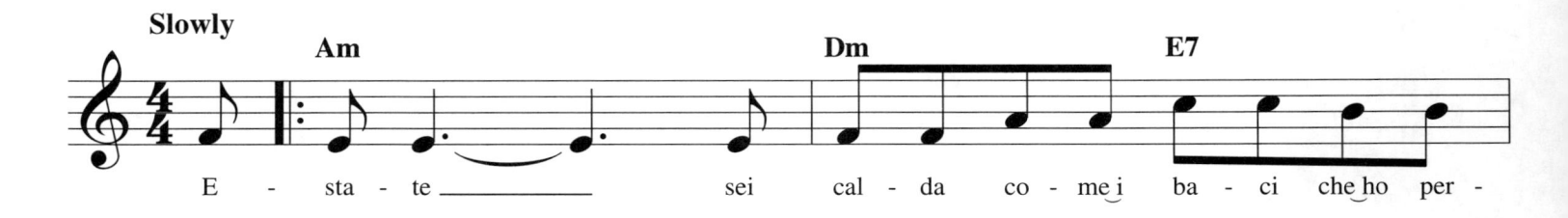

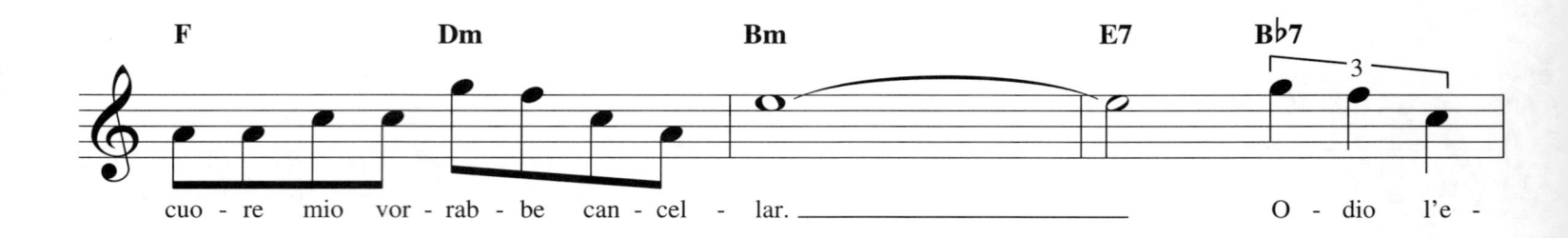

Copyright © 1960 SANTA CECILIA CASA MUSICALE
Copyright Renewed
All Rights for United States and Canada Controlled and Administered by UNIVERSAL MUSIC CORP.
All Rights Reserved   Used by Permission

Slowly

E - sta - te ___ sei cal - da co - me i ba - ci che ho per -
du - to ___ sei pie - na di un a - mo - re che è pas - sa - to ___ che il
cuo - re mio vor - rab - be can - cel - lar. ___ O - dio l'e -
sta - te! ___ Il so - le che o - gni gior - no ci scal - da - va, ___ che
splen - di - di tra - mon - ti di - pin - ge - va ___ a - des - so bru - ni a so - lo con fu -
ror... ___ Tor - ne - rá un al - tro in - ver - no, ___ ca -

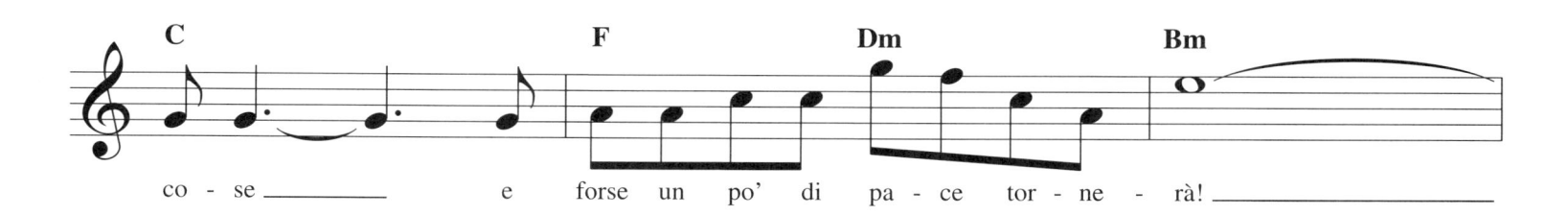

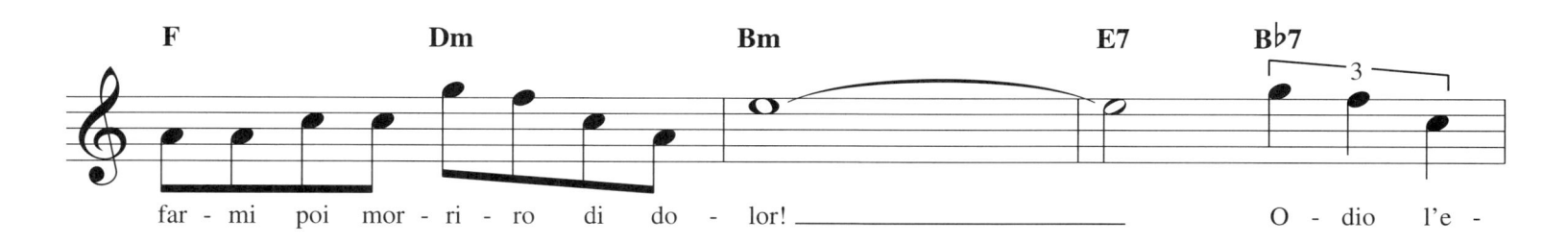

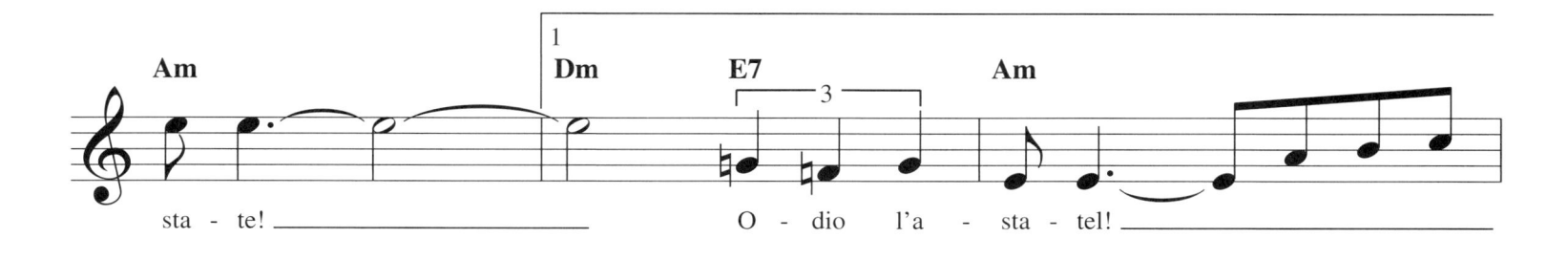

dran-no mil-le pe-ta-li di ro-se _____ la ne-ve co-pri-rà tut-te le

co-se _____ e forse un po' di pa-ce tor-ne-rà! _____

____ O - dio l'e - sta - te! _____ che ha da-to il suo pro-fu-mo ad o-gni

fio - re, _____ l'e - sta - te che ha crea-to il nos-tro a - mo - re _____ per

far - mi poi mor - ri - ro di do - lor! _____ O - dio l'e -

sta - te! _____ O - dio l'a - sta - te! _____

E - ____ O - dio l'e - sta - te! _____

FEELINGS
(¿Dime?)

Copyright © 1974 by Editora Augusta Ltda., Avenida Ipiranga,
1123, Sao Paulo, Brasil and Loving Guitar Music, Inc.
Copyright Renewed
International Copyright Secured   All Rights Reserved

English Words and Music by MORRIS ALBERT
and LOUIS GASTE
Spanish Words by THOMAS FUNDORA

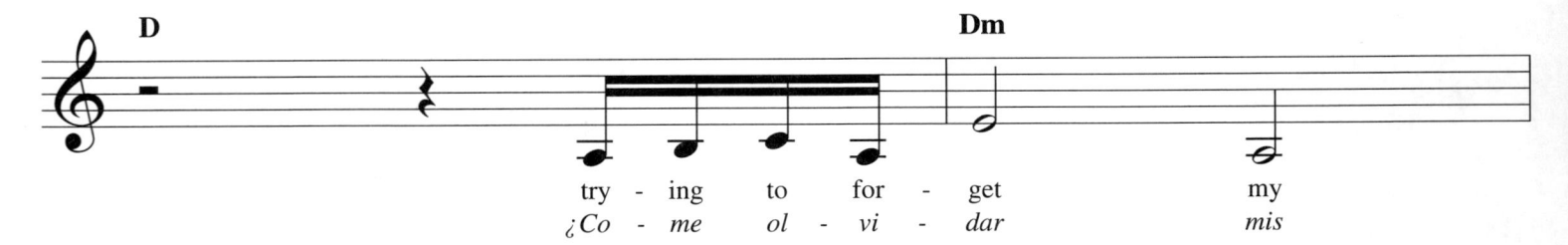

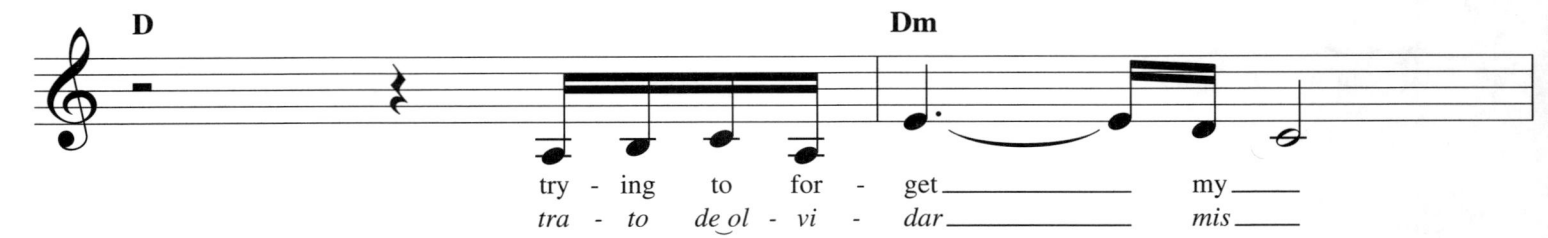

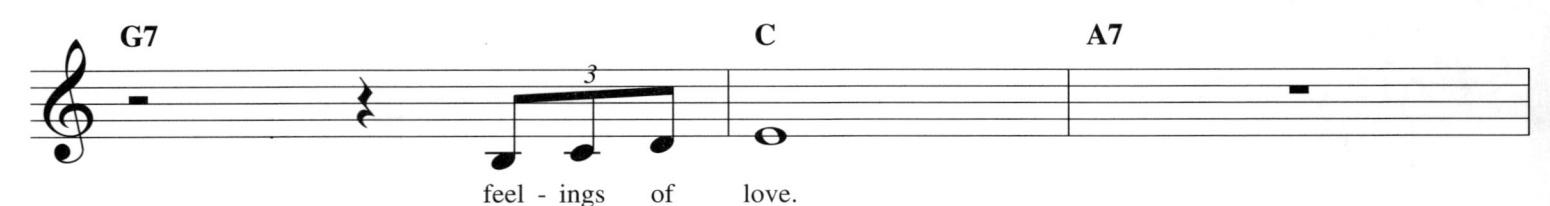

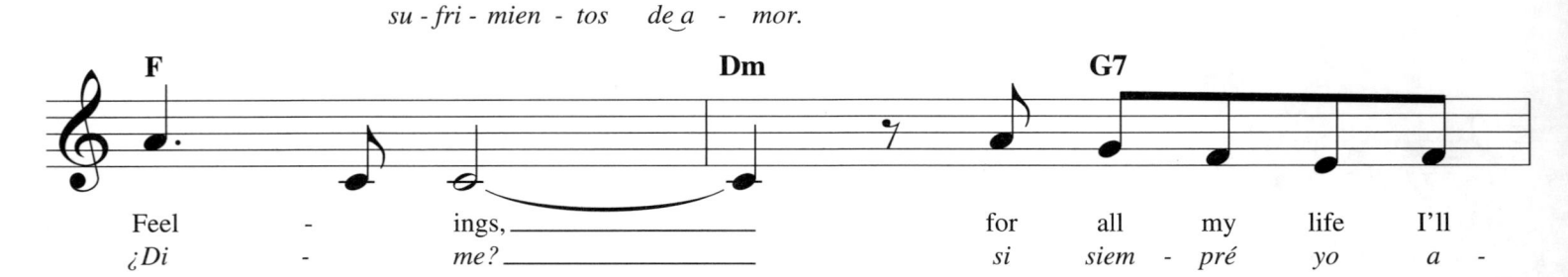

Moderately slow

Feel - ings,_____ noth - ing more than feel - ings,_____
¿Di - me?_____ ¿so - la - men - te di - me?_____

try - ing to for - get my
¿Co - me ol - vi - dar mis

feel - ings of love.
sen - ti - mien - tos de a - mor?

Tear - drops_____ roll - ing down on my face,_____
Lá - gri - mas_____ bro - tan de mis o - jos_____

try - ing to for - get_____ my_____
tra - to de ol - vi - dar_____ mis_____

feel - ings of love.
su - fri - mien - tos de a - mor.

Feel - ings,_____ for all my life I'll
¿Di - me?_____ si siem - pré yo a -

| Em | A7 | Dm |

feel it. I wish I'd nev-er met you girl;
sí te a-mé, ¿Por-que a-ho-ra sé lo ton - to que fuí?

| G7 | Em | A7 | F |

you'll nev-er come a-gain. Feel - ings,
Ja - más tú vol-ve - rás. ¿Di - me?

| Dm | G7 | Em | A7 |

wo wo wo, feel - ings, wo wo wo,
Wo wo wo ¿Di - me? Wo wo wo

| Dm | G7 | Bm |

feel you a - gain in my arms.
¿Di - me? A - quí en mis bra - zos.

| E7 | Am |

Feel - ings, feel-ings like I've
¿Di - me? Es que

| | D | |

nev - er lost you, and feel-ings like I'll
pien-so que ya te he per - di - do, y pre-sien - to que sin

| Dm | G7 |

nev - er have you a - gain in my
tí mi vi - da no no tie - ne ra -

heart. Feel - ings,
zón. *¿Di - me?*

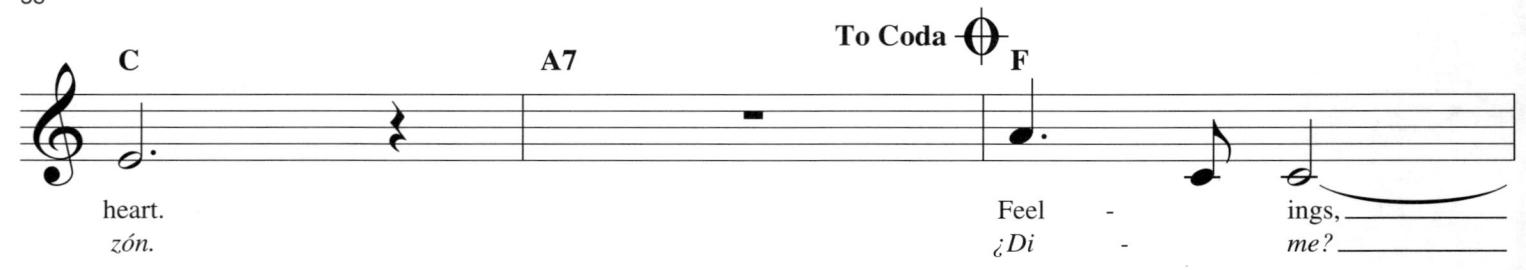

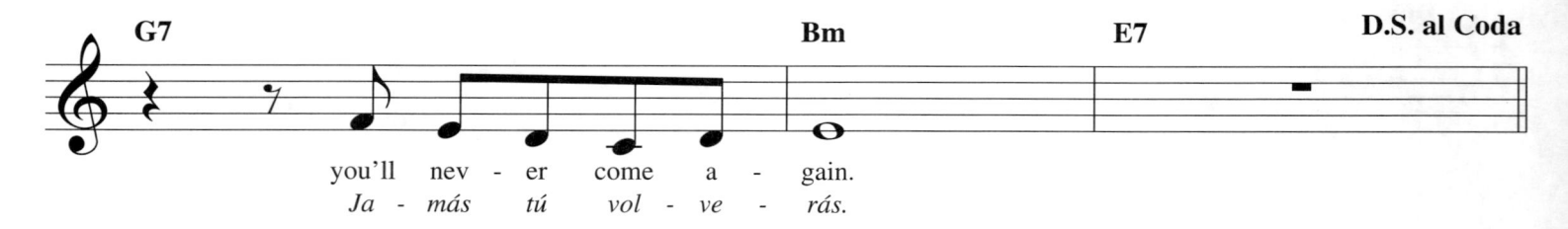

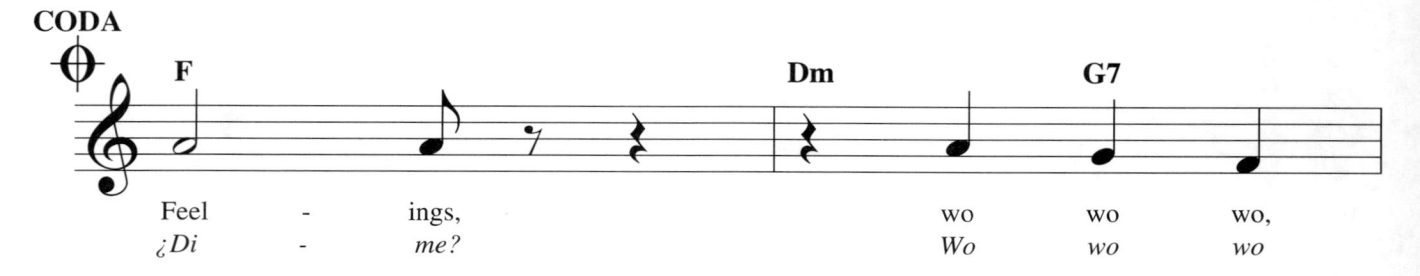

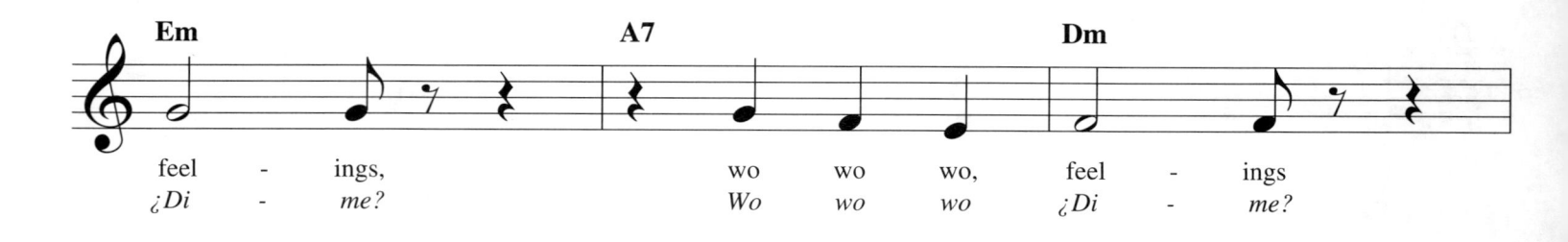

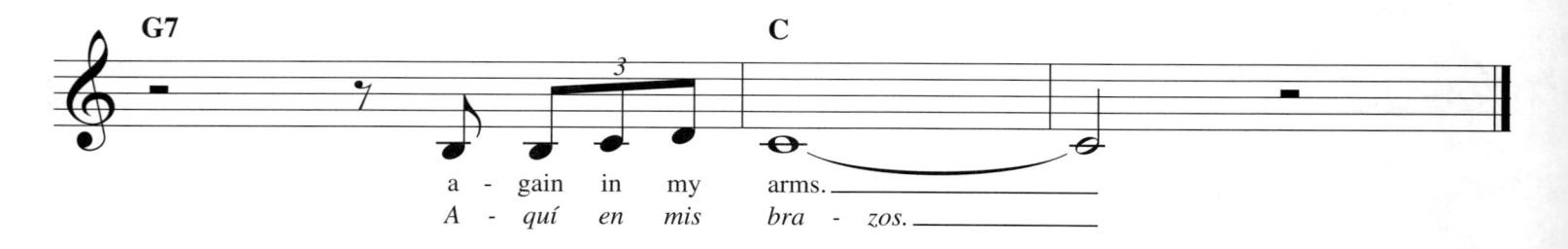

for all my life I'll feel it.
si siem - pre yo a - sí te a - mé,

I wish I'd nev - er met you, girl;
¿Por - que a - ho - ra se lo ton - to que fuí?

you'll nev - er come a - gain.
Ja - más tú vol - ve - rás.

Feel - ings, wo wo wo,
¿Di - me? *Wo wo wo*

feel - ings, wo wo wo, feel - ings
¿Di - me? *Wo wo wo ¿Di - me?*

a - gain in my arms.
A - quí en mis bra - zos.

FLAMINGO

Lyric by ED ANDERSON
Music by TED GROUYA

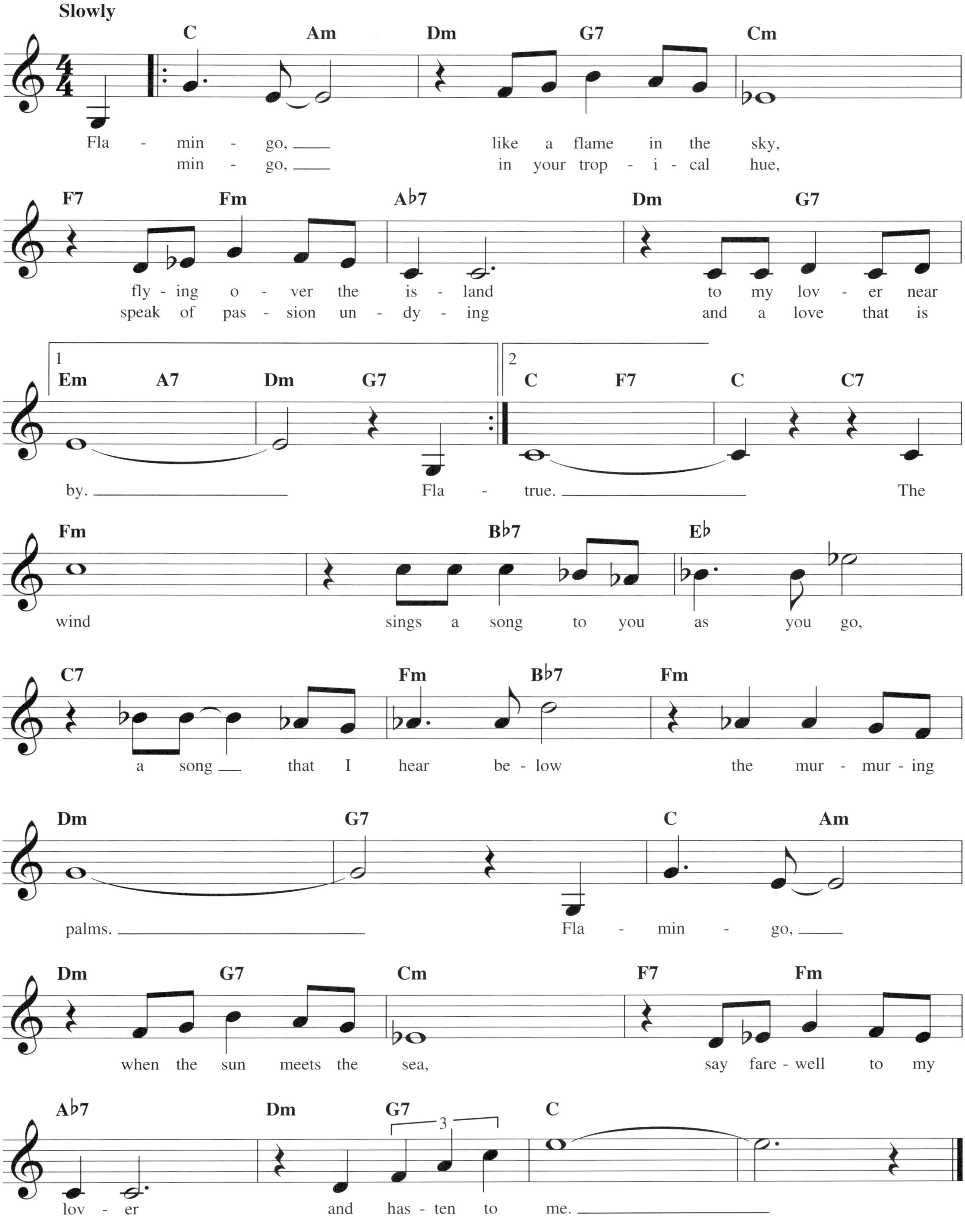

A FELICIDADE

Words and Music by VINICIUS DE MORAES
and ANTONIO CARLOS JOBIM

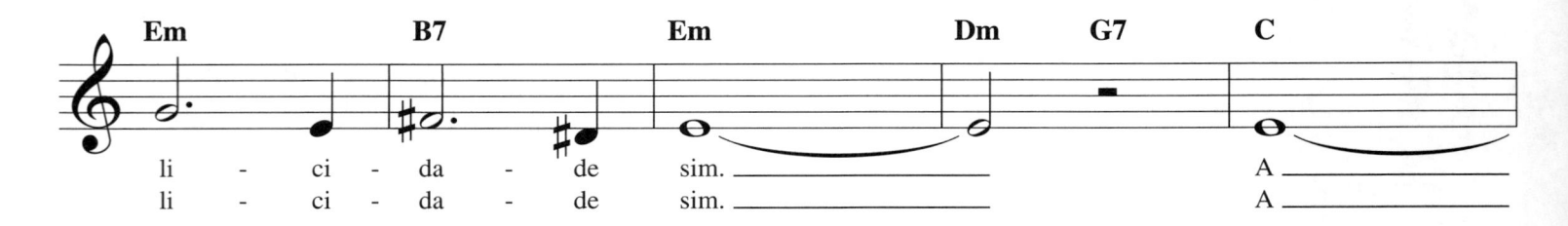

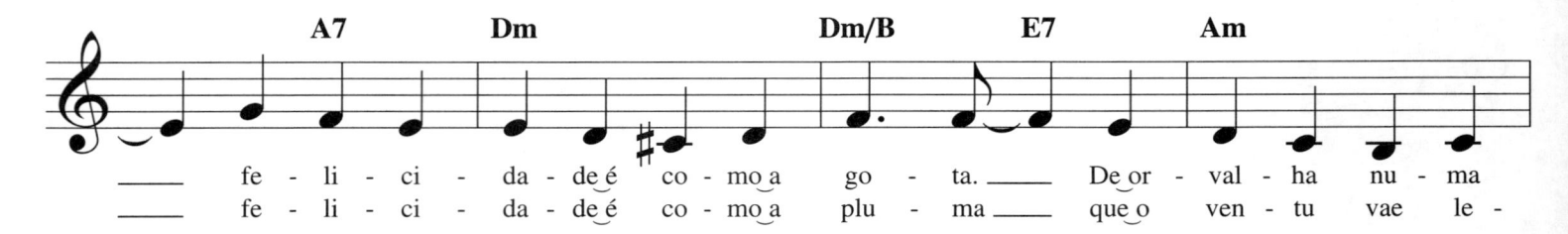

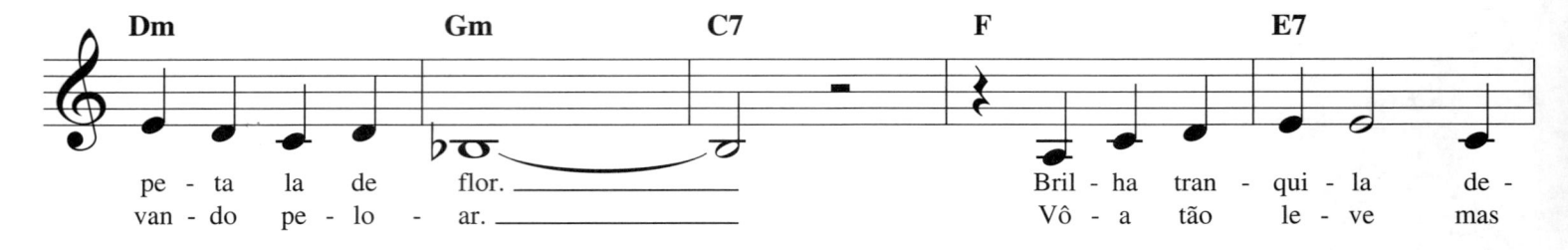

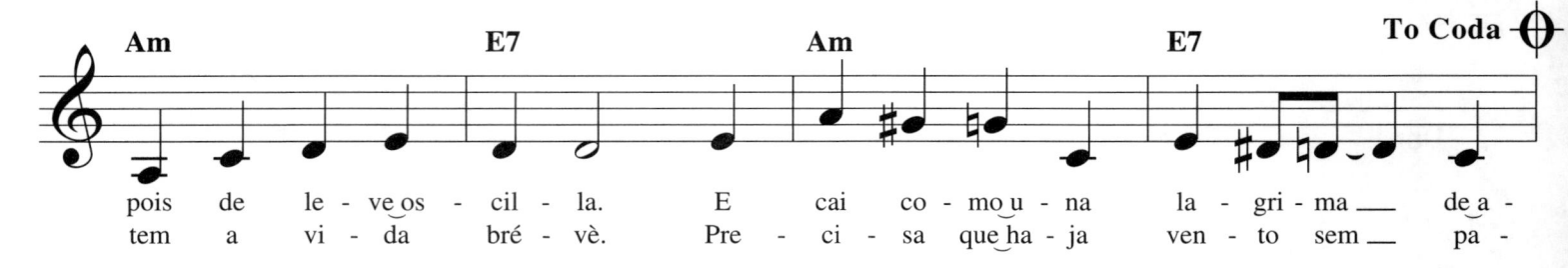

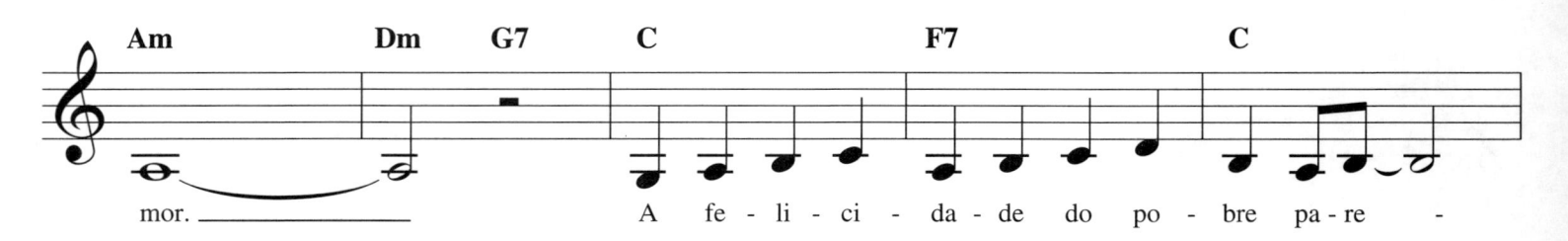

Copyright © 1959 by Les Nouvelles
Copyright Renewed, Assigned to Antonio Carlos Jobim and Vinicius de Moraes in the United States
All Rights for Antonio Carlos Jobim Administered by Corcovado Music Corp.
All Rights for Vinicius de Moraes Administered by VM Enterprises, Inc.
International Copyright Secured   All Rights Reserved

Moderate Bossa Nova

Tris - te _____ za não tem fim. _____ Fe -
te _____ za não tem fim. _____ Fe -

li - ci - da - de sim. _____ A _____
li - ci - da - de sim. _____ A _____

_____ fe - li - ci - da - de é co - mo a go - ta. _____ De or - val - ha nu - ma
_____ fe - li - ci - da - de é co - mo a plu - ma _____ que o ven - tu va e le -

pe - ta - la de flor. _____ Bril - ha tran - qui - la de -
van - do pe - lo ar. _____ Vô - a tão le - ve mas

pois de le - ve os - cil - la. E cai co - mo u - na la - gri - ma _____ de a -
tem a vi - da bré - vè. Pre - ci - sa que ha - ja ven - to sem _____ pa -

mor. _____ A fe - li - ci - da - de do po - bre pa - re -

ce. A gran - de i lu - são do car - na - val. _____ A

Dm G7 C
gen - te tra - bal - ha o a - ho en tei - ro. Por
B7 Gm/E A7 Dm G7
un mo - men - to de - son - ho. Pra - fa - zer a fan - ta - si - a. De
C E7
rei ou de pi - ra ta ou jar - di - nei - ra. E
Am E7 Am D.S. al Coda
tu - do se a - ca - bar na quar - ta fei - ra Tris -
CODA
Am E7
rar. Pre - ci - sa que ha - ja ven - to sem pa -
Am E7
rar. Pre - ci - sa que ha - ja ven - to sem pa -
Am F7
rar. Tris - te - za não tem
Am
fim.

THE FOOL ON THE HILL

Words and Music by JOHN LENNON and PAUL McCARTNEY

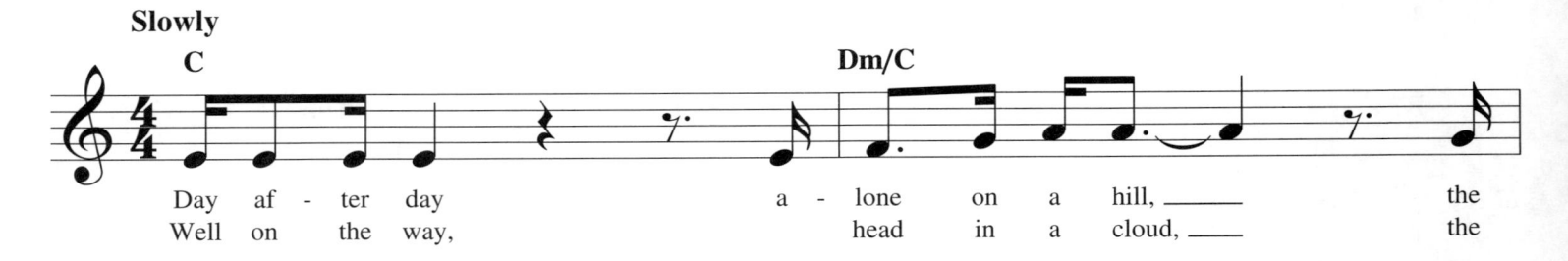

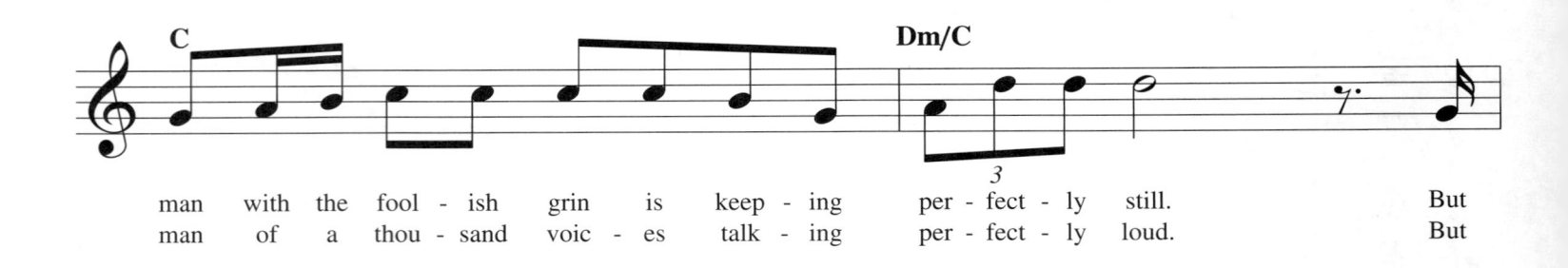

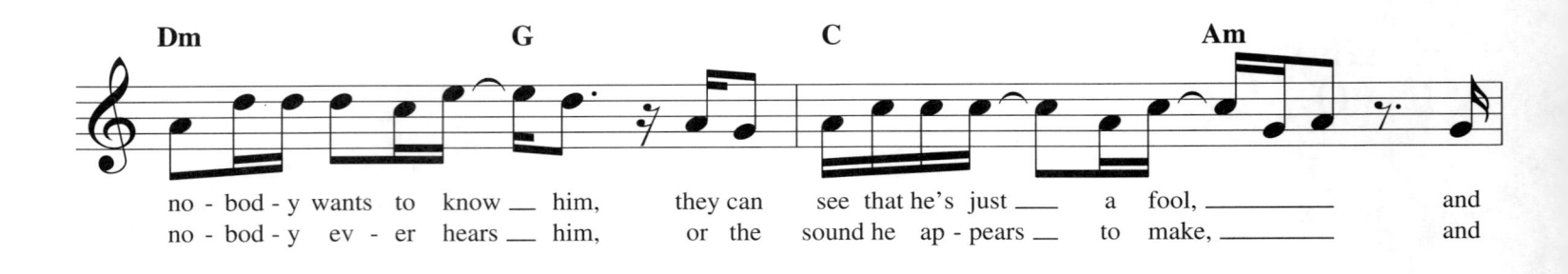

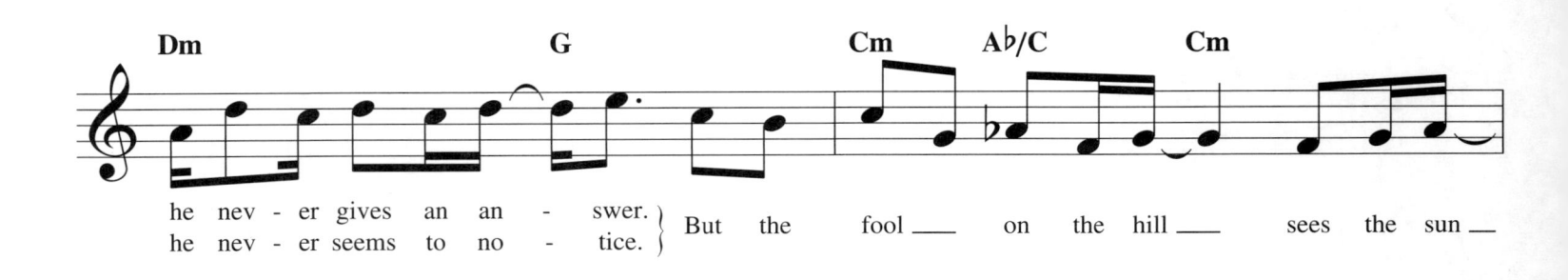

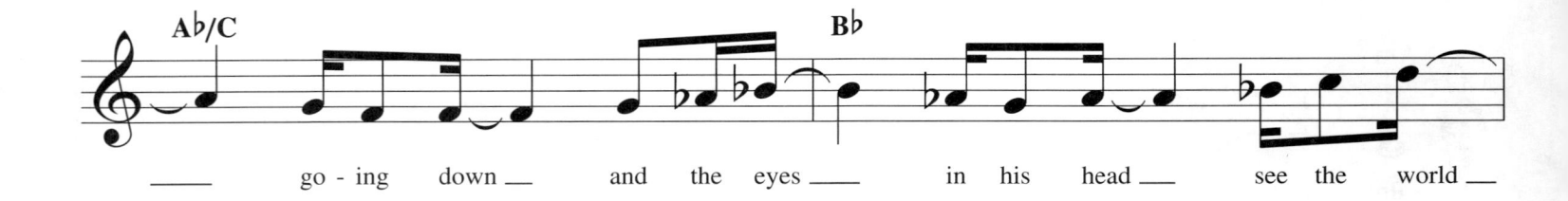

Copyright © 1967 Sony/ATV Music Publishing LLC
Copyright Renewed
All Rights Administered by Sony/ATV Music Publishing LLC, 8 Music Square West, Nashville, TN 37203
International Copyright Secured   All Rights Reserved

[Sheet music: lead sheet in 4/4, marked "Slowly", key of C. Chord progression includes C, Dm/C, Dm, G, Am, Cm, A♭/C, B♭.]

spin-ning 'round.

(Instrumental)

No-bod-y seems to like ___ him, they can tell what he wants ___ to do, ___ and
He nev-er lis-tens to ___ them, he knows _ that they're _ the fools. ___

he nev-er shows his feel - ings,
They don't like ___ him, } but the fool ___ on the hill ___ sees the sun ___

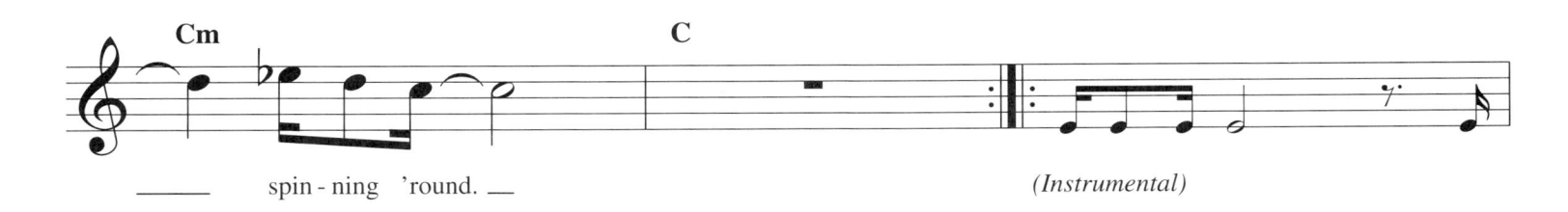

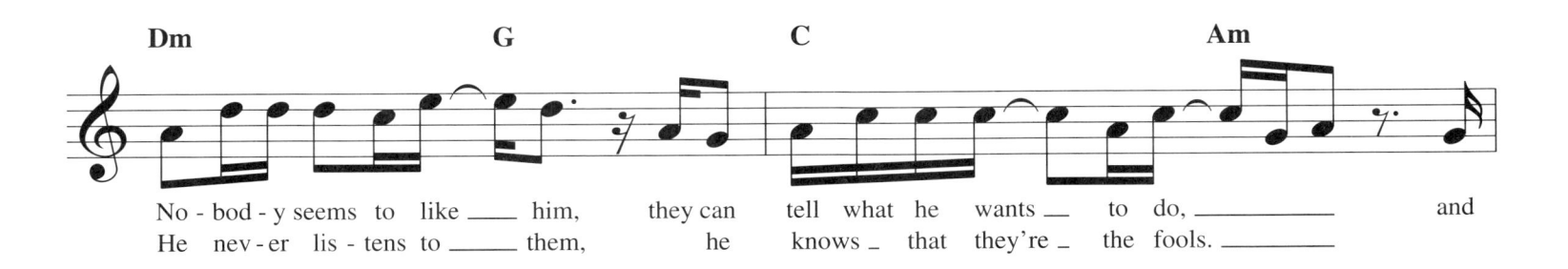

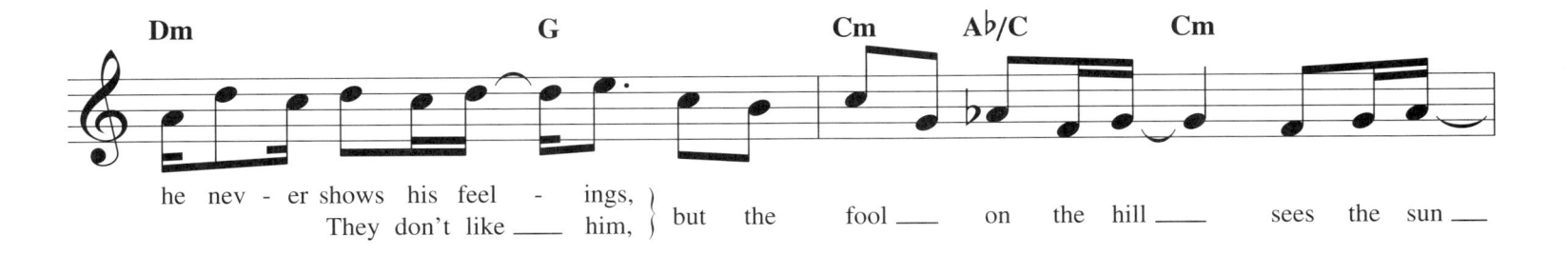

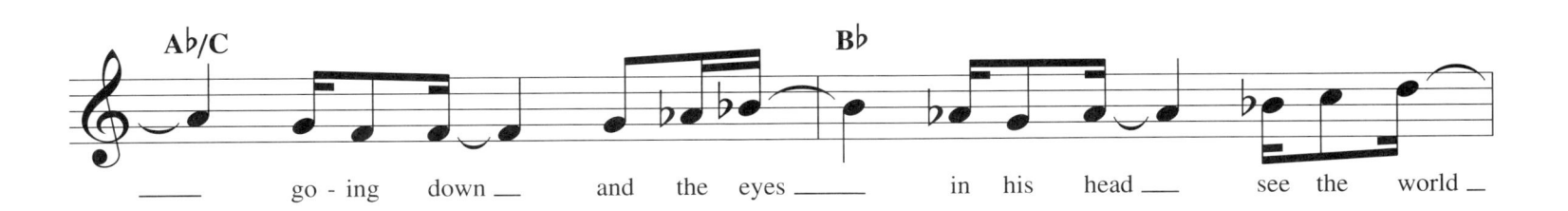

___ go - ing down ___ and the eyes ___ in his head ___ see the world ___

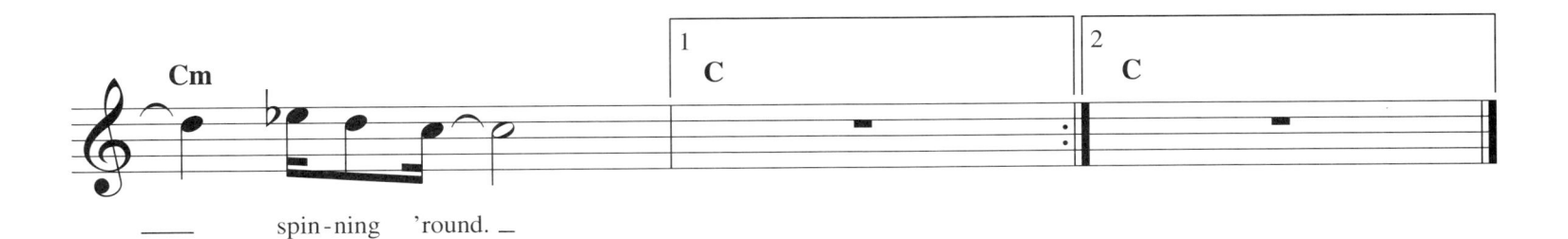

___ spin-ning 'round. ___

FRENESÍ

Copyright © 1939 by Peer International Corporation
Copyright Renewed
International Copyright Secured   All Rights Reserved

English Words by LEONARD WHITCUP
Original Spanish version by ALBERTO DOMINGUEZ

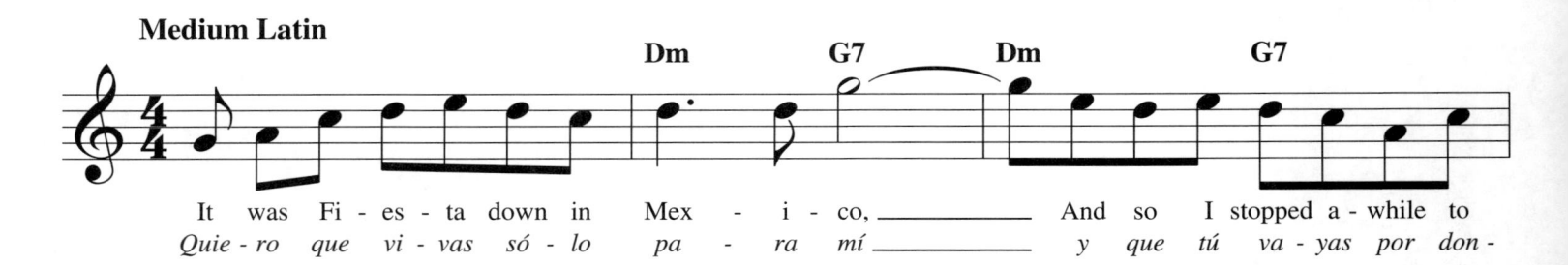

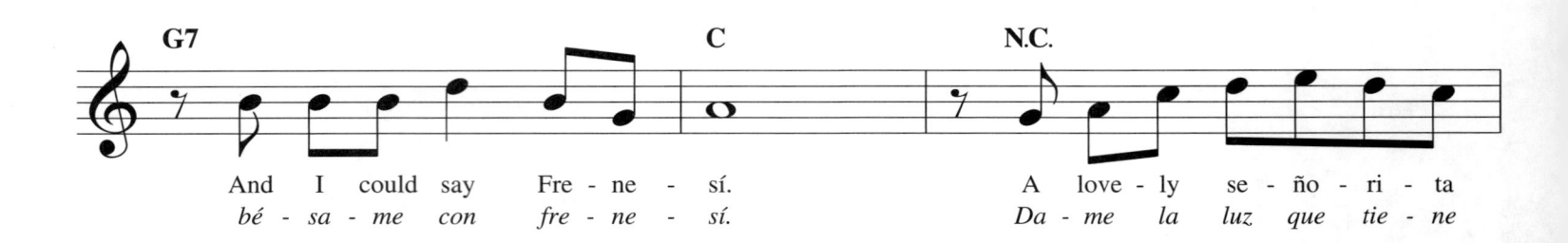

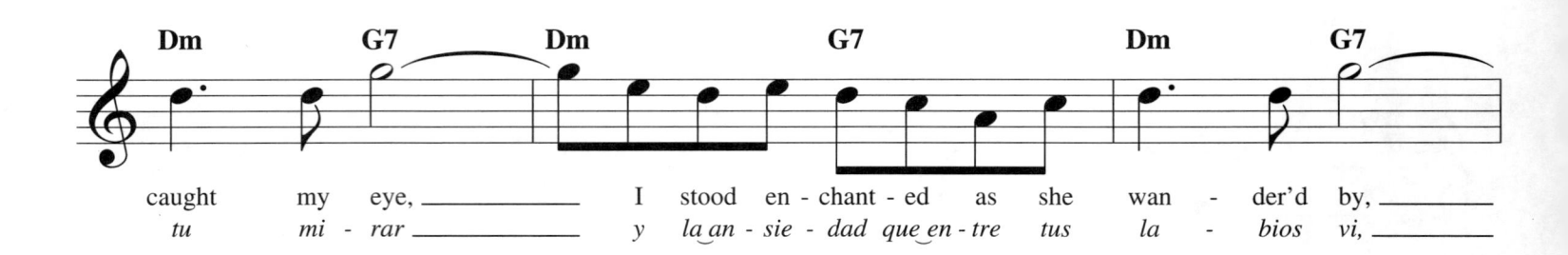

Medium Latin

It was Fi - es - ta down in Mex - i - co, _____ And so I stopped a - while to see the show, _____ I knew that Fre - ne - sí meant "please love me" And I could say Fre - ne - sí. A love - ly se - ño - ri - ta caught my eye, _____ I stood en - chant - ed as she wan - der'd by, _____ And nev - er know - ing that it came from me I gen - tly sighed Fre - ne - sí.

Quie - ro que vi - vas só - lo pa - ra mí _____ y que tú va - yas por don - de yo voy, _____ pa - ra que mi_al - ma sea no más de ti, bé - sa - me con fre - ne - sí. Da - me la luz que tie - ne tu mi - rar _____ y la_an - sie - dad que_en - tre tus la - bios vi, _____ e - sa lo - cu - ra de vi - vir y_a - mar, que es más que_a - mor, fre - ne - sí.

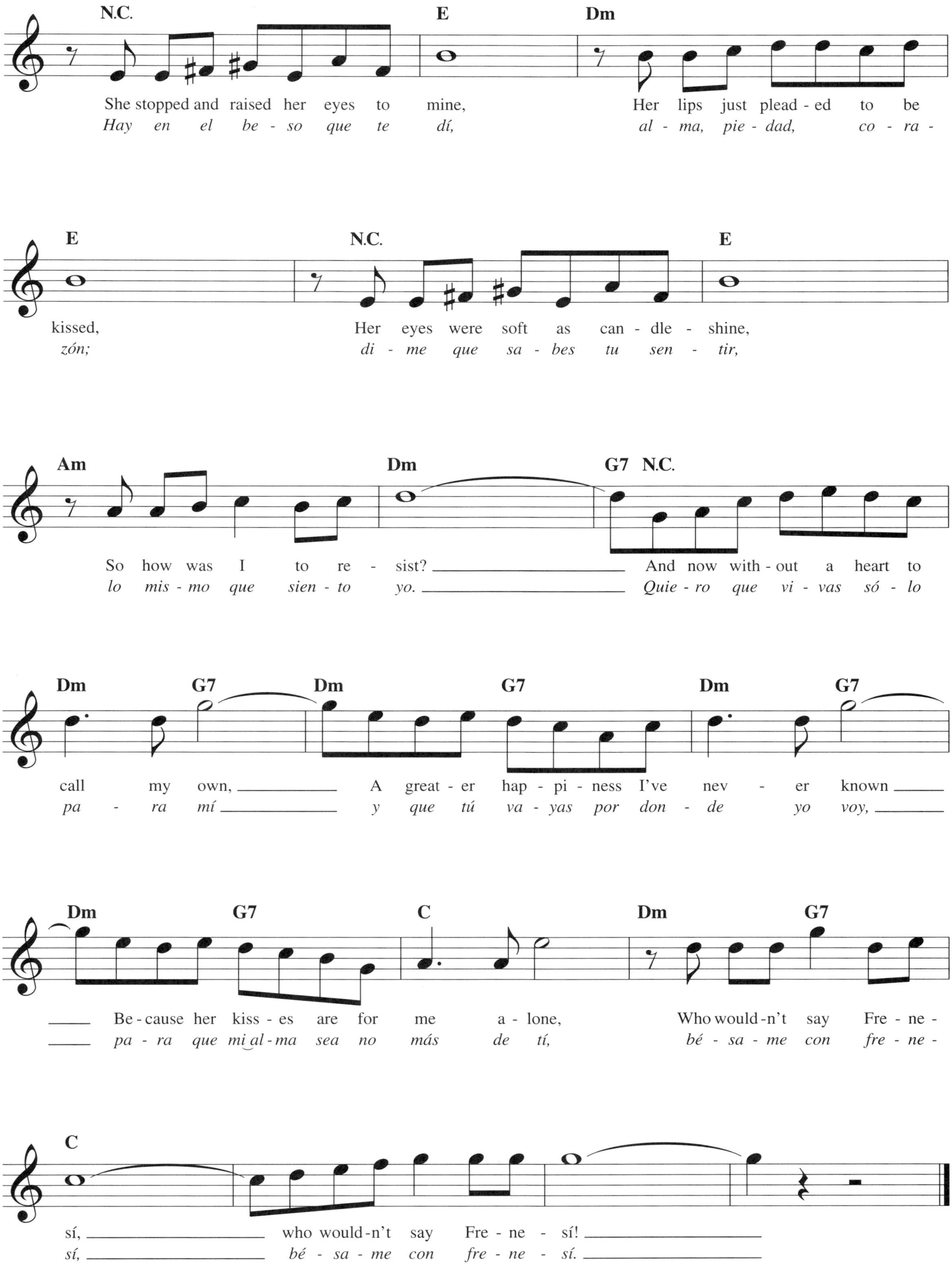
N.C.
E
Dm
She stopped and raised her eyes to mine, Her lips just plead - ed to be
Hay en el be - so que te dí, al - ma, pie - dad, co - ra -
E
N.C.
E
kissed, Her eyes were soft as can - dle - shine,
zón; di - me que sa - bes tu sen - tir,
Am
Dm
G7 N.C.
So how was I to re - sist? And now with - out a heart to
lo mis - mo que sien - to yo. Quie - ro que vi - vas só - lo
Dm G7 Dm G7 Dm G7
call my own, A great - er hap - pi - ness I've nev - er known
pa - ra mí y que tú va - yas por don - de yo voy,
Dm G7 C Dm G7
Be - cause her kiss - es are for me a - lone, Who would - n't say Fre - ne -
pa - ra que mi al - ma sea no más de tí, bé - sa - me con fre - ne -
C
sí, who would - n't say Fre - ne - sí!
sí, bé - sa - me con fre - ne - sí.

A GAY RANCHERO

Copyright © 1936 by Edward B. Marks Music Company
Copyright Renewed
International Copyright Secured All Rights Reserved
Used by Permission

Words by ABE TUVIM and FRANCIA LUBAN
Music by J.J. ESPINOSA

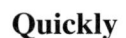

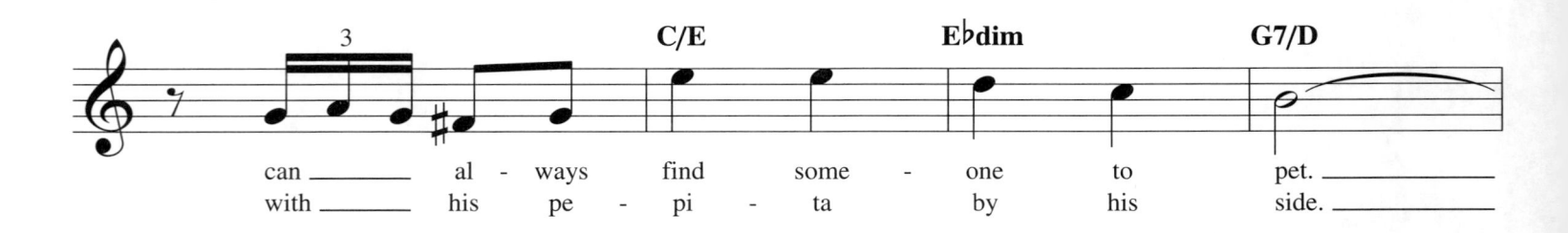

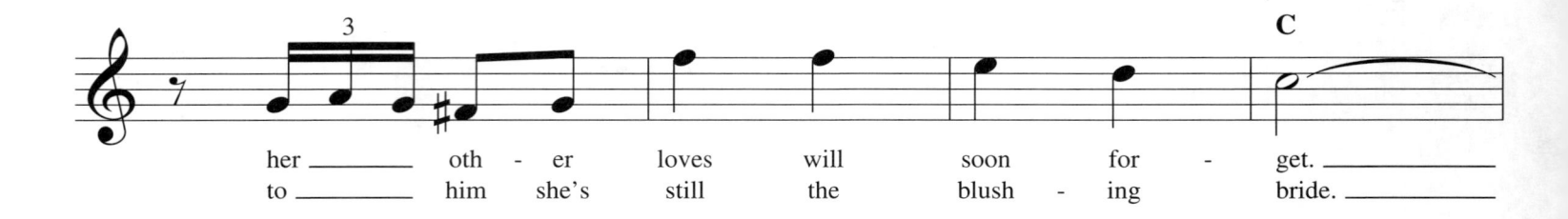

Quickly

A ___ gay ran - cher - o, a ___ cab - al - ler - o
ranch - o, we ___ now find Pan - cho

can ___ al - ways find some - one to pet. ___
with ___ his pe - pi - ta by his side. ___

A ___ señ - or - it - a, a ___ sweet Pe - pi - ta
She ___ thinks he's hand - some, worth ___ an - y ran - som

her ___ oth - er loves will soon for - get. ___
to ___ him she's still the blush - ing bride. ___

If ___ he's in - sis - tent and ___ she's not dis - tant
Our ___ gay ran - cher - o, our ___ cab - al - ler - o

the ___ señ - or - it - a will con - fess ___
still ___ tells the world of how they met. ___

_____ her gay ranch - er - o, _____ her cab - al - ler - o _____
_____ This gay ranch - er - o, _____ this cab - al - ler - o _____

_____ need on - ly ask and she'll say yes. _____
_____ says he has noth - ing to re - gret. _____

Soon there'll be a fies - ta with a blush - ing bride
Now to end the sto - ry that I once was told

and a gay ran - cher - o stand - ing by her side. If they find the
here's a lit - tle se - cret that I must un - fold. For they found the

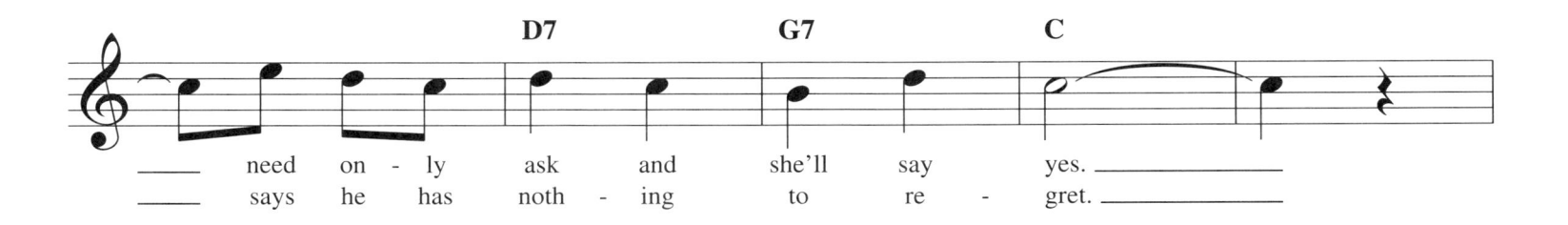

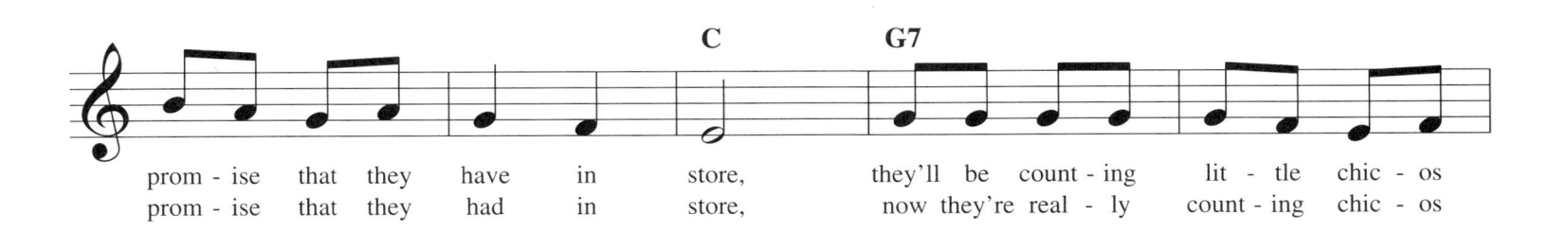

prom - ise that they have in store, they'll be count - ing lit - tle chic - os
prom - ise that they had in store, now they're real - ly count - ing chic - os

by the score. Back _____ on his
by the score.

THE GIFT!
(Recado Bossa Nova)

Music by DJALMA FERREIRA
Original Lyric by LUIZ ANTONIO
English Lyric by PAUL FRANCIS WEBSTER

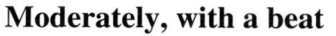

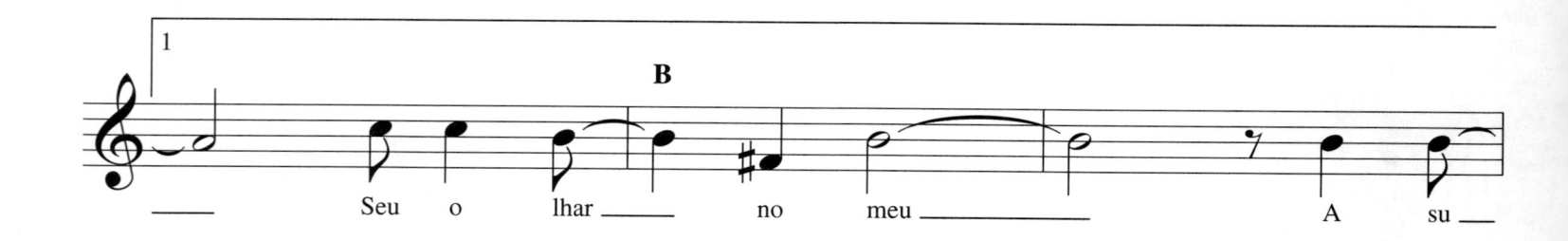

Moderately, with a beat

1. Você errou quando olhou prà mim. Uma esperança fer nascer em mim. Depois levou pra tão longe de nós. Seu olhar no meu. A su-
2., D.S. deixou sem querer, deixou uma saudade enorme em seu lugar. Depois nós dois cada qual a mercê

E7
a vór. Vo - cê
2
do seu des - ti
Gm
no vo - cê seu
E7
mim eu sem vo - cê.
To Coda
Am
A7
Sau da - de meu ma be - que de re - ca -
Dm
- do Não
B7
di - ga que eu me en - con
tro nêss - e es ta - do. Vo - cê
Em
E7
D.S. al Coda
(take 2nd ending)
CODA
Am
cê. Do seu des - ti no vo - cê seu
3
E7
mim eu sem vo - cê.
Am

THE GIRL FROM IPANEMA
(Garôta De Ipanema)

Music by ANTONIO CARLOS JOBIM
English Words by NORMAN GIMBEL
Original Words by VINICIUS DE MORAES

Moderate Bossa Nova

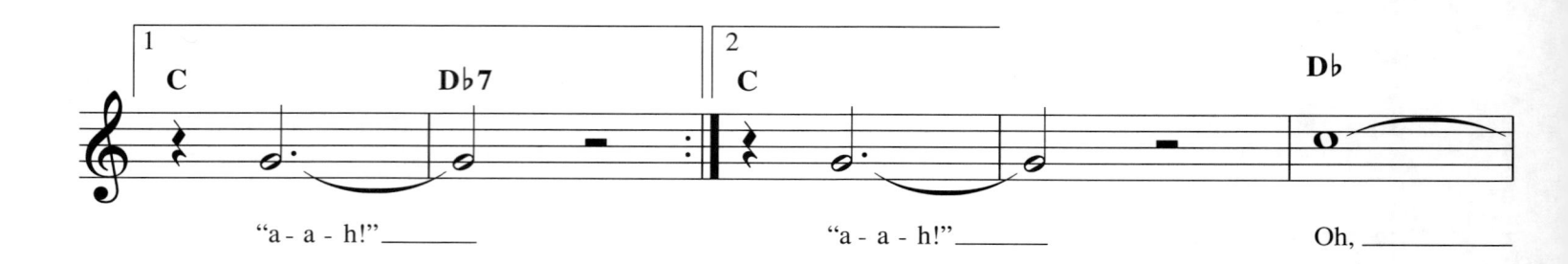

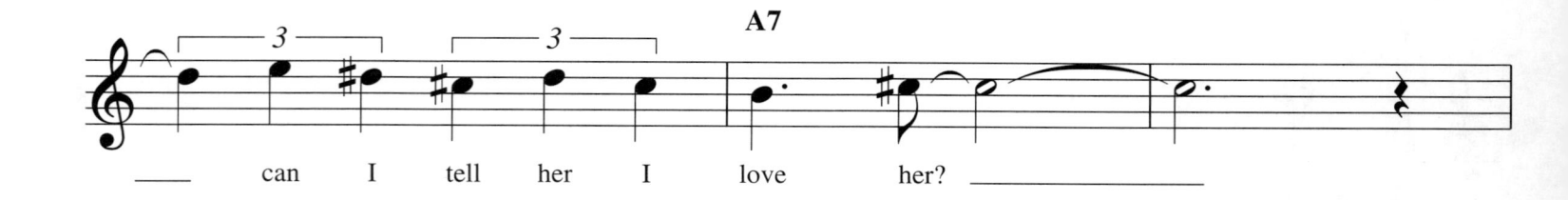

Tall and tan and young and love-ly, the girl from I-pa-ne-ma goes walk-ing, and when she pass-es, each one she pass-es goes "a-a-h!"

When she walks she's like a sam-ba that swings so cool and sways so gen-tle, that when she pass-es, each one she pass-es goes "a-a-h!"

Oh, but I watch her so sad-ly.

How can I tell her I love her?

Dm
Yes,
I would give my heart
Bb7
glad - ly,
but each
Em
day when she walks to the
A7
sea,
she
Dm
looks straight a - head not at
G7
me.
C
Tall and tan and young and love - ly, the
D7
girl from I - pa - ne - ma goes walk-ing, and
Dm
when she pass - es I
Db7
smile, but she does - n't
C
see.
Db7
She just does - n't
C
see.
Db7
No, she does - n't
C
see.

GITANERIAS
from the Spanish Suite ANDALUCIA

By ERNESTO LECUONA

1
2
Dm
B♭
E
Dm
B♭
E
Am
E7
Am
E
Am
B♭
Am
E7
Am
N.C.
E
Am
N.C.
E
Am
N.C.
D.C. al Coda
CODA
E7
Am
E
Am

GRANADA

Spanish Words and Music by AGUSTIN LARA
English Words by DOROTHY DODD

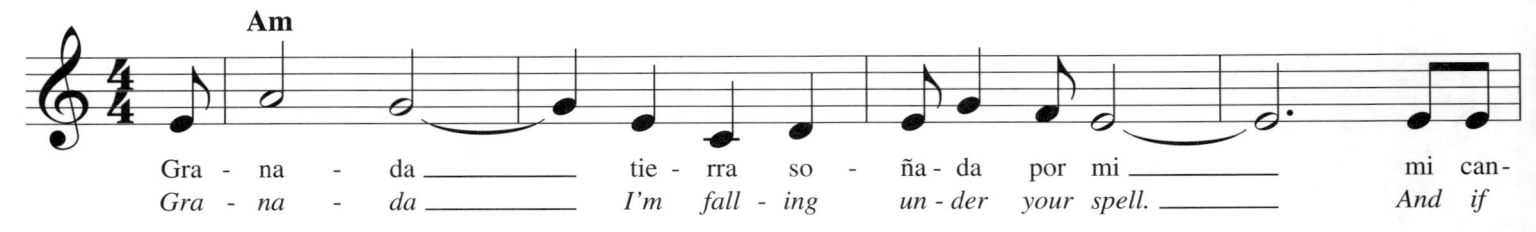

Gra - na - da tie - rra so - ña - da por mi mi can -
Gra - na - da I'm fall - ing un - der your spell. And if

tar - se vuel - ve gi - ta - no cuan - do es pa - ra ti
you could speak, what a fas - ci - nat - ing tale you would tell,

mi can - tar he - cho de fan - ta - si - a
of an age the world has long for - got - ten,

mi can - tar flor de me - lan - co - lí - a que yo te
of an age that weaves a si - lent mag - ic in Gra -

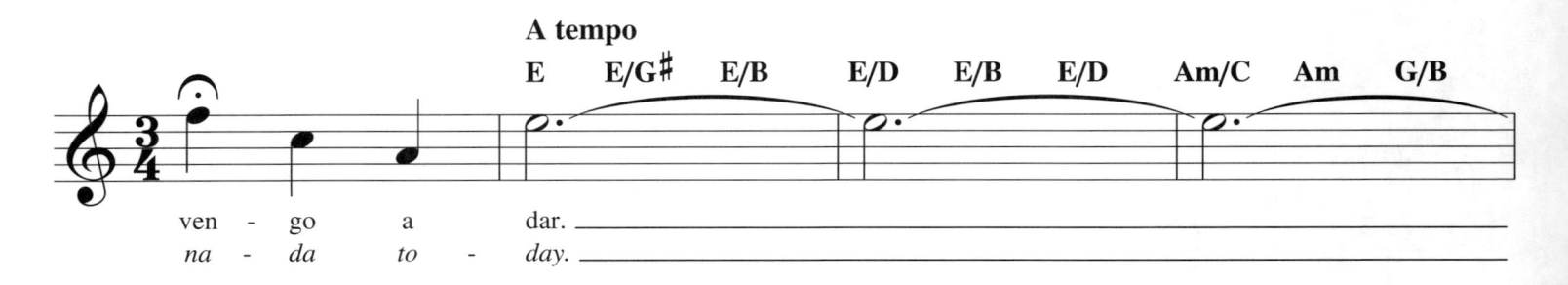

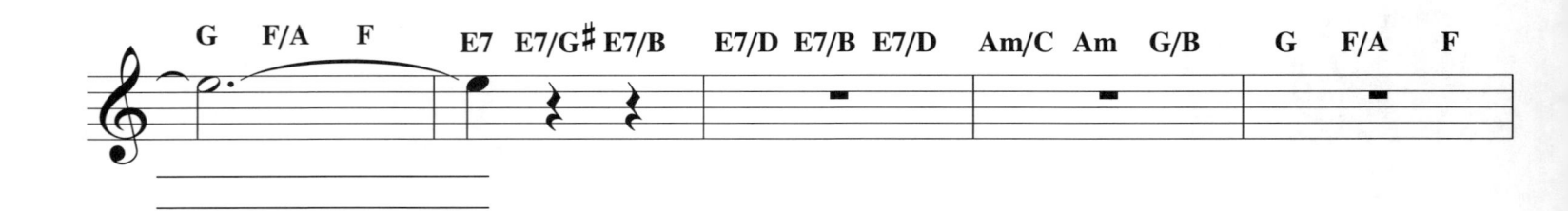

ven - go a dar.
na - da to - day.

E
Tempo di Habanera
N.C.
G7
C
D7
G
C
Gra - na - da tie - rra en - san - gren -
The dawn in the sky greets the
C/E
E♭dim
G7
3
ta - da en tar - des de to - ros.
day with a sigh for Gra - na - da,
Mu - jer que con - ser - va el em - bru - jo de
for she can re - mem - ber the splen - dor that
C
los o - jos mo - ros. De
once was Gra - na - da. It

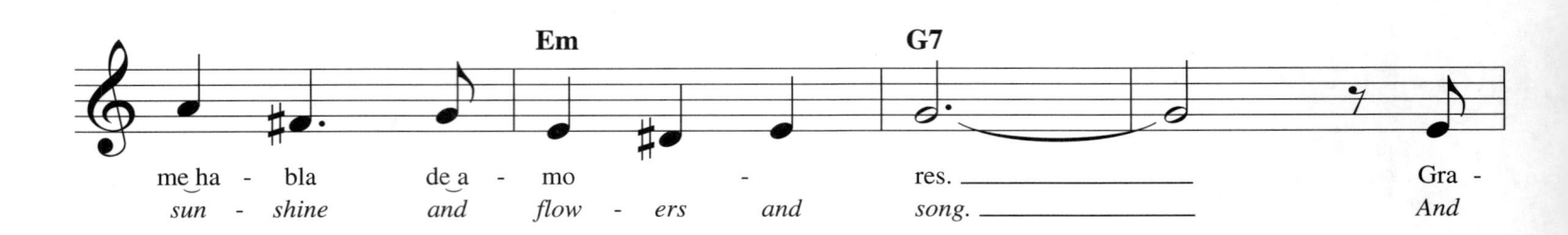

sue - ño re - bel - de y gi - ta - na cu - bier - ta de
still can be found in the hills all a - round as I

Em   **B7/D♯**

flo - res _____ y be - so tu
wan - der a - long, _____ en - tranc'd by the

Em   **B7/D♯**

bo - ca de gra - na _____ ju - go - sa man - za - na que
beau - ty be - fore _____ me, ___ en - tranc'd by a land full of

Em   **G7**

me ha - bla de a - mo - res. _____ Gra -
sun - shine and flow - ers and song. _____ And

C   **C/E**   **E♭dim**

na - da ma - no - la can - ta - da en co - plas pre -
when day is done and the sun starts to set in Gra -

G7

cio - sas. _____ No
na - da, _____ I

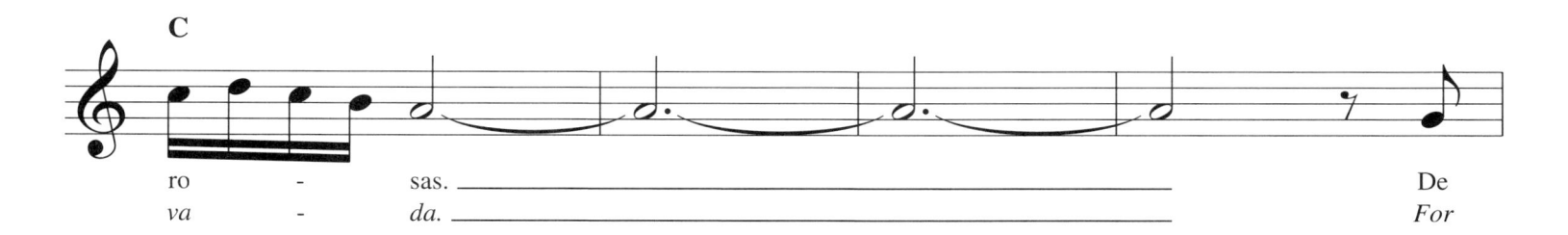

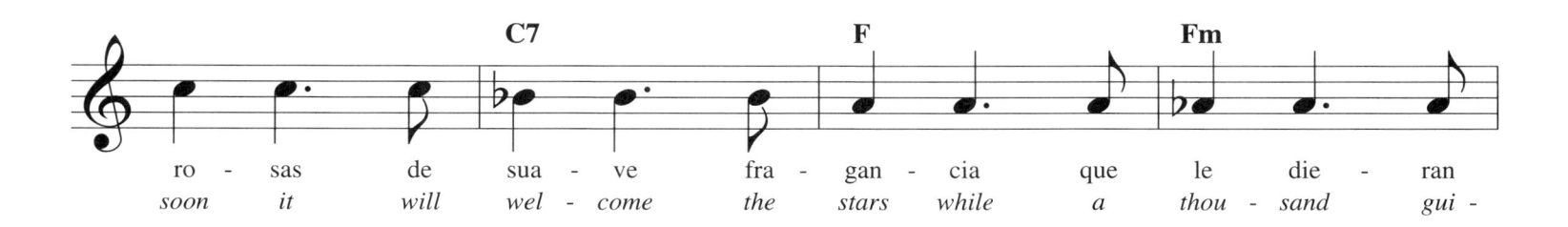

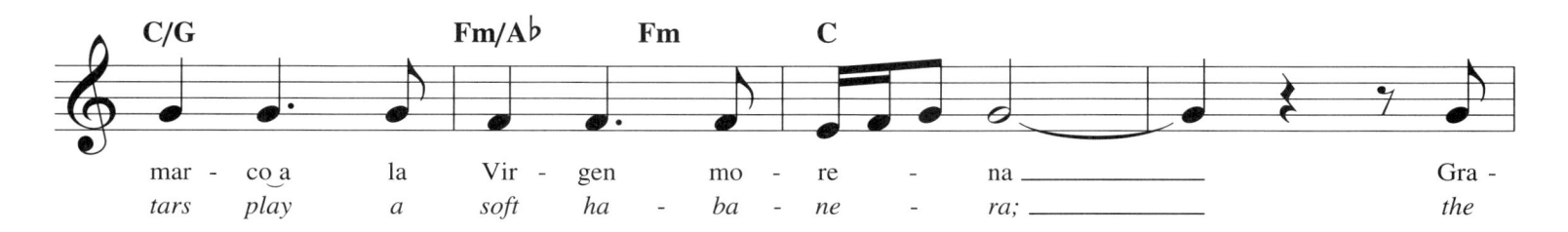

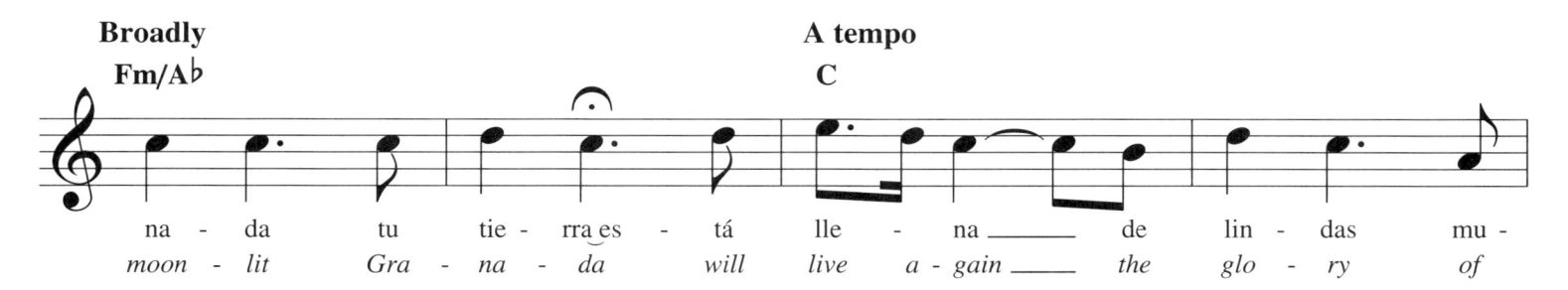

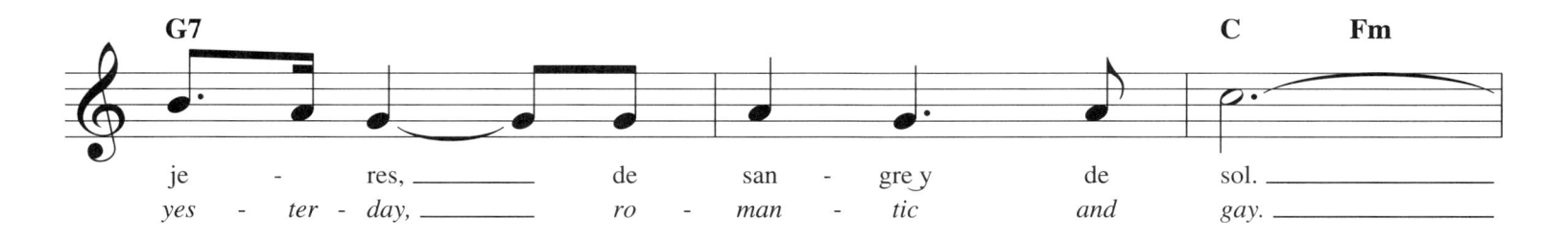

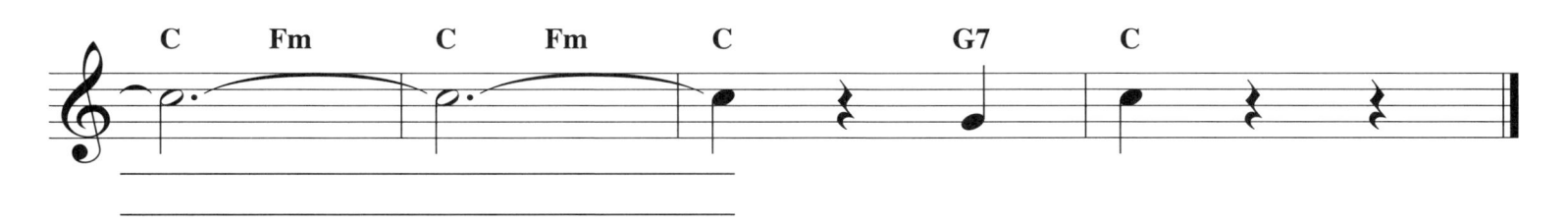

tengo otra cosa que darte que un ramo de
en - vy the blush of the snow - clad Si - er - ra Ne -

C
ro - sas. De
va - da. For

C7   **F**   **Fm**
ro - sas de sua - ve fra - gan - cia que le die - ran
soon it will wel - come the stars while a thou - sand gui -

C/G   **Fm/A♭**   **Fm**   **C**
mar - co a la Vir - gen mo - re - na Gra -
tars play a soft ha - ba - ne - ra; the

Broadly
Fm/A♭   **A tempo**   **C**
na - da tu tie - rra es - tá lle - na de lin - das mu -
moon - lit Gra - na - da will live a - gain the glo - ry of

G7   **C**   **Fm**
je - res, de san - gre y de sol.
yes - ter - day, ro - man - tic and gay.

C   **Fm**   **C**   **Fm**   **C**   **G7**   **C**

GUADALAJARA

Words and Music by
PEPE GUIZAR

Copyright © 1937 by Peer International Corporation
Copyright Renewed
International Copyright Secured All Rights Reserved

Moderately

(Instrumental)

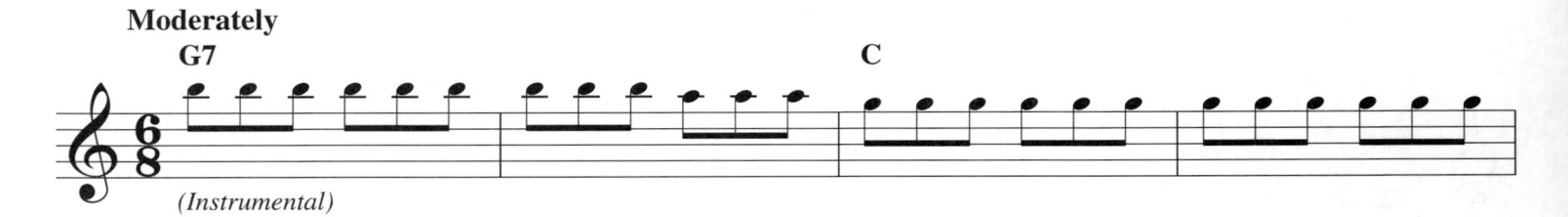

Gua - da - la - ja - ra, Gua - da - la - ja - ra. _____ Gua - da - la - ja - ra, Gua - da - la - ja - ra _____

tie - nes el al - ma de pro - vin - cia - na hue - les a lim - pio a ro - sa tem - pra - na a ver - de ja - ra fres - ca del ri - o son mil pa - lo - mos tu ca - se - rí - o. Gua - da - la - ja - ra, Gua - da - la - ja - ra sa - bes a pu - ra tie - rra mo - ja - da.

D.C. al Coda I
(take repeat)

CODA I

Ay!

Co - lo - mi - tos le - ja - nos.

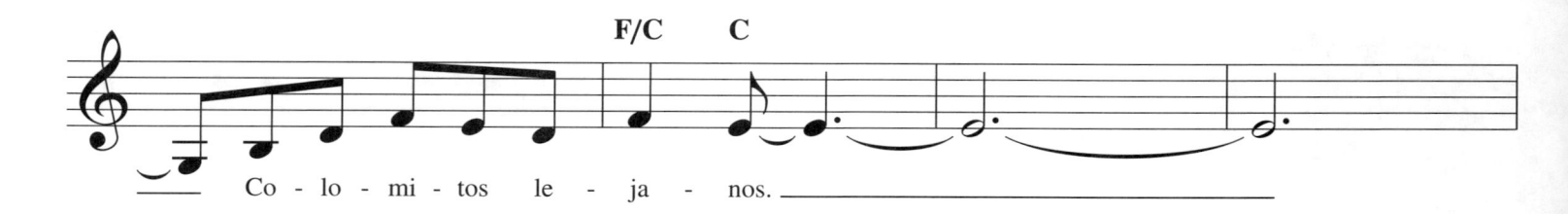

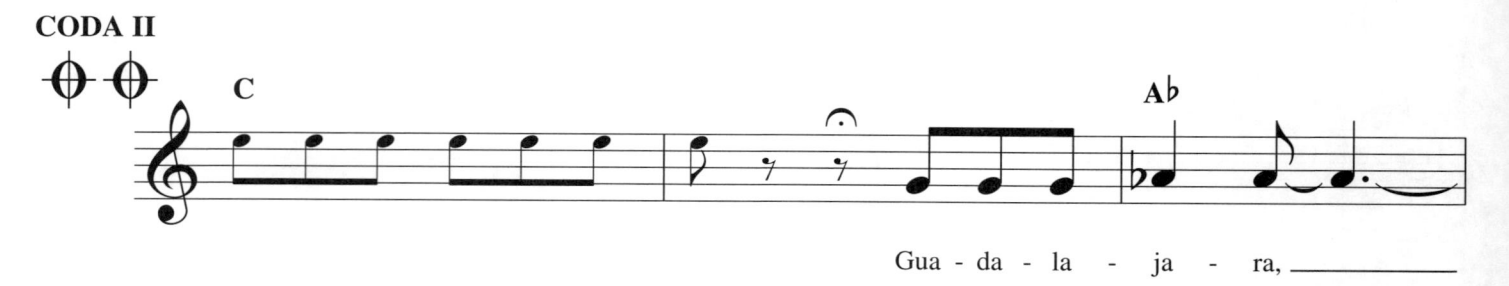

Ay! o - ji - tos de a-gua her - ma - nos.

Ay! Co - lo - mi - tos i - nol - vi - da - bles i - nol - vi - da - bles co - mo las tar - des en que la llu - via des - de la lo - ma ir - nos ha

ci - a has - ta Za - po - pam.

CODA II

Gua - da - la - ja - ra,

Gua - da - la - ja - ra.

GUANTANAMERA

Cuban Folksong

Guantanamera, guajira Guantanamera.
Guantanamera, guajira Guantanamera.
Yo soy un hombre sincero, de donde crece la palma.
Yo soy un hombre sincero, de donde crece la palma.
Y antes de morir me quiero, Echar mis versos del alma.
Guantanamera, guajira Guantanamera.
Guantanamera, guajira Guantanamera.

I GET IDEAS

Words by DORCAS COCHRAN
Music by JULIO C. SANDERS

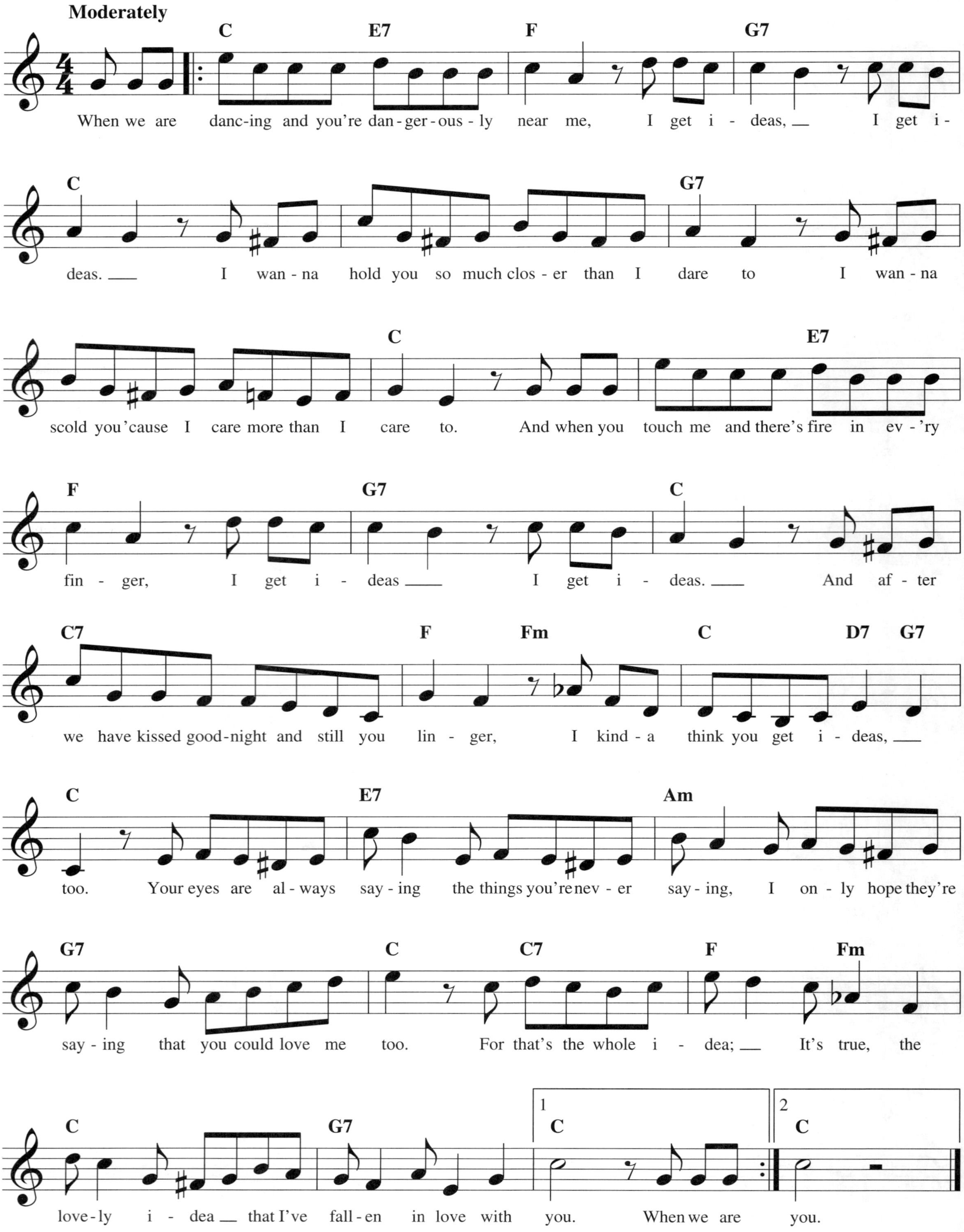

LA CUCARACHA

Mexican Revolutionary Folksong

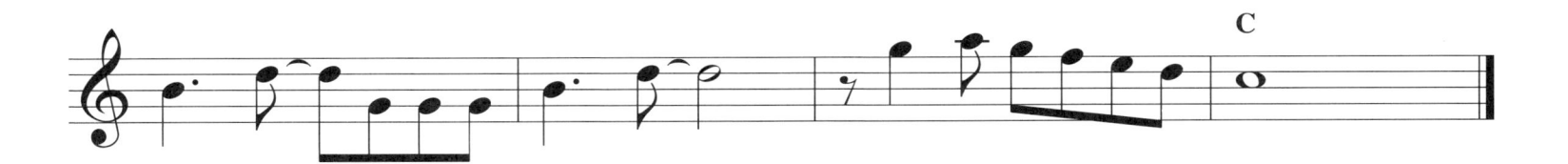

HOW INSENSITIVE
(Insensatez)

Copyright © 1963, 1964 ANTONIO CARLOS JOBIM and VINICIUS DE MORAES, Brazil
Copyright Renewed and Assigned to SONGS OF UNIVERSAL, INC.
and NEW THUNDER MUSIC, INC.
All Rights for NEW THUNDER MUSIC, INC. Administered by GIMBEL MUSIC GROUP, INC.
(P.O. Box 15221, Beverly Hills, CA 90209-1221 USA)
All Rights Reserved Used by Permission

Music by ANTONIO CARLOS JOBIM
Original Words by VINICIUS DE MORAES
English Words by NORMAN GIMBEL

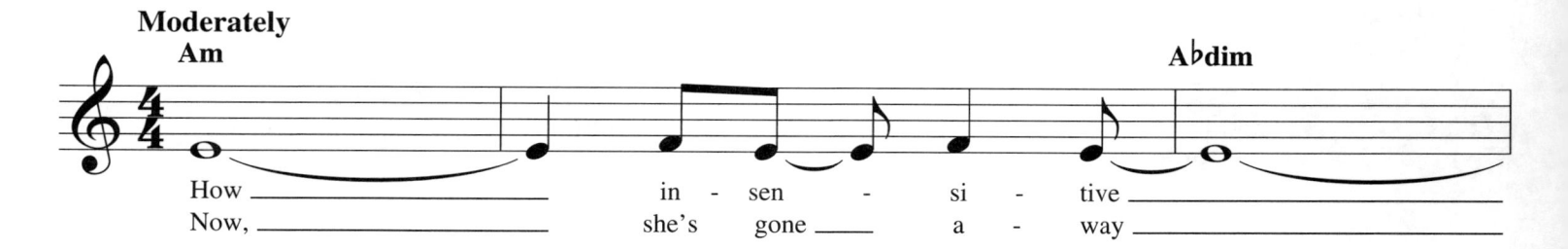

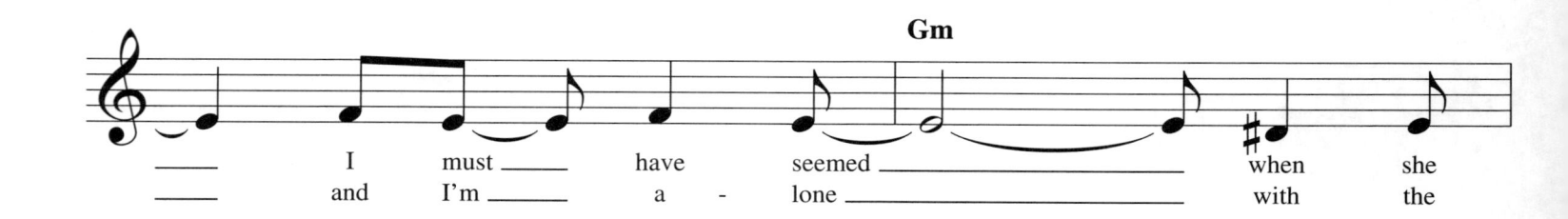

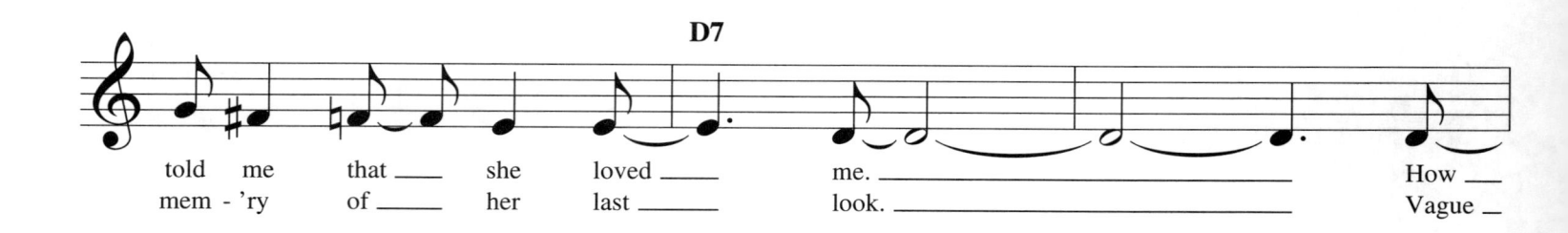

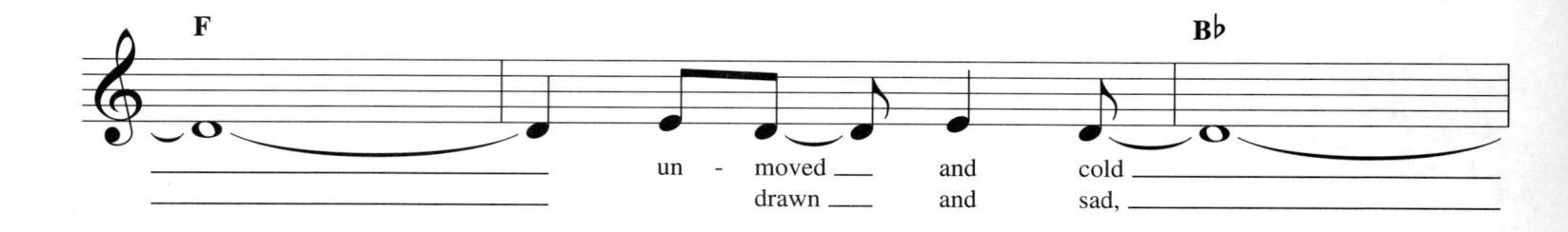

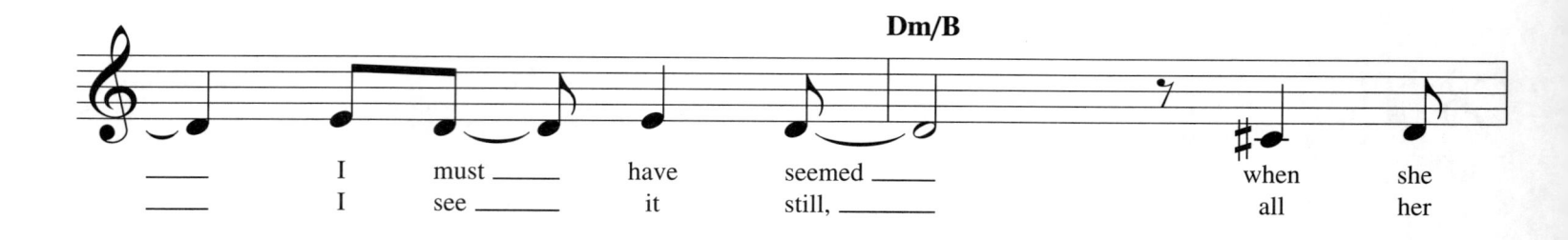

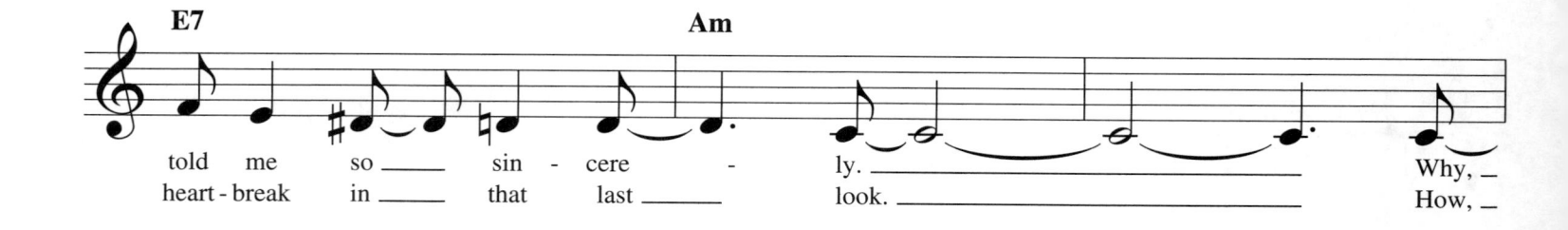

Moderately

Am / A♭dim

How _____ in - sen - si - tive _____
Now, _____ she's gone _____ a - way _____

Gm

_____ I must _____ have seemed _____ when she
_____ and I'm _____ a - lone _____ with the

D7

told me that _____ she loved _____ me. _____ How _____
mem - 'ry of _____ her last _____ look. _____ Vague

F / B♭

un - moved _____ and cold _____
drawn _____ and sad, _____

Dm/B

_____ I must _____ have seemed _____ when she
I see _____ it still, _____ all her

E7 / Am

told me so _____ sin - cere - ly. _____ Why, _____
heart - break in _____ that last _____ look. _____ How, _____

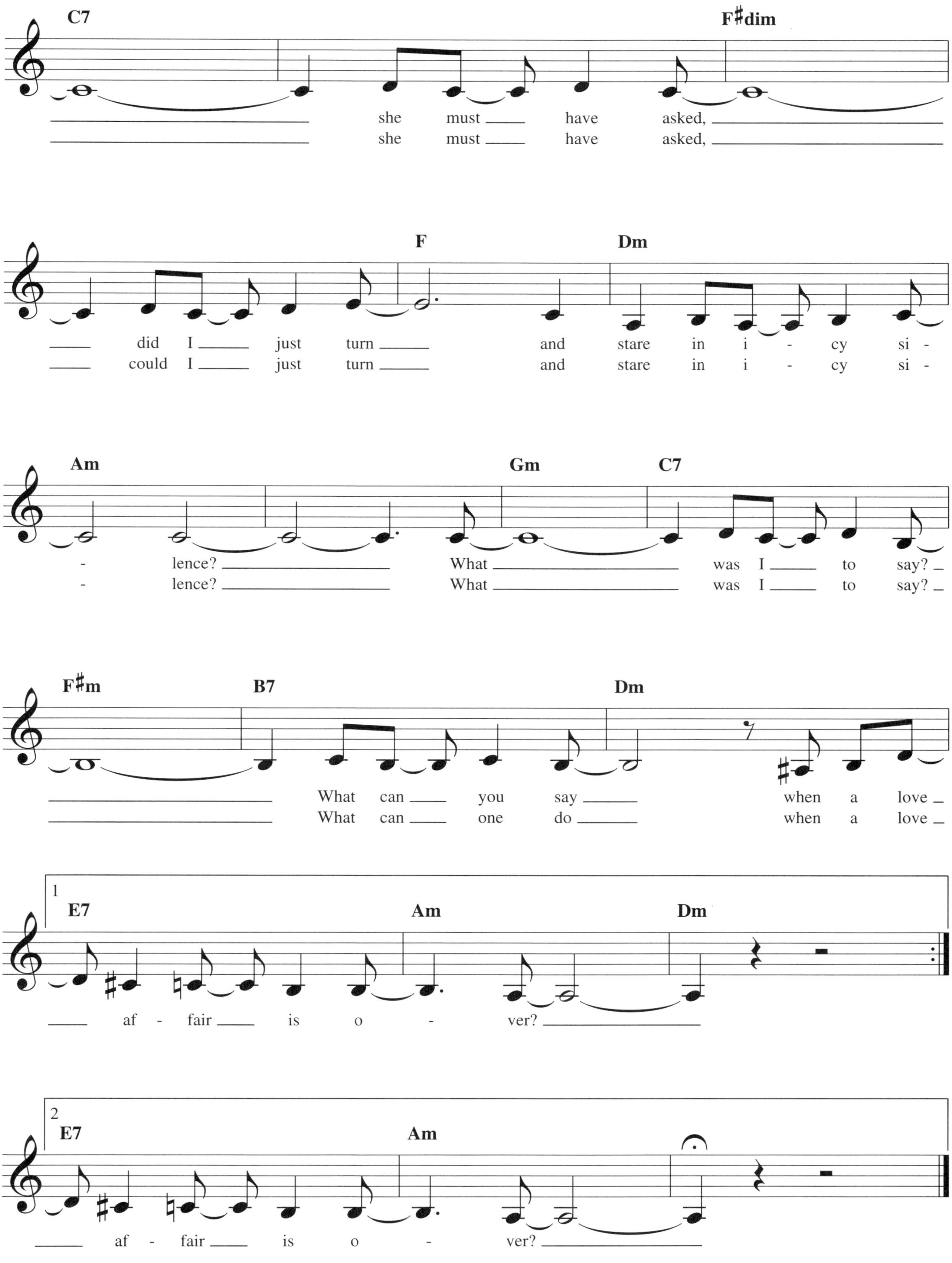
C7
F♯dim
she must have asked,
she must have asked,
F
Dm
did I just turn and stare in i - cy si -
could I just turn and stare in i - cy si -
Am
Gm
C7
- lence? What was I to say?
- lence? What was I to say?
F♯m
B7
Dm
What can you say when a love
What can one do when a love
1
E7
Am
Dm
af - fair is o - ver?
2
E7
Am
af - fair is o - ver?

IT'S IMPOSSIBLE
(Somos Novios)

English Lyric by SID WAYNE
Spanish Words and Music by ARMANDO MANZANERO

Slowly, with expression

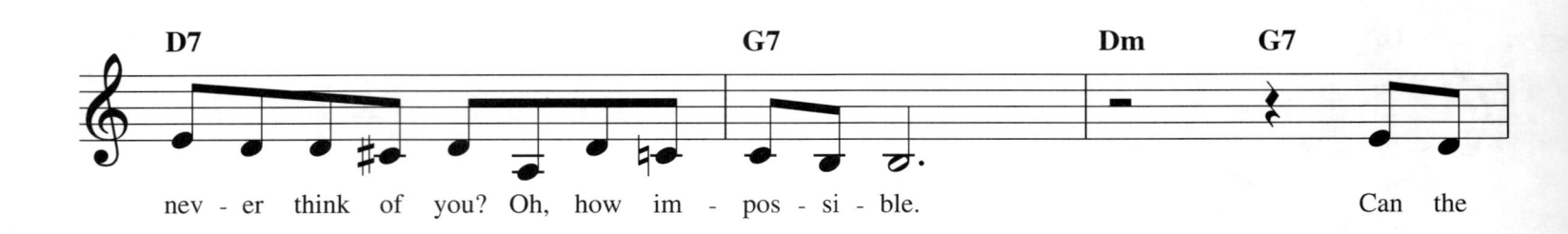

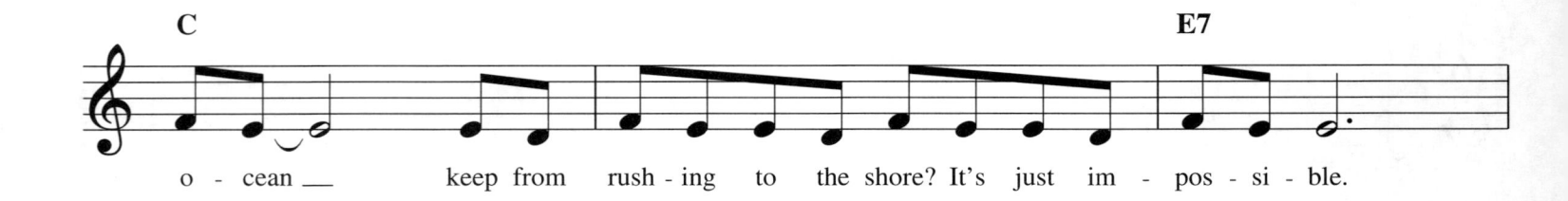

It's im-pos-si-ble, tell the sun to leave the sky. It's just im-pos-si-ble.

It's im-pos-si-ble, ask a ba-by not to cry. It's just im-pos-si-ble.

Can I hold you clos-er to me, and not feel you go-ing through me, split the sec-ond that I nev-er think of you? Oh, how im-pos-si-ble.

Can the o-cean keep from rush-ing to the shore? It's just im-pos-si-ble.

Am
Gm
C7
If I had you, could I ev - er want for more? It's just im -
Gm
A7
Dm
pos - si - ble. And to - mor - row, should you
Fm
C
A7
ask me for the world, some-how I'd get it. I would sell my ver - y soul and not re -
Dm
G7
C
gret it. For to live with-out your love is just im - pos - si - ble, im -
Am
Dm
G7
C
pos - si - ble. Mm, im - pos - si - ble.

KISS OF FIRE

Copyright © 1952 SONGS OF UNIVERSAL, INC.
Copyright Renewed
All Rights Reserved   Used by Permission

Words and Music by LESTER ALLEN
and ROBERT HILL
(Adapted from A.G. VILLOLDO)

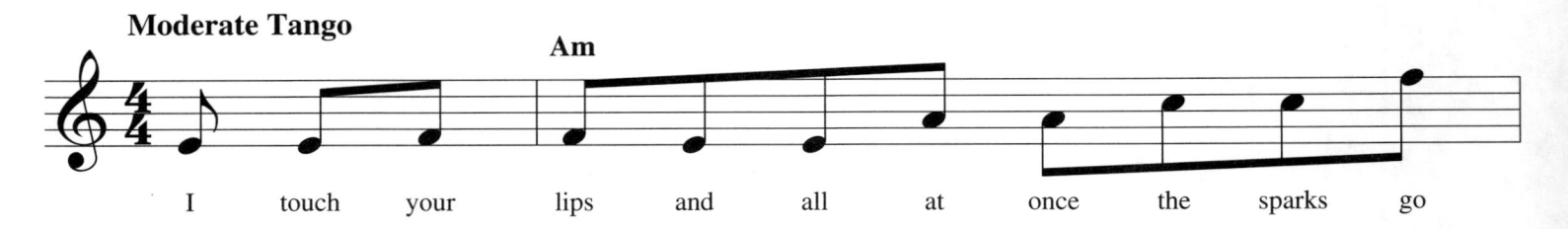

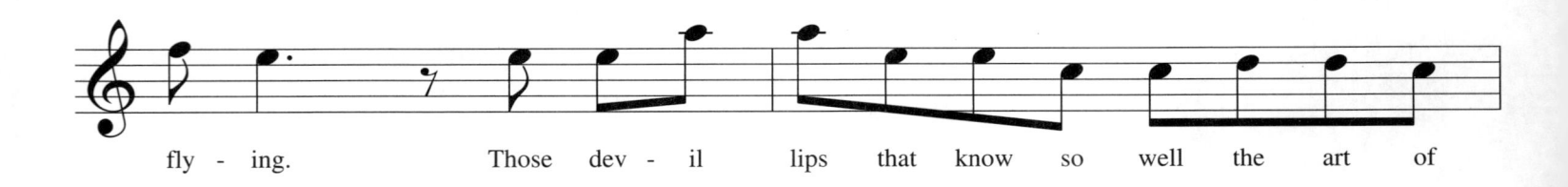

Moderate Tango

I touch your lips and all at once the sparks go fly - ing. Those dev - il lips that know so well the art of ly - ing, and tho' I see the dan - ger, still the flame grows high - er. I know I must sur - ren - der to your kiss of fire. Just like a torch, you set the soul with - in me burn - ing. I must go on a - long this road of no re -

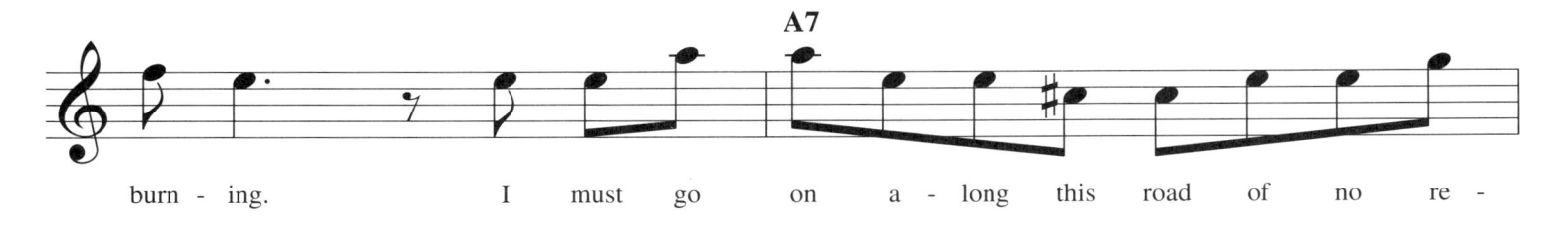

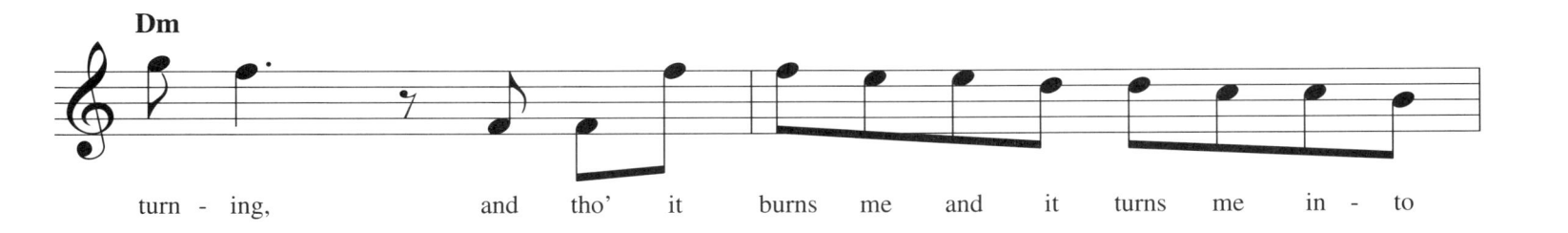

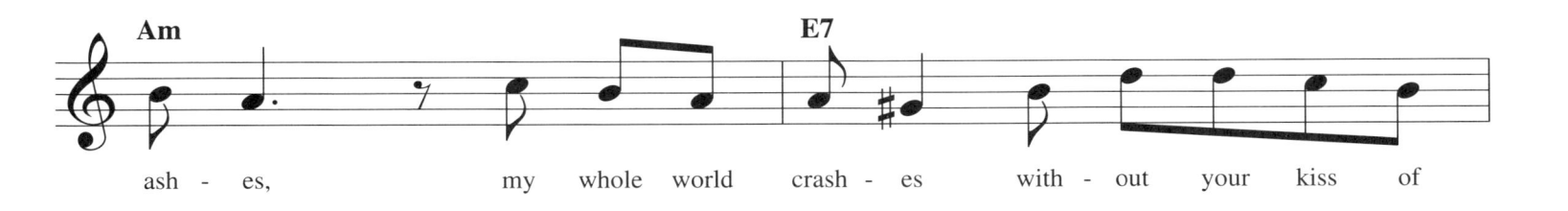

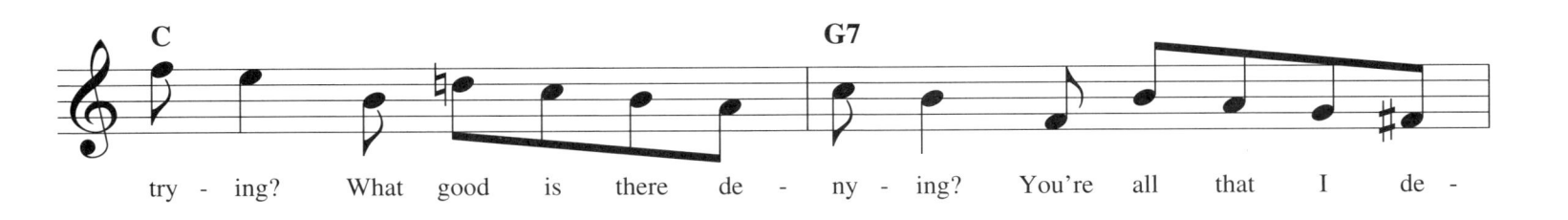

turn - ing, and tho' it burns me and it turns me in - to

ash - es, my whole world crash - es with - out your kiss of

fire. I can't re - sist you; what good is there in

try - ing? What good is there de - ny - ing? You're all that I de -

sire. ___ Since first I kissed you my heart was yours com -

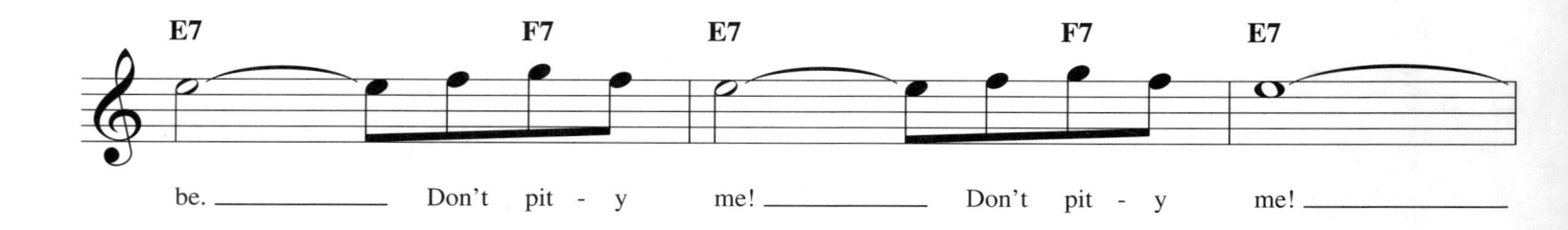

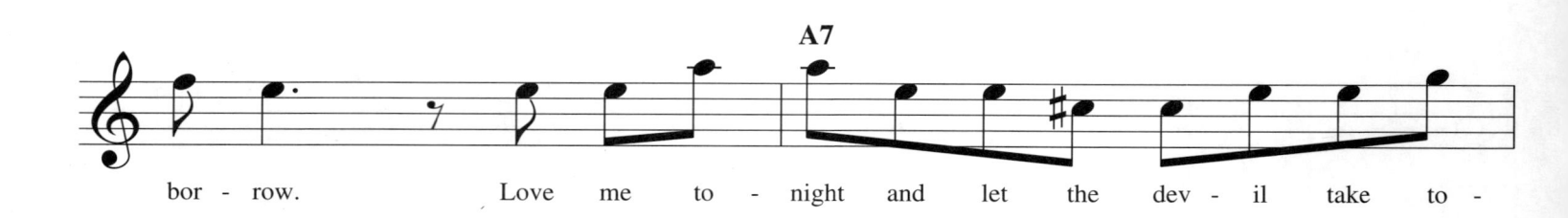

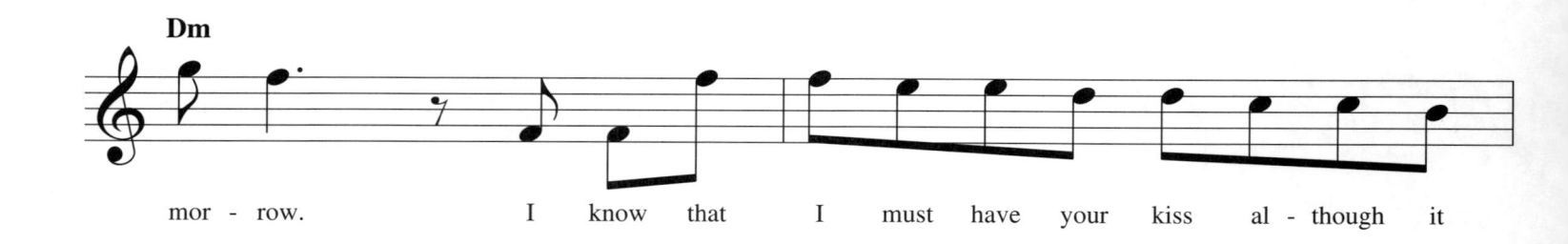

plete-ly. If I'm a slave then it's a slave I want to be. Don't pit-y me! Don't pit-y me! Give me your lips, the lips you on-ly let me bor-row. Love me to-night and let the dev-il take to-mor-row. I know that I must have your kiss al-though it dooms me, tho' it con-sumes me, your kiss of fire.

LITTLE BOAT
(O Barquinho)

Original Words by RONALDO BOSCOLI
English Words by BUDDY KAYE
Music by ROBERTO MENESCAL

Copyright © 1963 EDITIONS SACHA S.A.R.L.
Copyright Renewed
All Rights for the U.S. and Canada Controlled and Administered by SONGS OF UNIVERSAL, INC.
All Rights Reserved   Used by Permission

Bouncy

My lit-tle boat is like a note bounc-ing mer-ri-ly a-long, hear it splash-in' up a song. The sails are white, the sky is bright head-in' out in-to the blue with a crew of on-ly two. Where we can share love's salt-y air on a lit-tle par-a-dise that's a-float, not a care have we in my lit-tle boat.

The wind is still, we feel the thrill of a voy-age heav-en bound, tho' we on-ly drift a-round. Warmed by the sun, two hearts as one beat-ing with en-chant-ed bliss, melt-ing in each oth-er's kiss. When day-light ends, and sly-ly sends lit-tle stars to twin-kle bright-ly a-bove, it's good-bye to my lit-tle boat of love. Good-bye lit-tle boat. Good-bye lit-tle boat.

LISBON ANTIGUA
(In Old Lisbon)

English Lyric by HARRY DUPREE
Music by RAUL PORTELA,
J. GALHARDO and AMADEU DO VALE

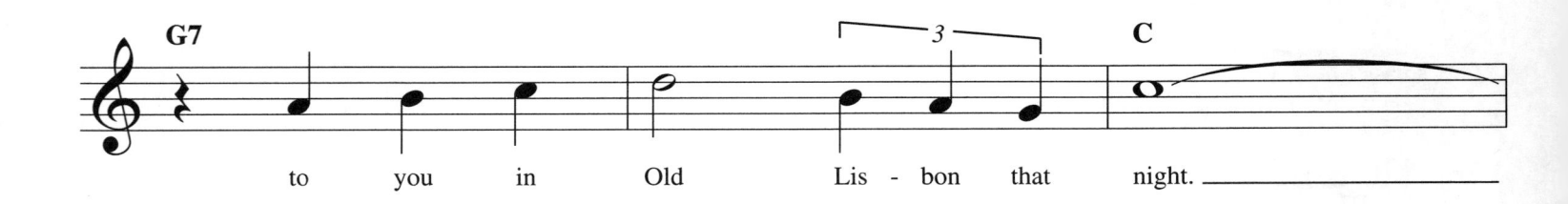

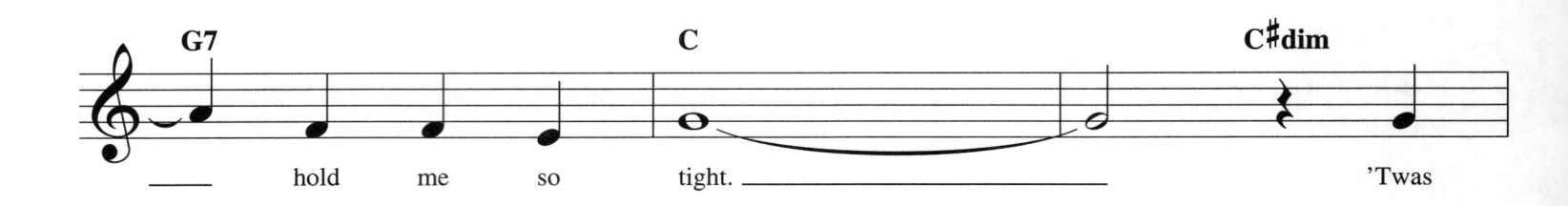

Moderately bright

I gave my heart to you in Old Lisbon that night. Under the spell of your charms, I felt your arms hold me so tight. 'Twas heaven to find such bliss in each kiss. _____

I lost my heart but I found one so

true, _____ in Old Lis - bon with

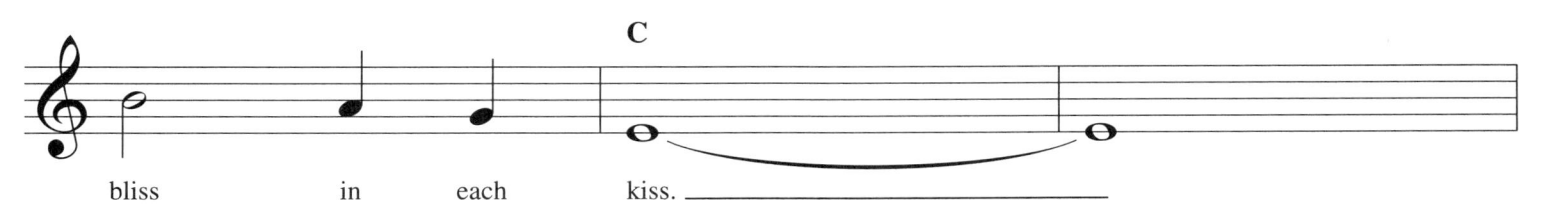

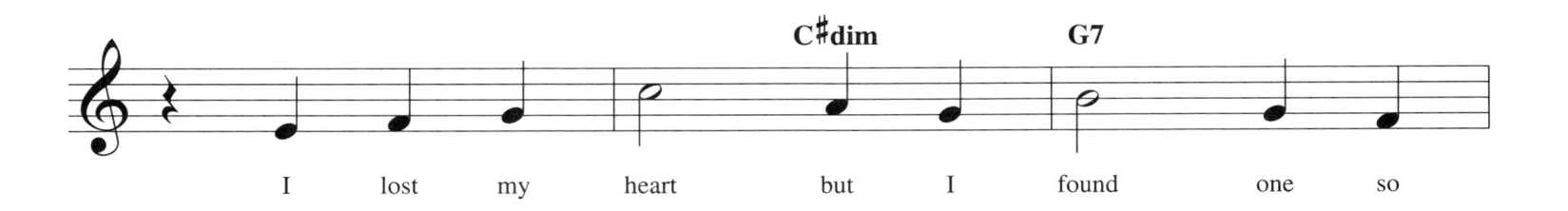

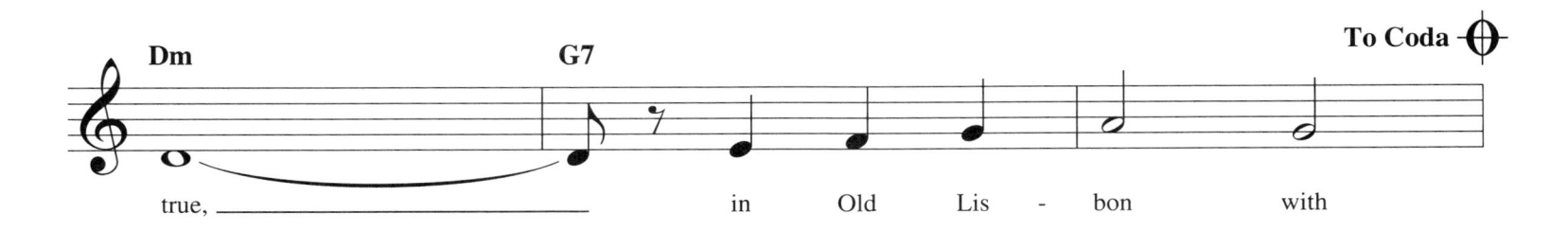

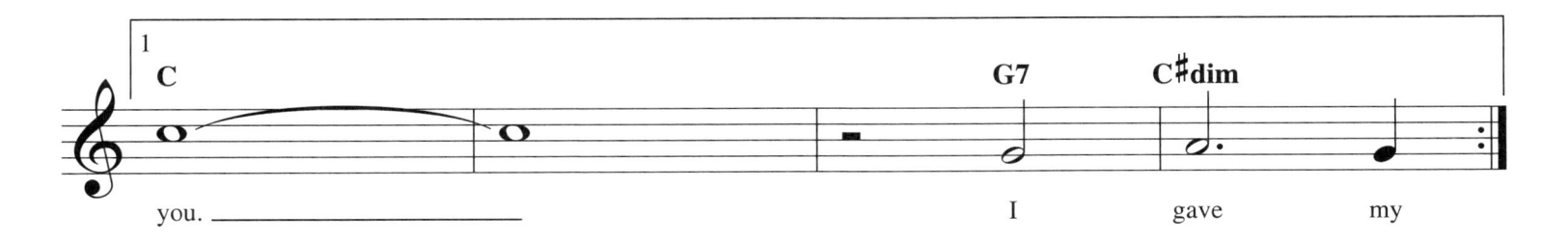

1.
you. _____ I gave my

2.
you. _____ It hap - pened

one night in Por - tu - gal, _____

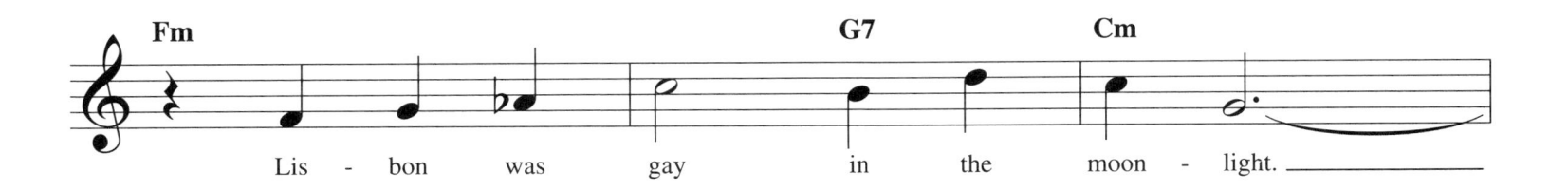

Lis - bon was gay in the moon - light. _____

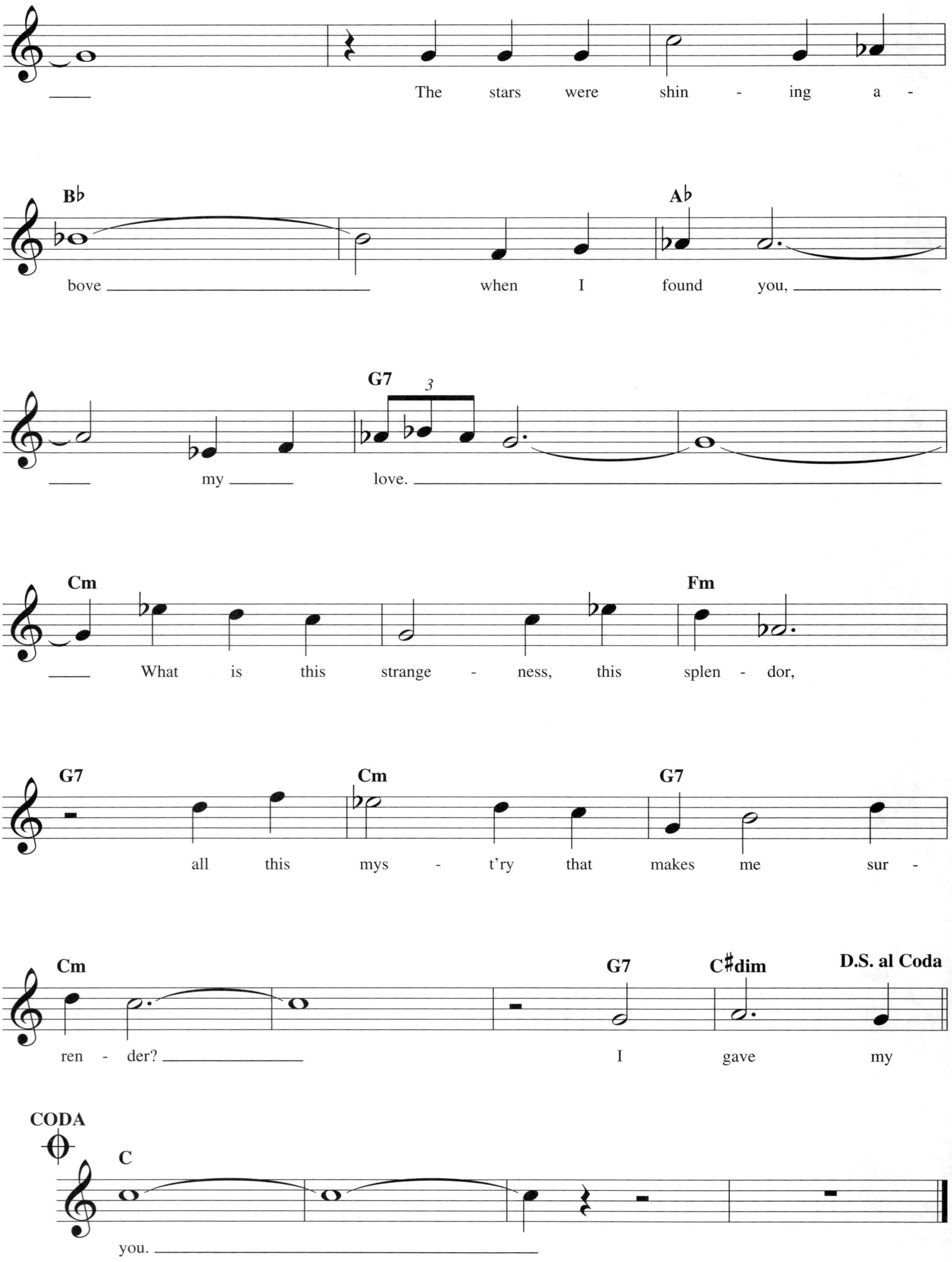
The stars were shin - ing a -
B♭
A♭
bove when I found you,
G7
3
my love.
Cm
Fm
What is this strange - ness, this splen - dor,
G7
Cm
G7
all this mys - t'ry that makes me sur -
Cm
G7
C♯dim
D.S. al Coda
ren - der? I gave my
CODA
C
you.

MAMBO #5

Words and Music by
DÁMASO PÉREZ PRADO

Copyright © 1948 by Editorial Mexicana de Musica Internacional, S.A.
Copyright Renewed
All Rights Administered by Peer International Corporation
International Copyright Secured All Rights Reserved

THE LOOK OF LOVE
from CASINO ROYALE

Words by HAL DAVID
Music by BURT BACHARACH

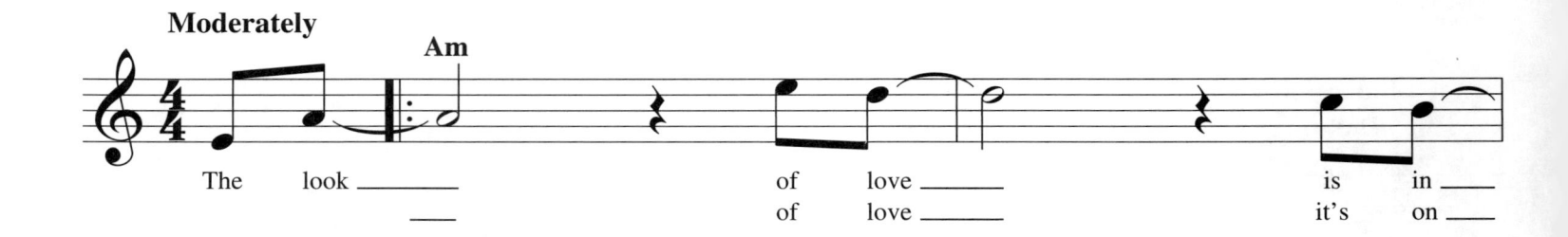

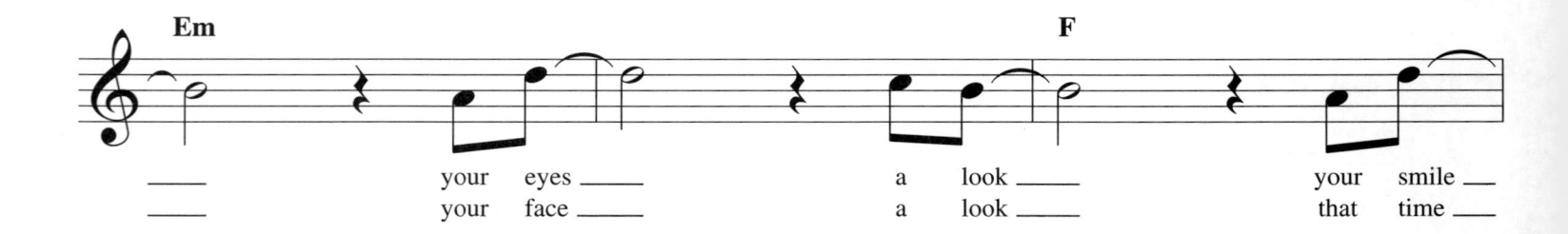

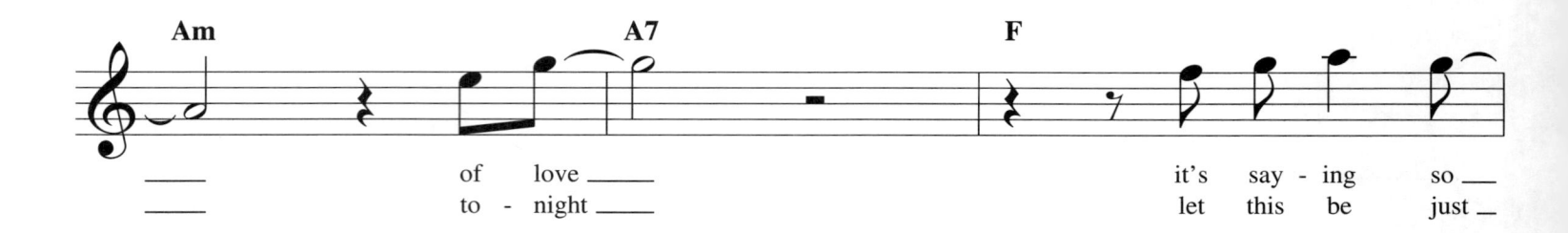

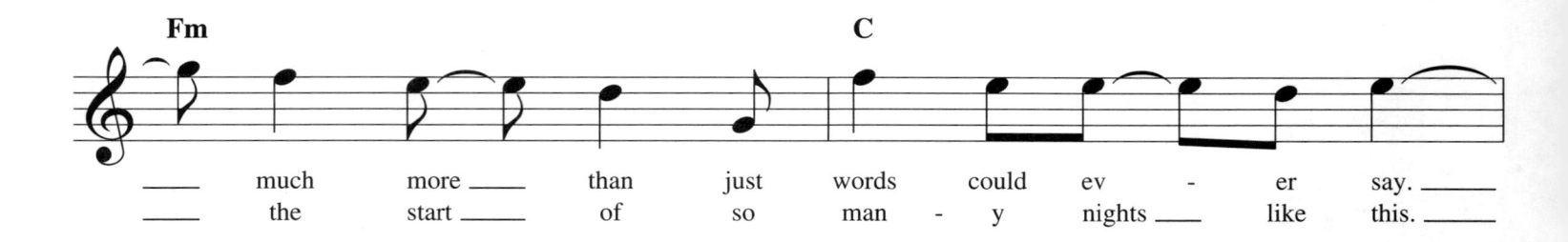

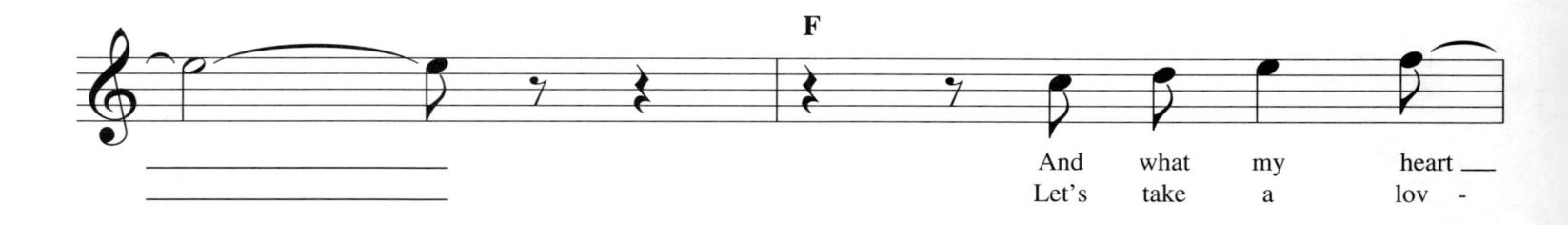

Moderately

Am
The look _____ of love _____ is in _____
_____ of love _____ it's on _____

Em _____ your eyes _____ a look _____ your smile _____
_____ your face _____ a look _____ that time _____

F

E7
_____ can't dis - guise. _____ The look _____
_____ can't e - rase. _____ Be mine _____

Am **A7** **F**
_____ of love _____ it's say - ing so _____
_____ to - night _____ let this be just _____

Fm **C**
_____ much more _____ than just words could ev - er say. _____
_____ the start _____ of so man - y nights _____ like this. _____

F
_____ And what my heart _____
_____ Let's take a lov -

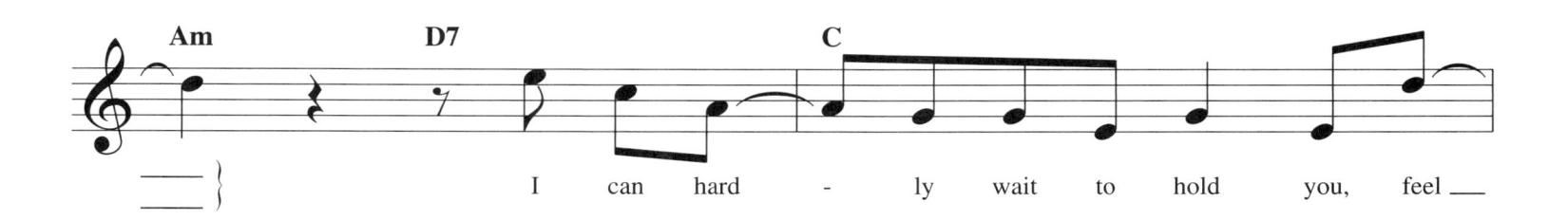

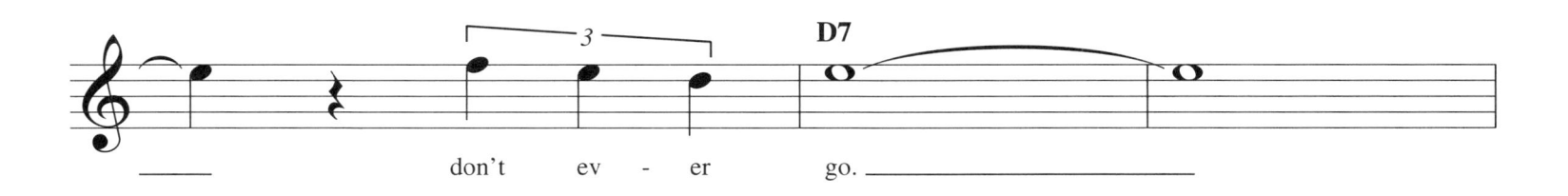

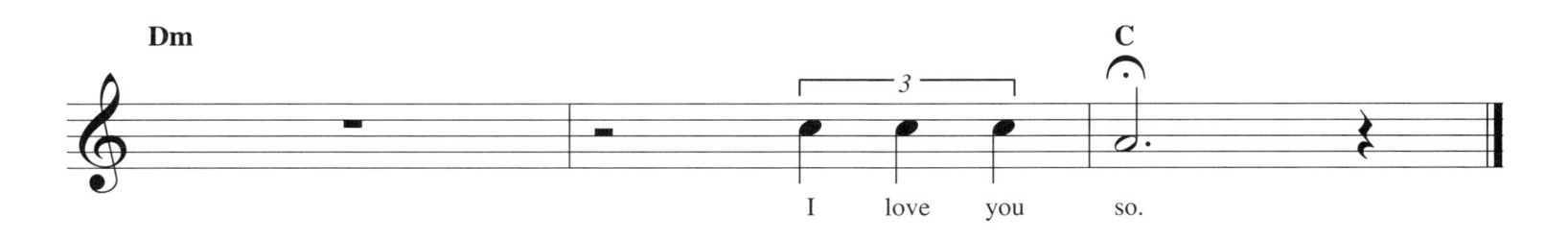

E7
___ has heard, ___ well, it takes my breath ___ a - way. ___
- er's vow ___ and then seal it with ___ a kiss. ___

Am **D7** **C**

I can hard - ly wait to hold you, feel ___

Dm/G

___ my arms a - round you, how long ___ I have wait - ed,

C **Dm/G**

wait - ed just to love you, now ___ that I have found you, ___

1. ___ you've got the look ___ *2.* ___ don't ev - er go ___ **Am**

D7

don't ev - er go. ___

Dm **C**

I love you so.

LOVE ME WITH ALL YOUR HEART
(Cuando Calienta El Sol)

Original Words and Music by CARLOS RIGUAL
and CARLOS A. MARTINOLI
English Words by SUNNY SKYLAR

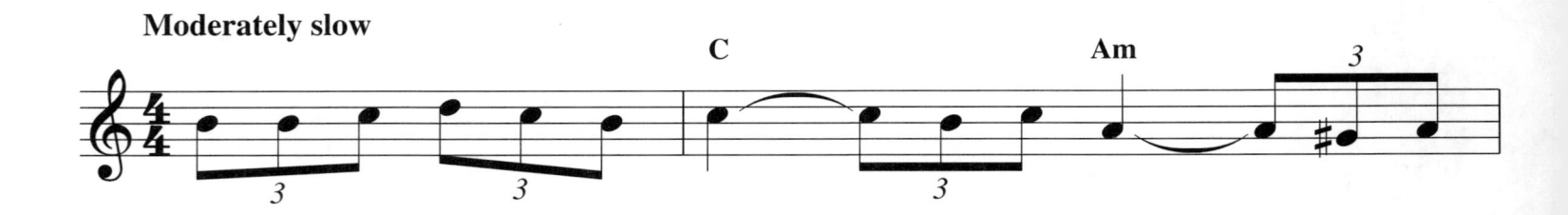

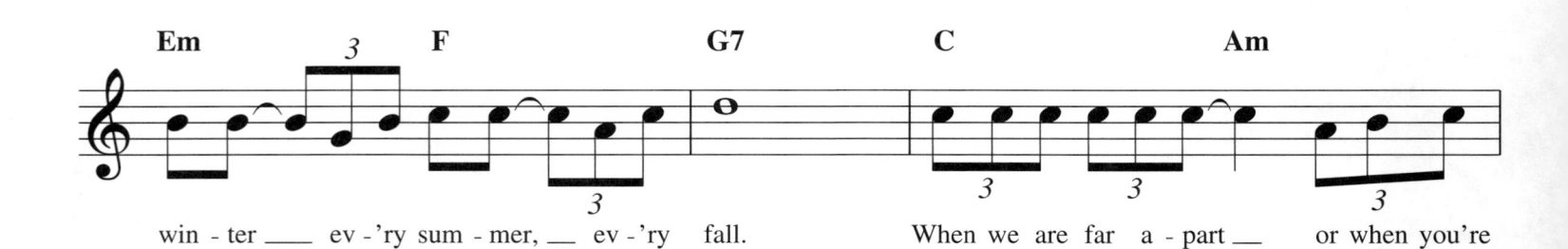

Love me with all your heart, ___ that's all I want, love. ___ Love me with all of your heart or not at all. ___ Just promise me this: ___ that you'll give me ___ all your kisses, ___ ev'ry winter ___ ev'ry summer, ___ ev'ry fall. When we are far apart ___ or when you're near me, _____ Love me with all of your heart as I love you. _____

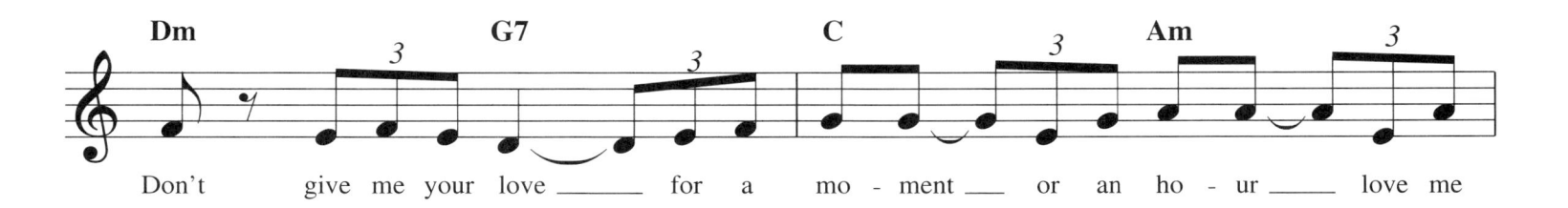

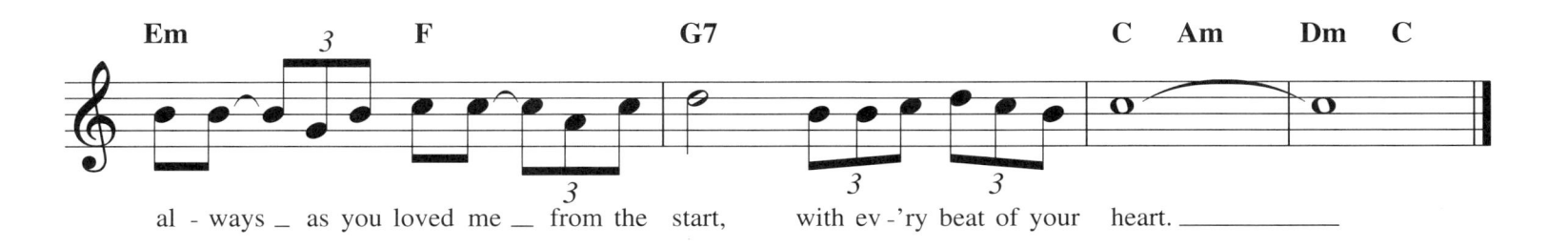

Don't give me your love ___ for a mo-ment __ or an ho-ur ___ love me

al-ways _ as you loved me _ from the start, with ev-'ry beat of your heart. _____

Spanish Lyrics

Cuando calienta el sol aqui en la playa
Siento tu cuerpo vibrar cerca de mí
Es tu palpitar es tu cara es tu pelo
Son tus besos me estremezco - o - o - o
Cuando calienta el sol aqui en la playa
Siento tu cuerpo vibrar cerca de mí
Es tu palpitar tu recuerdo mi locura
Mi delirio me estremezco - o - o - o
Cuando calienta el sol.

MALAGUEÑA
from the Spanish Suite ANDALUCIA

Music and Spanish Lyric by
ERNESTO LECUONA
English Lyric by MARIAN BANKS

Copyright © 1928 by Edward B. Marks Music Company
Copyright Renewed
International Copyright Secured All Rights Reserved
Used by Permission

Moderately slow

"Fly a-way!" Said my care-free heart. "To the place where the day-dreams start. "Fly a-way!" Said my heart to me. "To the shore of the moon-lit sea." 'Tis the gyp-sy code to be fan-cy free; when I see a road, oh that's the road for me! *(Instrumental)*

Flamenco tempo–in 4

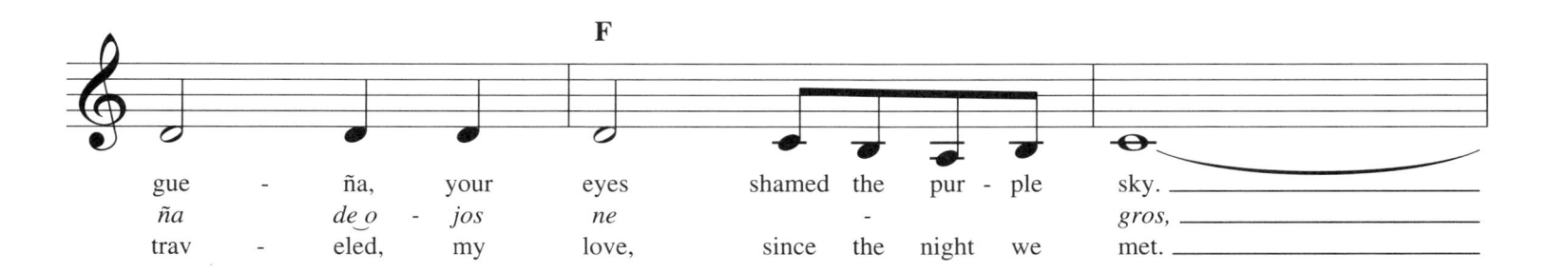

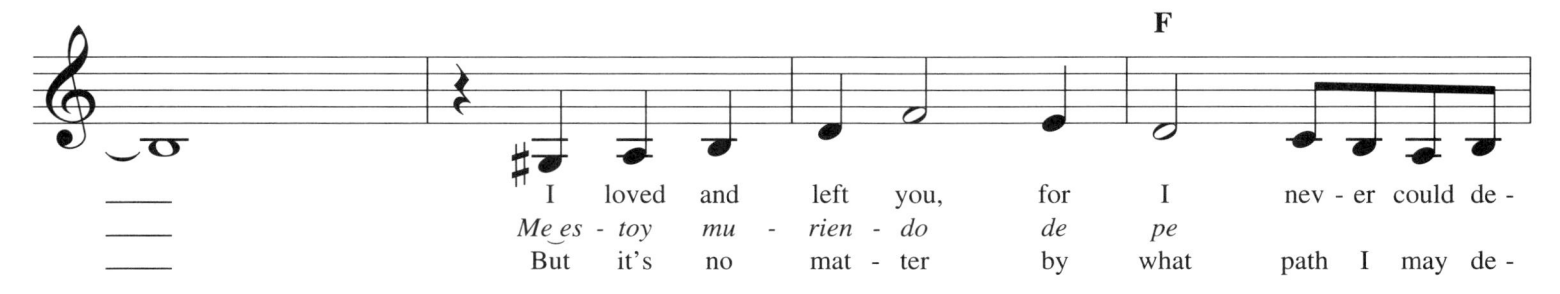

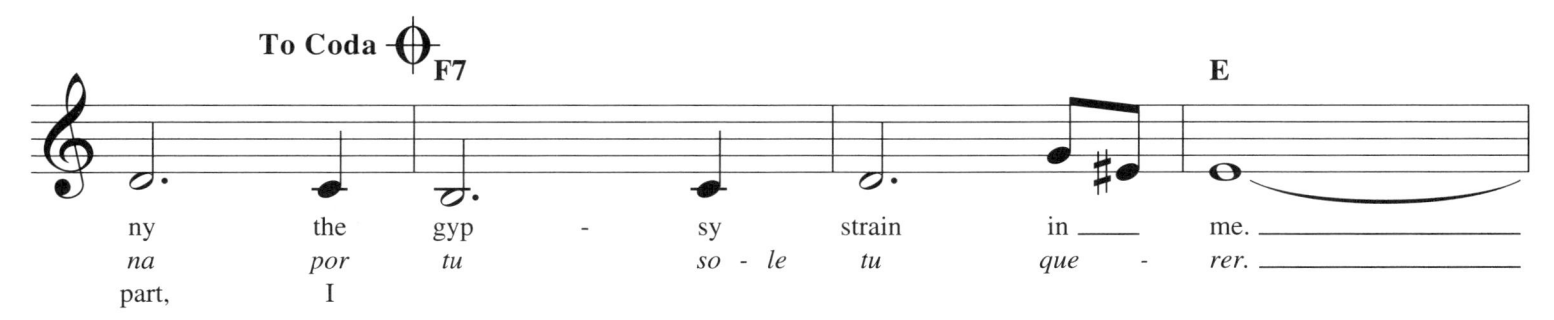

1. My Mala-
1.,2. Ma - la - gue
2. Long have I

gue - ña, your eyes shamed the pur - ple sky.
ña de o - jos ne - gros,
trav - eled, my love, since the night we met.

You were as fair as I dreamed you would be;
Ma - la - gue - na de mis sue - ños.
Seek - ing in wan - d'ring a way to for - get.

I loved and left you, for I nev - er could de-
Me es - toy mu - rien - do de pe
But it's no mat - ter by what path I may de-

To Coda

ny the gyp - sy strain in me.
na por tu so - le tu que - rer.
part, I

Light - ly as a
La la la la la

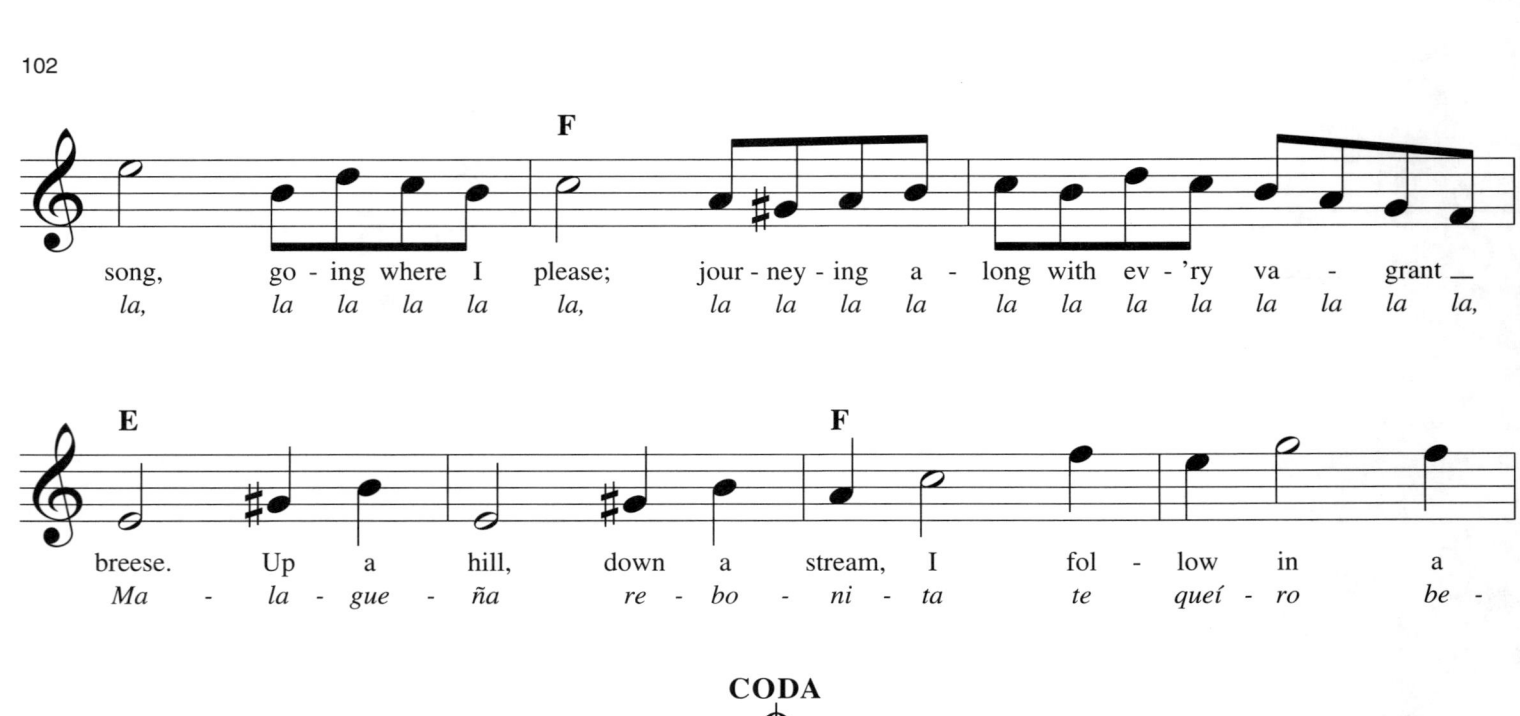

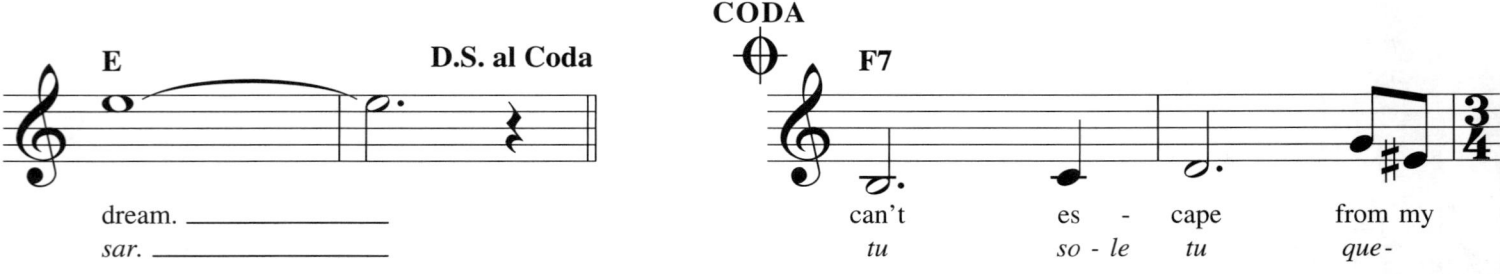

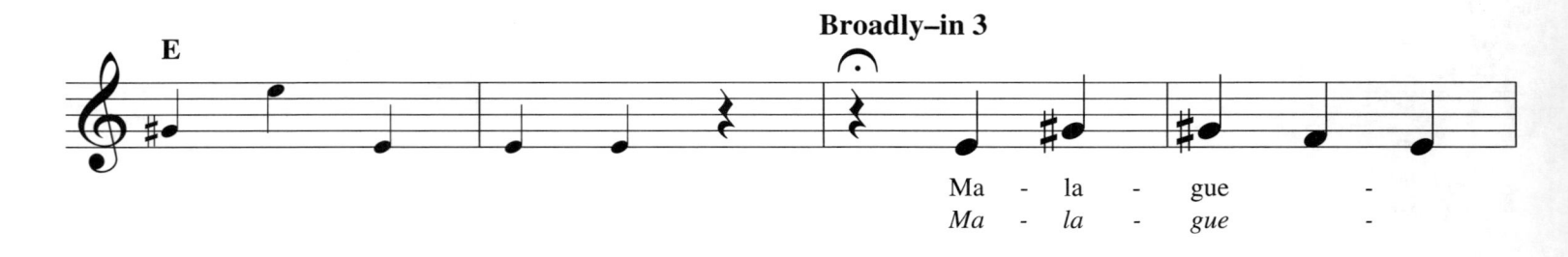

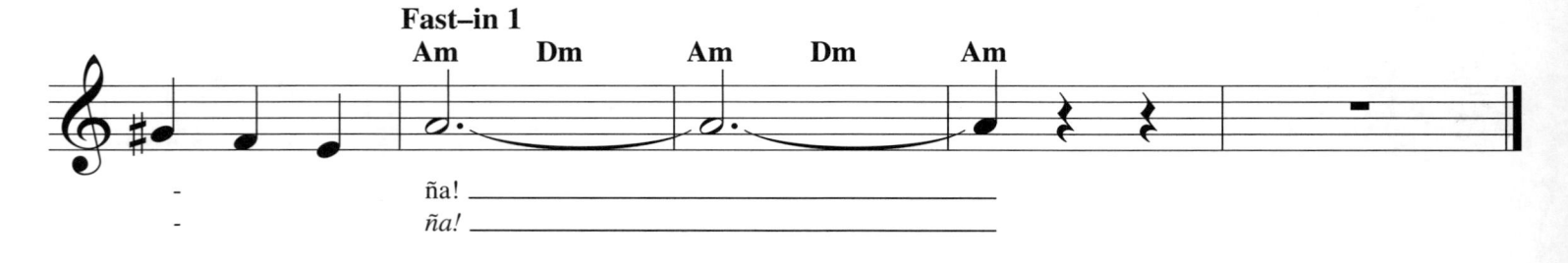

song, go - ing where I please; jour - ney - ing a - long with ev - 'ry va - grant
la, la la la la la, la la la la la la la la la la la la,

breese. Up a hill, down a stream, I fol - low in a
Ma - la - gue - ña re - bo - ni - ta te queí - ro be -

D.S. al Coda **CODA**

dream. can't es - cape from my
sar. tu so - le tu que -

heart. *(Instrumental)*
rer.

Broadly–in 3

Ma - la - gue -
Ma - la - gue -

Fast–in 1

ña!
ña!

MAÑANA

Words and Music by PEGGY LEE
and DAVE BARBOUR

Copyright © 1948 by Denslow-Music, Inc. and Criterion Music Corp.
Copyright Renewed
All Rights for Denslow-Music, Inc. Administered by Universal Music - MGB Songs
International Copyright Secured   All Rights Reserved

Samba

1. The fau-cet she is drip-ping and the fence she's fall-ing down. My pock-et needs some mon-ey so I can't go in to town. My broth-er is-n't work-ing and my sis-ter does-n't care. The car she needs a mo-tor so I can't go an-y-where.

Ma-ña-na, Ma-ña-na, Ma-ña-na is soon e-nough for me.

2. My moth-er's al-ways work-ing; she's work-ing ver-y hard. But ev-'ry time she looks for me I'm sleep-ing in the yard. My moth-er thinks I'm la-zy and may-be she is right. I'll go to work Ma-ña-na, but I got-ta sleep to-night.

3. Oh, once I had some mon-ey but I gave it to my friend. He said he'd pay me dou-ble, it was on-ly for a lend. But he said a lit-tle lat-er that the horse she was so slow. Why he gave the horse my mon-ey is some-thing I don't know.

4. My broth-er took his suit-case and he went a-way to school. My fa-ther said he on-ly learn'd to be a sil-ly fool. My fa-ther said that I should learn to make a chi-li pot. But then I burn'd the house down; the chi-li was too hot.

5. The win-dow she is bro-ken and the rain is com-ing in. If some-one does-n't fix it I'll be soak-ing to my skin. But if we wait a day or two the rain may go a-way. And we don't need a win-dow on such a sun-ny day.

MAMA INEZ

Words by L. WOLFE GILBERT
Music by ELISEO GRENET

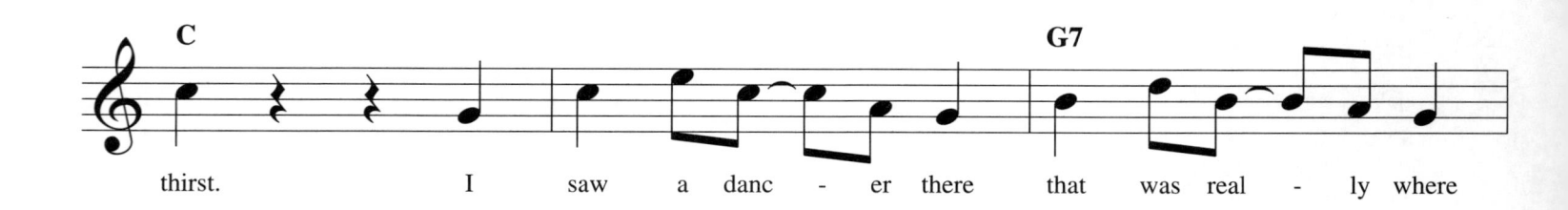

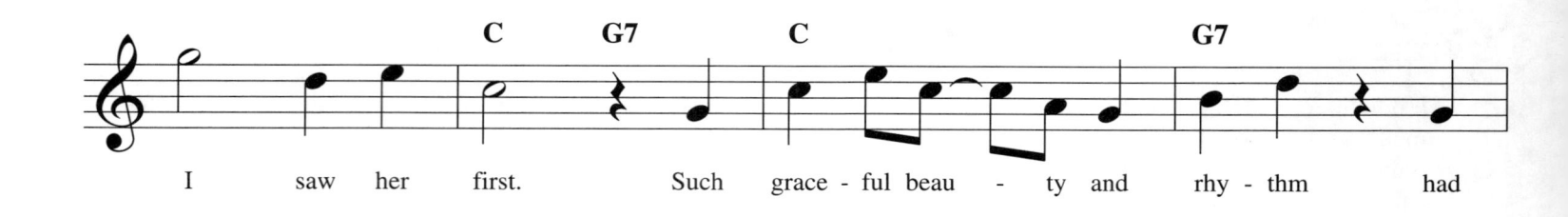

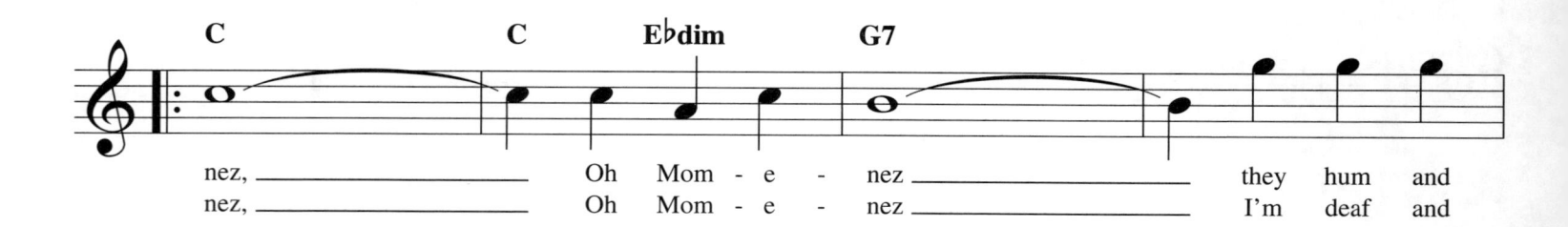

Copyright © 1932 by Edward B. Marks Music Company
Copyright Renewed
International Copyright Secured All Rights Reserved
Used by Permission

Briskly

In Slop-py Joe's in Ha-van-a I lin-gered quench-ing my thirst. I saw a danc-er there that was real-ly where I saw her first. Such grace-ful beau-ty and rhy-thm had nev-er come to my sight. She made me want to stay, danced my heart a-way most ev-'ry night. Oh Mom-e-nez, Oh Mom-e-nez they hum and
Oh Mom-e-nez, Oh Mom-e-nez I'm deaf and

strum that la rum - ba for you. _____ Oh Mom - e -
dumb when la rum - ba I see. _____ Oh Mom - e -

nez, _____ Oh Mom - e - nez _____ though oth - ers
nez, _____ Oh Mom - e - nez _____ my limbs get

come, their la rum - ba won't do. _____ When
numb, oh la rum - ba for me. _____ Ha -

I first saw _ this she - bang - o I fell so hard _ for the
wai - ians dance _ in a crude way the Af - ri - cans _ in a

tan - go. But now this brand _ new fan - dang - o's got _ me like
lewd way. And though you dance _ in a new way ev - ery - one

noth - in' got _ me be - fore, Oh Mom - e - nez, _____
loves your won - der - ful style. Oh Mom - e - nez, _____

_____ Oh Mom - e - nez _____ no Cu - ban rum like la
_____ Oh Mom - e - nez _____ I'm blue and glum, dance la

rum - ba for me. _____ Oh Mom - e -
rum - ba for me. _____

MAMBO JAMBO
(Que Rico El Mambo)

English Words by RAYMOND KARL
and CHARLIE TOWNE
Original Words and Music by DÁMASO PÉREZ PRADO

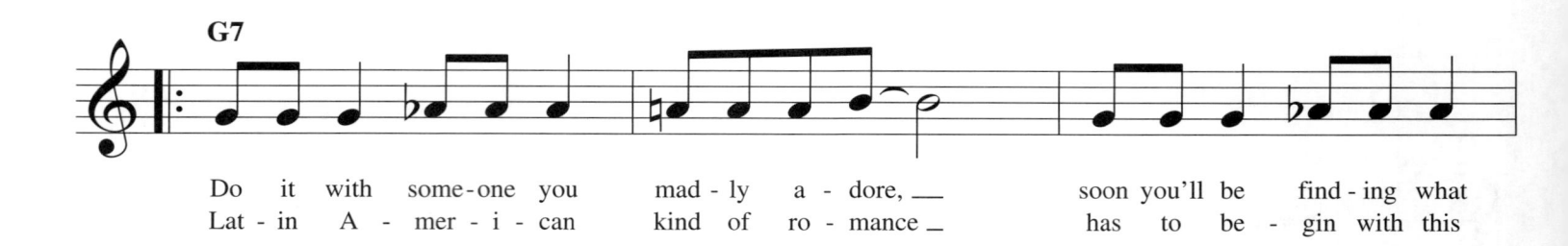

Fast Latin

Do the mambo, do the mambo, mambo jambo, mambo jambo.

Do it with someone you madly adore, soon you'll be finding what
Latin American kind of romance has to begin with this

you've waited for. For when you sway with her, holding her close,
fabulous dance. Wonderful rhythm she'll never resist.

she'll be reluctant to say "adios."
Here is the part where she'll want to be kissed.

Dif'rent from any rhumba, better than any samba,

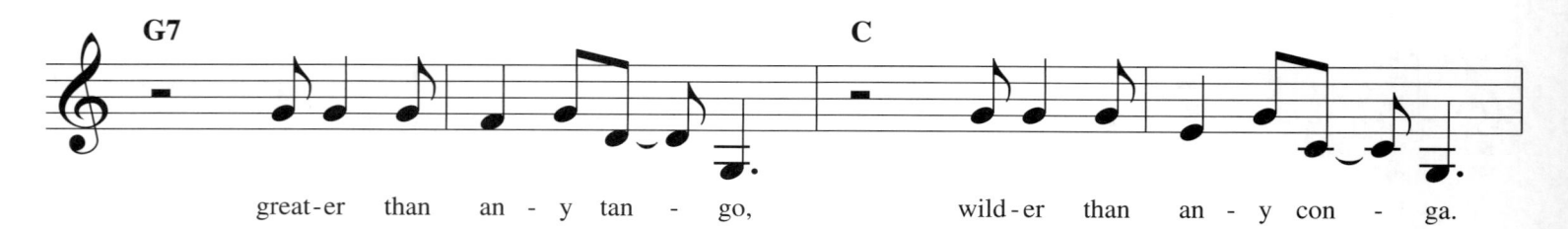

greater than any tango, wilder than any conga.

Fm | **C**

The min-ute that you be-gin, ____ you'll find it be-
You'll find at the break of day, ____ your heart has been

F A/E Dm A7/C♯ Dm/C G7/B F/A G7 C

neath your skin ____ like the hoo-doo of a voo-doo drum.
flown a-way ____ to a land where on-ly lov-ers dwell.

Fm

It teach-es your heart the beat, ____
The mo-ment your love is found, ____

C | **F A/E Dm A7/C♯**

then goes to your head and feet ____ like a shak-er
the mo-ment your heart is bound, ____ you will bless the

To Coda ⊕

Dm/C G7/B F/A G7 C

of Ja-mai-ca rum. You
mam-bo jam-bo

C7 | **F**

do the mam-bo jam-bo, you
do the mam-bo jam-bo, all

C7 | **F**

dance to break of day, day,
night you hol-ler hey! Hey!

1. day, day. You **2.** Ho- **D.S. al Coda** lay!

C

spell. ____

A MAN AND A WOMAN
(Un Homme Et Une Femme)
from A MAN AND A WOMAN

Original Words by PIERRE BAROUH
English Words by JERRY KELLER
Music by FRANCIS LAI

Copyright © 1966 EDITIONS SARAVAH, Paris, France
Copyright Renewed
All Rights in the U.S. and Canada Controlled and Administered by UNIVERSAL MUSIC CORP.
All Rights Reserved Used by Permission

Moderately

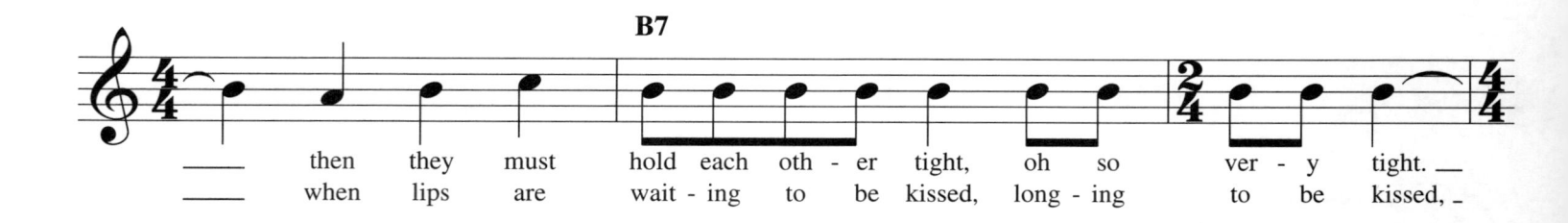

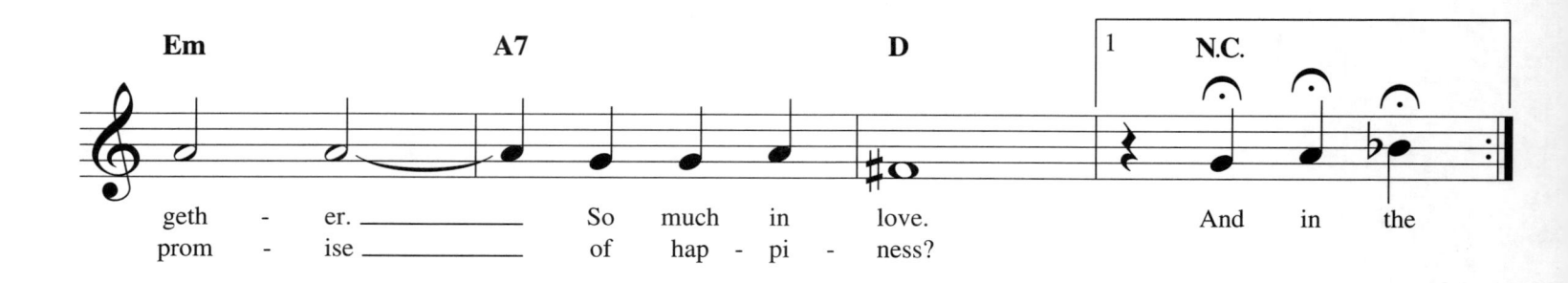

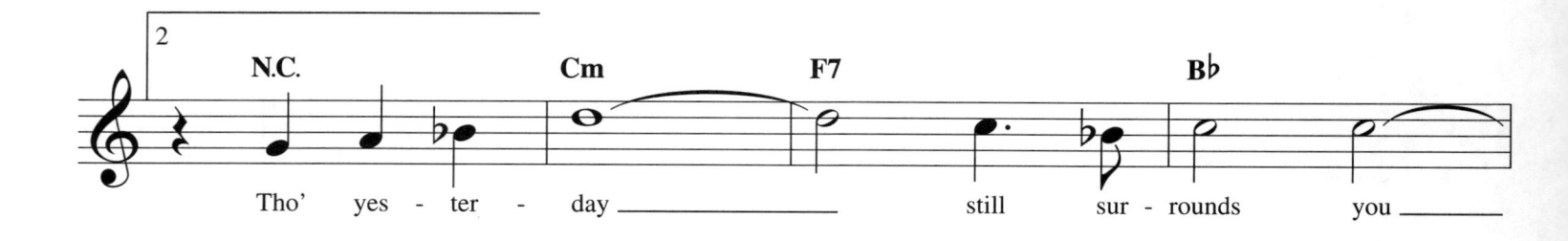

When hearts are pass-ing in the night, in the lone-ly night
si-lence of the mist, of the morn-ing mist,

then they must hold each oth-er tight, oh so ver-y tight.
when lips are wait-ing to be kissed, long-ing to be kissed,

And take a chance that in the light in to-mor-row's light they'll stay to-
where is the rea-son to re-sist and de-ny a kiss that holds a

geth-er. So much in love. And in the
prom-ise of hap-pi-ness?

Tho' yes-ter-day still sur-rounds you

_____ with a warm and pre - cious mem - o - ry, _____

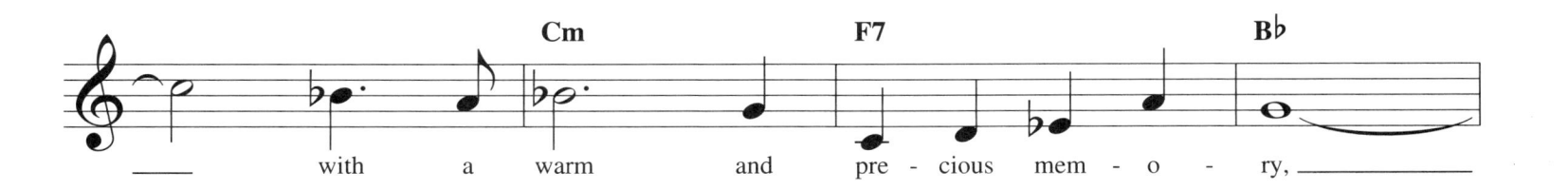

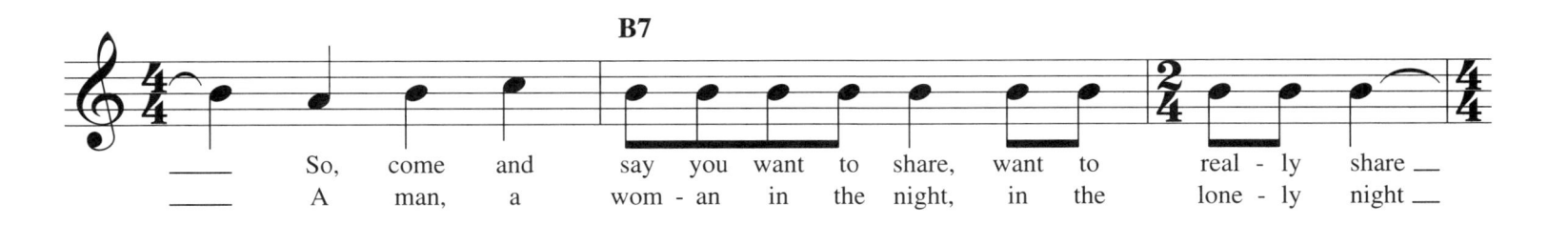

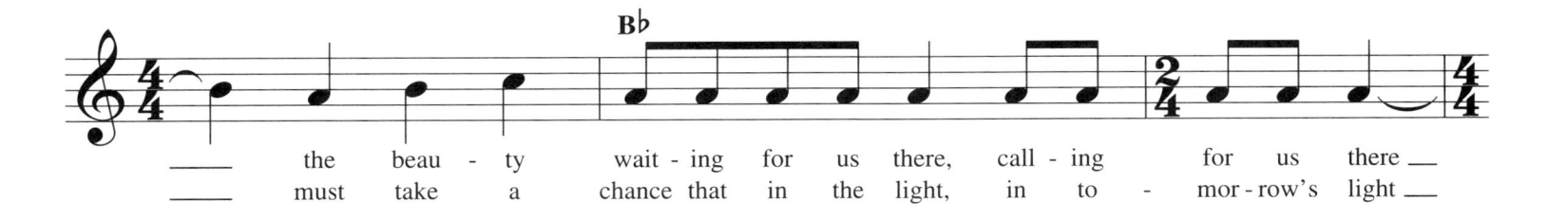

_____ may - be _____ for to - mor - row _____

_____ we can build a new dream _____ for you and me.

This glow we feel is some - thing rare, some - thing real - ly rare. _____
pass - ing in the night, in the rush - ing night. _____

_____ So, come and say you want to share, want to real - ly share _____
_____ A man, a wom - an in the night, in the lone - ly night _____

_____ the beau - ty wait - ing for us there, call - ing for us there _____
_____ must take a chance that in the light, in to - mor - row's light _____

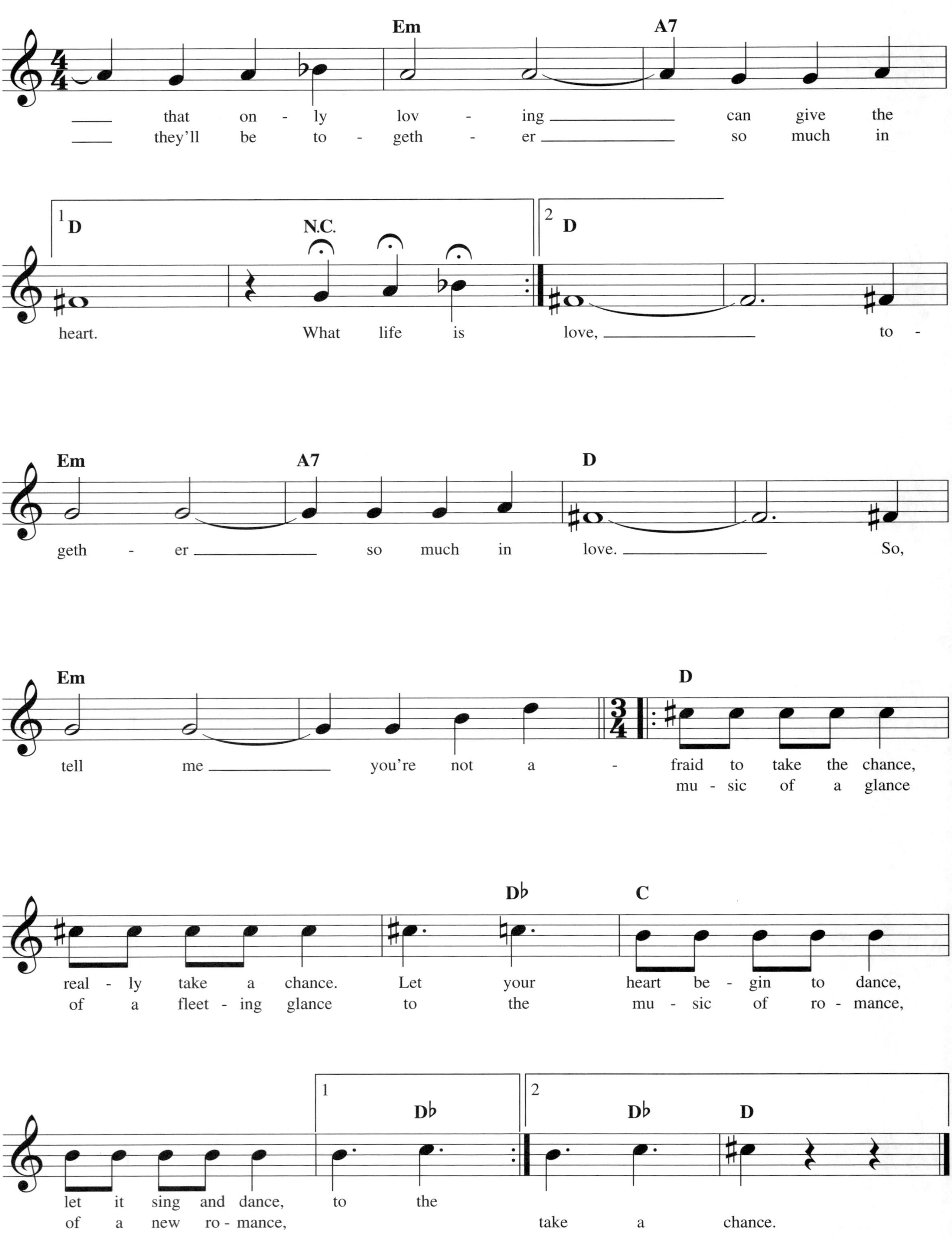
Em A7
that on - ly lov - ing can give the
they'll be to - geth - er so much in
1 D N.C. 2 D
heart. What life is love, to -
Em A7 D
geth - er so much in love. So,
Em D
tell me you're not a - fraid to take the chance,
mu - sic of a glance
D♭ C
real - ly take a chance. Let your heart be - gin to dance,
of a fleet - ing glance to the mu - sic of ro - mance,
1 D♭ 2 D♭ D
let it sing and dance, to the
of a new ro - mance, take a chance.

MI VIDA

By ERNESTO LECUONA

Mi vi - da, te a - mo des - de que yo te ví, Mi vi - da,
Mi vi - da, I loved you the mo - ment we met. Mi vi - da,

tu e - res la i - lu - sión pa - ra mí Co - mo un sue - ño a - zul vi -
dreams came true the mo - ment we met. In some mag - ic way, you

nis - te fu - gaz, Den - tro de mi ser yo sien - to que tu es -
came from a - far. You are here to - day, will you be here to -

tás Mi vi - da, mi des - ti - no fue tu pa - sión,
mor - row? Mi vi - da, I knew we were des - tined to meet.

Tu a - mor que pa - ra mi la vi - da ha de ser, Nun - ca mi
With you, my life could be com - plete - ly com - plete. This heart of

co - ra - zón ha - brá de ol - vi - dar. A - que - lla
mine will nev - er let me for - get You and the

vez que te ví. | *ví.*
moment we met. | met.

MARIA ELENA

Copyright © 1932 by Peer International Coporation
Copyright Renewed
International Copyright Secured   All Rights Reserved

English Words by S.K. RUSSELL
Music and Spanish Words by LORENZO BARCELATA

Moderately

Ma - ri - a E - le - na, you're the an - swer to a pray'r.

Ma - ri - a E - le - na, can't you see how much I care?

To me your voice is like the ech - o of a

sigh, and when you're near my heart can't speak a - bove a

sigh. Ma - ri - a E - le - na, say that we will nev - er part.

Ma - ri - a E - le - na, take me to your heart.

A love like mine is great e - nough for two.

To share this love is real - ly all I ask of you.

ST. THOMAS

By SONNY ROLLINS

MAS QUE NADA

Copyright © 1963 by Peermusic Do Brasil Edicoes Musicais Ltda.
Copyright Renewed
All Rights Administered by Peer International Corporation
International Copyright Secured   All Rights Reserved

Words and Music by
JORGE BEN

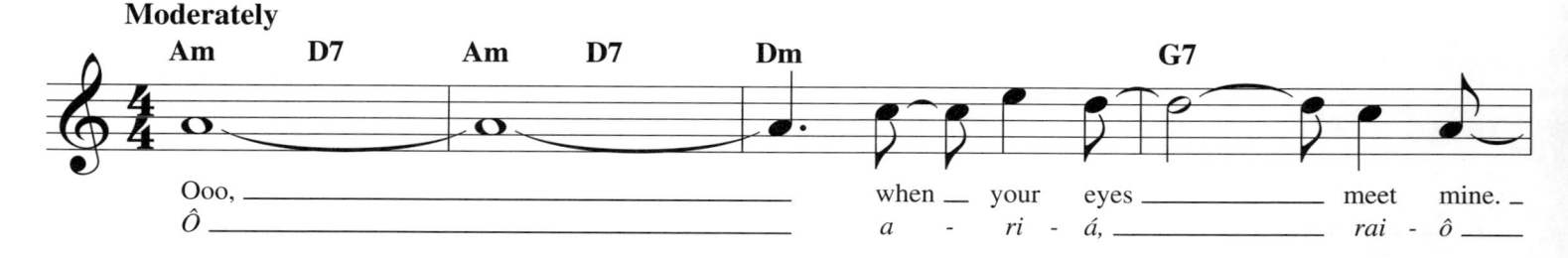

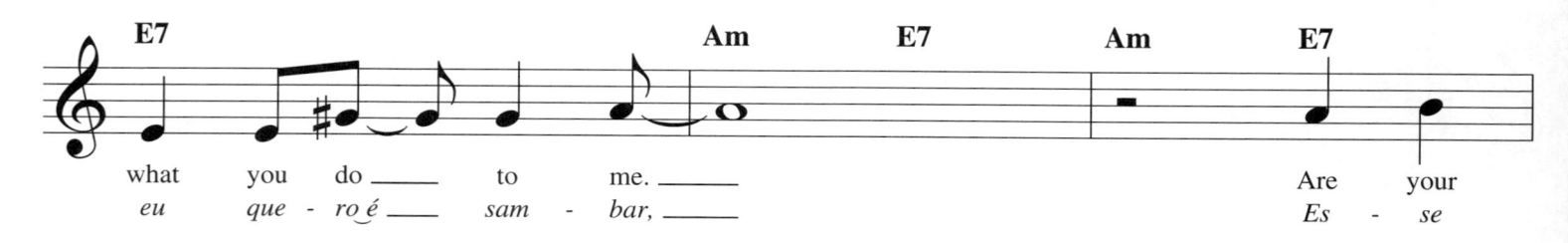

Moderately

Ooo, _____ when your eyes _____ meet mine.
Ô _____ a - ri - á, _____ rai - ô _____

_____ Pow! Pow! Pow!
ô - bá, ô - bá, ô - bá.

Ooo _____ I _____ could lose _____ my mind. _____
Ô _____ a - ri - á _____ rai - ô _____

_____ Ow! Ow! Ow!
ô - bá, ô - bá, ô - bá.

It's a feel - ing that be - gins to grow an' grow an' grow in - side _____
Mas Que Na - da sai da mi - nha fren - te que eu que - ro pas -

_____ me 'til I feel like I'm gon - na ex - plode. _____ Oh, this is
- sar, pois o sam - ba es - tá a - ni - ma - do. O que

what you do _____ to me. _____ Are your
eu que - ro é _____ sam - bar, _____ Es - se

Dm G7 C
lips say - ing things that you feel in your heart?
sam - ba que é mix - to de ma - ra ca - tú,
D7 G Em
If your heart is beat - ing mad - ly, then let the mu - sic start.
é sam - ba de pre - to ve - lho, sam - ba de pre - to tú.
Am E7 Am
Hold me, hold me! It's
Mas Que Na - da, um
E7 Am E7
heav - en, ooo, it's heav - en when you hold me! I want you night and
sam - ba co - mo es - se tão le - gal, vo - cê não vai que -
Am E7 Am E7
day. Ooo, I want you here to stay.
rer que eu che - gue no fi - nal.
1 Am E7
2 Am E7
D.C. al Coda
CODA
Am D7
ô -
Am D7
Ow! Ow! Ow!
bá, ô - bá, ô - bá. Ô -
Repeat and Fade
Am D7 Am D7 Am D7
Pow! Pow! Pow!
bá, ô - bá, ô - bá. Ô -

MEDITATION
(Meditação)

Music by ANTONIO CARLOS JOBIM
Original Words by NEWTON MENDONÇA
English Words by NORMAN GIMBEL

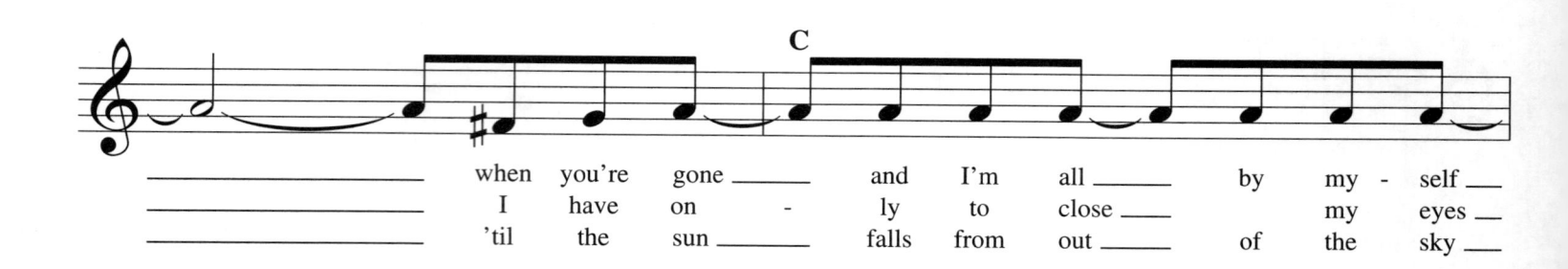

Copyright © 1963, 1964 ANTONIO CARLOS JOBIM
and MRS. NEWTON MENDONÇA, Brazil
Copyright Renewed and Assigned to SONGS OF UNIVERSAL, INC. and NEW THUNDER MUSIC, INC.
All Rights for NEW THUNDER MUSIC, INC. Administered by GIMBEL MUSIC GROUP, INC.
(P.O. Box 15221, Beverly Hills, CA 90209-1221 USA)
All Rights Reserved   Used by Permission

Moderately

[C] [B7]
In my loneliness
Though you're far a-way,
I will wait for you

[C]
when you're gone and I'm all by myself
I have on-ly to close my eyes
'til the sun falls from out of the sky

[Em] [A7]
and I need your ca-ress,
and you are back to stay.
for what else can I do?

[Dm] [Fm]
I just think of you
I just close my eyes
I will wait for you

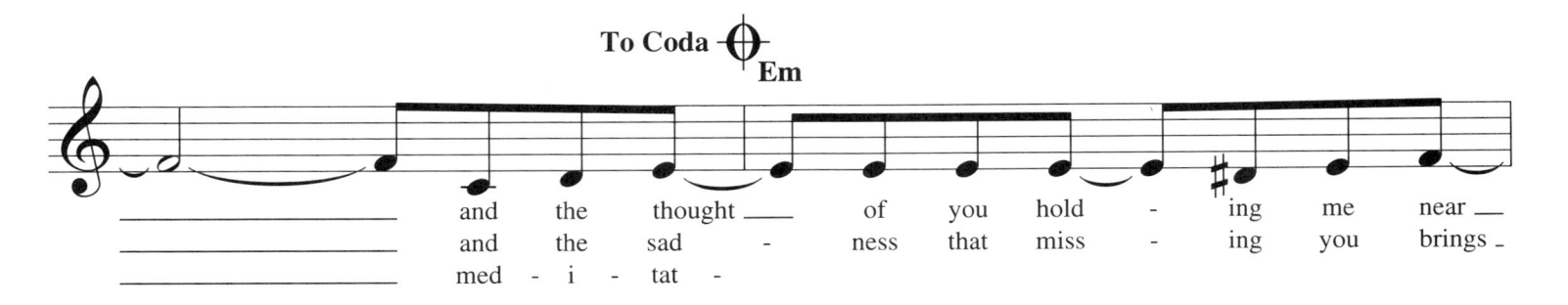

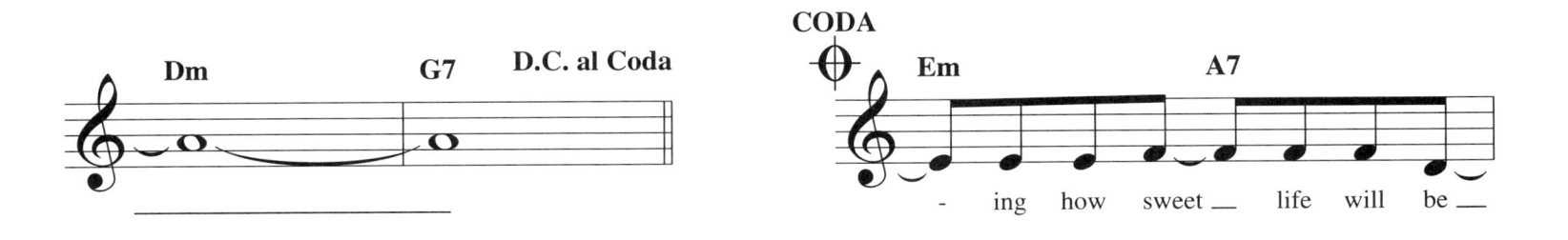

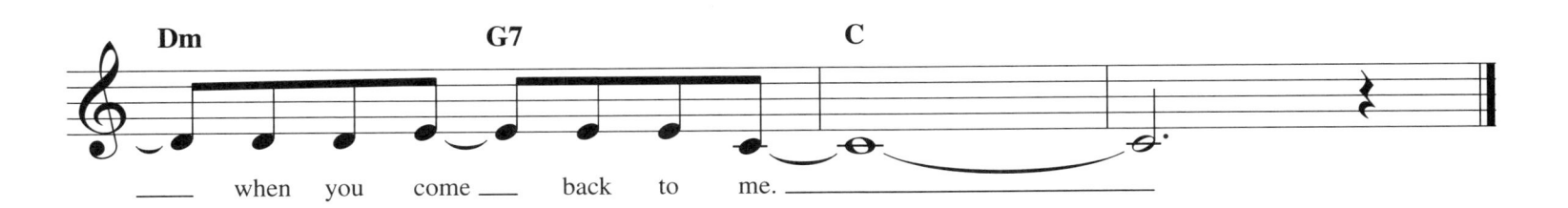

and the thought of you hold-ing me near
and the sad-ness that miss-ing you brings
med-i-tat-
makes my lone-li-ness soon dis-ap-pear.
soon is gone and this heart of mine sings.

Yes, I love you so
and that for me is all I need to know.

D.C. al Coda

CODA
-ing how sweet life will be
when you come back to me.

MIAMI BEACH RUMBA

Words by ALBERT GAMSE
Music by IRVING FIELDS

Up tempo Rhumba

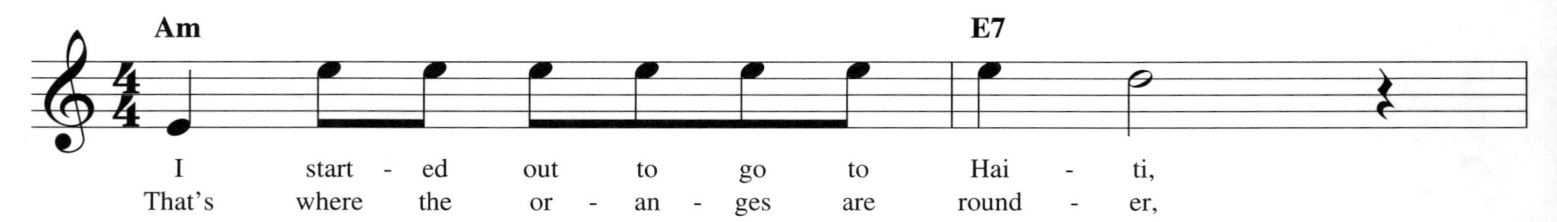

I start-ed out to go to Hai - ti,
That's where the or - an - ges are round - er,

soon I was at Mi - am - i Beach. There, not so ver - y far from
that's where the win - ter days are warm. That's where I caught a hun - dred

Hai - ti, quaint are the danc - es they teach!
pound - er we danced in true Lat - in form.

Here was all the charm of Hai - ti, the trop - ic sky was just as

fair. The temp - 'ra - ture was o - ver eight - y, which

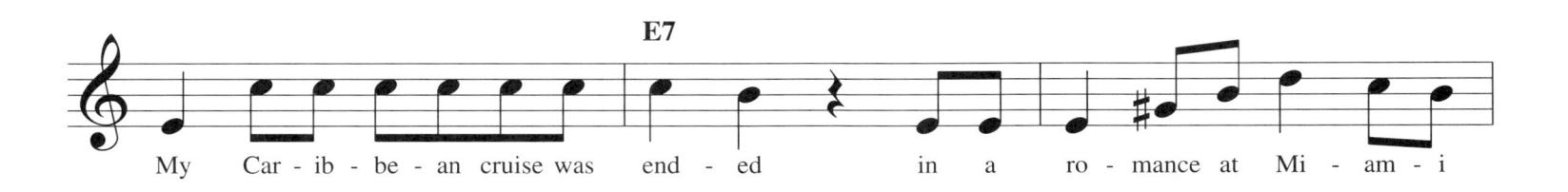

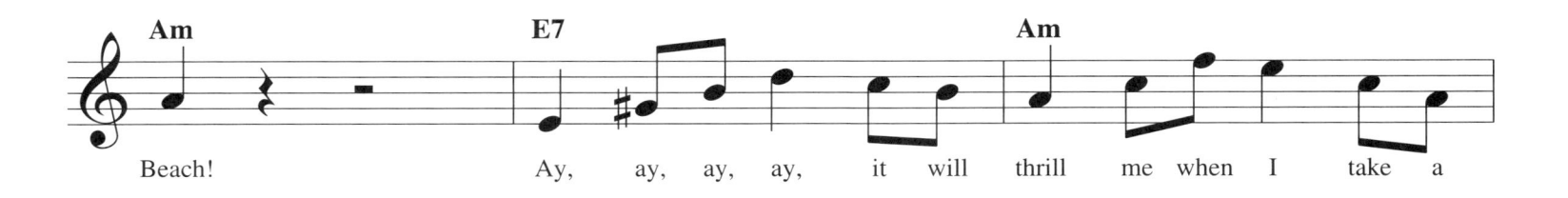

they call cool down there! I didn't go where I intended, far greater joy was in my reach.

My Caribbean cruise was ended in a romance at Miami Beach! Ay, ay, ay, ay, it will thrill me when I take a flight through the sky to Miami by the sea. Ay, ay, ay, ay, it will thrill me to fly to the place where my love waits for me.

MORE
(Ti Guarderò Nel Cuore)
from the film MONDO CANE

Copyright © 1962 by C.A.M. S.r.l. - Rome (Italy), Via Cola di Rienzo, 152
International Copyright Secured   All Rights Reserved

Music by NINO OLIVIERO and RIZ ORTOLANI
Italian Lyrics by MARCELLO CIORCIOLINI
English Lyrics by NORMAN NEWELL

Smoothly

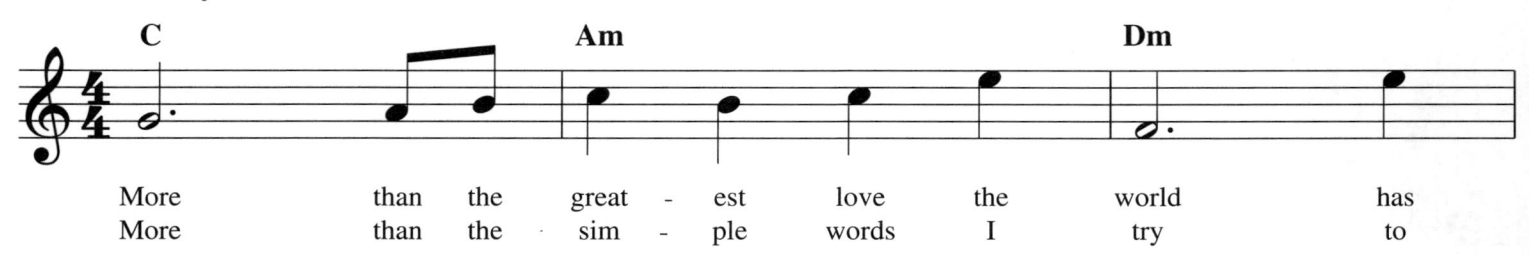

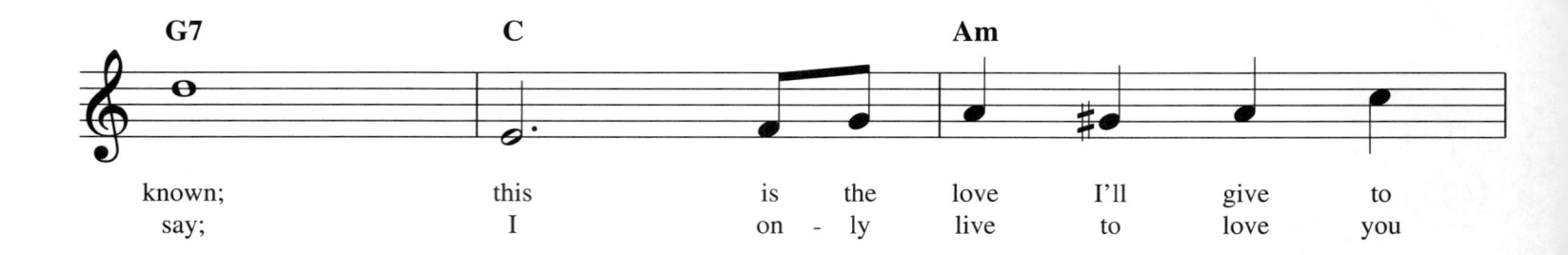

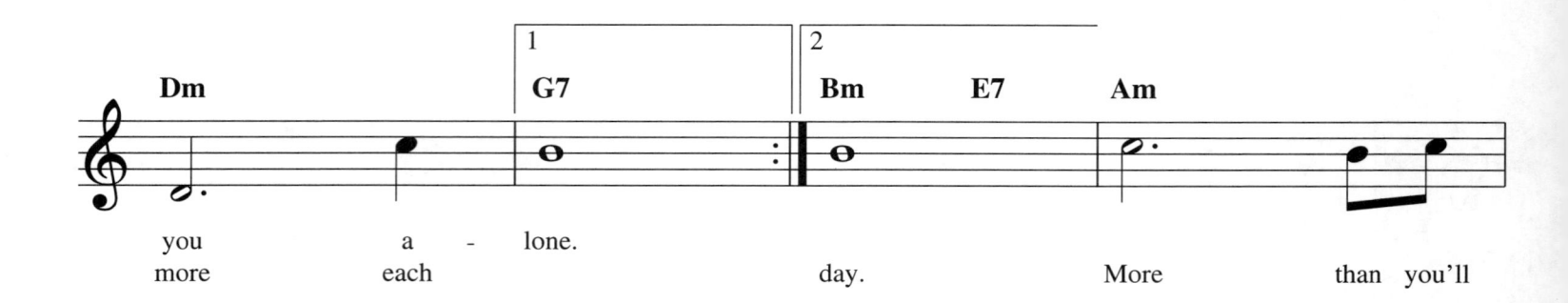

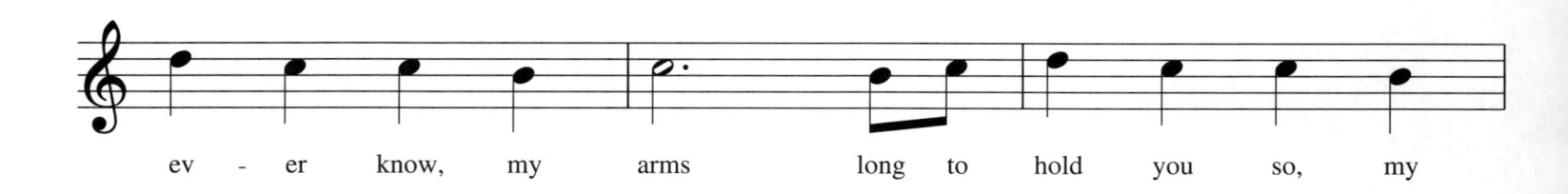

More than the great-est love the world has known;
More than the sim-ple words I try to say;

this is the love I'll give to you a-lone.
I on-ly live to love you more each day.

More than you'll ev-er know, my arms long to hold you so, my life will be in your keep-ing wak-ing, sleep-ing, laugh - ing, weep - ing. Long - er than al - ways is a long, long time; but far be - yond for - ev - er you'll be mine. I know I nev - er lived be - fore and my heart is ver - y sure no one else could love you more.

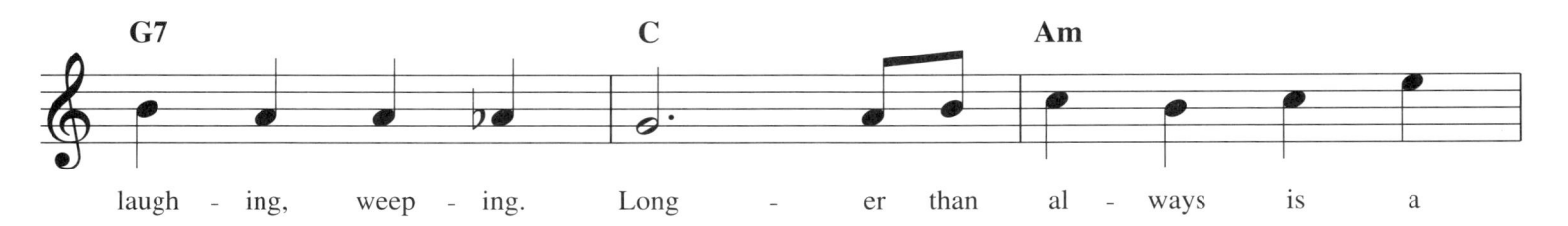

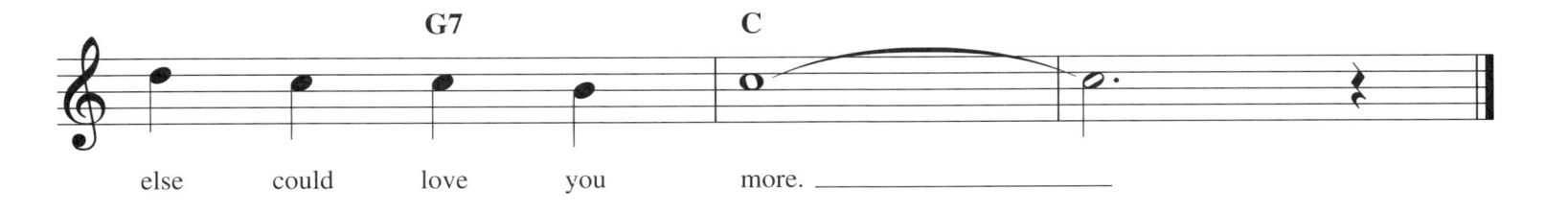

MY SHAWL

Copyright © 1936 by Edward B. Marks Music Company
Copyright Renewed
International Copyright Secured   All Rights Reserved
Used by Permission

English Lyric by STANLEY ADAMS
Spanish Lyric by PEDRO BERRIOS
Music by XAVIER CUGAT

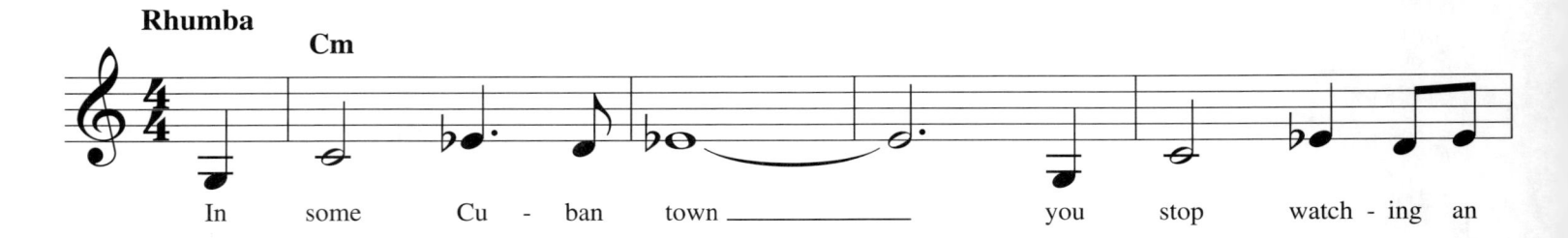

Rhumba

In some Cuban town _____ you stop watching an old maker of shawls. _____ A quaint little man _____ whose gay colored bazaar stands near the walls. _____ He smiles thru his beard _____ and spins heavenly dreams for ev'ry maid. _____ A shawl in his hand _____ his call reaches their

hearts as they pa - rade. _____ My

shawl _____ pret - ty la - dy _____

_____ try it on you. _____ Buy my shawl _____

_____ spun in mag - ic _____ wish - es come true. _____

_____ It's glo - ry _____ weaves a sto -

ry of love dreams _____ old but new. _____

_____ My shawl _____ brings a ro - mance _____

_____ may - be for you. _____ My

NEGRA CONSENTIDA
(My Pet Brunette)

Copyright © 1919 by L. Wagner y Levien
This arrangement Copyright © 1945 by Edward B. Marks Music Company
Copyright Renewed
International Copyright Secured All Rights Reserved
Used by Permission

English Words by MARJORIE HARPER
Spanish Words and Music by
JOAQUIN PARDAVE
Arranged by ELMER SCHOEBET

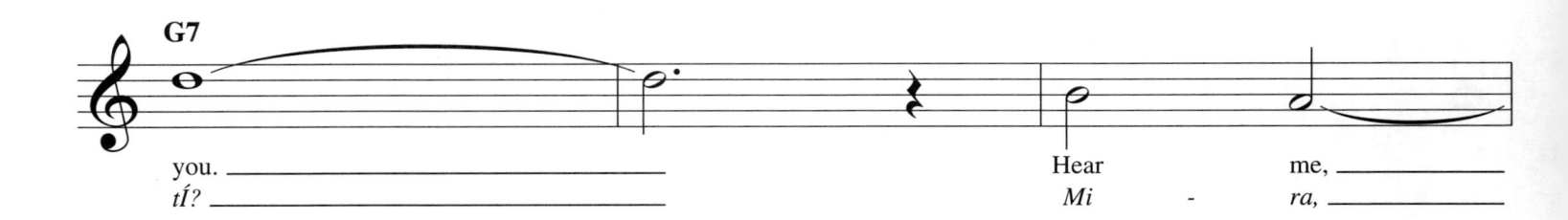

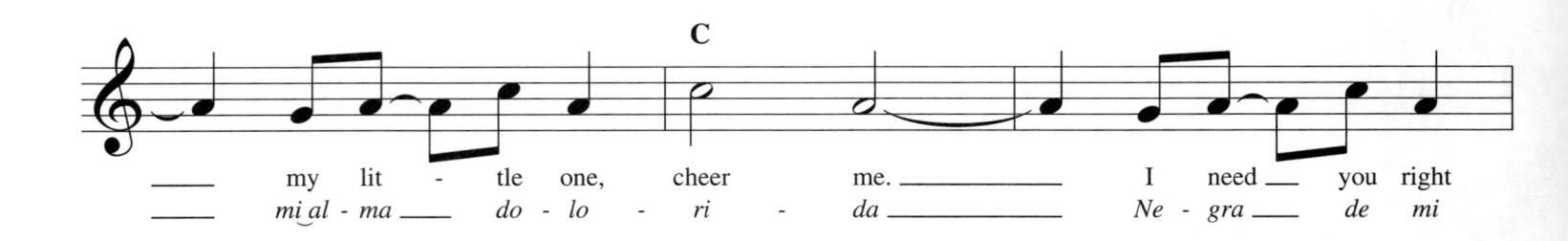

Medium Beguine

Love me, my pet brunette, love me and al-ways think of me as I think of you. Hear me, my lit-tle one, cheer me. I need you right near me. I want you I do.

Ne-gra, ne-gra de mi vi-da, Ne-gra Con-sen-ti-da, Quien te quie-re a tí? Mi-ra, mi al-ma do-lo-ri-da Ne-gra de mi vi-da, Y so-lo por tí.

Take me. My pet brunette, take me. How can you forsake me. Why won't you be true? See, dear, have pity on me, dear, and answer my plea, dear. I love only you. you.

Negra, negra de mi vida. Negra Consentida. Deja de llorar. Mira, que mi pecho amante. Esta dellrante, De felicidad. dad.

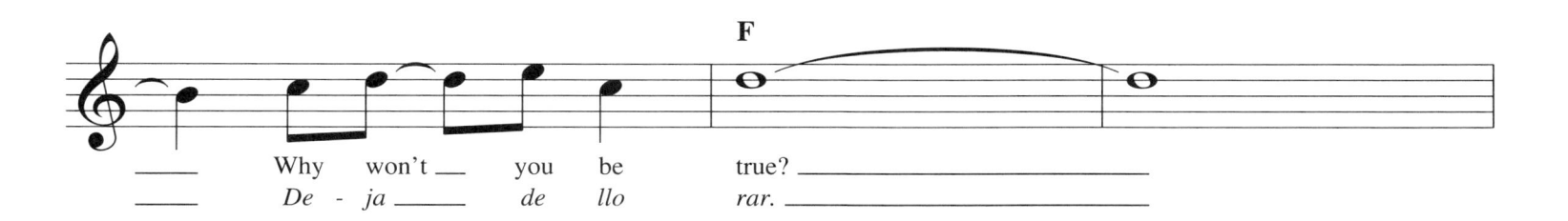

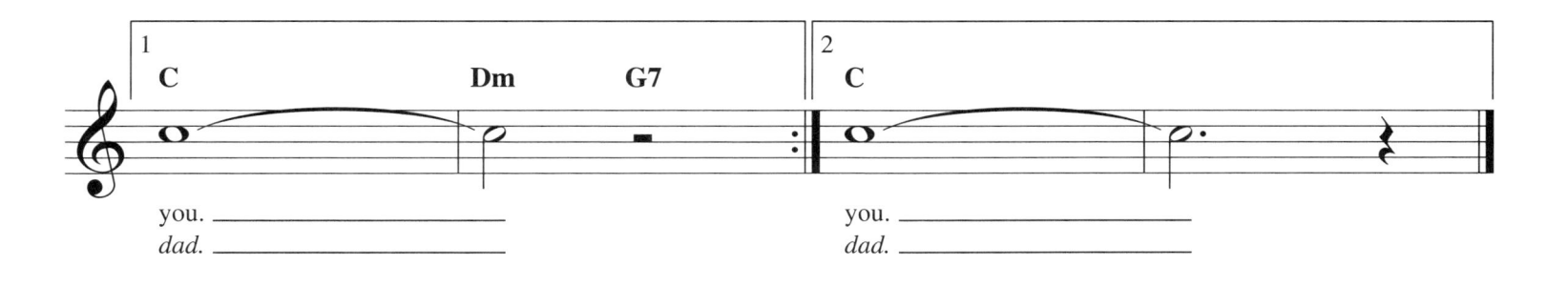

NEVER ON SUNDAY
from Jules Dassin's Motion Picture NEVER ON SUNDAY

© 1960 (Renewed) LLEE CORP. and EMI UNART CATALOG INC.
All Rights Reserved

Words by BILLY TOWNE
Music by MANOS HADJIDAKIS

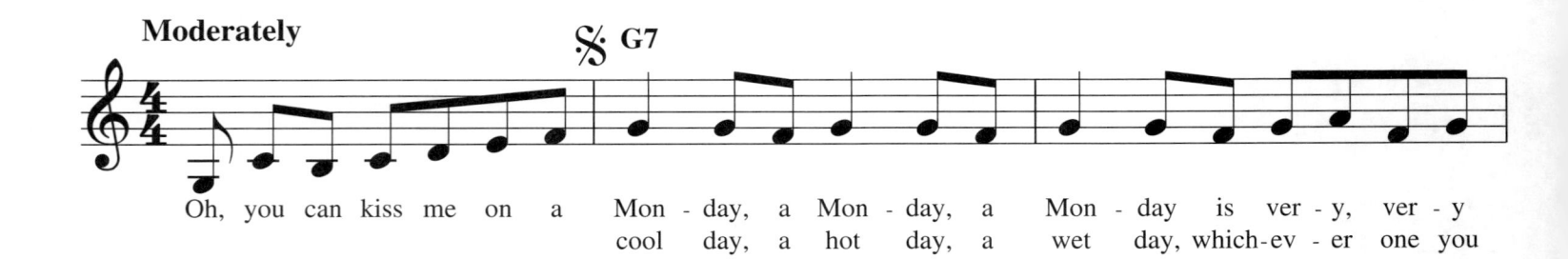

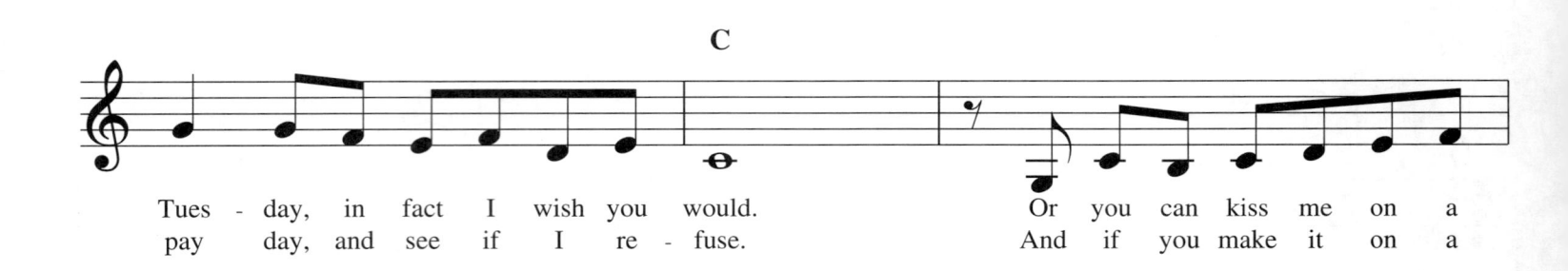

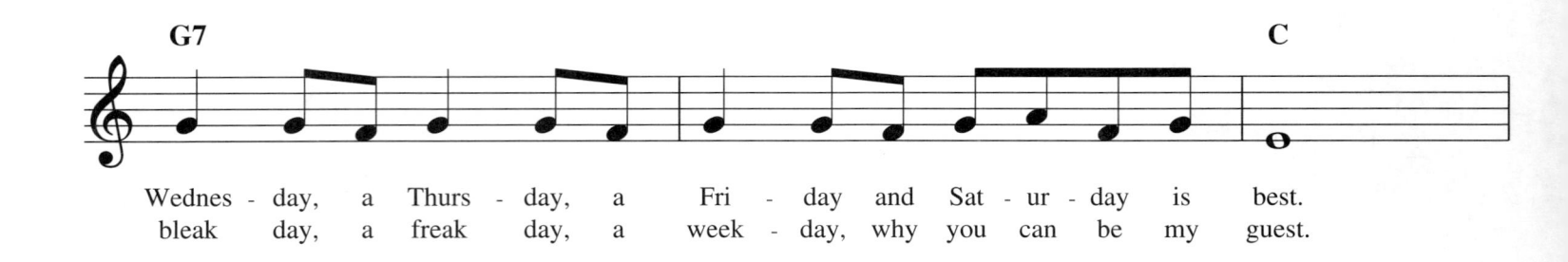

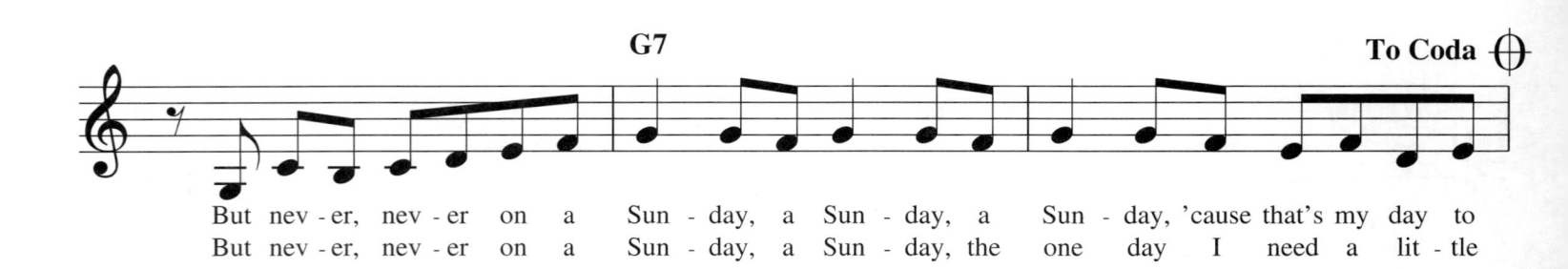

Moderately

Oh, you can kiss me on a Mon-day, a Mon-day, a Mon-day is ver-y, ver-y good.
cool day, a hot day, a wet day, which-ev-er one you choose.

Or you can kiss me on a Tues-day, a Tues-day, a Tues-day, in fact I wish you would.
Or try to kiss me on a gray day, a May day, a pay day, and see if I re-fuse.

Or you can kiss me on a Wednes-day, a Thurs-day, a Fri-day and Sat-ur-day is best.
And if you make it on a bleak day, a freak day, a week-day, why you can be my guest.

To Coda

But nev-er, nev-er on a Sun-day, a Sun-day, a Sun-day, 'cause that's my day to
But nev-er, nev-er on a Sun-day, a Sun-day, the one day I need a lit-tle

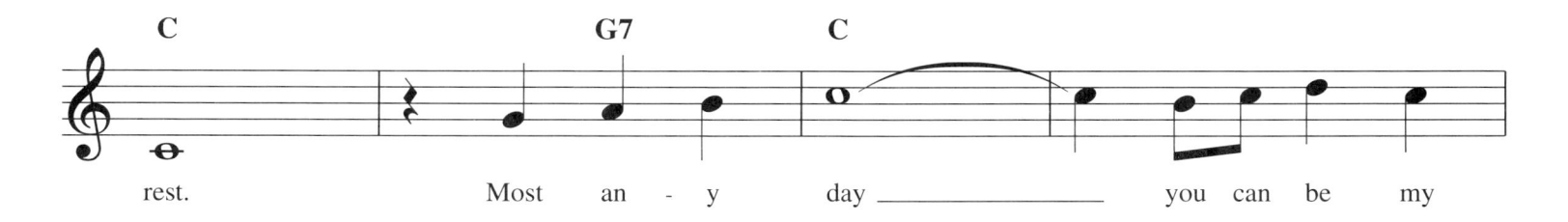

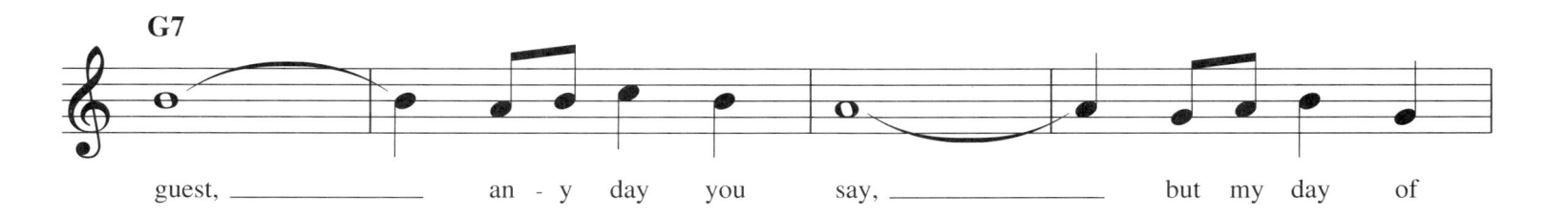

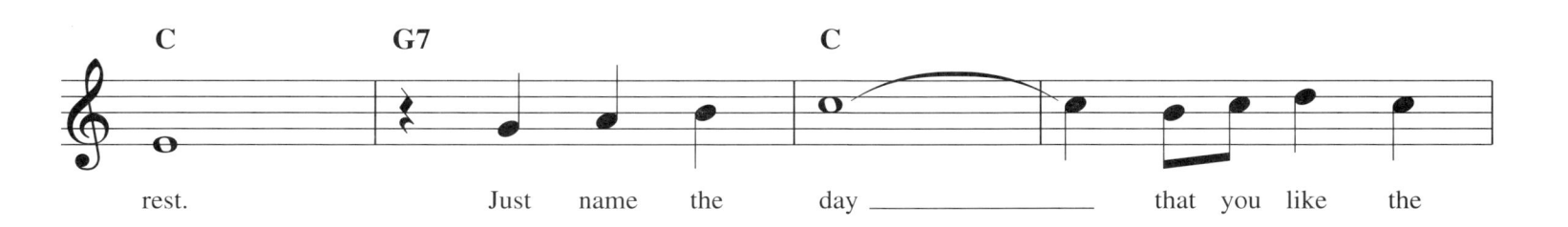

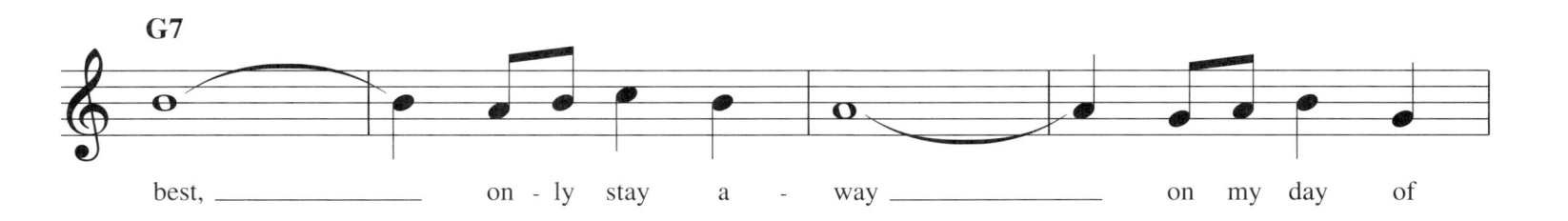

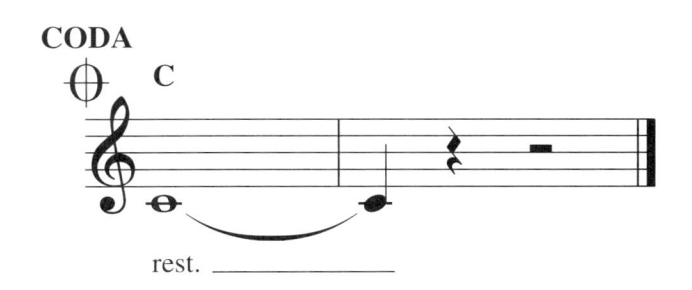

rest. Most an-y day _____ you can be my guest, _____ an-y day you say, _____ but my day of rest. Just name the day _____ that you like the best, _____ on-ly stay a-way _____ on my day of rest. Oh, you can kiss me on a rest. _____

D.S. al Coda

CODA

NOCHE AZUL
(Blue Night)

By ERNESTO LECUONA

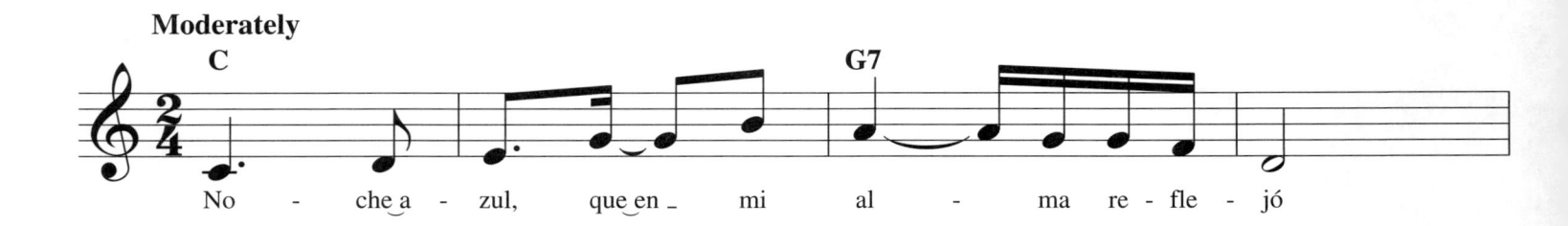

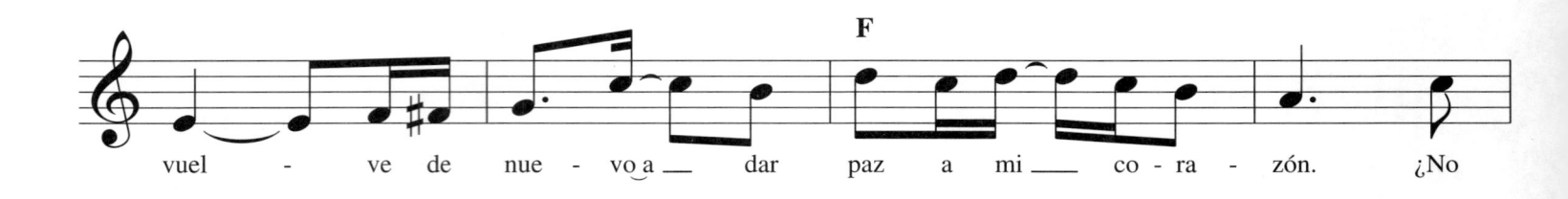

Copyright © 1929, 1941 by Edward B. Marks Music Company
Copyright Renewed
International Copyright Secured   All Rights Reserved
Used by Permission

Moderately

No - che a - zul, que en mi al - ma re - fle - jó

la pa - sión que so - ña - ba a - ca - ri - ciar,

vuel - ve de nue - vo a dar paz a mi co - ra - zón. ¿No

ves que mue - ro de do - lor?

Ven no - che a - zul, ven o - tra vez a que me

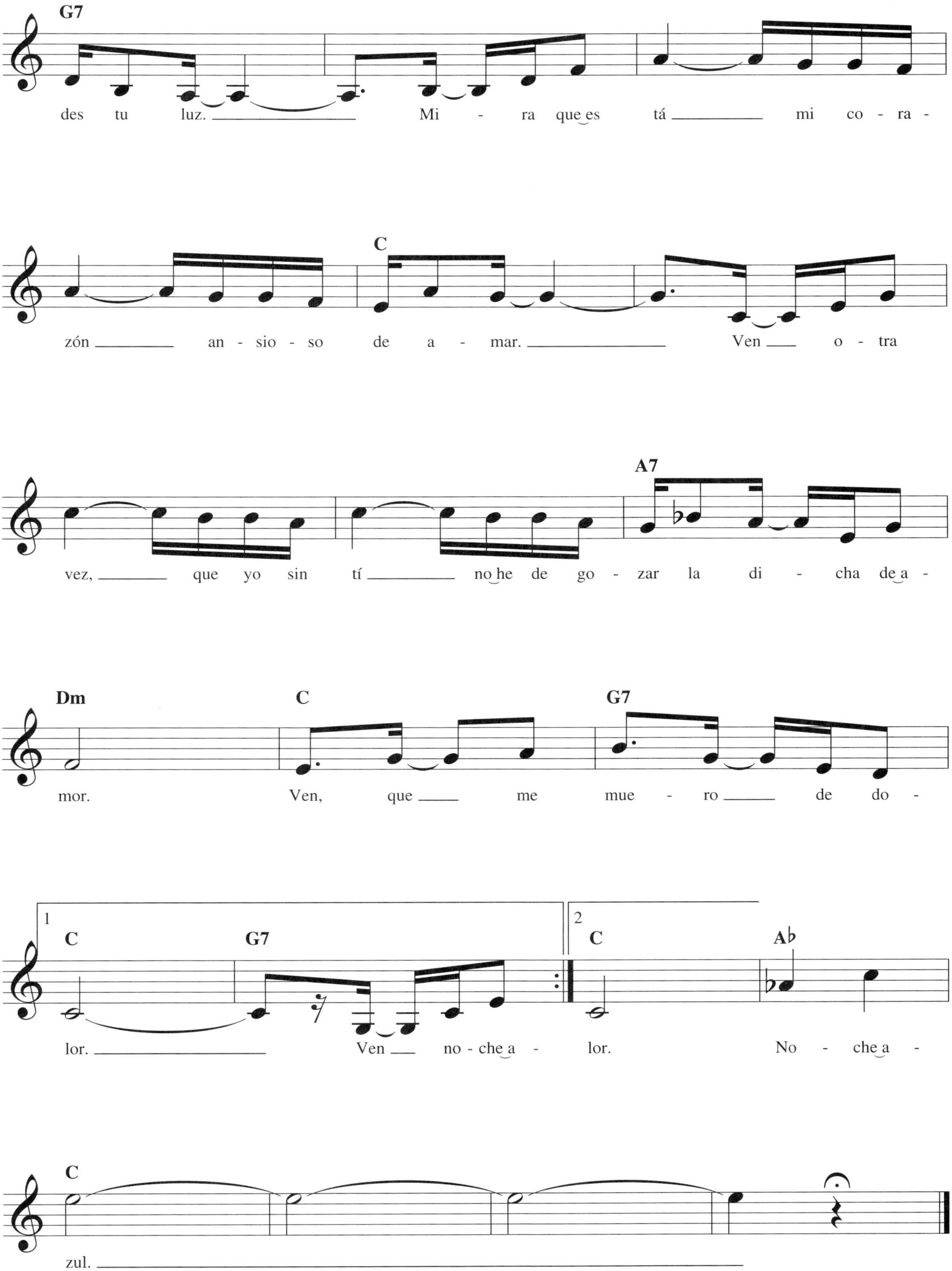
G7
des tu luz. Mi - ra que es tá mi co - ra -
zón an - sio - so de a - mar. Ven o - tra
C
vez, que yo sin tí no he de go - zar la di - cha de a -
A7
Dm C G7
mor. Ven, que me mue - ro de do -
1 C G7
lor. Ven no - che a -
2 C A♭
lor. No - che a -
C
zul.

NOCHE DE RONDA
(Be Mine Tonight)

Original Words and Music by
MARIA TERESA LARA
English Words by SUNNY SKYLAR

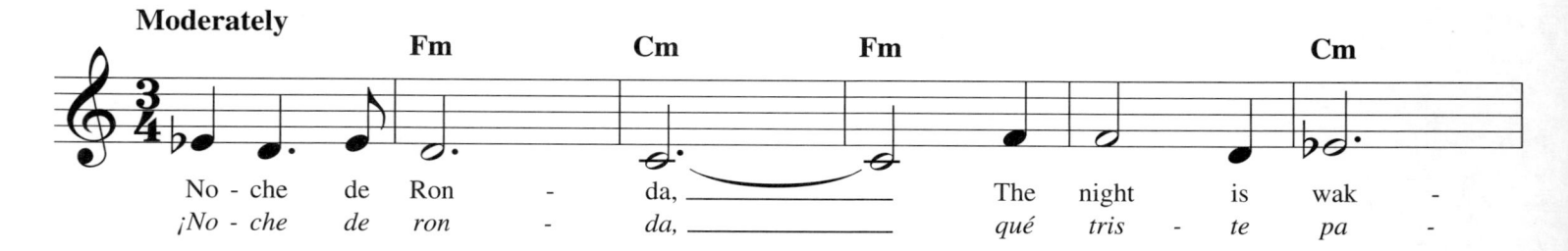

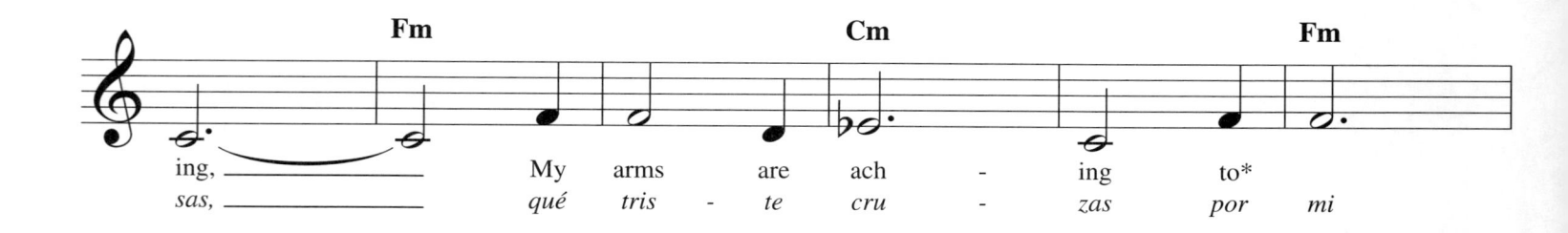

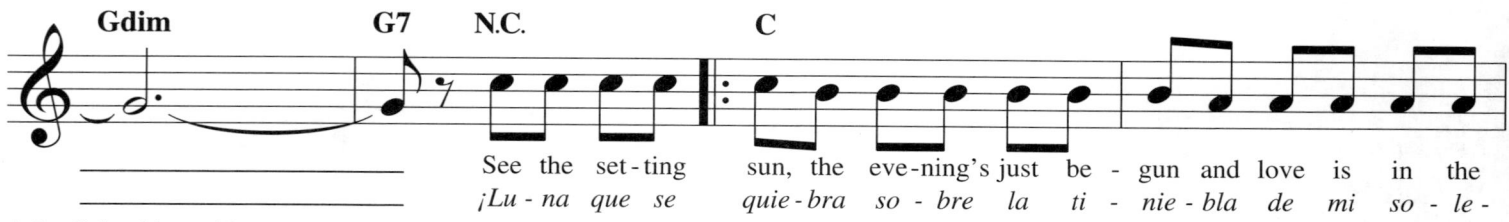

Copyright © 1935 by Promotora Hispano Americana de Musica, S.A.
Copyright © 1951 by Peer International Corporation
Copyright Renewed
All Rights Administered by Peer International Corporation
International Copyright Secured   All Rights Reserved

Moderately

No - che de Ron - da, _____ The night is wak -
¡No - che de ron - da, _____ qué tris - te pa -

ing, _____ My arms are ach - ing to*
sas, _____ qué tris - te cru - zas por mi

bal - cón! _____ ¡No - che de ron -

da, _____ có - mo me hie - res, _____

**hold you near. _____
có - mo las - ti - mas mi co - ra - zón. _____

_____ See the set - ting sun, the eve - ning's just be - gun and love is in the
_____ ¡Lu - na que se quie - bra so - bre la ti - nie - bla de mi so - le -

*English: skip to **

air: be mine to- night.
dad! ¿A - don - de vas?

At a time like this, would you re-fuse the kiss I'm beg-ging you to share;
¿Di - me si_es - ta no - che tú le vas de ron - da co - mo_e - lla se fué,

be mine to- night. Prom-ise this, my
con quien es - tá? Di - le que la

own, be-fore the night has flown, you'll tell me that you care and
quie - ro, di - le que me mue - ro de tan - to_es - pe - rar, que

hold me tight. Whis-per love words,
vuel - va ya, que las ron - das

oh, so ten-der, give your kiss - es
no son bue - nas, que_ha - cen da - ño,

in sur-ren-der, let your heart be mine to-
que dan pe - nas, que se_a - ca - ba por llo -

1
night. See the set - ting
rar. ¡Lu - na que se

2
night.
rar.

ONCE I LOVED
(Amor Em Paz)
(Love in Peace)

Copyright © 1963 Antonio Carlos Jobim and Vinicius de Moraes
English lyrics Copyright © 1965 Ipanema Music Corp.
Copyright Renewed, Assigned to Corcovado Music Corp., Ipanema Music Corp. and VM Enterprises, Inc.
International Copyright Secured   All Rights Reserved

Music by ANTONIO CARLOS JOBIM
Portuguese Lyrics by VINICIUS DE MORAES
English Lyrics by RAY GILBERT

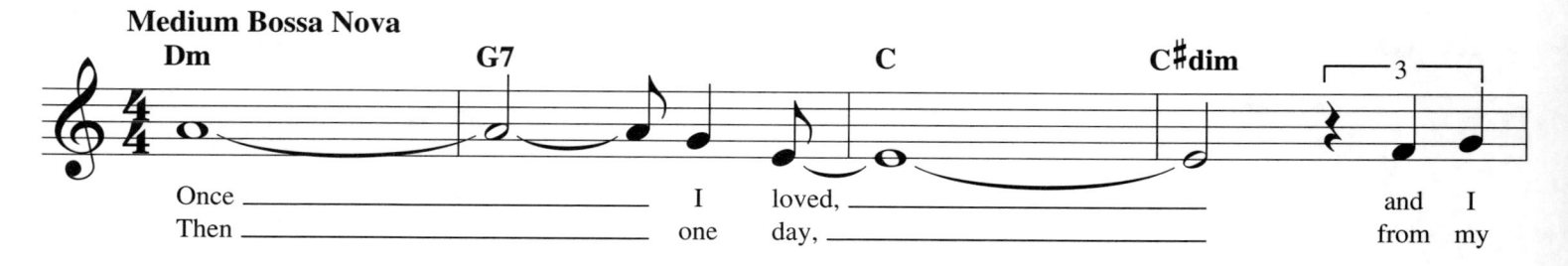

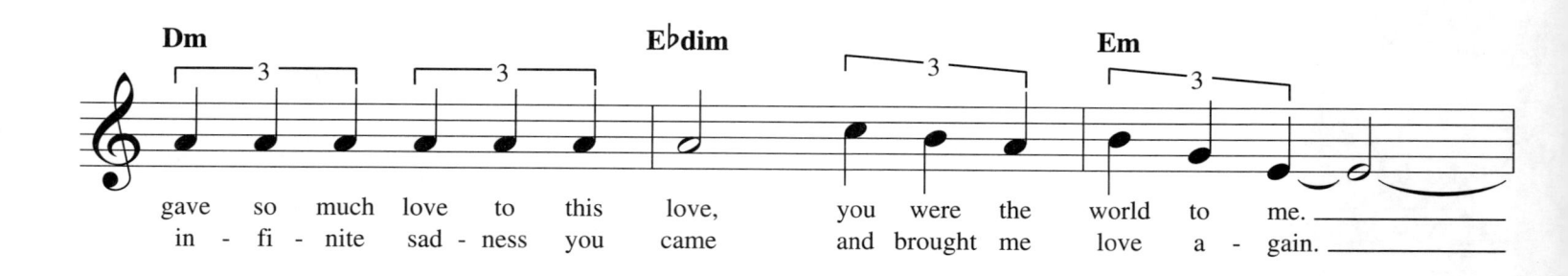

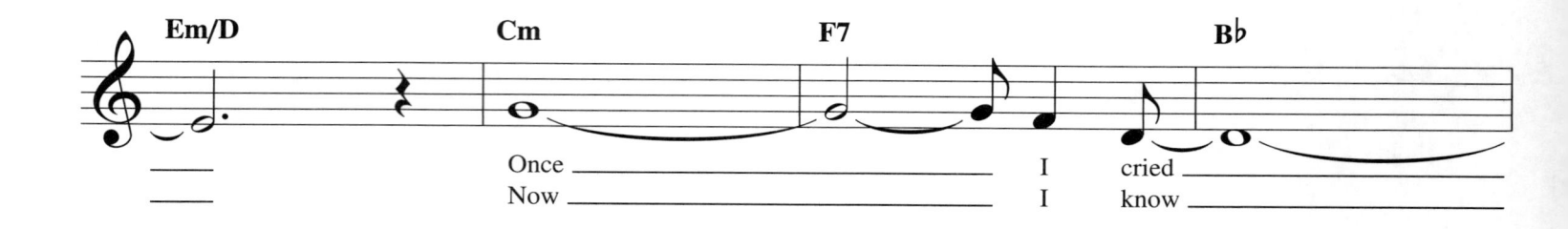

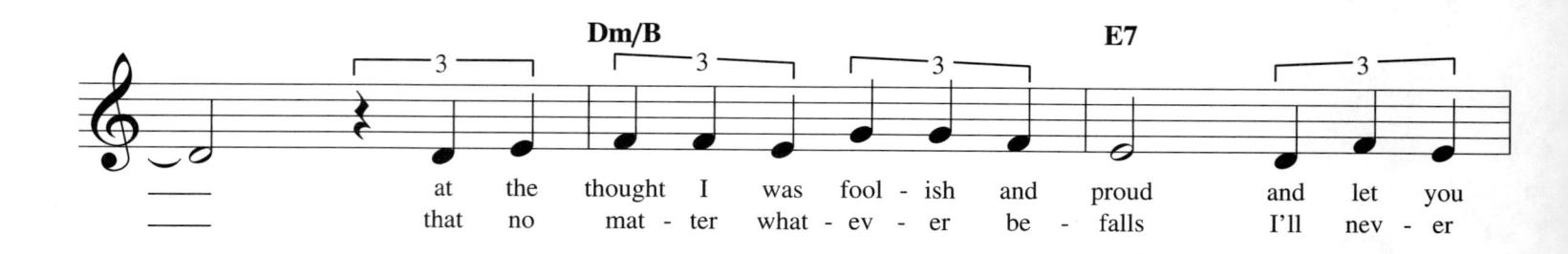

Medium Bossa Nova

Once I loved, and I gave so much love to this love, you were the world to me. Once I cried at the thought I was foolish and proud and let you say good-bye.

Then one day, from my infinite sadness you came and brought me love again. Now I know that no matter whatever befalls I'll never let you go,

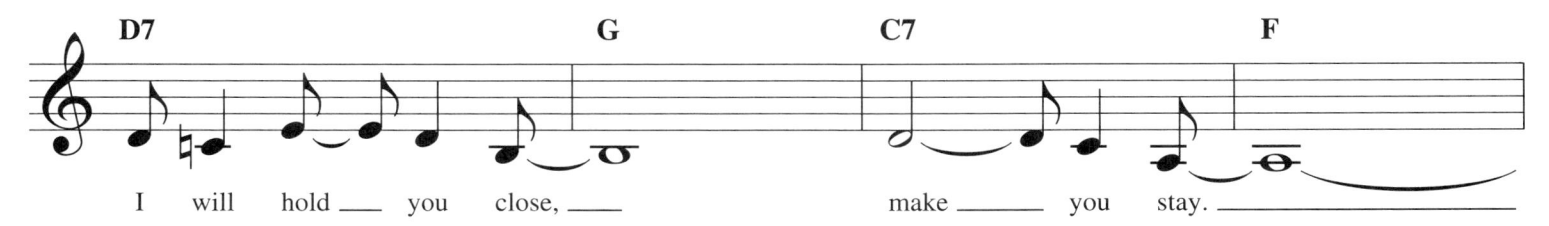

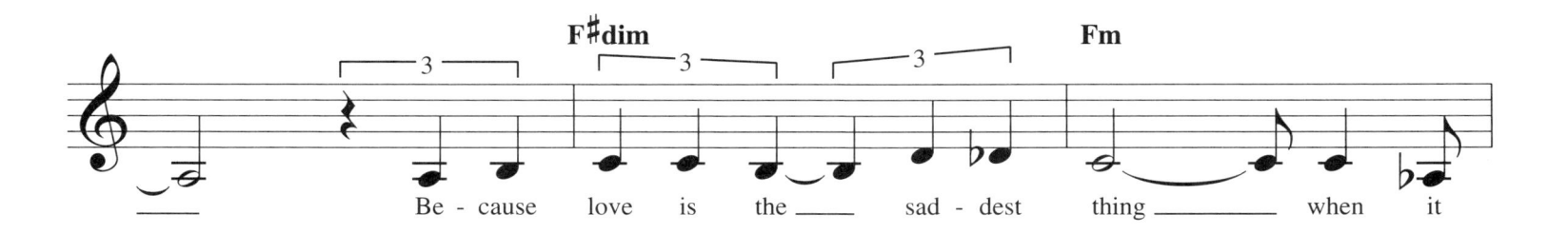

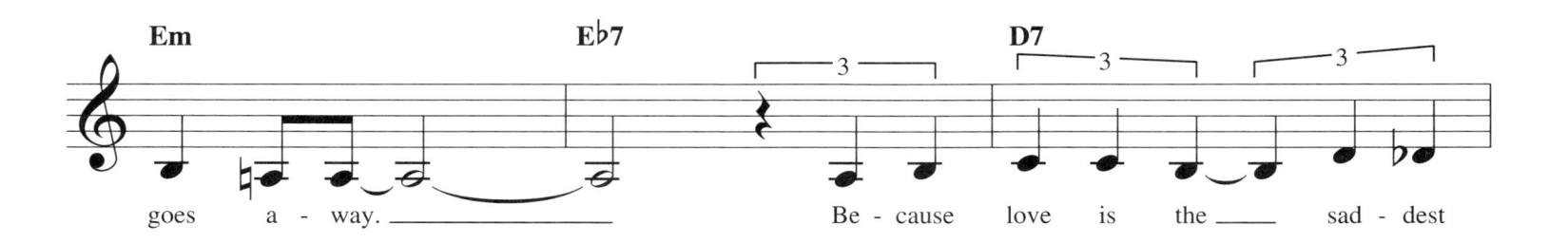

Portuguese Lyrics

Eu amei E amei muito mais Do que devia amar
E chorei ao sentir que eu iria sofrer e me dese perar

Fol, então que da minha infinita trizteza aconteceu você
Encontrei em você a razão de viver e de amar em paz

E não sofrer mais Nunca mais
Porque o amor é a coisa mais triste quando se destaz
O amor é a coisa mais triste quando se desfaz

ONE NOTE SAMBA
(Samba De Una Nota So)

Original Lyrics by NEWTON MENDONÇA
English Lyrics by ANTONIO CARLOS JOBIM
Music by ANTONIO CARLOS JOBIM

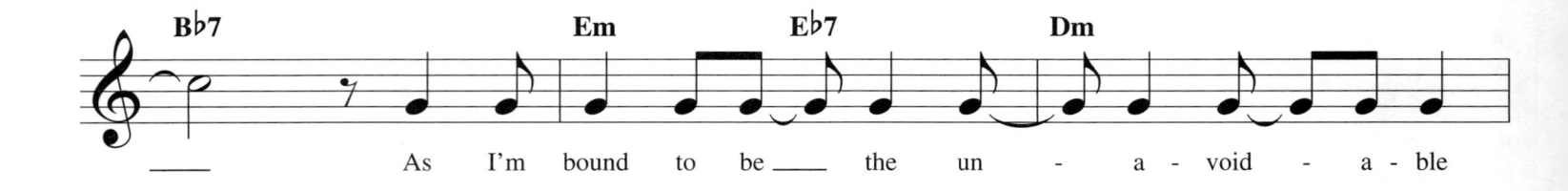

Copyright © 1961, 1962 ANTONIO CARLOS JOBIM and MRS. MENDONÇA
Copyright Renewed
All Rights for English Speaking Countries Controlled and Administered by SONGS OF UNIVERSAL, INC.
All Rights Reserved   Used by Permission

Samba

This is just a lit - tle sam - ba built up - on a sin - gle note. Oth - er notes are bound to fol - low but the root is still that note. Now this new one is the con - se - quence of the one we've just been through. As I'm bound to be the un - a - void - a - ble con - se - quence of you. There's so man - y peo - ple who can talk and talk and talk and just say noth - ing, or near - ly noth-ing. _____ I have used up all the scale I

know and at the end I've come to noth-ing, or near-ly

noth-ing. So I come back to ____ my first ____ note, as I

must come back ___ to you. ____ I will pour in-to ____ that one __

____ note all the love I feel ___ for you. ____ An-y-

one who wants ___ the whole ____ show Re, Mi,

Fa, Sol, La, ___ Ti, Do, ____ he will find him-self ___ with no __

____ show. Bet-ter play ____ the note ___ you know. ____

ONLY TRUST YOUR HEART

Words by SAMMY CAHN
Music by BENNY CARTER

Copyright © 1964 UNIVERSAL MUSIC CORP.
Copyright Renewed
All Rights Reserved   Used by Permission

Moderate Latin

Nev - er trust the stars_____ when you're a - bout to fall in love. Look for hid - den signs_____ be - fore you start to sigh._____

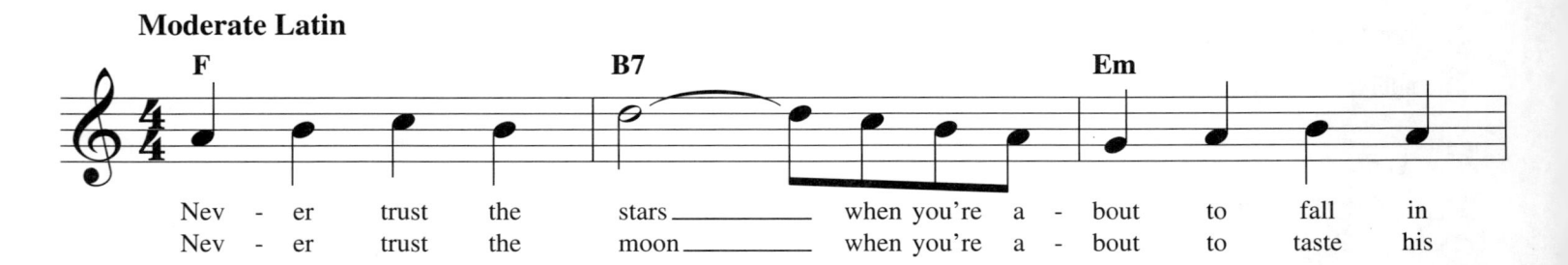

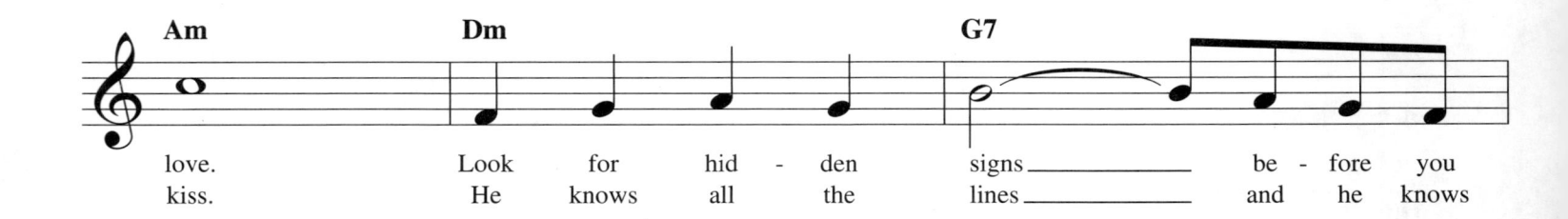

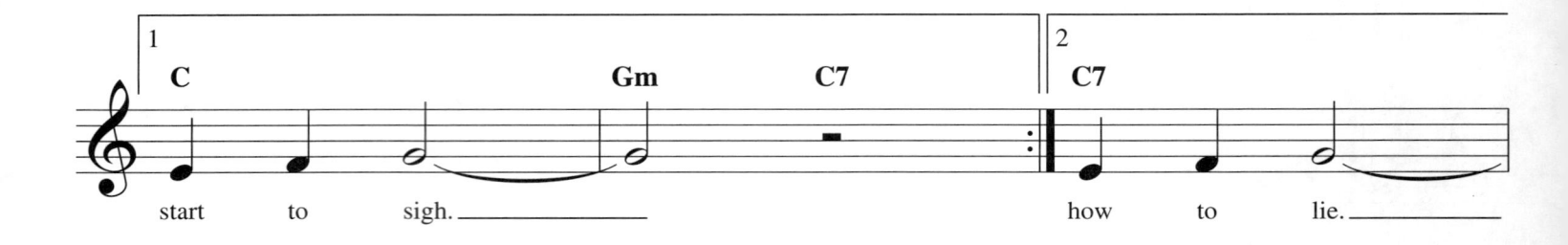

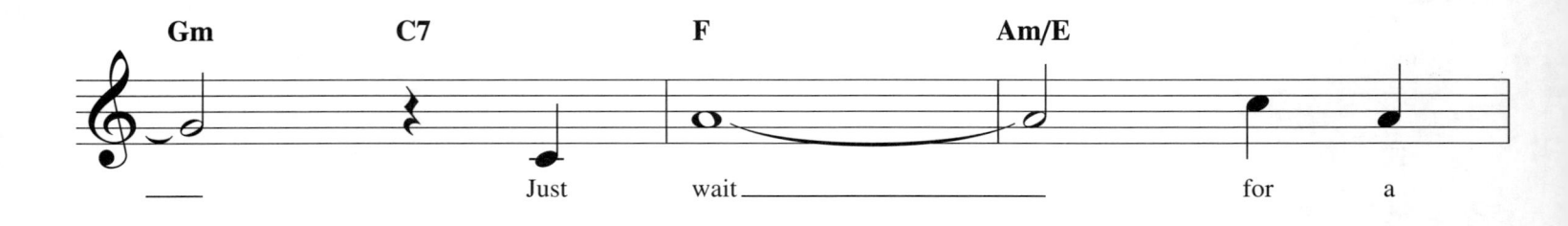

Nev - er trust the moon_____ when you're a - bout to taste his kiss. He knows all the lines_____ and he knows how to lie._____

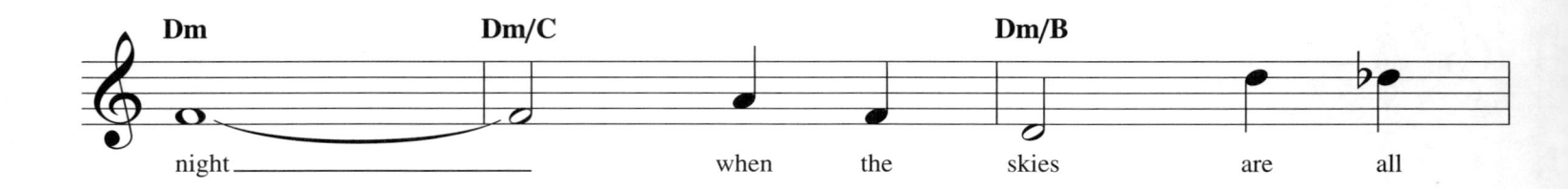

Just wait_____ for a night_____ when the skies are all

| E7 | Am | A♭m | Gm | C7 |

bare and then if you care.

| F | B7 | Em |

Nev-er trust your dreams____ when you're a-bout to fall in

| Am | Dm | G7 |

love. For your dreams may quick - ly fall a-

| B♭7 | A7 | Dm |

part.____ So, if you're smart,____

| Fm | B♭7 | C | Em | A7 |

____ real - ly smart,____

| A♭7 | G7 | C |

on - ly trust____ your heart.____

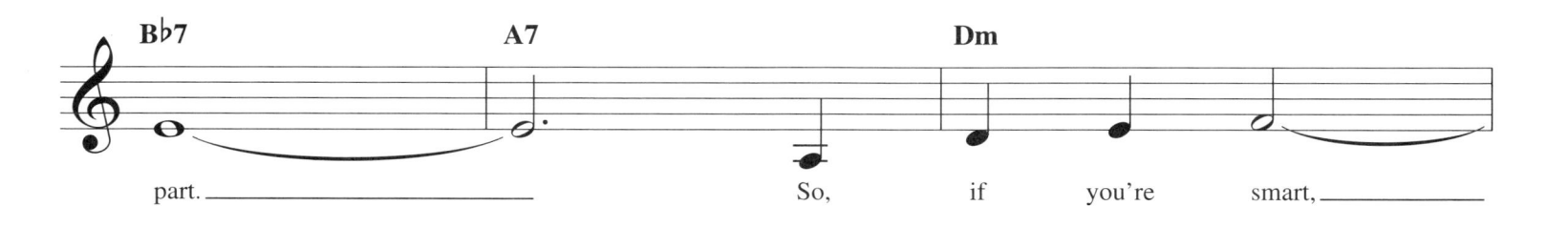

OUR LANGUAGE OF LOVE
from IRMA LA DOUCE

Music by MARGUERITE MONNOT
Original French Words by ALEXANDRE BREFFORT
English Words by JULIAN MORE,
DAVID HENEKER and MONTY NORMAN

No need to speak, no need to sing, when just a glance means ev'ry-thing. Not a word need be spo-ken in our lan-guage of love. I'll touch your cheek, you'll hold my hand and on-ly we will un-der-stand that the si-lence is bro-ken by our lan-guage of love. It's clear to you, it's clear to me this pre-cious mo-ment had to be, oth-er mo-ments out-class-ing guard-ian an-gels are pass-ing. No words will do, no lips can say the ten-der mean-ing we con-vey, "I love you" is un-spo-ken, in our lan-guage of love.

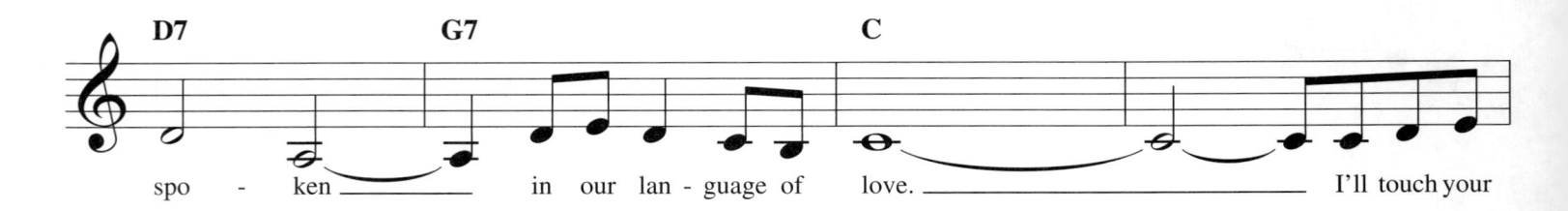

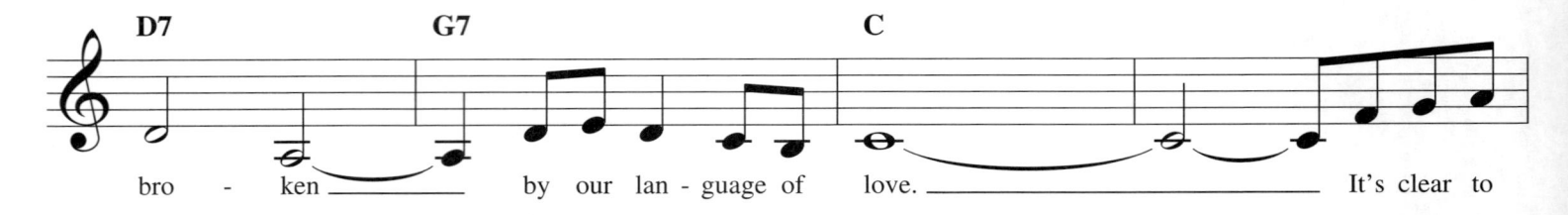

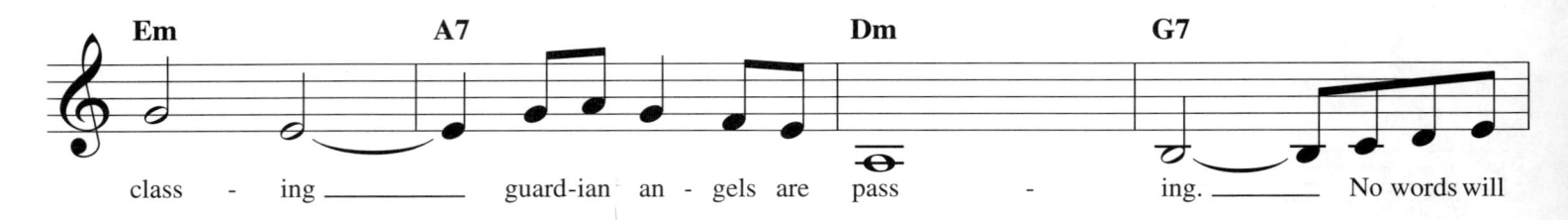

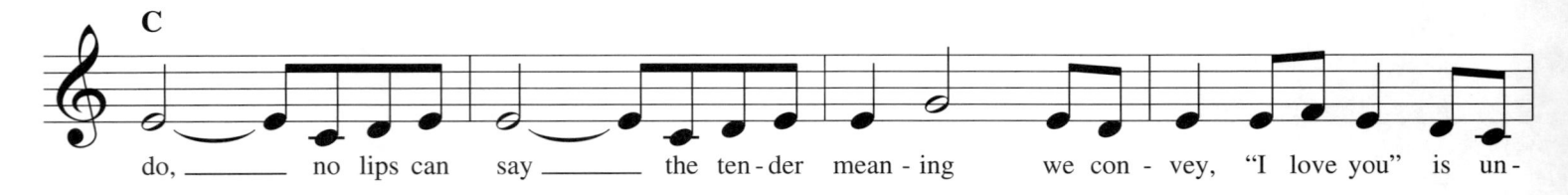

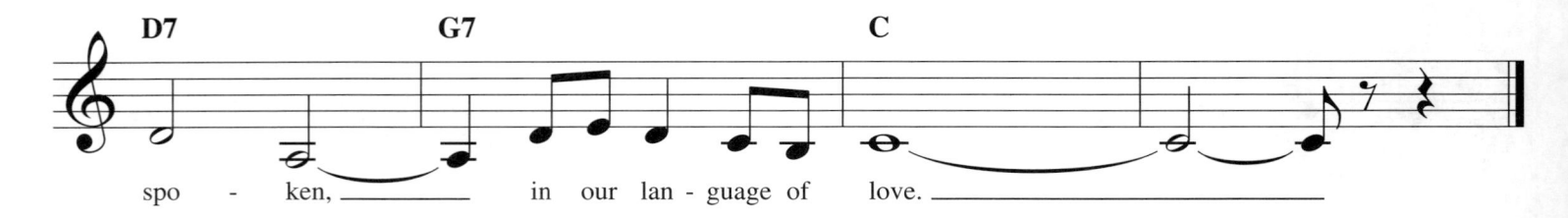

WHAT A DIFF'RENCE A DAY MADE

English Words by STANLEY ADAMS
Music and Spanish Words by MARIA GREVER

Copyright © 1934 by Edward B. Marks Music Company
Copyright Renewed and Assigned to Stanley Adams Music, Inc. and Grever Music Publishing S.A. De C.V.
All Rights for Stanley Adams Music, Inc. Administered by The Songwriters Guild Of America
All Rights for Grever Music Publishing S.A. De C.V. in the U.S. Administered by Universal Music - Z Tunes LLC
All Rights for the World Excluding U.S. Administered by Edward B. Marks Music Company
International Copyright Secured   All Rights Reserved
Used by Permission

Relaxed

What a dif-f'rence a day made, twen-ty four lit-tle ho-urs.
day makes, there's a rain-bow be-fore me.

Brought the sun and the flow-ers, where there used to be
Skies a-bove can't be storm-y since that mo-ment of

rain. My yes-ter-day was blue, dear, to-day I'm part of

you, dear. My lone-ly nights are through, dear,

since you said you were mine. What a dif-f'rence a

CODA

bliss, that thrill-ing kiss. It's heav-en when you

find ro-mance on your men-u. What a dif-f'rence a

day made, and the dif-f'rence is you.

PERFIDIA

Copyright © 1939 by Peer International Corporation
Copyright Renewed
International Copyright Secured   All Rights Reserved

Words and Music by
ALBERTO DOMINGUEZ

Moderately

To you, _____ my heart cries out, "Per-
Mu - jer, _____ si pue - des tú con

fi - di - a," _____ For I found you, the
Dios ha - blar, _____ pre - gún - ta - le si

love of my life, in some - bod - y else - 's
yo al - gu - na vez te he de - ja - do de a - do -

arms; _____ Your eyes _____
rar. _____ Y el mar, _____

_____ are ech - o - ing "Per - fi - di - a," _____
_____ es - pe - jo de mi co - ra - zón, _____

_____ For - get - ful of our prom - ise of love, you're
_____ las ve - ces que me ha vis - to llo - rar la

sharing another's charms. With a
per - fi - dia de tu a - mor. *Te he bus -*

sad lament, my dreams have faded like a broken melo-
ca - do don - de quie - ra - que yo voy y no te pue - do ha -

dy; While the gods of love look down and laugh at
llar. ¿Pa - ra qué quie - ro o - tros be - sos si tus

what romantic fools we mortals be; And
la - bios no me quie - ren ya be - sar? Y

now I know my love was not for you,
tú. ¡Quién sa - be por don - de an - da - rás,

And so I'll take it back with a sigh, per-
¿quién sa - be qué a - ven - tu - ra ten - drás, qué

fid - i - ous one, good - bye.
le - jos es - tás de mí.

POINCIANA
(Song of the Tree)

Words by BUDDY BERNIER
Music by NAT SIMON

Copyright © 1936 by Chappell & Co.
Copyright Renewed
International Copyright Secured All Rights Reserved

Moderately

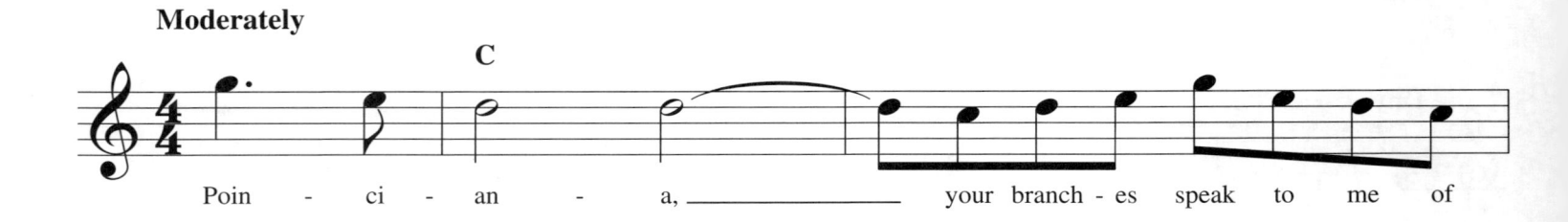

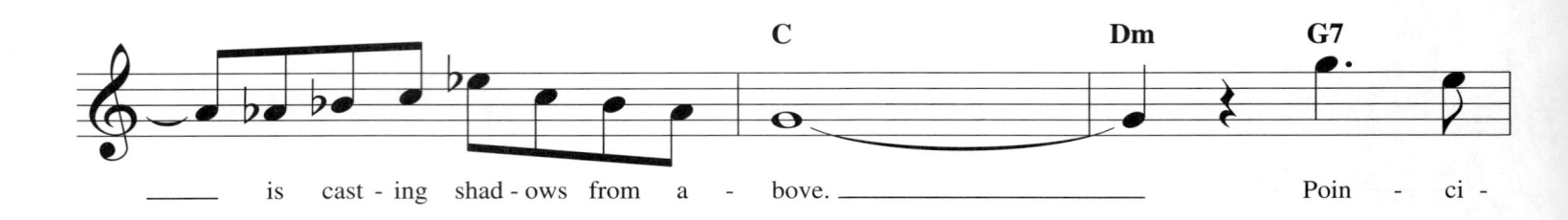

Poin - ci - an - a, _____ your branch - es speak to me of love. _____ Pale moon _____ is cast - ing shad - ows from a - bove. _____ Poin - ci - an - a, _____ some - how I feel the jun - gle heat. _____ With - in me _____ there grows a rhyth - mic sav - age beat. Love is ev-'ry-where, its mag-ic per-fume fills the air. To and fro you sway, my heart's in time, I've learned to care. Poin-ci-an-a, though skies may turn from blue to gray, my love will live for-ev-er and a day.

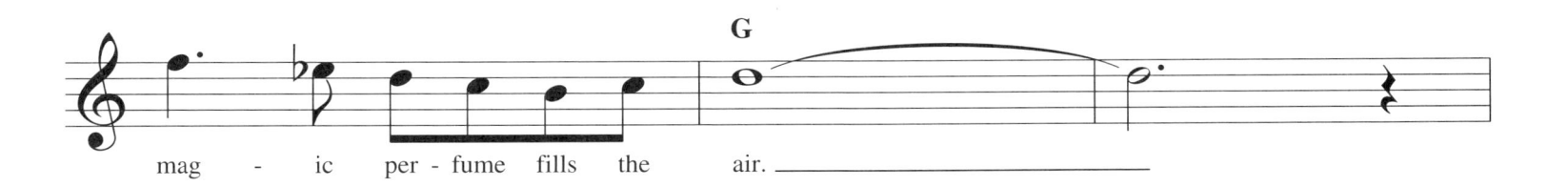

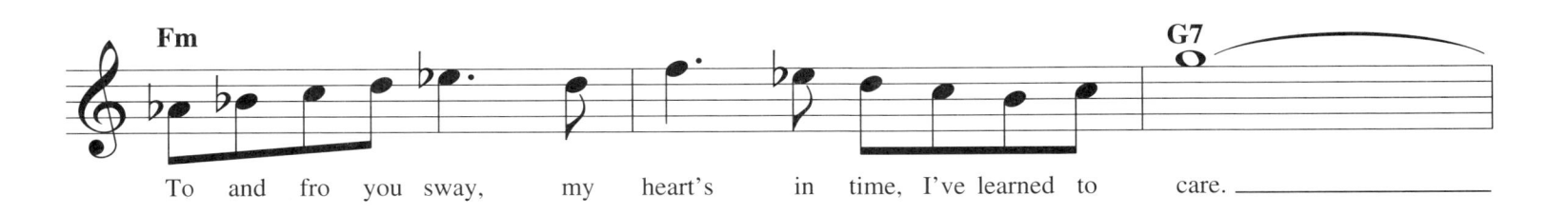

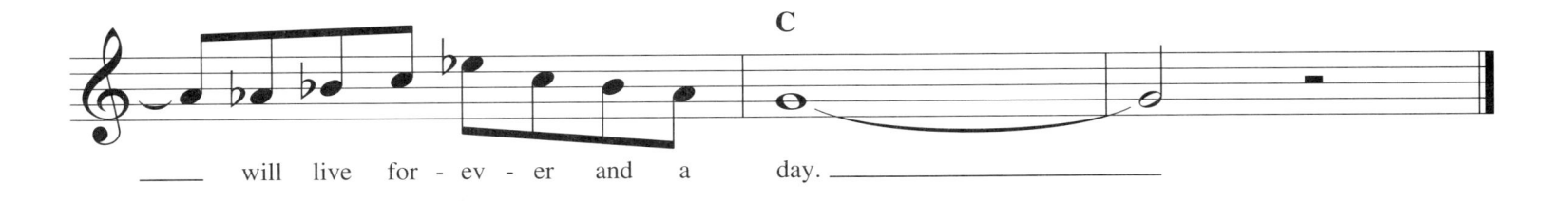

QUIET NIGHTS OF QUIET STARS
(Corcovado)

English Words by GENE LEES
Original Words and Music by ANTONIO CARLOS JOBIM

Moderately slow

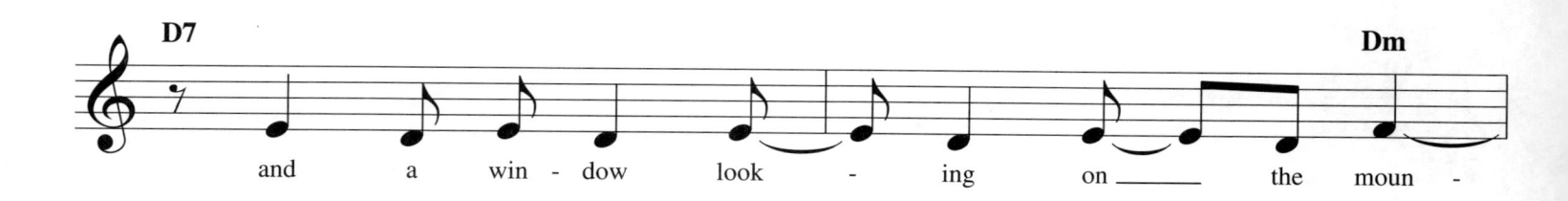

[D7] Qui-et nights of qui-et stars, [Abdim] qui-et chords from my
gui-tar [Gm] float-ing on the si-lence that [Gb] sur-rounds
[F] us. [Fm] Qui-et thoughts and qui-
-et dreams, [Em] qui-et walks by [A7] qui-et streams,
[D7] and a win-dow look-ing on [Dm] the moun-
[Abdim] -tains and the sea. How love-ly!

D7

This is where I want to be.

A♭dim

Here, with you so close to me un- til

Gm — 3 — **G♭**

the fi- nal flick- er of life's em-

F **Fm**

-ber. I, who was lost and

Em **Am**

lone- ly, be- liev- ing life was on- ly

Dm **G7**

a bit- ter trag- ic joke, have found with you

Em **A7** **Dm**

the mean- ing of ex-

G7 **C**

-ist- ence. Oh, my love.

QUIZÁS, QUIZÁS, QUIZÁS
(Perhaps, Perhaps, Perhaps)

Copyright © 1947 by Southern Music Pub. Co. Inc.
Copyright Renewed
International Copyright Secured All Rights Reserved

Music and Spanish Words by OSVALDO FARRES
English Words by JOE DAVIS

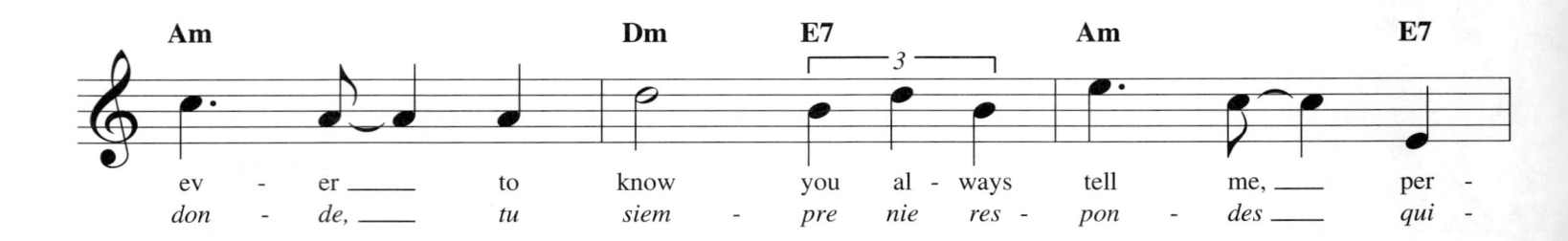

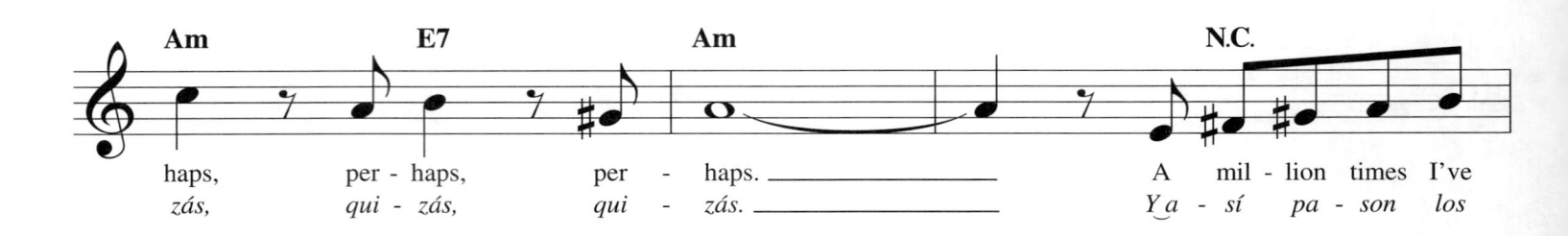

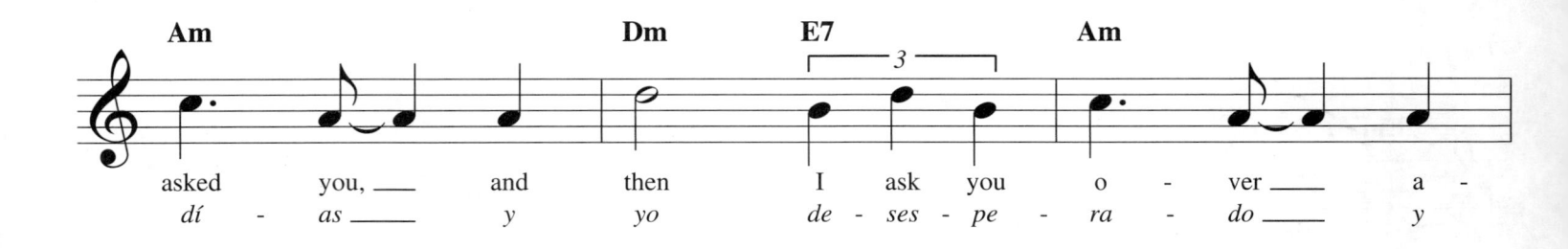

Moderately

You won't admit you love me, and so how am I ever to know you always tell me, perhaps, perhaps, perhaps. A million times I've asked you, and then I ask you over again, you only answer, perhaps, perhaps, per-

Siempre que te pregunto que cuando, como y donde, tu siempre nie respondes quizás, quizás, quizás. Ya así pason los días y yo desesperado y tú, tú contestando quizás, quizás, qui-

haps. _____ If you can't make your mind up, ___ we'll
zás. _____ Es - tás per - dien - do el tiem - po ___ pen -

nev - er ___ get start - ed, _____ and I don't want to
san - do, ___ pen - san - do; _____ por lo que mas tú

wind up, ___ be - ing part - ed, ___ bro - ken - heart - ed. _____
quie - ras ___ has - ta cuan - do, ___ has - ta cuan - do. _____

___ So, if you real - ly love me, ___ say "yes," but if you
___ Ya - sí pa - san los dí - as ___ y yo de - ses - pe -

don't dear, ___ con - fess, and please don't tell me, ___ per - haps, per - haps, per -
ra - do ___ y tú, tú con - tes - tan - do ___ qui - zás, qui - zás, qui -

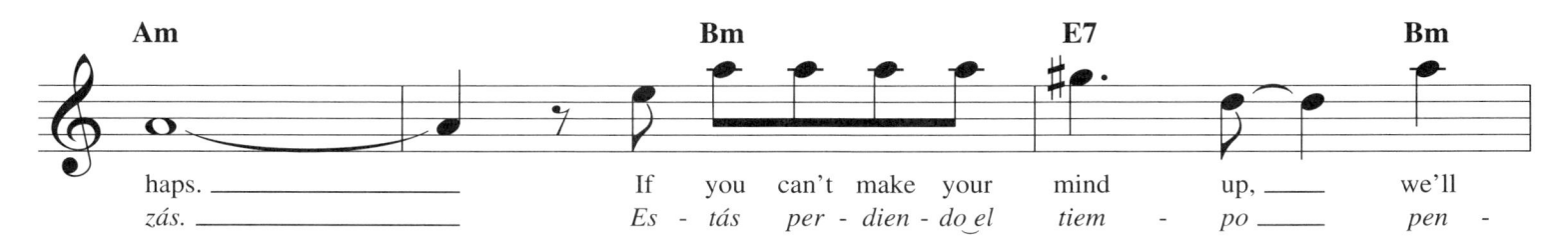

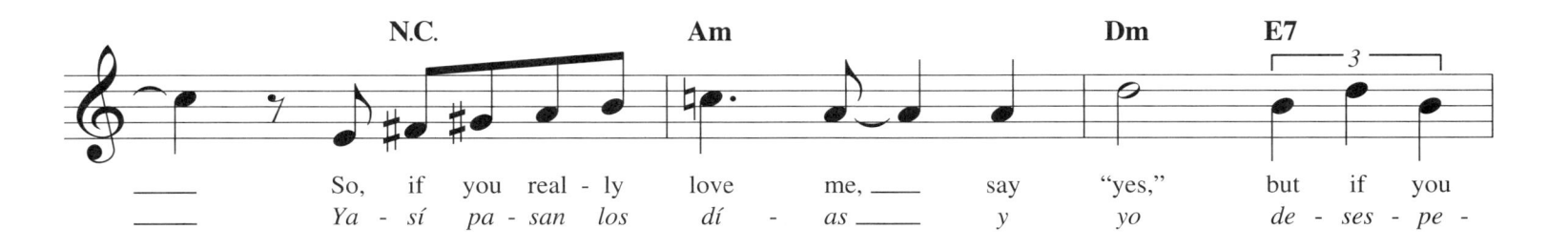

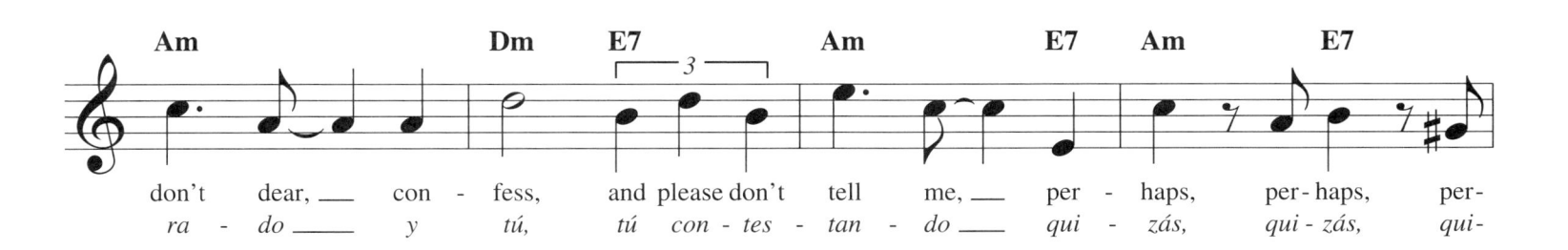

1. haps. _____ You won't ad - mit you
zás. _____ Siem - pre que te pre

2. haps. _____
zás. _____

RETRATO EM BRANCO E PRETO

Copyright © 1968 Antonio Carlos Jobim and Chico Buarque de Hollanda
Copyright Renewed
Published by Corcovado Music Corp. and Marola Edicoes Musicais
International Copyright Secured   All Rights Reserved

Words by CHICO BUARQUE DE HOLLANDA
Music by ANTONIO CARLOS JOBIM

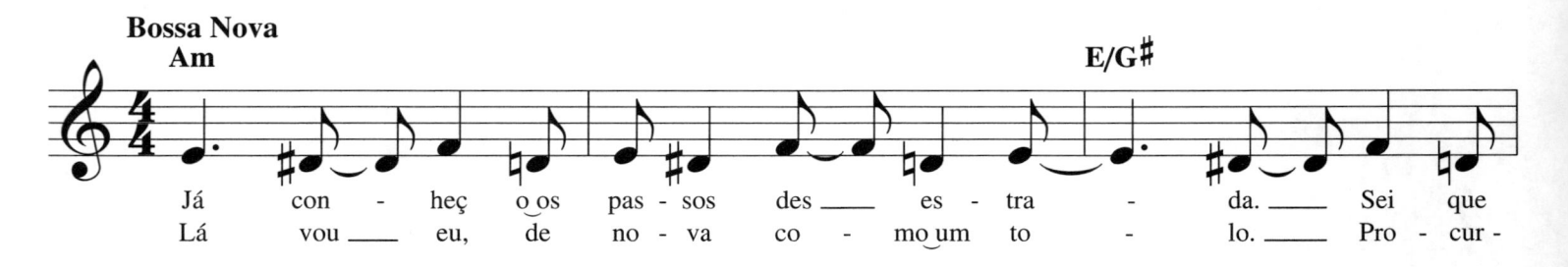

Bossa Nova

Já con-heç o os pas-sos des-sa es-tra-da. Sei que
Lá vou eu, de no-va co-mo um to-lo. Pro-cur-

não vai dar em na-da. Seus seg-re-dos sei de cor.
ar a des-con so-lo. Que cansel de con-he-cer.

Sá con-heç o as
No-vos di-as

ped-ras do cam-inho. E sei tam-bém que al-i soz-in-
tris-tes, noit-es cla-ras. Ver-sos car-tas, min-ha ca-

-ho. Eu vou fic-ar tan-to pi-or. O que é
-ra. Ain-da vol-ta ihe es-crev-er. Pra lhe diz-

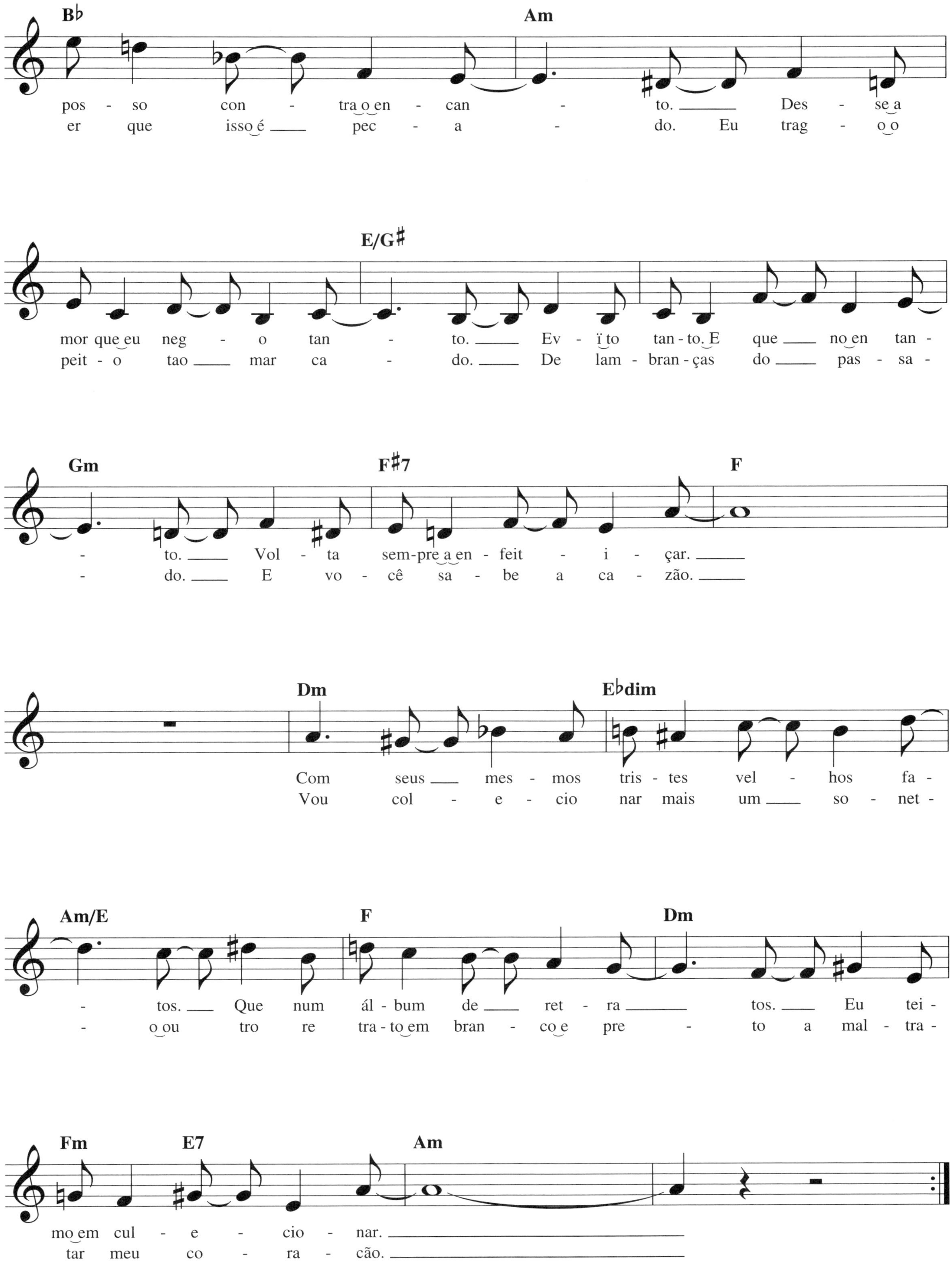
B♭
Am
pos - so con - tra o en - can - to. Des - se a
er que isso é pec - a - do. Eu trag - o o
E/G♯
mor que eu neg - o tan - to. Ev - ï to tan - to. E que no en tan -
peit - o tao mar ca - do. De lam - bran - ças do pas - sa -
Gm
F♯7
F
- to. Vol - ta sem-pre a en - feit - i - çar.
- do. E vo - cê sa - be a ca - zão.
Dm
E♭dim
Com seus mes - mos tris - tes vel - hos fa -
Vou col - e - cio nar mais um so - net -
Am/E
F
Dm
- tos. Que num ál - bum de ret - ra tos. Eu tei -
- o ou tro re tra - to em bran - co e pre - to a mal - tra -
Fm
E7
Am
mo em cul - e - cio - nar.
tar meu co - ra - cão.

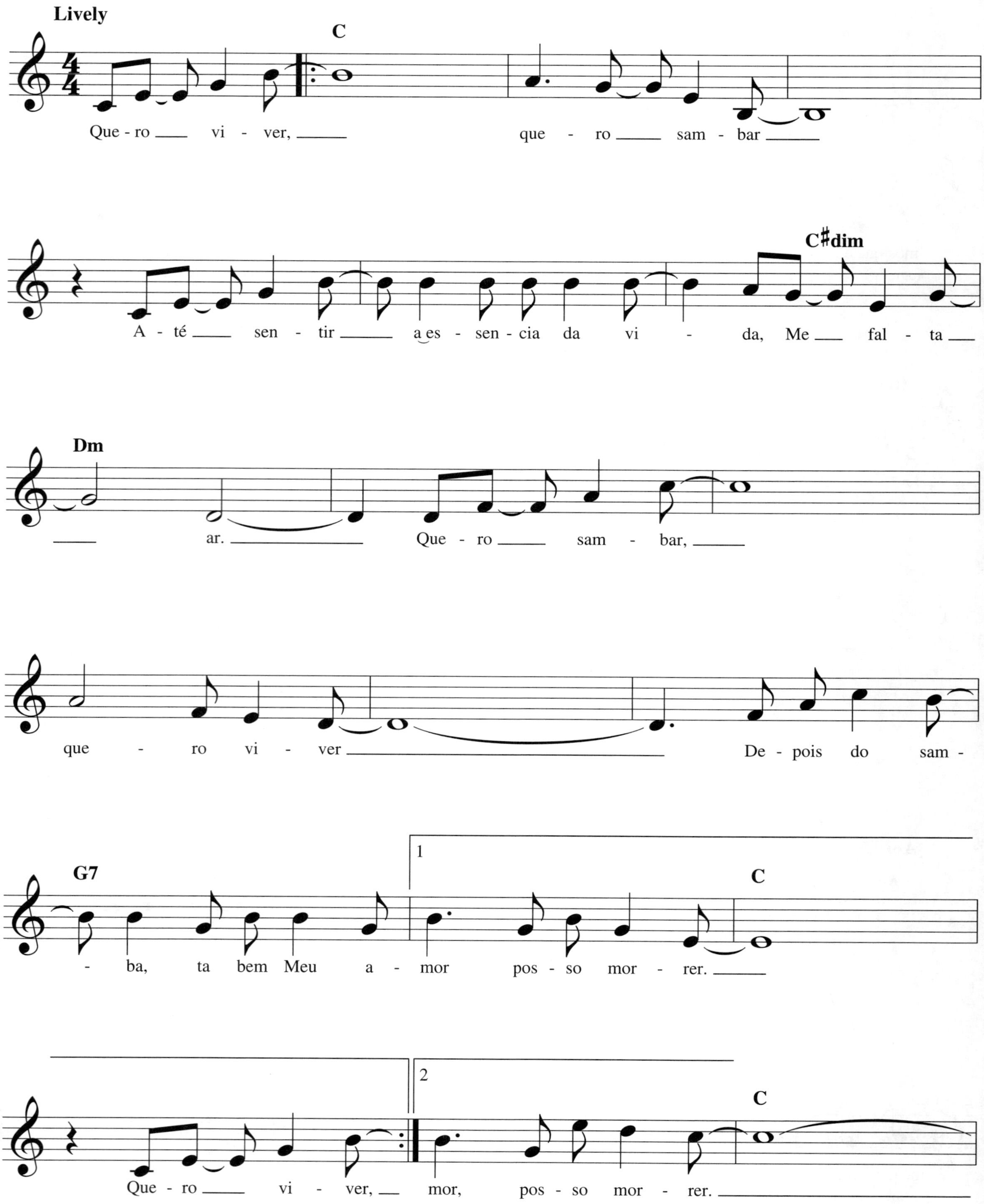

Quem qui - zer _____ gos - tar ___ de mim.
Se qui - zer _____ vai - ser ___ as - sim
Va - mos ___ vi - ver, ___
va - mos ___ sam - bar _____ Se a fan - ta - sia
ras - gar, Meu a - mor, ___ eu com - pro ou - tra
Va - mos ___ sam - bar _____ va - mos vi - ver
O sam - ba é ___ livre, Eu sou livre tam -
bem, A - te mor - rer.

SAY "SÍ, SÍ"

Copyright © 1936 by Edward B. Marks Music Company
Copyright Renewed
International Copyright Secured   All Rights Reserved
Used by Permission

Music by ERNESTO LECUONA
Spanish Words by FRANCIA LUBAN
English Words by AL STILLMAN

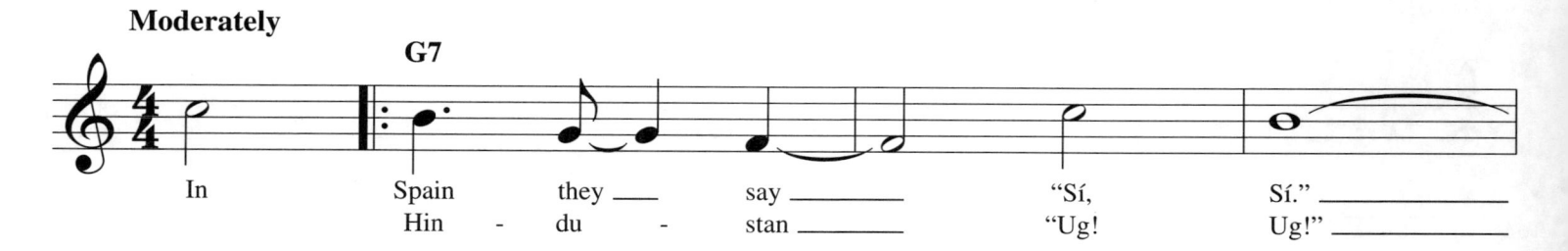

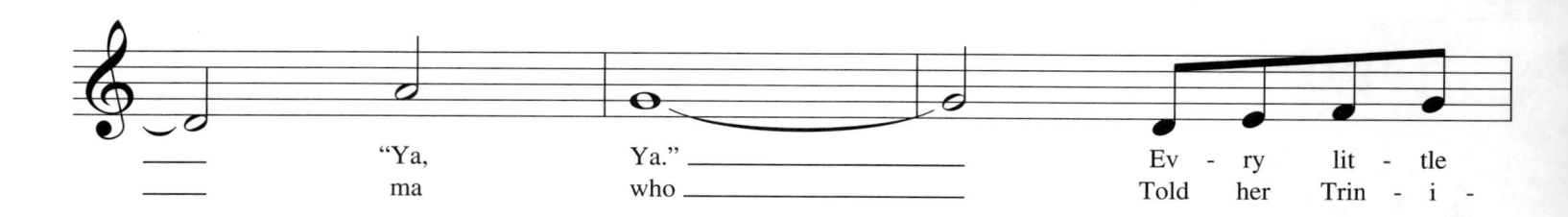

Moderately

In Spain they say "Sí, Sí." In France you'll hear "Wee, Wee." Ev-'ry lit-tle Dutch girl says "Ya, Ya." Ev-'ry little Da-nish doll says "Da."

Hin-du-stan "Ug! Ug!" means "O. K., babe, let's hug." Nev-er was a Pan-a-ma ma who Told her Trin-i-dad-dy, "No can do!"

G7
But sweet - heart tell me
On ev - 'ry Vir - gin
C
why, no mat - ter how
Isle they say it with
G7 C
I try. You won't lis - ten
a smile. But you nev - er
F C
to my plea won't say "yes" in an - y lan - guage to
hear my plea, won't say "yes" in an - y lan - guage to
G7
me. When will you say "Sí,
me. When will you say "Sí,
1 C
Sí?" In
2 C
Sí?"

SHE'S A CARIOCA

Lyric by RAY GILBERT
Music by ANTONIO CARLOS JOBIM
Portuguese Lyric by VINICIUS DE MORAES

Copyright © 1965 Corcovado Music Corp., VM Enterprises, Inc.
and Ipanema Music Corp.
Copyright Renewed
International Copyright Secured All Rights Reserved

Moderate Bossa Nova

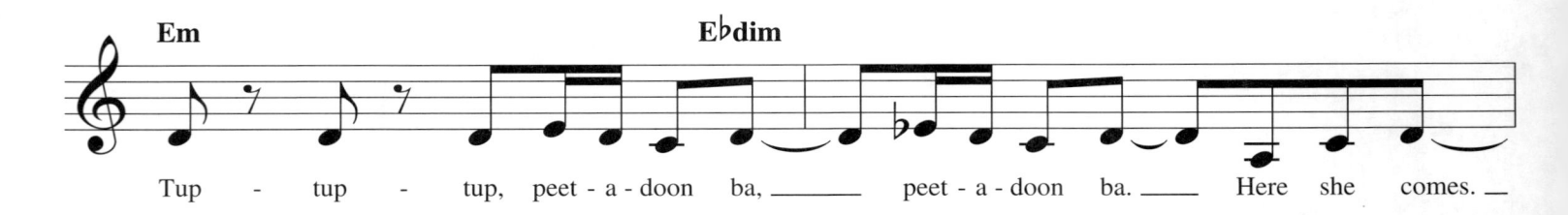

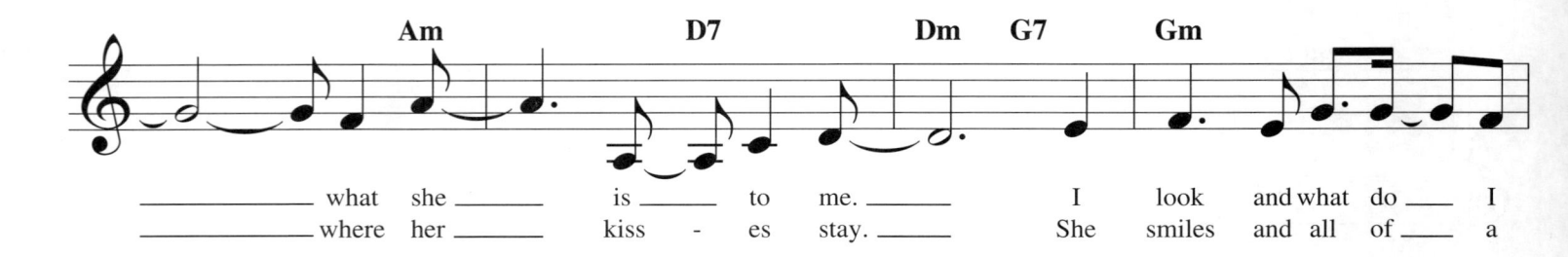

Tup - tup - tup, peet - a - doon ba, peet - a - doon ba, peet - a - doon.

Tup - tup - tup, peet - a - doon ba, peet - a - doon ba. Here she comes.

Here she comes. E - la

car - i - o - ca. She's a car - i - o - ca.
on - ly that, I'm in love with her

Just see the way she walks. No - bod - y else can be
the most ex - cit - ing way. It's writ - ten on my lips

what she is to me. I look and what do I
where her kiss - es stay. She smiles and all of a

| C7 | D7 | Fm | C | B7 |

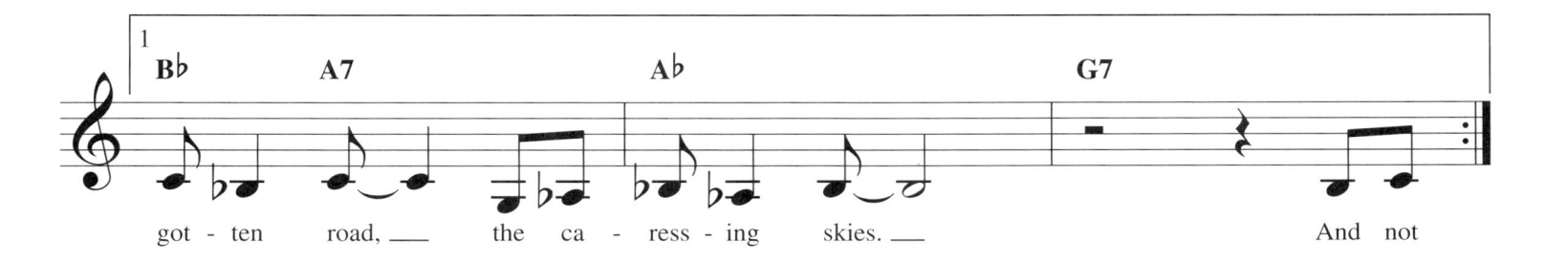

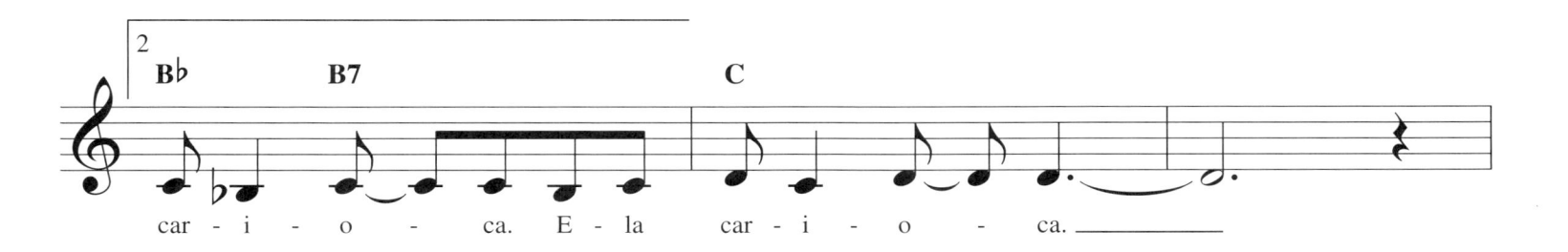

see when I look deep in her eyes? I can see the sea, a for-
sud-den the world is smil-ing for me. And you know what else? She's a

1. | Bb A7 | Ab | G7 |

got-ten road, the ca-ress-ing skies. And not

2. | Bb B7 | C | |

car-i-o-ca. E la car-i-o-ca.

| D7 | | Fm | |

Tup-tup-tup, peet-a-doon-ba, peet-a-doon ba, peet-a-doon.

| Em | | Bbdim | |

Tup-tup-tup, peet-a doon ba, peet-a-doon ba. There she goes.

| D7 | G7 | C | |

There she goes.

SIMILAU
(See–me–lo)

Words by HARRY COLEMAN
Music by ARDEN CLAR

© 1948 (Renewed) CHERIO CORP.
All Rights Reserved

Afro–Cuban tempo

Spir-it in de wood beat de hol-low cane. Spir-it in de wood float a-way de pain. Make de bod-y ripe and a-live a-gain.
Spir-it in de heart make de blood flow fast. Spir-it in de heart make de mus-cle last. Keep de hope a-live when de youth go past.

Ay, Sim-i-lau. When de wom-an come up-on de scene drop de pet-al from de tree.

Fling de moun-tain up in-to de sky. Spill de riv-er in de sea. Spir-it in de wood let de hol-low cane ech-o in de af-ter glow. Wait-ing for de flame to burn a-gain.

Ay, Sim-i-lau.

YOURS
(Cuando Se Quiere De Veras)

Copyright © 1931, 1937 by Edward B. Marks Music Company
Copyright Renewed
International Copyright Secured All Rights Reserved
Used by Permission

Words by ALBERT GAMSE and JACK SHERR
Music by GONZALO ROIG

Dreamily

Yours till the stars lose their glo-ry!

Yours till the birds fail to sing!

Yours to the end of life's sto-ry, this pledge to

you, dear, I bring! Yours in the

gray of De-cem-ber here or on

far dis-tant shores! I've nev-er

loved an-y-one the way I love you! How could I?

When I was born to be just yours.

SLIGHTLY OUT OF TUNE
(Desafinado)

Copyright © 1959, 1962 Editora Musical Arapua, Sao Paulo, Brazil
Copyrights Renewed
All Rights for the U.S. Controlled and Administered by Corcovado Music Corp. and Bendig Music Corp.
All Rights for Canada Controlled and Administered by Bendig Music Corp.
International Copyright Secured   All Rights Reserved

English Lyric by JON HENDRICKS and JESSIE CAVANAUGH
Original Text by NEWTON MENDONCA
Music by ANTONIO CARLOS JOBIM

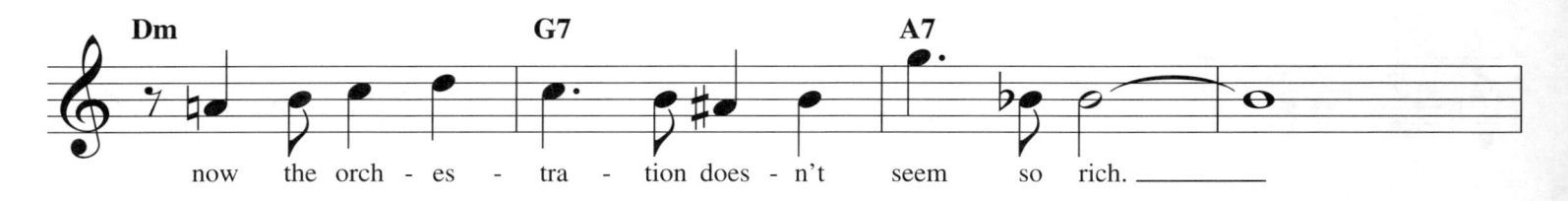

Bossa Nova

Love is like a nev-er-end-ing mel-o-dy.

Po-ets have com-pared it to a sym-pho-ny,

a sym-pho-ny con-duct-ed by the light-ing of the moon,

but our song of love is slight-ly out of tune.

Once your kiss-es raised me to a fe-ver pitch,

now the orch-es-tra-tion does-n't seem so rich.

Seems to me you've changed the tune we used to sing.

Like the Bos-sa No-va love should swing. We

| E | Fdim | F#m | B7 |

used to har-mo-nize ___ two souls in per - fect time. ___

| E | C#m | F#m | B7 |

Now the song is dif-f'rent and the words don't e-ven rhyme. ___ 'Cause

| G | G#dim | Am | D7 |

you for-got the mel-o-dy our hearts would al - ways croon. ___ And so what

| Dm | C#dim | D7 | G7 |

good's a heart that's slight-ly out of tune. ___

| C | | D7 | |

Tune your heart to mine the way it used to be. ___

| Dm | G7 | Gm/E | A7 |

Join with me in har-mo-ny and sing a song of lov - ing. We're

| Dm | Fm | C | Am |

bound to get in tune a-gain be - fore too long. There'll be

| D7 | | B♭7 | |

no De-sa-fi-na-do when your heart be - longs to me com-plete-ly. ___ Then you

| D7 | Dm | G7 | C |

won't be slight-ly out of tune. ___ You'll sing a - long with me. ___

SÓ DANÇO SAMBA
(Jazz 'n' Samba)
from the film COPACABANA PALACE

Copyright © 1962, 1963, 1965 Edizioni Suvini Zerboni, Milan, Italy
Copyrights Renewed
Corcovado Music Corp. and VM Enterprises, Inc. control all publication rights for the U.S.A.
International Copyright Secured   All Rights Reserved

English Lyric by NORMAN GIMBEL
Original Text by VINICIUS DE MORAES
Music by ANTONIO CARLOS JOBIM

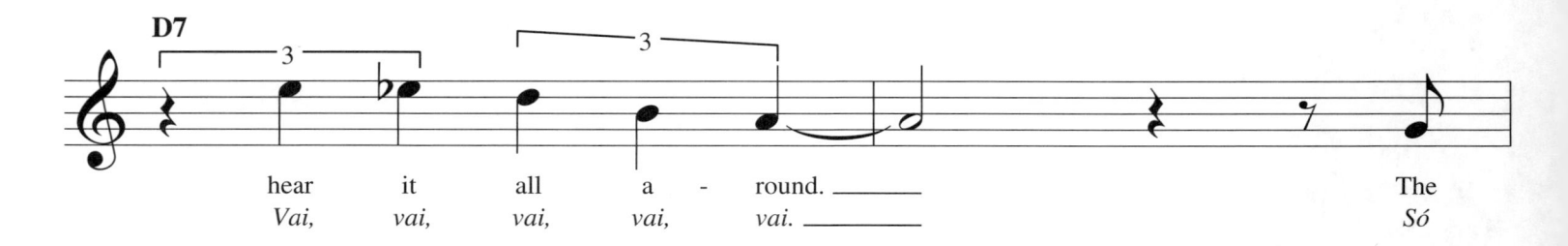

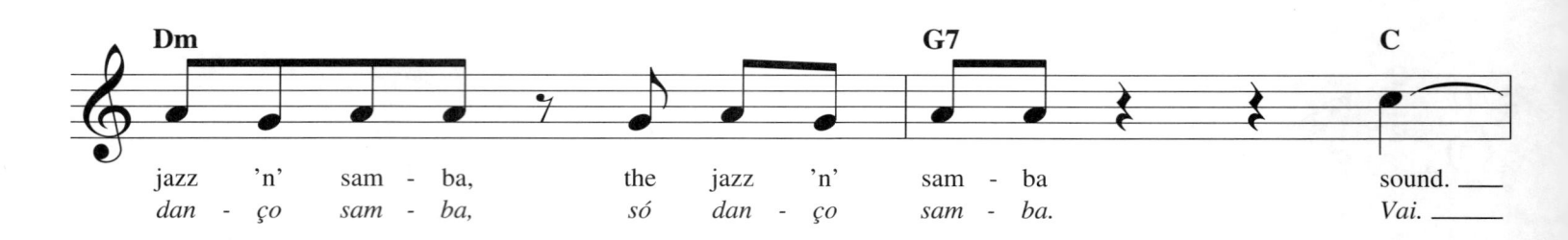

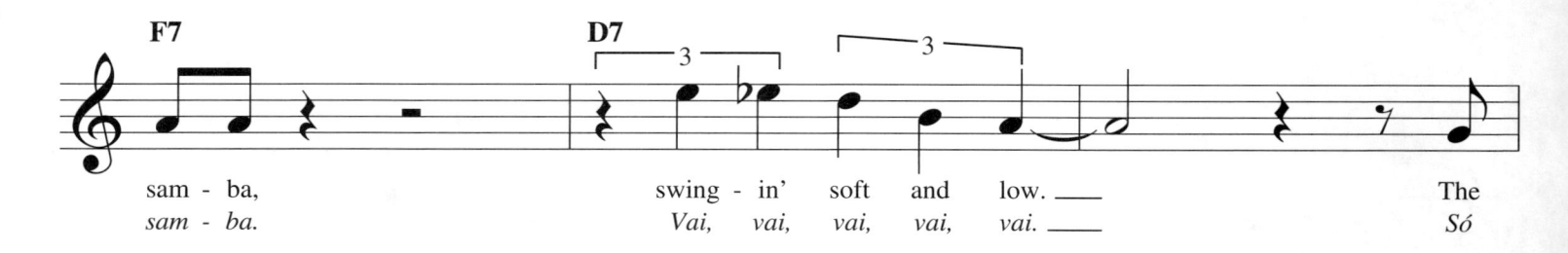

Samba

The jazz 'n' samba, the jazz 'n' samba,
Só danço samba, só danço samba.

hear it all a-round. ____ The
Vai, vai, vai, vai, vai. ____ Só

jazz 'n' samba, the jazz 'n' samba sound. ____
danço samba, só danço samba. Vai. ____

The jazz 'n' samba, the jazz 'n'
Só danço samba, só danço

samba, swing-in' soft and low. ____ The
samba. Vai, vai, vai, vai, vai. ____ Só

jazz 'n' samba, the jazz 'n' samba, go! ____
danço samba, só danço samba, Vai. ____

Gm
Jet from Ri - o, non -
Já dan - cei o twist
C7
F
- stop U. S. A.
a - té de - mais.
Am
D7
This new sound came one day, and it's
Mas não sei me can - sei do ca -
G7
clear that it's here to stay. It's
lip - so ao chá chá chá. Só
C
F7
jazz 'n' sam - ba, it's so re - fresh - ing,
dan - ço sam - ba, só dan - ço sam - ba.
D7
3
3
like a new per - fume. It's
Vai, vai, vai, vai, vai. Só
Dm
G7
jazz 'n' sam - ba, it's jazz 'n' sam - ba,
dan - ço sam - ba, só dan - ço sam - ba.
C
1
F7
2
ummm! The
Vai. Só

162

SO NICE
(Summer Samba)

Copyright © 1965, 1966 MARCOS VALLE and PAULO SERGIO VALLE, Brazil
Copyright Renewed and Assigned to UNIVERSAL MUSIC CORP. and NEW THUNDER MUSIC, INC.
All Rights for NEW THUNDER MUSIC, INC. Administered by GIMBEL MUSIC GROUP, INC.
 (P.O. Box 15221, Beverly Hills, CA 90209 USA)
All Rights Reserved   Used by Permission

Original Words and Music by MARCOS VALLE
and PAULO SERGIO VALLE
English Words by NORMAN GIMBEL

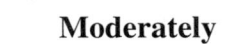

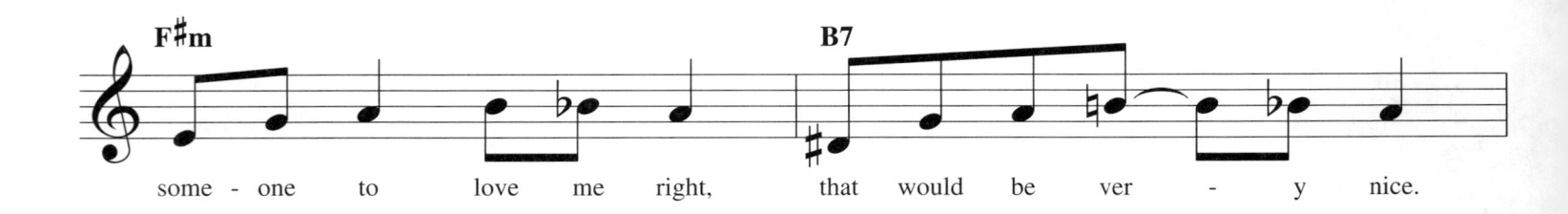

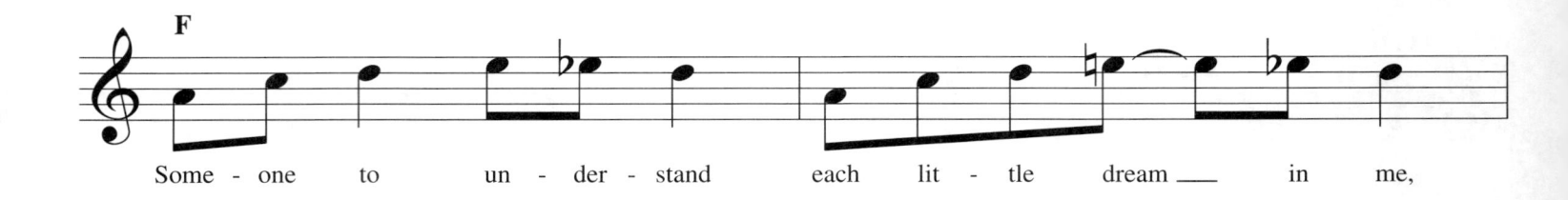

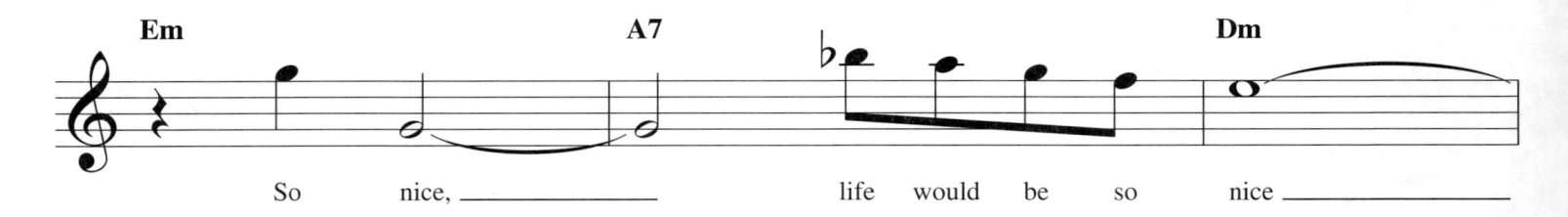

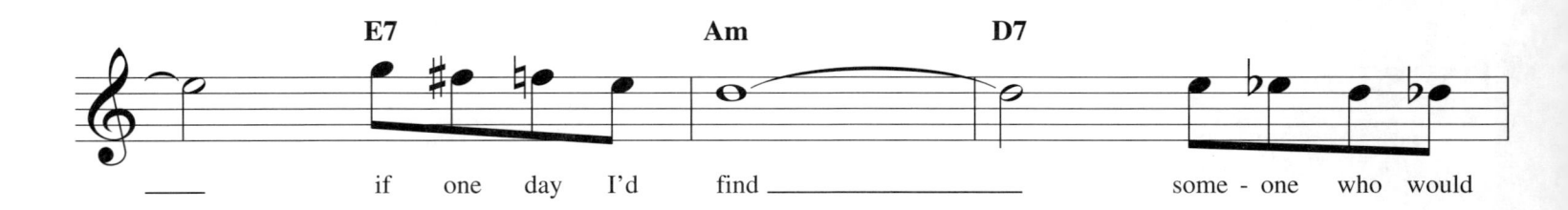

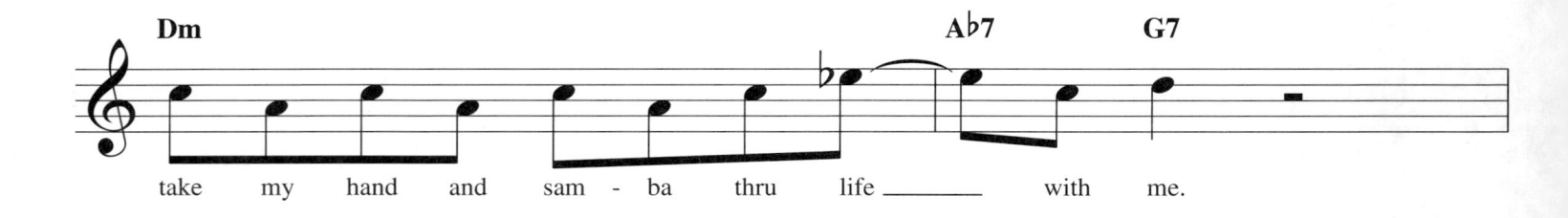

Moderately

(C) Some-one to hold me tight, that would be ver-y nice,

(F#m) some-one to love me right, (B7) that would be ver-y nice.

(F) Some-one to un-der-stand each lit-tle dream in me,

(Bb7) some-one to take my hand, to be a team with me.

(Em) So nice, (A7) life would be so nice (Dm)

(E7) if one day I'd find (Am) some-one (D7) who would

(Dm) take my hand and sam-ba thru (Ab7) life (G7) with me.

[Sheet music]

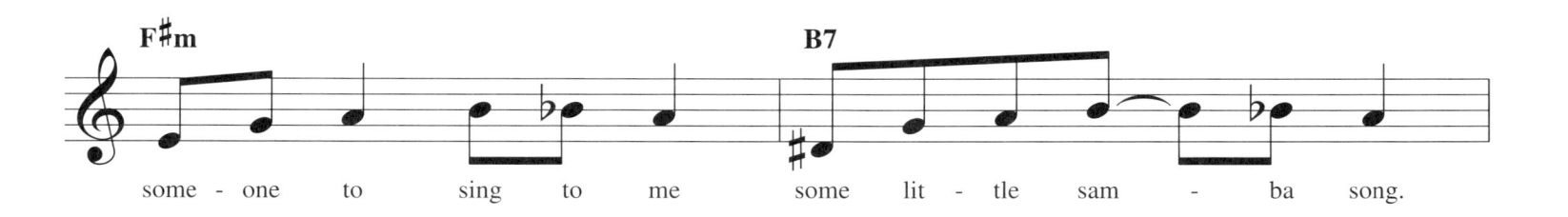

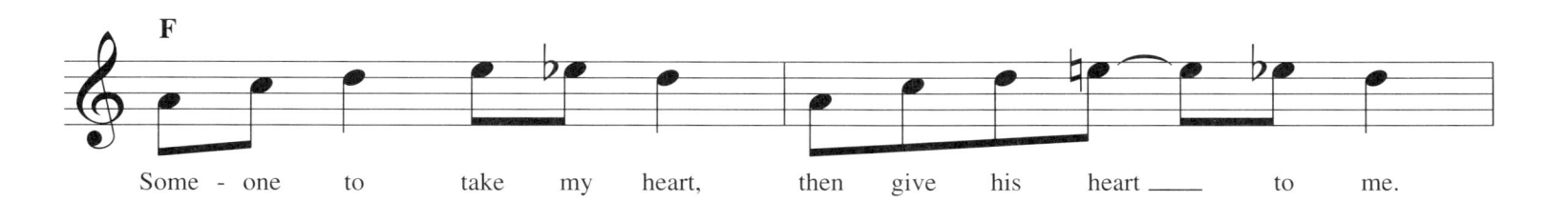

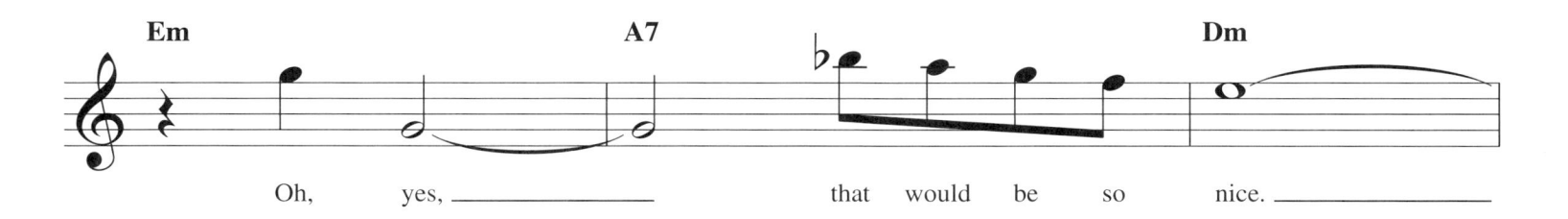

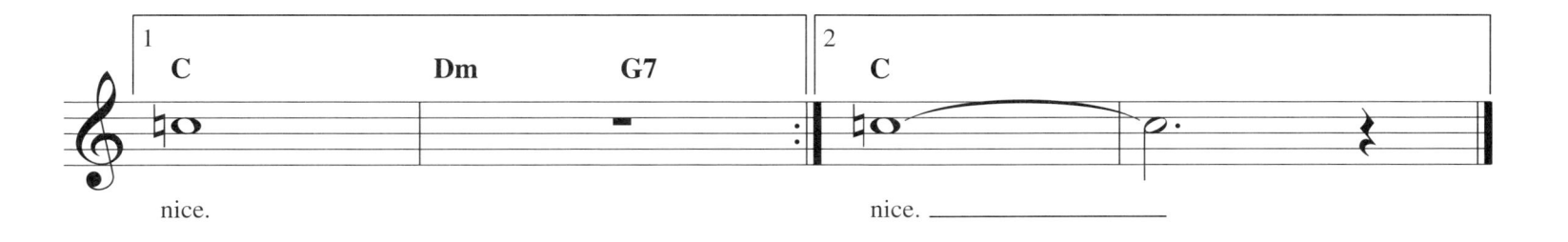

C
Some-one to cling to me, stay with me right ___ or wrong,

F#m ... **B7**
some-one to sing to me some lit-tle sam-ba song.

F
Some-one to take my heart, then give his heart ___ to me.

Bb7
Some-one who's read-y to give love a start ___ with me.

Em ... **A7** ... **Dm**
Oh, yes, ___ that would be so nice. ___

G7 ... **C** ... **F7**
___ Should it be you and me, I could see it would be

1. **C** ... **Dm** **G7**
nice.

2. **C**
nice. ___

SOMEONE TO LIGHT UP MY LIFE
(Se Todos Fossem Iguais A Voce)

English Lyric by GENE LEES
Original Text by VINICIUS DE MORAES
Music by ANTONIO CARLOS JOBIM

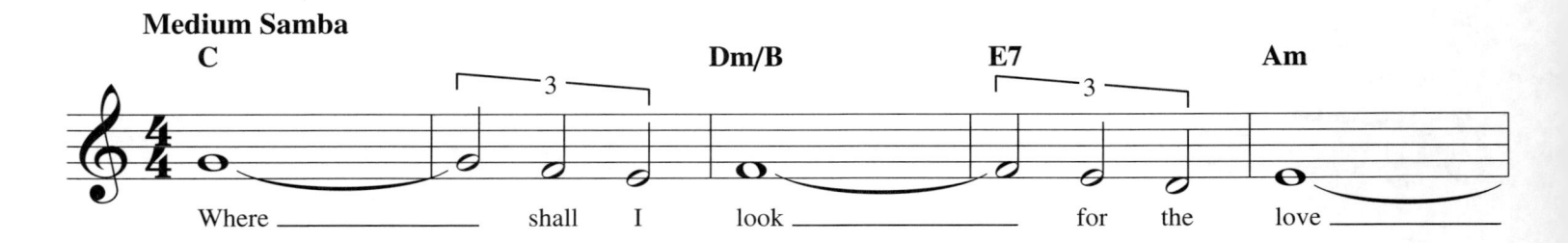

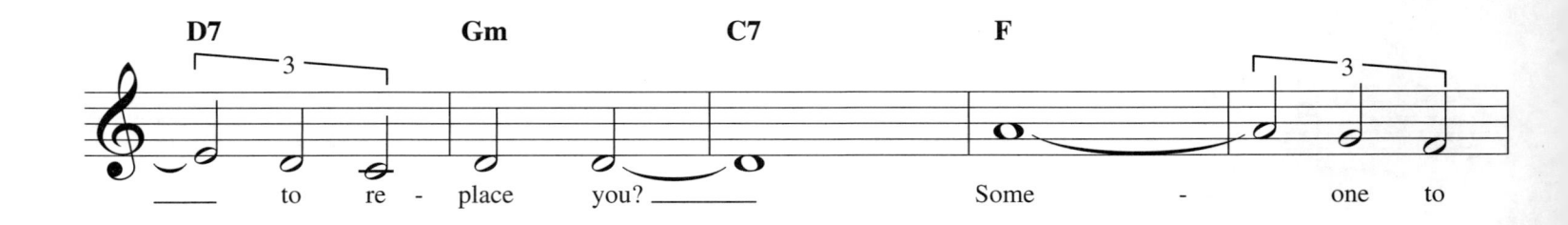

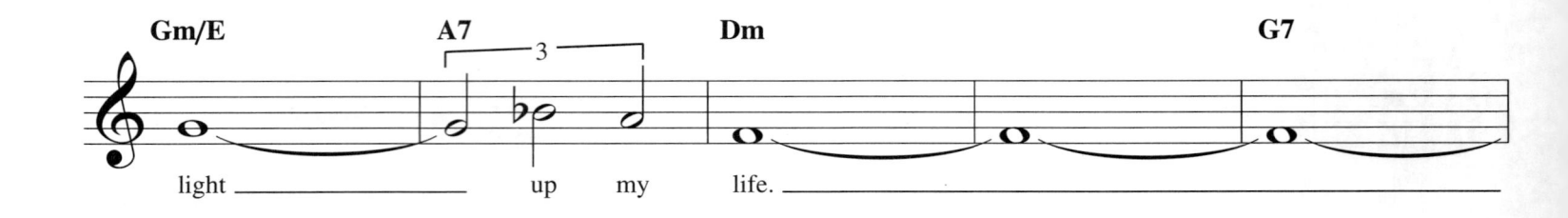

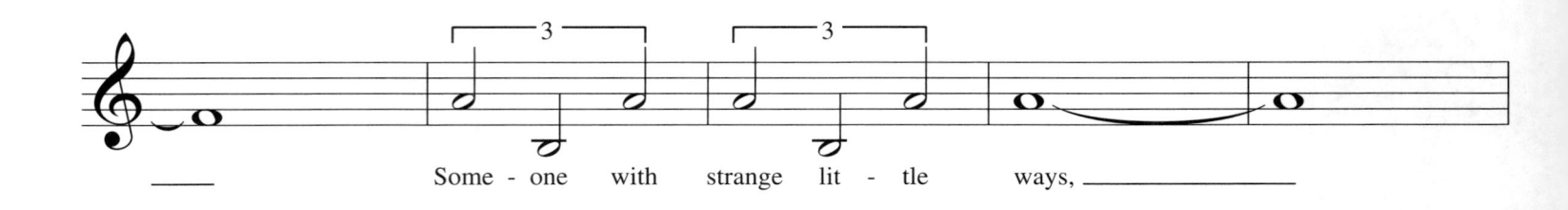

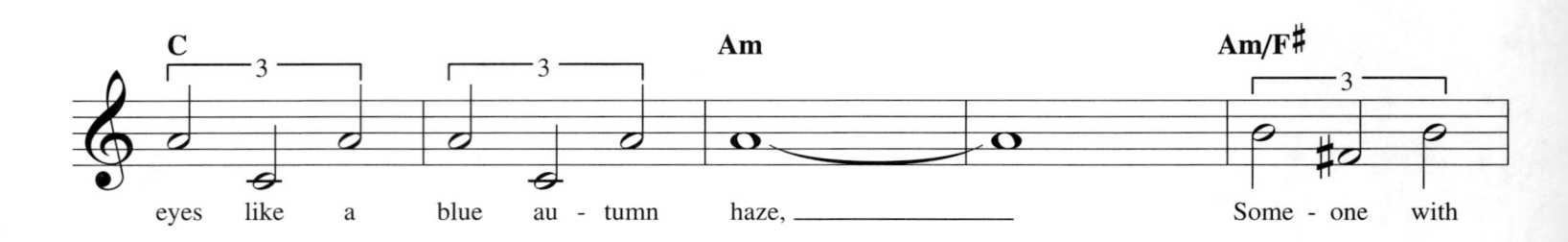

© Copyright 1958 (Renewed), 1964 (Renewed) and 1965 (Renewed) Antonio Carlos Jobim and Vinicius de Moraes
TRO - Hollis Music, Inc., New York, NY, Corcovado Music Corp., New York, NY
and VM Enterprises, New York, NY control all publication rights for the U.S.A.
International Copyright Secured
All Rights Reserved   Used by Permission

Medium Samba

Where ____ shall I look ____ for the love ____ to re-place you? Some-one to light ____ up my life. ____ Some-one with strange lit-tle ways, ____ eyes like a blue au-tumn haze, ____ Some-one with your laugh-ing style ____ and a smile that I

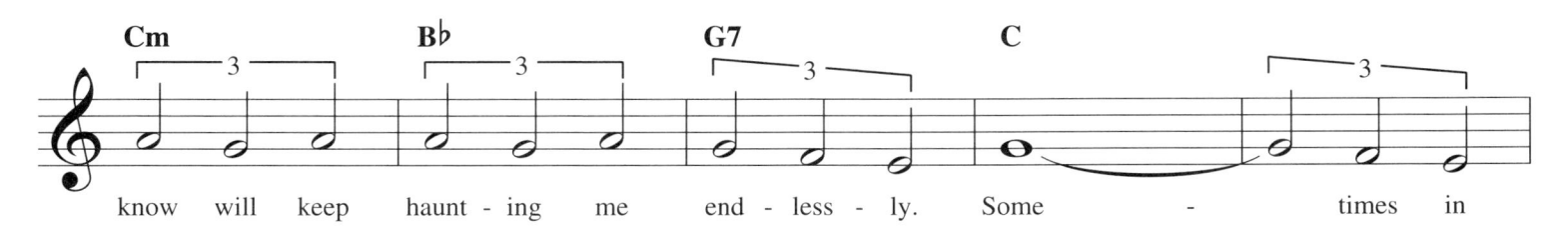

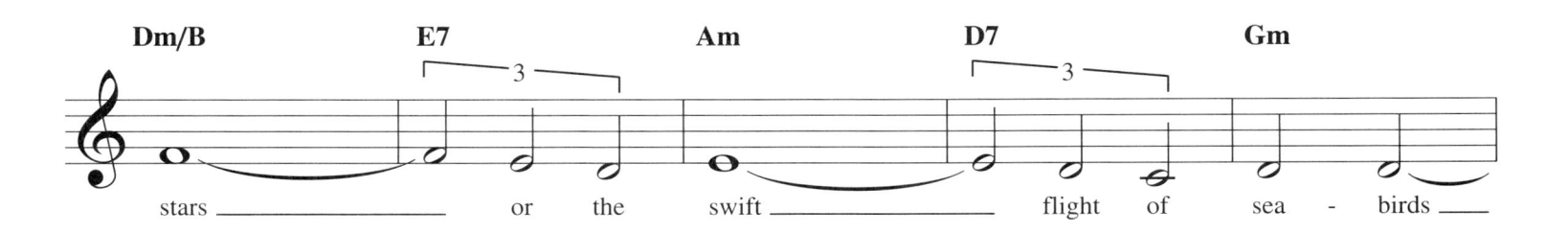

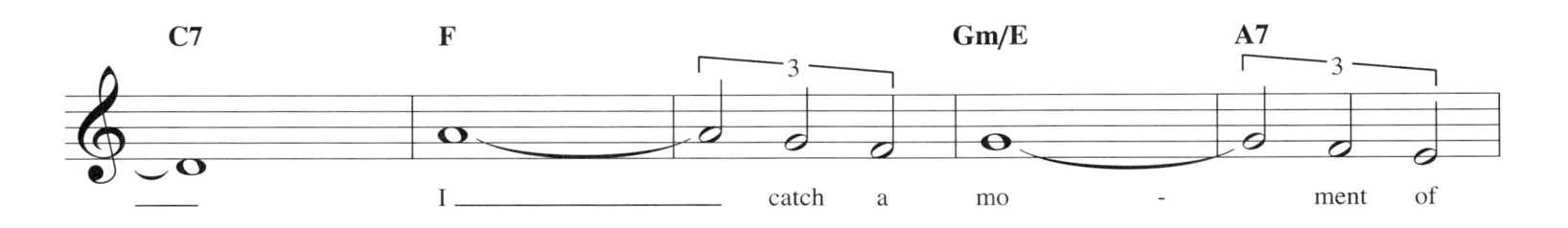

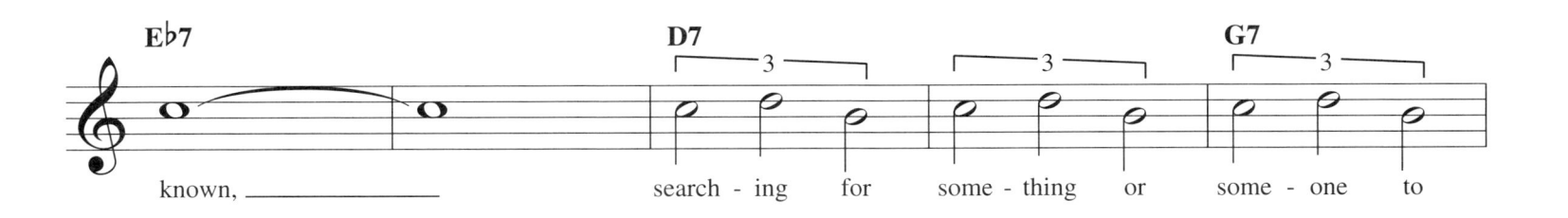

Cm	B♭	G7	C	
know will keep	haunt - ing me end - less - ly.		Some -	times in

Dm/B	E7	Am	D7	Gm
stars	or the swift	flight of	sea -	birds

C7	F	Gm/E	A7	
	I	catch a mo -	ment of	

F				Am/F#
you.				That's why I

	Fm		C	
walk all a -	lone,		search - ing for	some - thing un -

E♭7	D7		G7	
known,	search - ing for	some - thing or	some - one to	

	C			
light up my	life.			

SONG OF THE JET
(Samba Do Avião)
from the film COPACABANA PALACE

English Lyric by GENE LEES
Original Text and Music by
ANTONIO CARLOS JOBIM

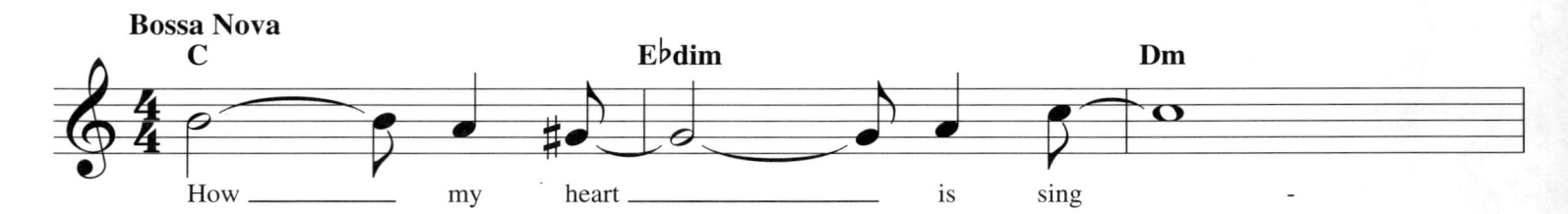

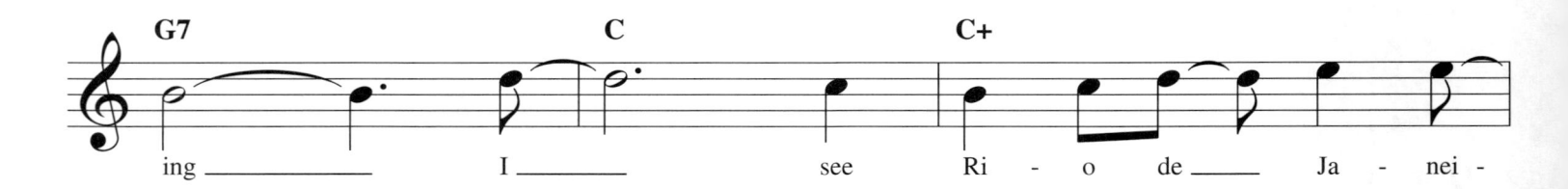

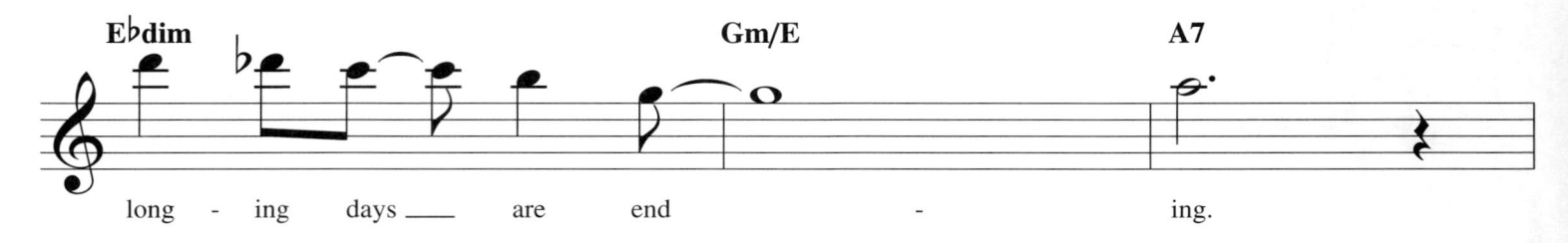

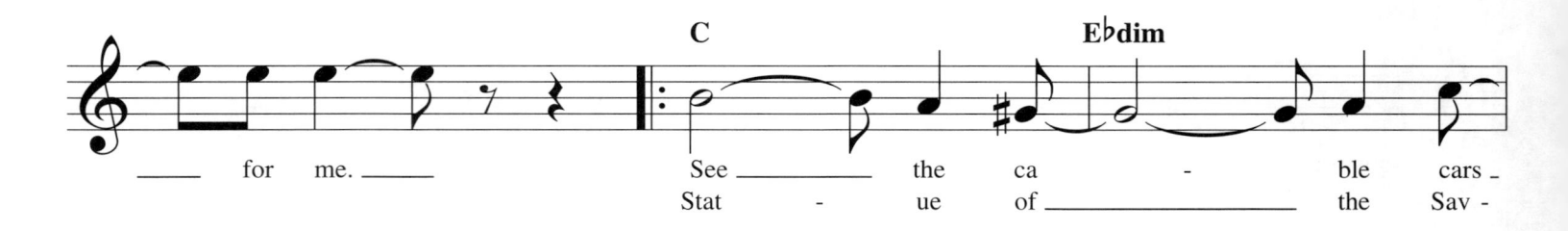

Bossa Nova

How my heart is sing-ing I see Ri-o de Ja-nei-ro. My lone-ly long-ing days are end-ing. Ri-o my love, there by the sea. Ri-o my love, wait-ing for me.

See the ca-ble cars that sway a-bove the
Stat-ue of the Sav-ior with o-pen arms a-

Chord	Lyric line 1	Lyric line 2
C+ ... F ... Fm	Bay of Gua - na - ba - ra.	bove the yel - low sea - shore.
F ... Fm ... C	Ti - ny sail - boats far be - low dance the sam - ba as	Su - gar Loaf in maj - es - ty climb - ing from a sil -
E♭dim ... F ... Fm	they go. Shin - ing Ri - o, there you lie,	- ver sea. Dark - eyed girls who smile at me,
Em A7 Dm G7 Gm	cit - y of sun, of sea and sky. Moun - tains of green ris - ing	cit - y of love and mys - ter - ies; fas - ten seat - belts, no smok -
A7 F Dm G7	so high four min - utes more we'll be there at the air - port of	- ing please. Now we're de - scend - ing and ev - 'ry - thing's rush - ing and
Dm / D7 (1st ending)	Ga - le - ão,	now the wheels

1st ending (D7): Ri - o de Ja - nei - ro, Ri - o

G7: de Ja - nei - ro, Ri - o de Ja - nei - ro, Ri - o de Ja - nei - ro.

2nd ending — D7 | D♭7 | C: touch the ground.

SOUTH OF THE BORDER
(Down Mexico Way)

Copyright © 1939 The Peter Maurice Music Co., Ltd., London, England
Copyright Renewed and Assigned to Shapiro, Bernstein & Co., Inc., New York for U.S.A. and Canada
International Copyright Secured   All Rights Reserved
Used by Permission

Words and Music by JIMMY KENNEDY
and MICHAEL CARR

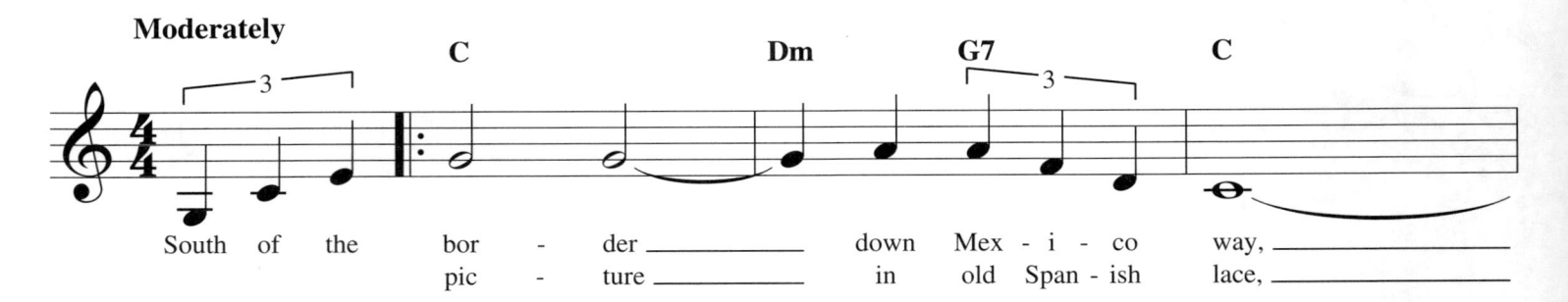

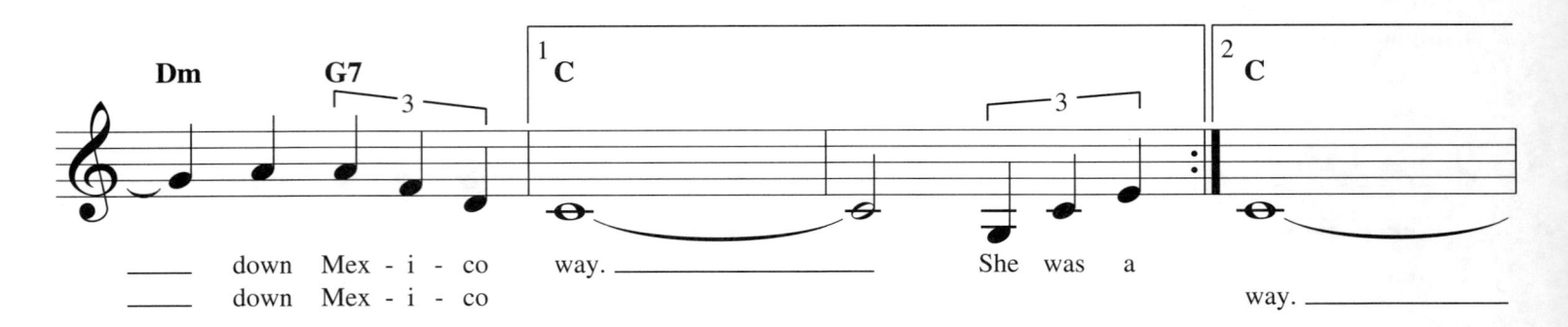

Moderately

South of the bor - der _____ down Mex - i - co way, _____
pic - ture _____ in old Span - ish lace, _____

_____ that's where I fell in love when stars a - bove came
_____ just for a ten - der while I kissed the smile up -

out to play. _____ And now as I wan - der, _____
on her face. _____ For it was Fi - es - ta _____

_____ my thoughts ev - er stray _____ south of the bor - der _____
_____ and we were so gay _____ south of the bor - der _____

_____ down Mex - i - co way. _____ She was a
_____ down Mex - i - co way. _____

Then she sighed as she whis - pered Ma - ña - na, nev - er

G7 C A7
dream - ing that we were part - ing. And I lied as I whis-pered Ma -
Dm C G7 C
ña - na, for our to - mor - row nev - er came. South of the
Dm G7 C
bor - der I rode back one day; there in a
C/E E♭dim G7
veil of white by can - dle-light she knelt to pray. The mis - sion bells
C C7 F
told me that I must - n't stay south of the
C Dm G7 C
bor - der down Mex - i - co way. Ay! Ay! Ay!
G7 C
Ay! Ay! Ay! Ay! Ay! Ay! Ay! Ay!
G7 C
Ay! Ay! Ay! Ay! Ay!

SPANISH EYES

Words by CHARLES SINGLETON and EDDIE SNYDER
Music by BERT KAEMPFERT

© 1965, 1966 (Renewed 1993, 1994) EDITION DOMA BERT KAEMPFERT
All Rights for the world, excluding Germany, Austria and Switzerland,
Controlled and Administered by SCREEN GEMS-EMI MUSIC INC.
All Rights Reserved   International Copyright Secured   Used by Permission

Moderately

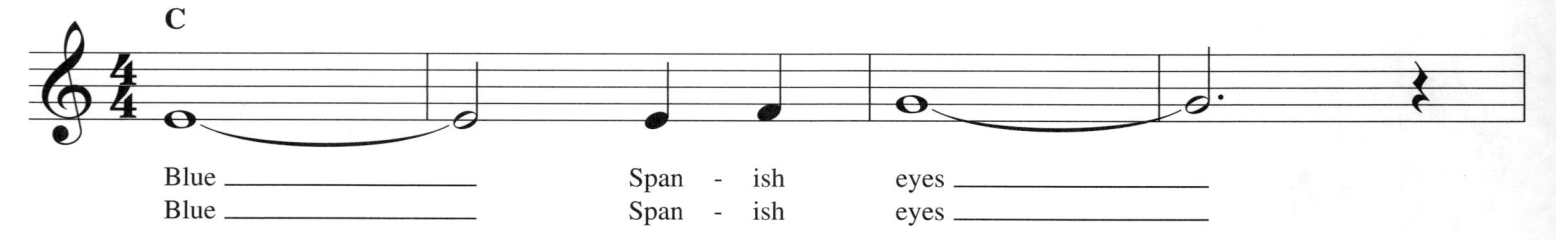

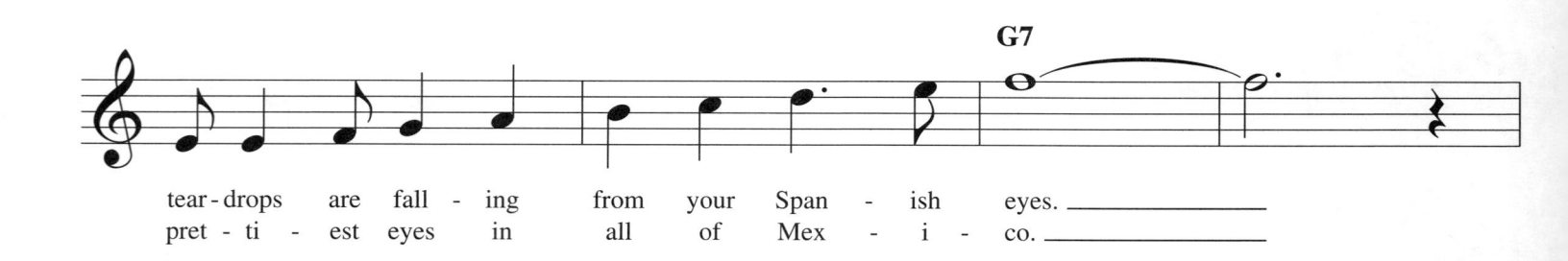

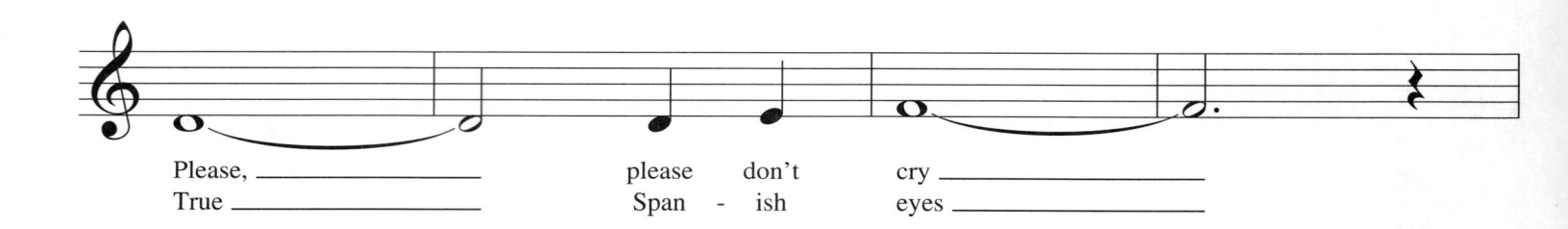

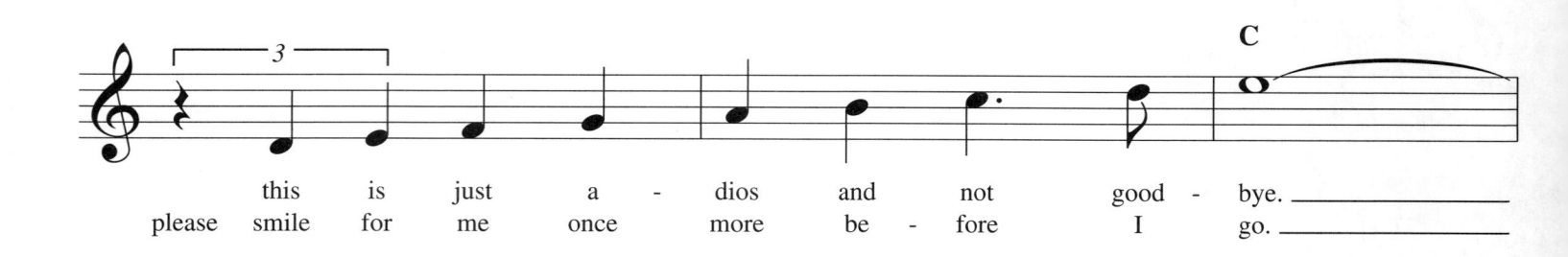

Blue _____ Span-ish eyes _____
Blue _____ Span-ish eyes _____

tear-drops are fall-ing from your Span-ish eyes.
pret-ti-est eyes in all of Mex-i-co.

Please, _____ please don't cry _____
True _____ Span-ish eyes _____

this is just a-dios and not good-bye.
please smile for me once more be-fore I go.

Soon _____ I'll re-turn _____

bring - ing you all the love your heart can

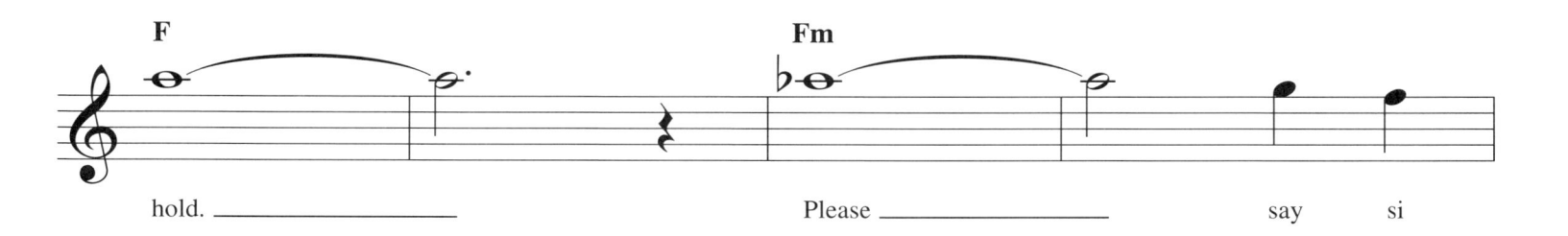

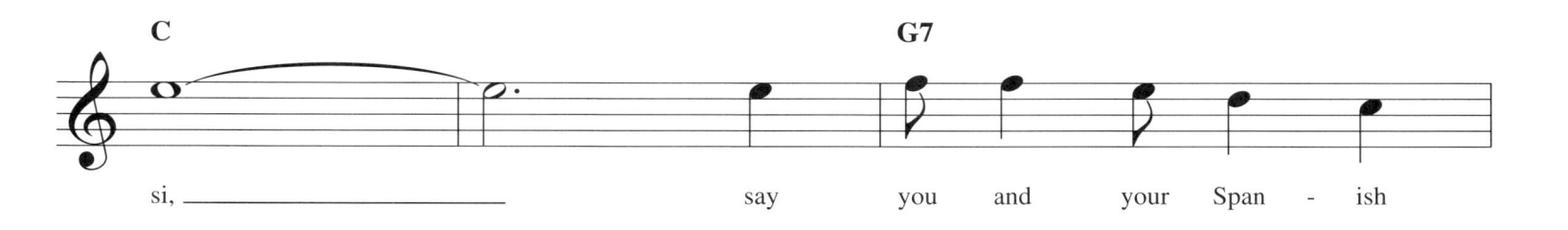

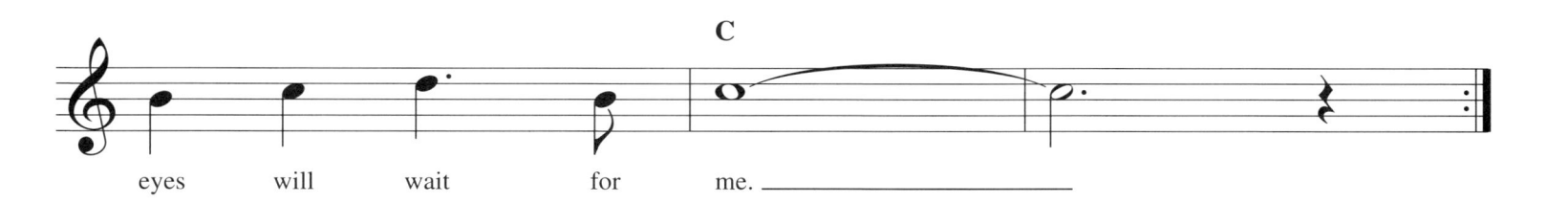

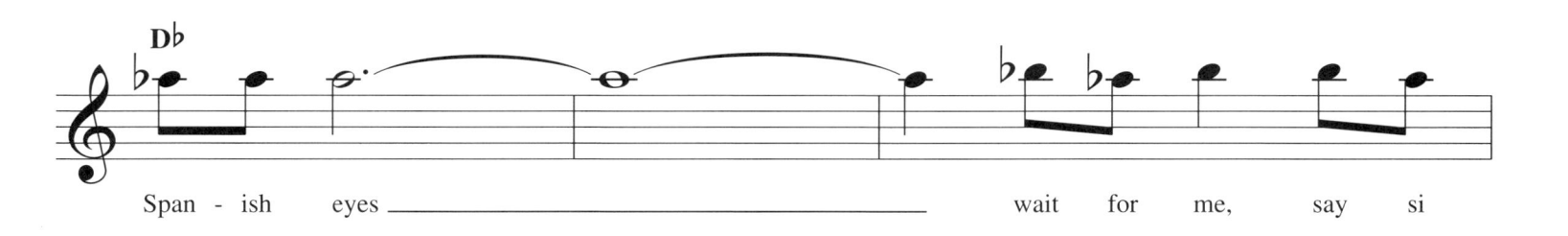

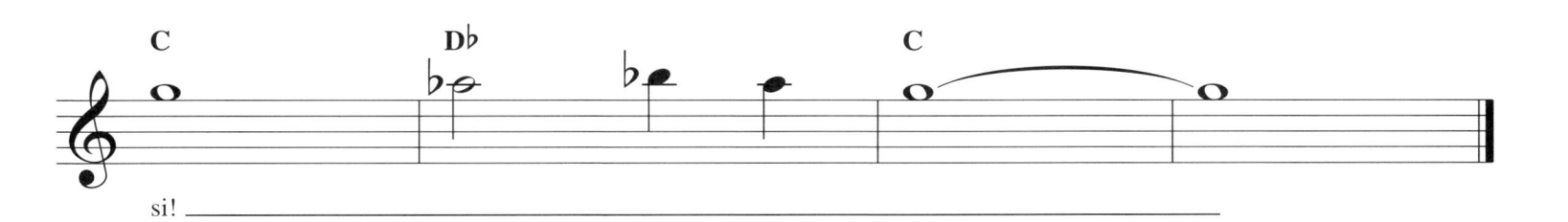

C7

F
hold. _____

Fm
Please _____ say si

C
si, _____ say you and your Span - ish

G7

C
eyes will wait for me. _____

D♭
Span - ish eyes _____ wait for me, say si

C **D♭** **C**
si! _____

SPEAK LOW
from the Musical Production ONE TOUCH OF VENUS

Words by OGDEN NASH
Music by KURT WEILL

TRO - © Copyright 1943 (Renewed) Hampshire House Publishing Corp.,
New York and Chappell & Co., Los Angeles, CA
International Copyright Secured
All Rights Reserved Including Public Performance For Profit
Used by Permission

Moderately slow

Speak low _____ when you speak,
low, _____ dar - ling, speak

love, _____ our sum - mer day with - ers a -
low, _____ love is a spark lost in the

way too soon, too soon. Speak
dark too soon, too soon. I

low _____ when you speak, love, _____
feel _____ wher - ev - er I go _____

our moment is swift, like ships a -
that to - mor - row is near, to - mor - row is

1. drift we're swept a - part too soon. Speak
   here and al - ways too

2. soon. _____ Time is so old _____

E♭m
and love so brief.
B♭ B7
Love is pure gold and time a
G7 Dm G7
thief. We're late, dar - ling, we're
Dm G7
late. The cur - tain de -
Dm G7 C
scends, ev - 'ry - thing ends too soon, too
A7 Fm B♭7
soon. I wait, dar - ling, I
C A7 D7
wait. Will you speak low to me, speak
G7 C
love to me and soon.

SWAY
(Quien Será)

Copyright © 1954 by Editorial Mexicana De Musica Internacional, S.A.
Copyright Renewed
All Rights Administered by Peer International Corporation

English Words by NORMAN GIMBEL
Spanish Words and Music by PABLO BELTRAN RUIZ

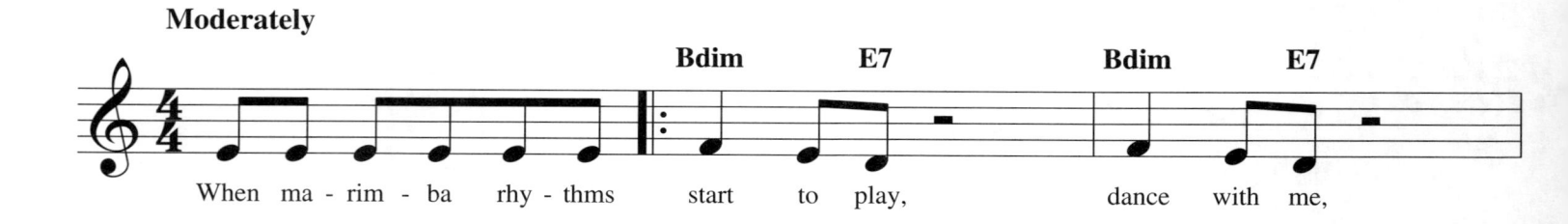

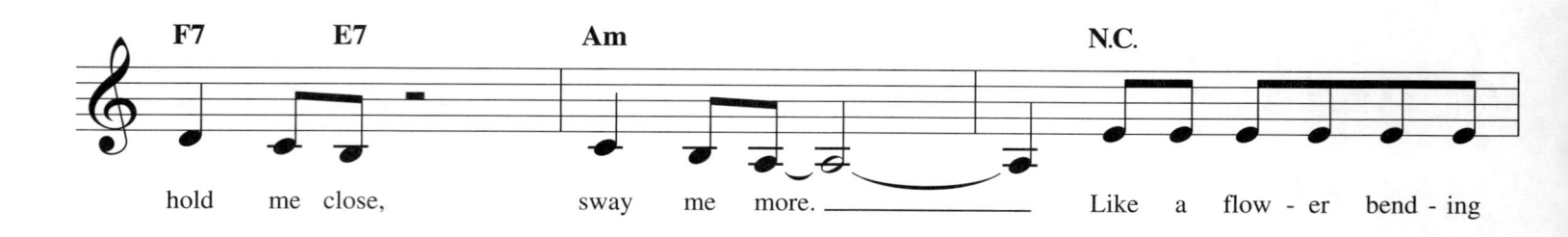

Moderately

When marimba rhythms start to play, dance with me, make me sway. Like the lazy ocean hugs the shore, hold me close, sway me more. Like a flower bending in the breeze, bend with me, sway with ease. When we dance you have a way with me, stay with me, sway with me. Other dancers may be on the floor, dear, but my eyes will see only you. Only you have that magic technique, when we sway I grow weak. *(Instrumental)* I can hear the sound of violins, long before it begins. Make me thrill as only you know how, sway me smooth, sway me now. When marimba rhythms Sway me now. Sway me smooth, sway me now.

Tango of Roses

Words by MARJORIE HARPER
Music by VITTORIO MASCHERONI

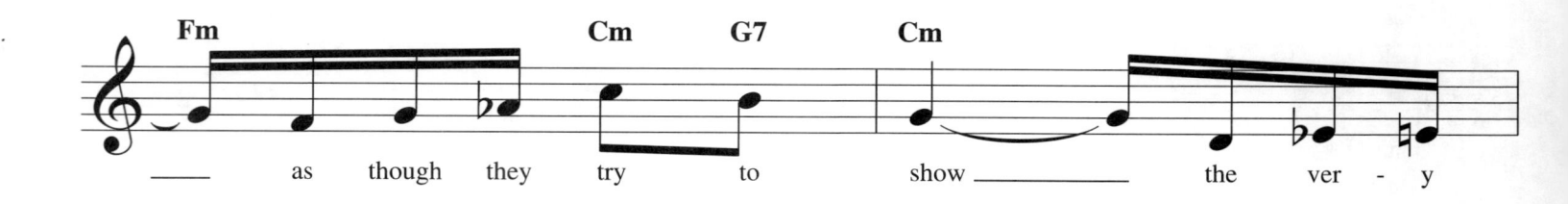

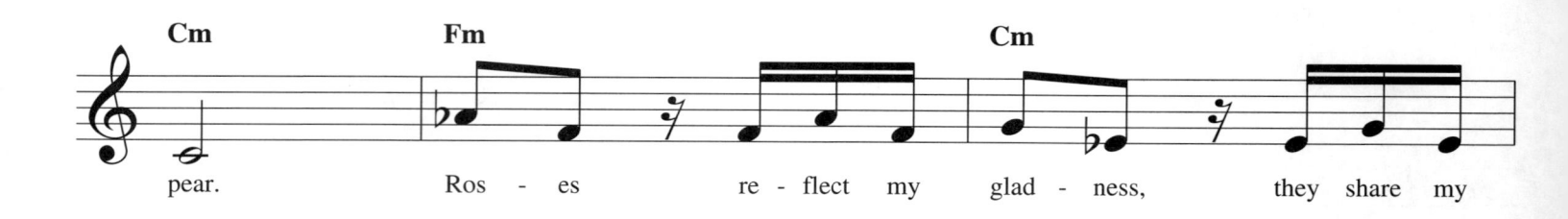

Moderately

See how red the roses grow, as though they try to show the very fire, the same desire, that you inspire when you appear. Roses reflect my gladness, they share my sadness when you're not near. They are the emblems of pas - sion, ro - mance and love. *(Instrumental)*

Ros - es try _____ to ech - o my de - vo - tion. _____

____ Ros - es seem _____ to mir - ror my e -

mo - tion. _____ Yet with - in _____ the dream - y tan - go of -

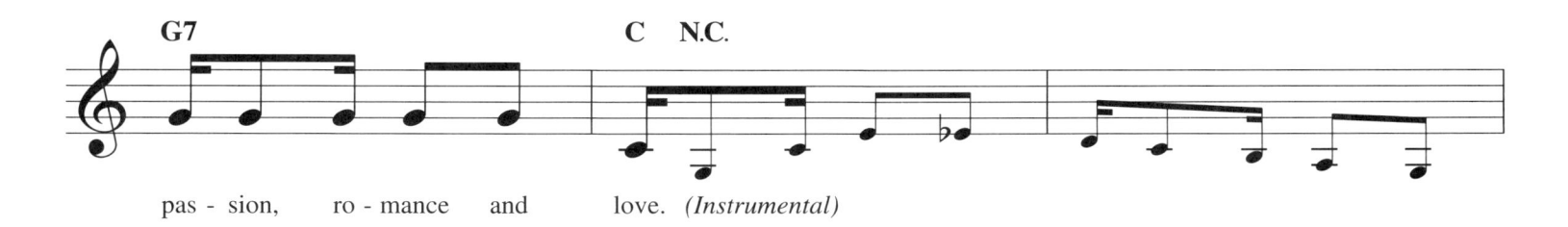

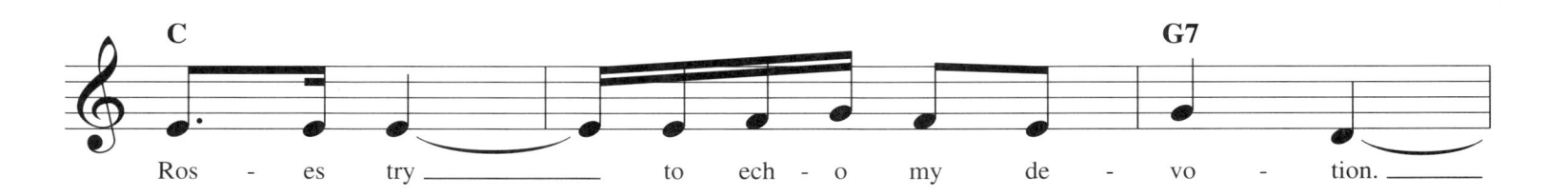

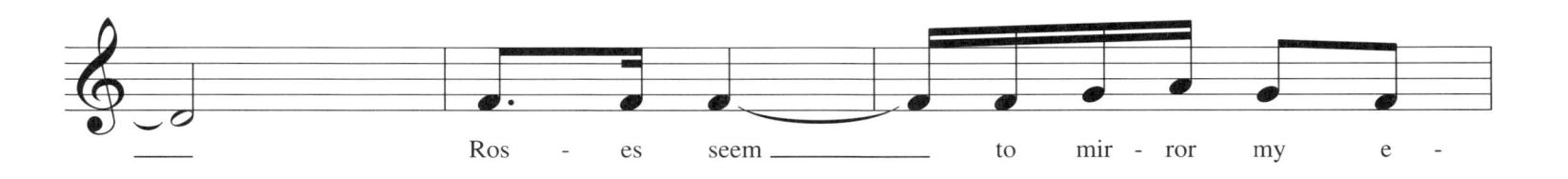

ros - es, my heart so will - ing - ly dis - clos - es;

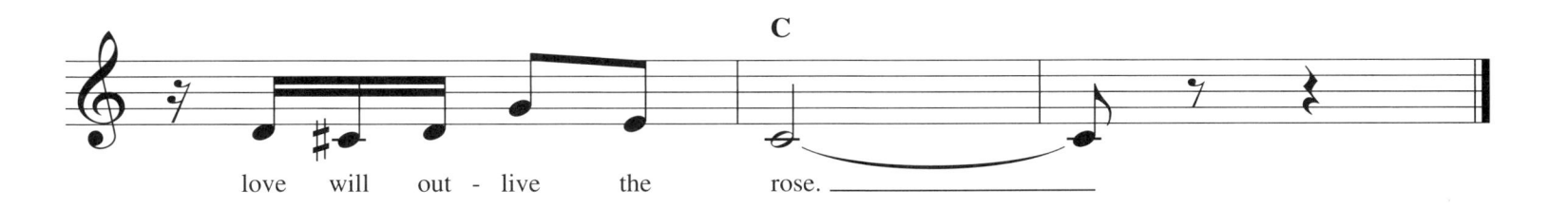

love will out - live the rose. _____

TELEPHONE SONG

English Words by NORMAN GIMBEL
Portuguese Words by RONALDO BOSCOLI
Music by ROBERTO MENESCAL

Copyright © 1965 by ON STAGE MUSIC, A Division of PAM PRODUCTIONS, INC.
Copyright Renewed
English Words Renewed 1993 by NORMAN GIMBEL and Assigned to
 GIMBEL MUSIC GROUP, INC. (P.O. Box 15221, Beverly Hills, CA 90209 USA) and
 ON STAGE MUSIC, A Division of PAM PRODUCTIONS, INC. for the world
All Rights Reserved   Used by Permission

Bossa Nova

Buzz, buzz, line is bus-y ev-'ry time that I phone. Buzz,
Tuem, tuem, oc-u-pa-do pe-la dec-im-a vez. Tuem,

he's the long-est talk-er I've ev-er known. Buzz,
tel-e-fon-e e não con-sig-o fal-ar. Tuem,

buzz, I've been try-ing now to reach him all day. Buzz,
tuem estou ou-vin-do há mui-to mais de um mês. Tuem,

when I get him I'll for-get what to say. (Should I call the op-er-
já com-e-ça quando eu pen-so em dis-car. (Eu já estou des-com-fi-

a-tor?) (Is the num-ber that I gave him my own?) Buzz,
an-do.) (Que e-la deu meu tel-e-fon-e p'ra mim.) Tuem,

buzz, I've been sit-ting here and dial-ing all day. Buzz,
tuem, e diz-er que a vid-a in-teir-a es-per-ei. Tuem,

got to get him and there must be a way. Buzz, buzz, if you heard the way he
que dei dur-o e me mat-ei p'ra en-con-trar. Tuem, tuem, tô-da a list-a quas e que

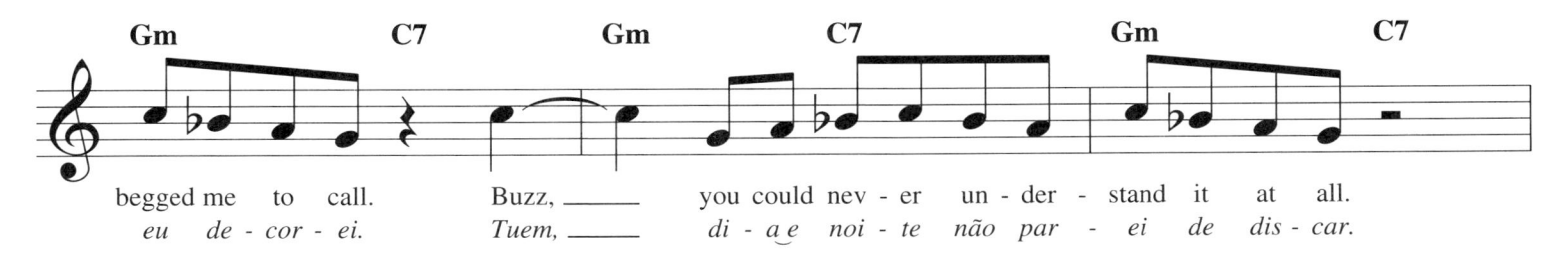

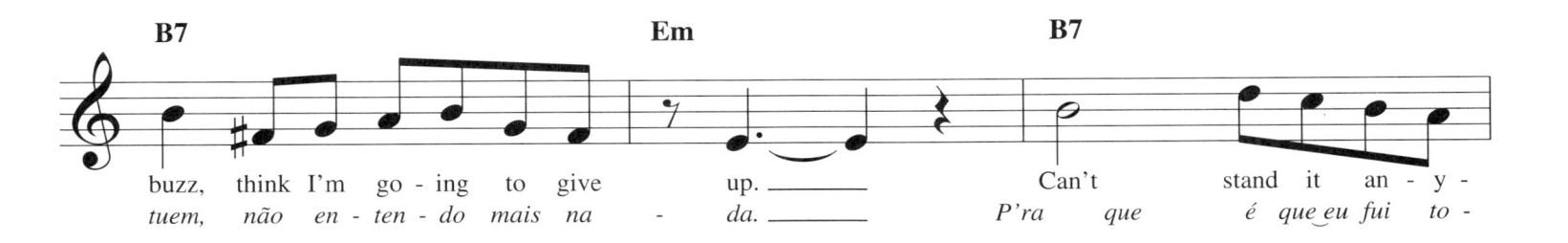

begged me to call. Buzz, _____ you could nev-er un-der-stand it at all.
eu de-cor-ei. Tuem, _____ di-a e noi-te não par-ei de dis-car.

(When I met him he was qui-et, _____ but now he learned to talk.) Buzz,
(E só vend-o com que jei-to, _____ Pe-dia p'ra eu lig-ar.) Tuem,

buzz, think I'm go-ing to give up. _____ Can't stand it an-y-
tuem, não en-ten-do mais na-da. _____ P'ra que é que eu fui to-

more. Buzz, buzz, I've de-cid-ed that our ro-mance is through.
par. Tuem, tuem, não me di-ga que a-gor-a at-en-deu.

Can it be true? The phone is ring-ing! I can't be-lieve it!
Se-rá, que eu? Eu com se-qui, a-gor-a en-con-trar! A

Wait till I say, "Hel-lo!" Buzz, lo!"
mo-ça at-en-deu, "A-lo." Tuem, lo."

TICO TICO
(Tico Tico No Fuba)

Copyright © 1943 by Irmaos Vitale S.A.
Copyright Renewed
All Rights Administered by Peer International Corporation
International Copyright Secured   All Rights Reserved

Words and Music by ZEQUINHA ABREU,
ALOYSIO OLIVEIRA and ERVIN DRAKE

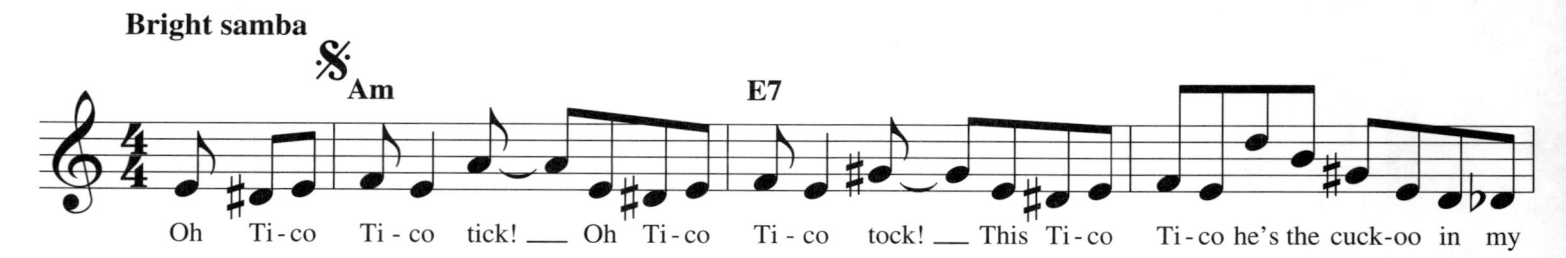

Bright samba

Oh Ti-co Ti-co tick! __ Oh Ti-co Ti-co tock! __ This Ti-co Ti-co he's the cuck-oo in my clock. And when he says: "Cuck-oo!" __ he means it's time to woo; __ it's "Ti-co time" for all the lov-ers in the block. I've got a heav-y date __ a tête-à-tête at eight, __ so speak, oh Ti-co, tell me is it get-ting late? If I'm on time: "Cuck-oo!" __ but if I'm late, "Woo-woo!" __ The one my heart has gone to may not want to wait! For just a bir-die, and a bir-die who goes no-where, he knows of ev-'ry Lov-ers' Lane and how to go there. For in af-fairs of the heart, __ my Ti-co's ter - ri - bly smart. He tells me: "Gent - ly sen - ti - ment - 'ly at the start!" Oh - oh, I hear my lit - tle Ti - co Ti - co call - ing, be - cause the time is right and shades of night are fall - ing. I love that not - so - cuck - oo cuck - oo in the clock: Ti - co Ti - co Ti - co Ti - co Ti - co tock. tock.

Interlude

TIME WAS

Copyright © 1936 by Southern Music Pub. Co. Inc.
Copyright Renewed
International Copyright Secured All Rights Reserved

English Words by S.K. RUSSELL
Music by MIGUEL PRADO

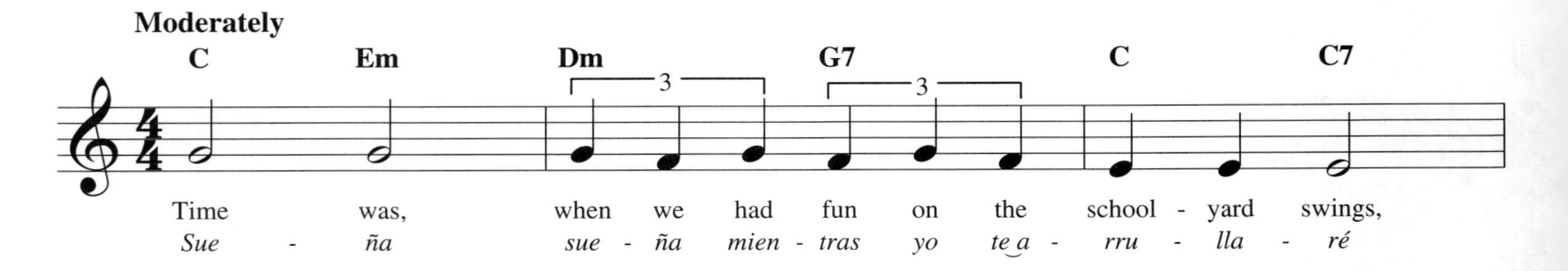

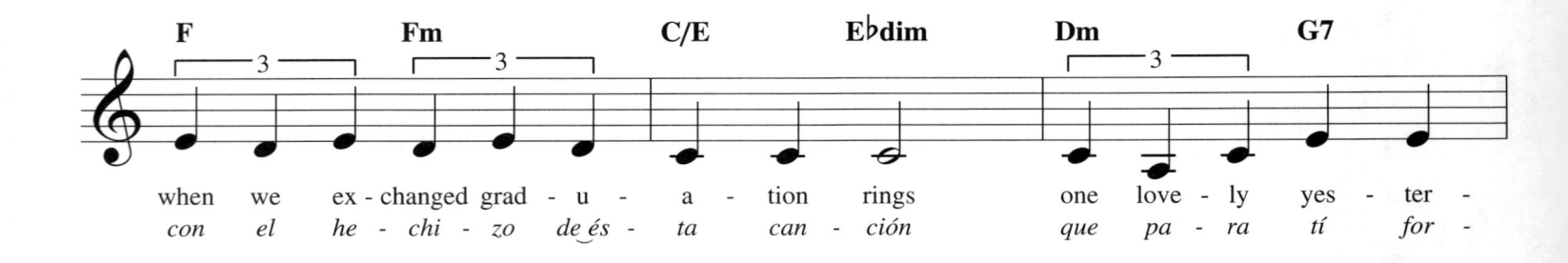

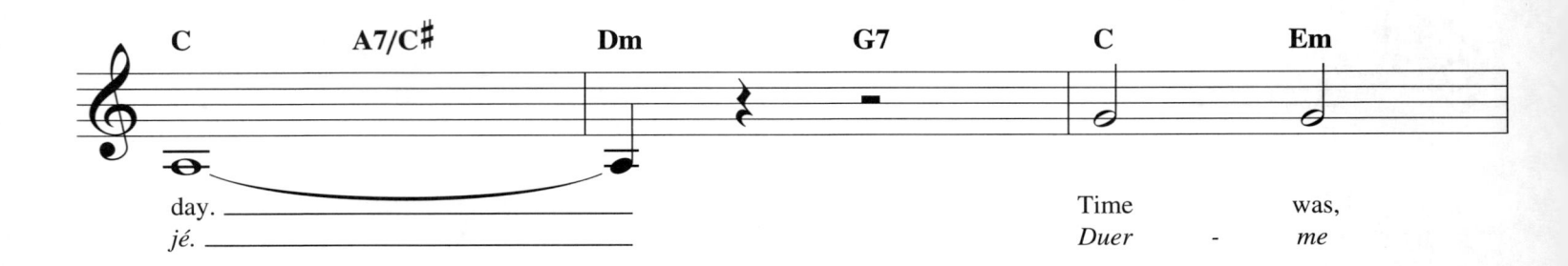

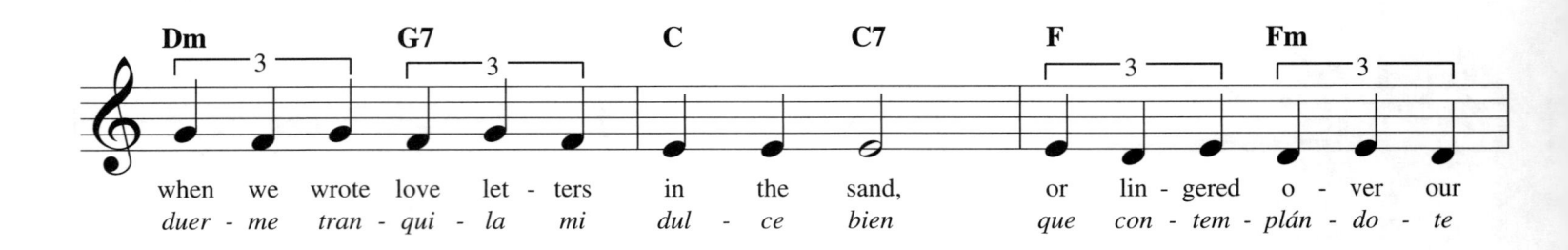

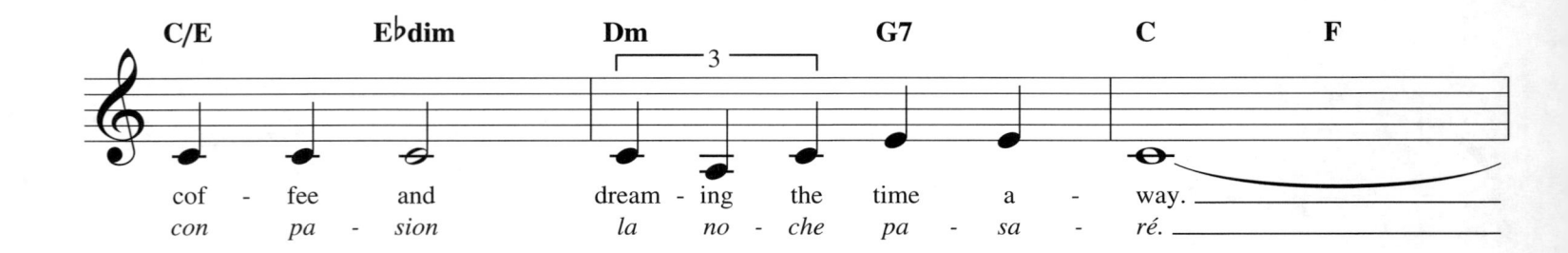

Moderately

Time was, when we had fun on the school-yard swings,
Sue - ña sue - ña mien - tras yo te a - rru - lla - ré

when we ex-changed grad-u-a-tion rings one love-ly yes-ter-
con el he - chi - zo de és - ta can - ción que pa - ra tí for -

day. Time was,
jé. Duer - me

when we wrote love let-ters in the sand, or lin-gered o-ver our
duer - me tran - qui - la mi dul - ce bien que con - tem - plán - do - te

cof - fee and dream-ing the time a - way.
con pa - sion la no - che pa - sa - ré.

183

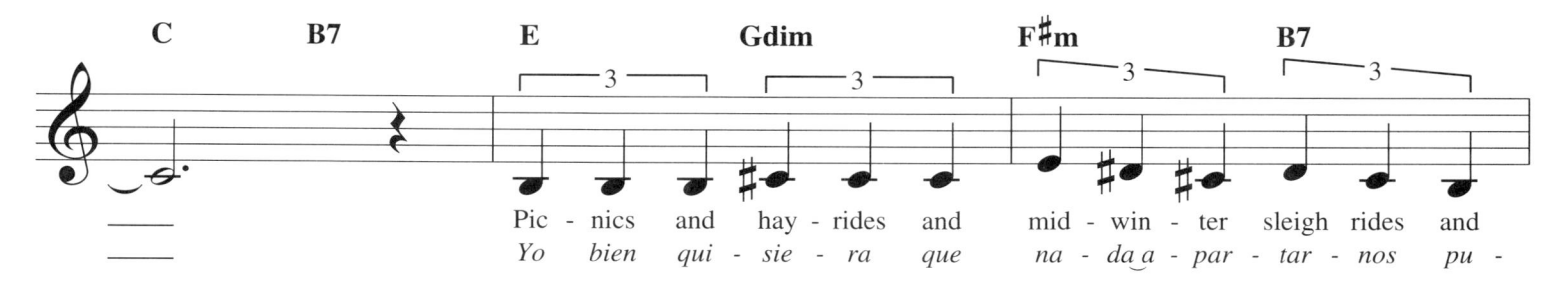

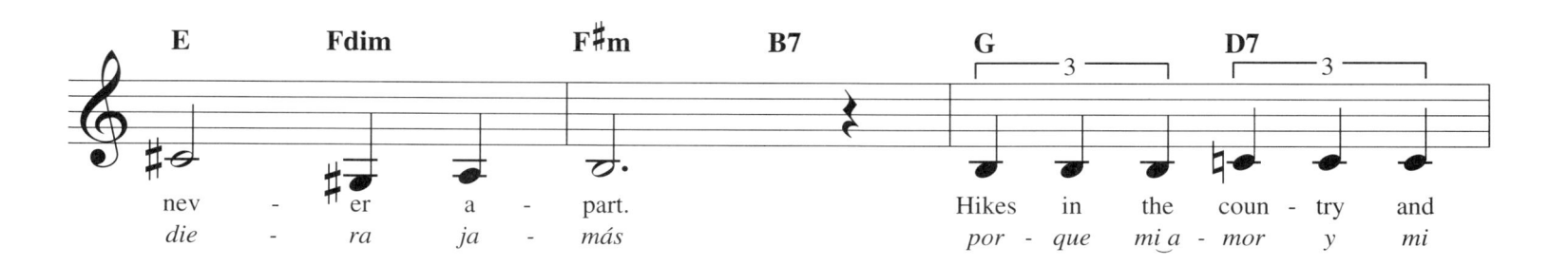

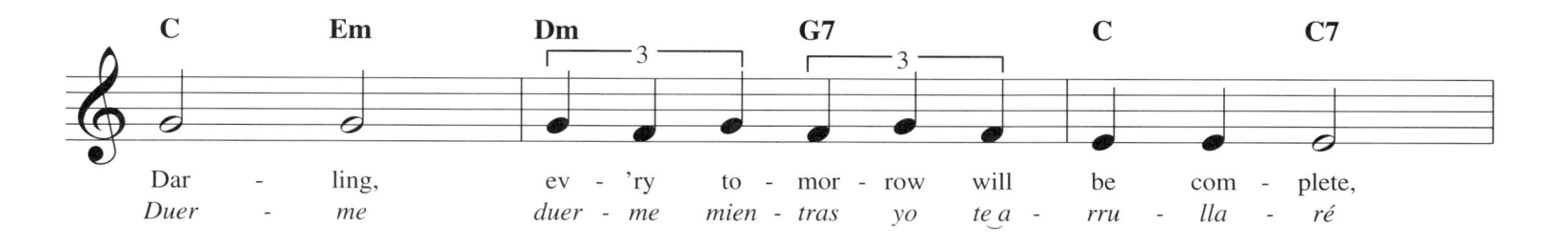

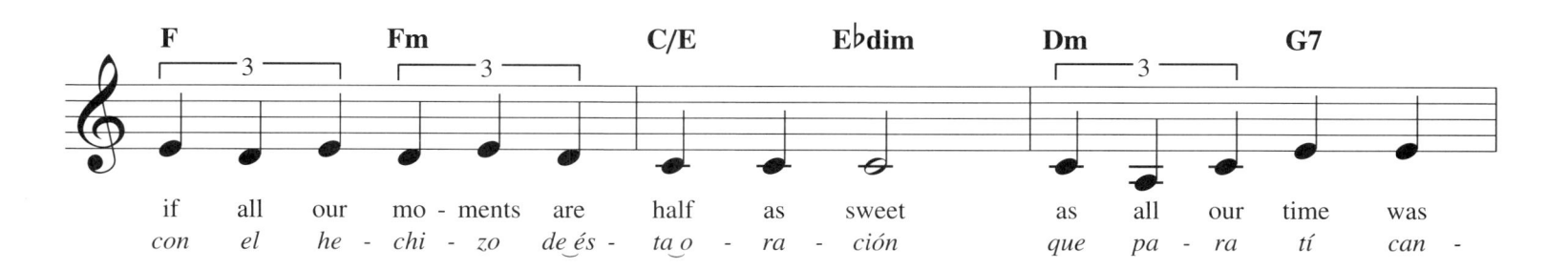

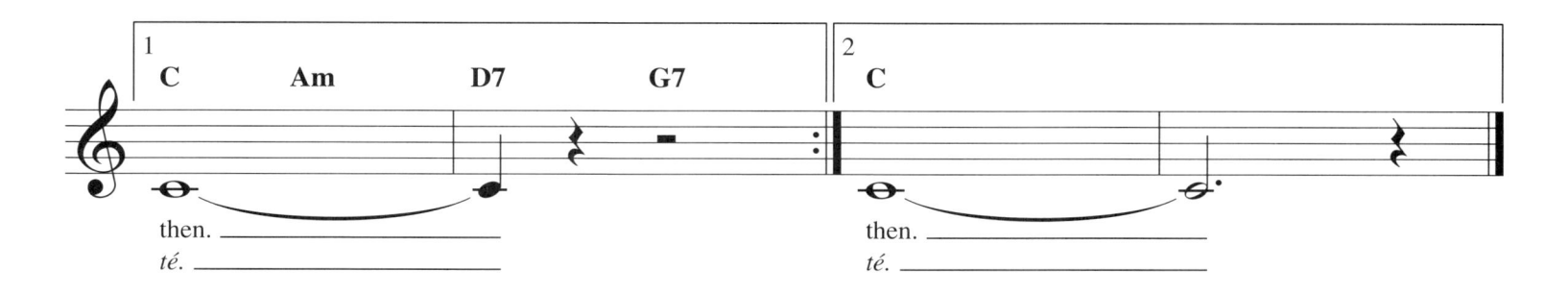

| | C | B7 | E | Gdim | F#m | B7 |

Pic - nics and hay - rides and mid - win - ter sleigh rides and
Yo bien qui - sie - ra que na - da a - par - tar - nos pu -

| E | Fdim | F#m | B7 | G | D7 |

nev - er a - part. Hikes in the coun - try and
die - ra ja - más por - que mi a - mor y mi

| G | D7 | G | G7 |

there's more than one tree on which I've a place in your heart.
vi - da y mi to - do e - res tú mu - jer - ci - ta i - deal.

| C | Em | Dm | G7 | C | C7 |

Dar - ling, ev - 'ry to - mor - row will be com - plete,
Duer - me duer - me mien - tras yo te a - rru - lla - ré

| F | Fm | C/E | E♭dim | Dm | G7 |

if all our mo - ments are half as sweet as all our time was
con el he - chi - zo de és - ta o - ra - ción que pa - ra tí can -

1. | C | Am | D7 | G7 | 2. | C |

then. _____
té. _____

then. _____
té. _____

TRISTE

By ANTONIO CARLOS JOBIM

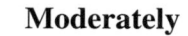

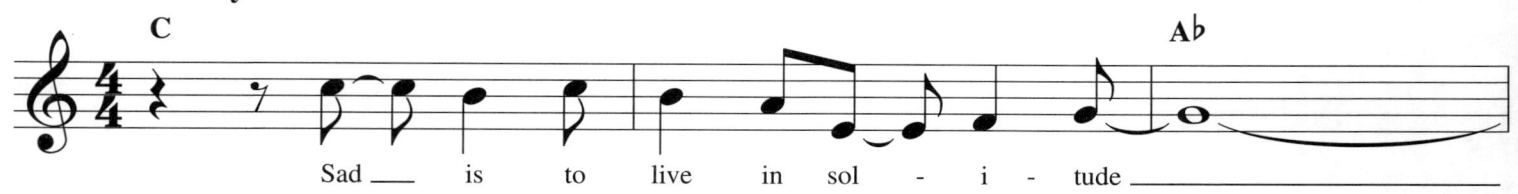

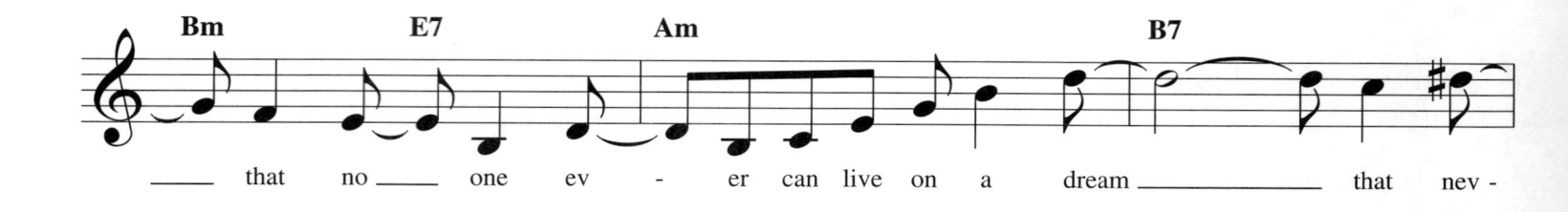

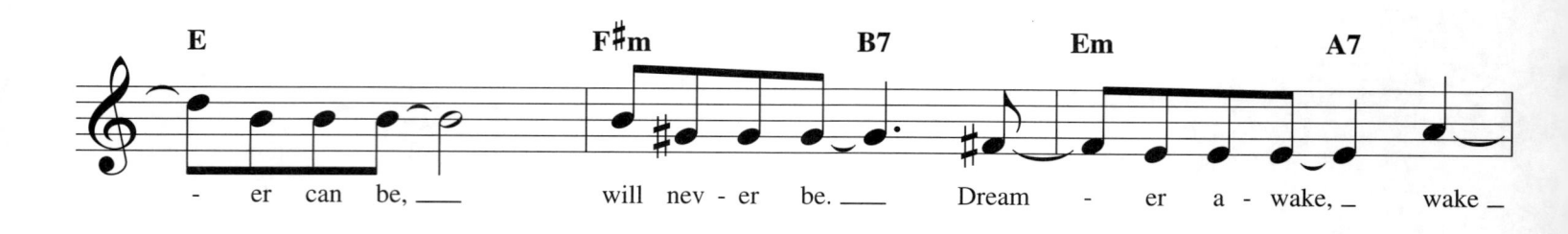

Moderately

Sad is to live in sol-i-tude far from your tran-quil al-ti-tude. Sad is to know that no one ev-er can live on a dream that nev-er can be, will never be. Dream-er a-wake, wake up and see. Your beau-ty is an aer-o-plane

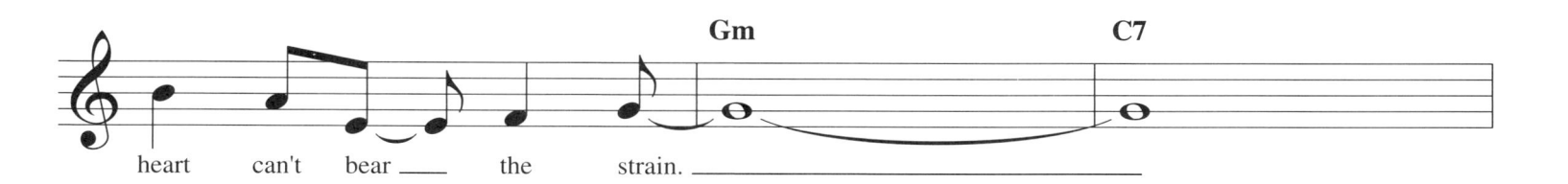

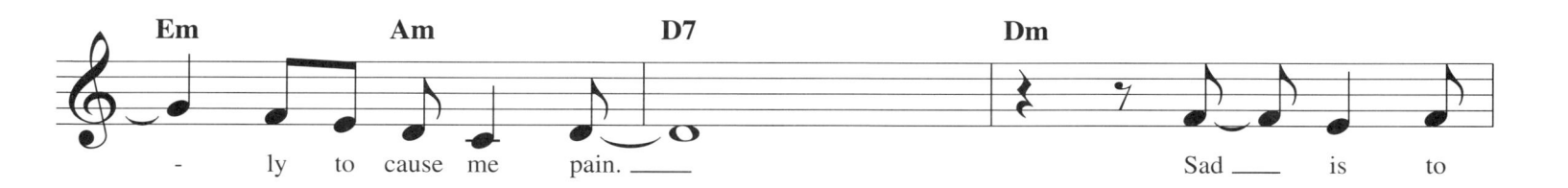

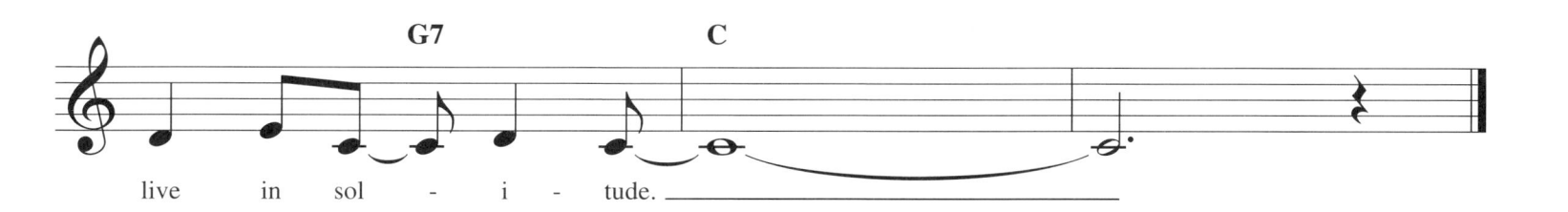

Portuguese Lyrics

Triste é viver a na solidão
Na dor cruel de uma paixão
Triste é saber que ninguem pade viver de ilusão
Que nunca vai ser, nunca dar
O sonhador tem que acordar.

Tua beleze é um auião
Demals prá um pobre coracao
Que para pra te ver passar
So pra se maltratar
Triste é viver na solidád.

VAYA CON DIOS
(May God Be with You)

Words and Music by LARRY RUSSELL, INEZ JAMES and BUDDY PEPPER

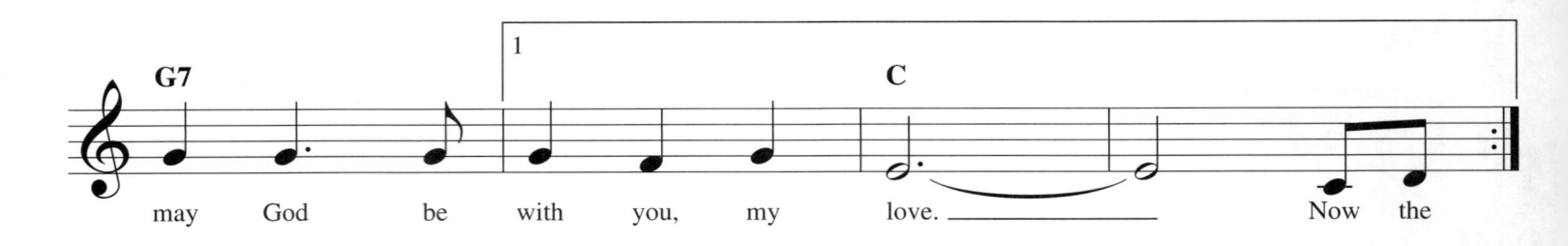

Copyright © 1953 by Beachaven Music and Jarest Music
Copyright Renewed 1981
International Copyright Secured   All Rights Reserved

Moderately

Now the ha-ci-en-da's dark, the town is sleep-ing.
vil-lage mis-sion bells are soft-ly ring-ing.

Now the time has come to part, the time for weep-ing.
If you lis-ten with your heart you'll hear them sing-ing.

Va-ya Con Di-os, my dar-ling,

may God be with you, my love. Now the

with you, my love. Wher-ev-er you may be

I'll be be-side you. Al-though you're man-y mil-lion

dreams a-way. Each night I'll say a pray'r, a pray'r to guide you to hasten ev'ry lonely hour of ev'ry lonely day. Now the dawn is breaking through a gray tomorrow. But the mem-o-ries we share are there to borrow. Vaya Con Dios, my darling, may God be with you, my love.

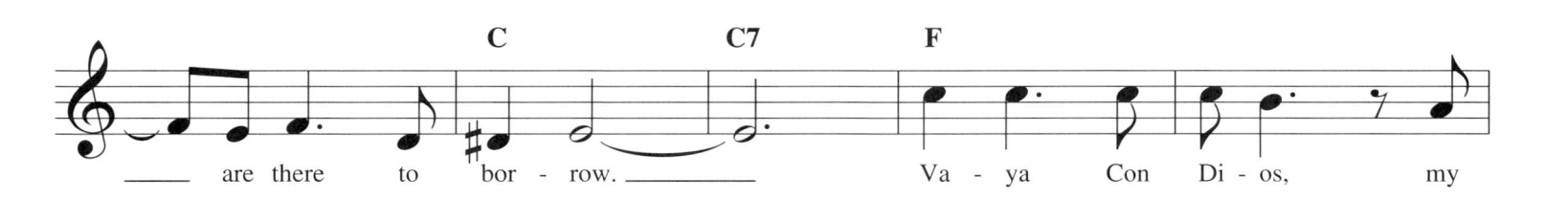

VIVO SONHANDO
(Dreamer)

Copyright © 1963, 1968 Antonio Carlos Jobim
Copyrights Renewed
Published by Corcovado Music Corp.
International Copyright Secured   All Rights Reserved

Words and Music by ANTONIO CARLOS JOBIM
English Lyrics by GENE LEES

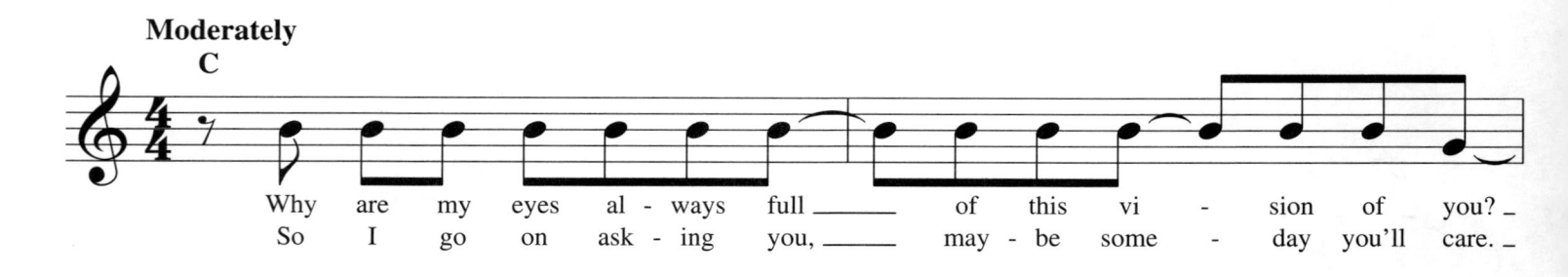

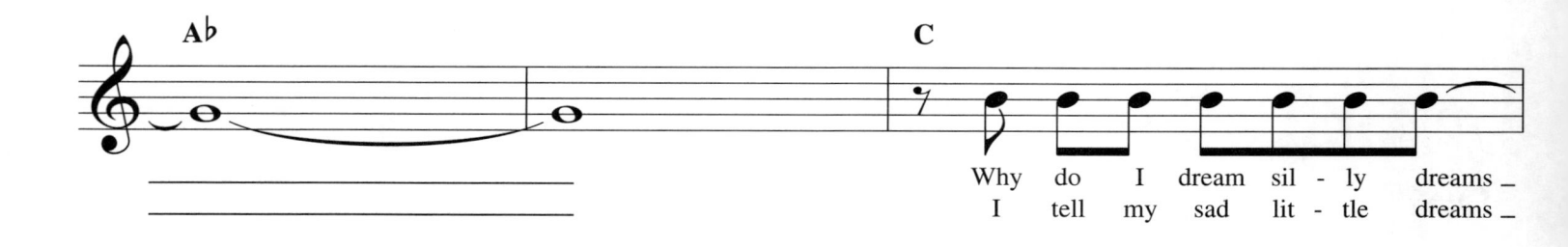

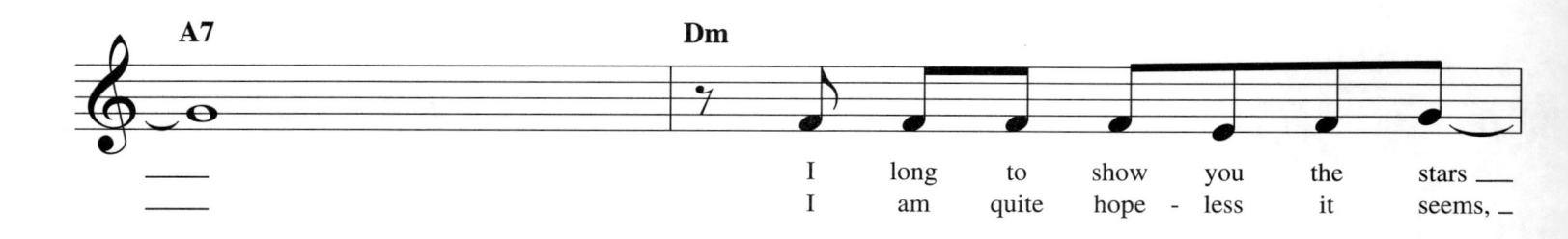

Moderately

Why are my eyes al - ways full of this vi - sion of you?
So I go on ask - ing you, may - be some - day you'll care.

Why do I dream sil - ly dreams
I tell my sad lit - tle dreams

that I fear won't come true?
to the soft eve - ning air.

I long to show you the stars
I am quite hope - less it seems,

1.
caught in the dark of the sea.

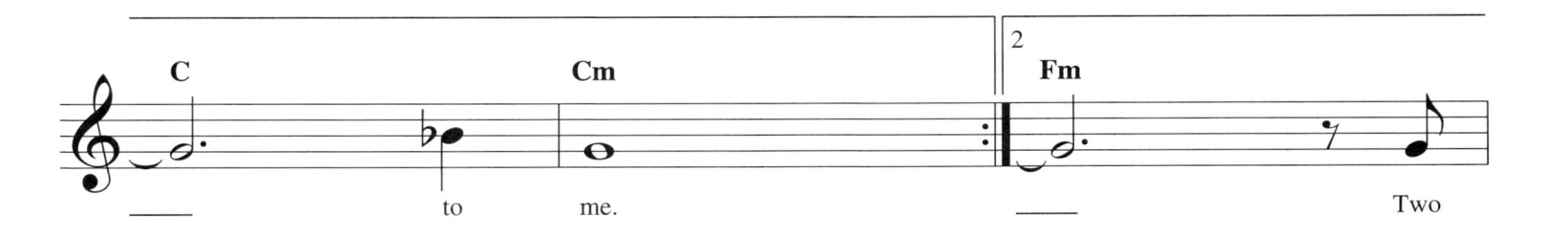

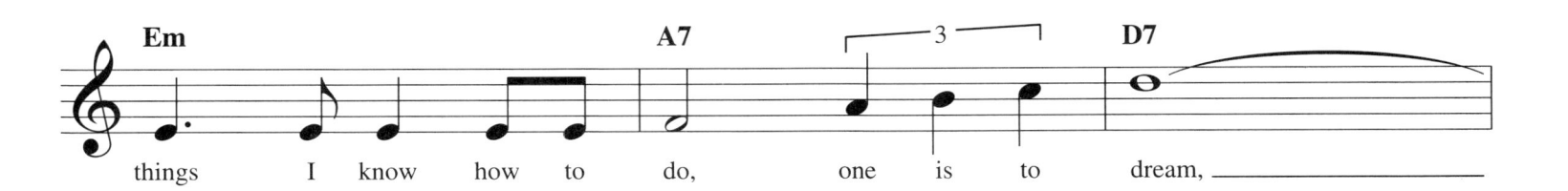

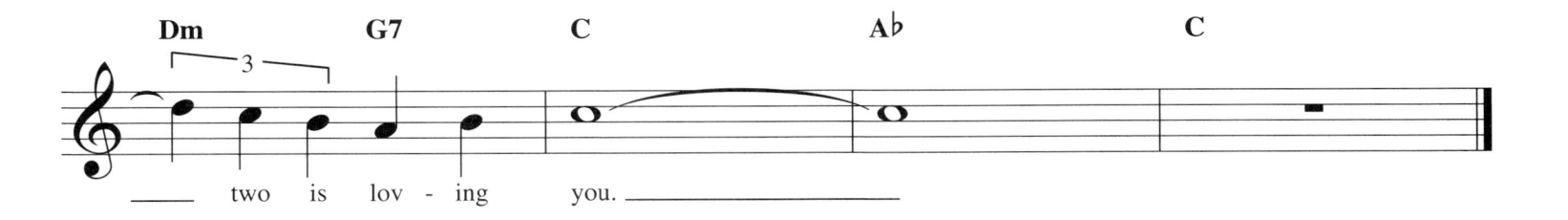

Portuguese lyrics

Vivo sonhando, Sonhando mil horas sem fim
Tempo em que vou perguntando Se gostas de mim
Tempo de falar em estrelas
Falar de um mar De um céu assim
Falar do bem que se tem mas você não vem
Não vem Você não vindo, Não vindo a vida tem fim
Gente que passa sorrindo zombando de mim
E eu a falar em estrelas, mar, amor, luar
Pobre de mim que só sei te a-mar

Watch What Happens
from THE UMBRELLAS OF CHERBOURG

Music by MICHEL LEGRAND
Original French Text by JACQUES DEMY
English Lyrics by NORMAN GIMBEL

Copyright © 1964 PRODUCTIONS MICHEL LEGRAND
and PRODUCTIONS FRANCIS LEMARQUE
Copyright © 1965 UNIVERSAL - SONGS OF POLYGRAM INTERNATIONAL, INC.
and JONWARE MUSIC CORP.
Copyright Renewed; English words Renewed 1993 by NORMAN GIMBEL and
Assigned to Gimbel Music Group, Inc. (P.O. Box 15221, Beverly Hills, CA 90209 USA)

Moderately

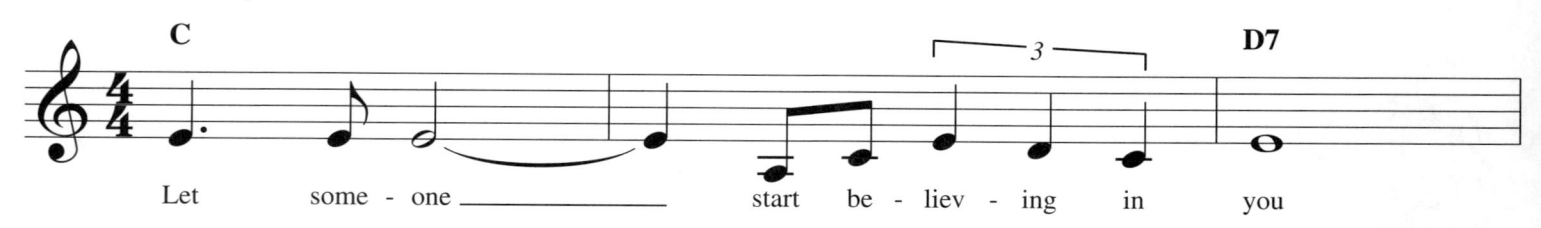

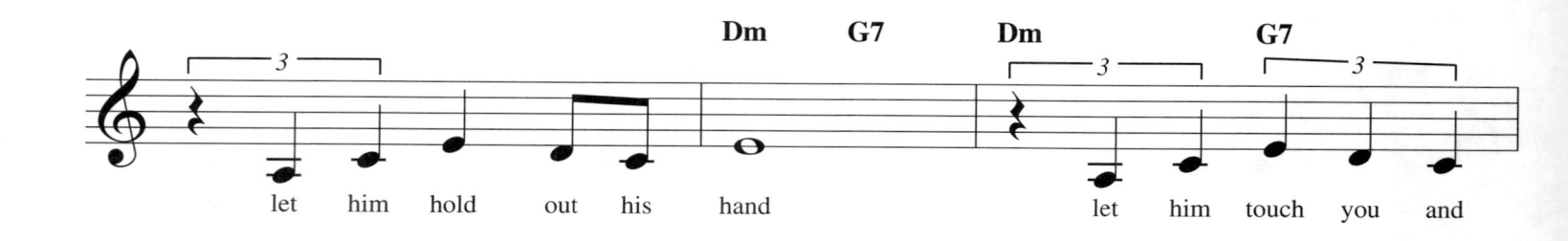

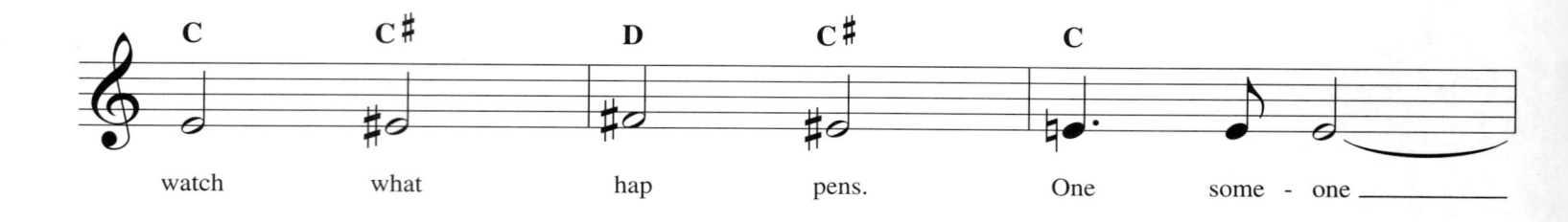

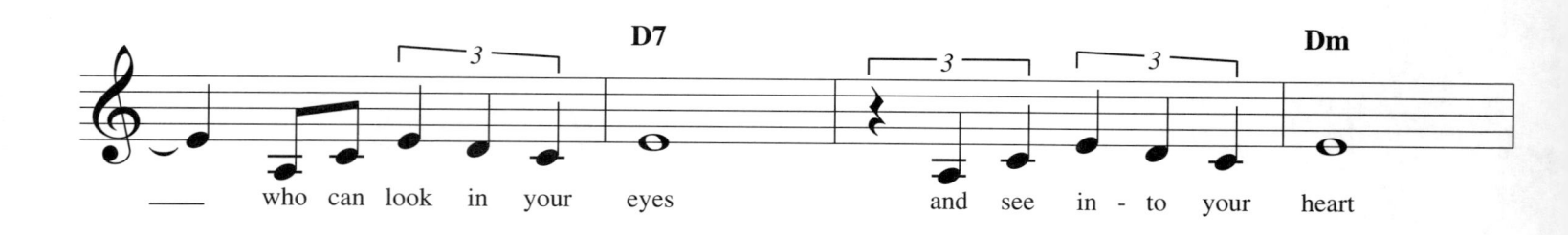

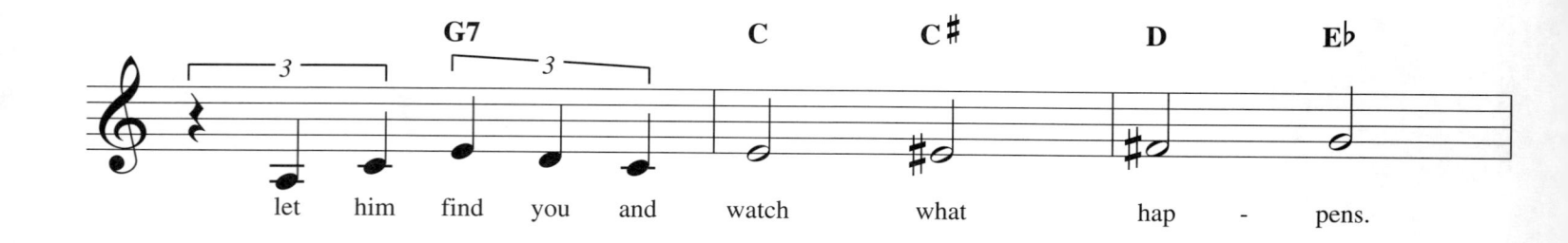

Let some - one _____ start be - liev - ing in you

let him hold out his hand let him touch you and

watch what hap pens. One some - one _____

who can look in your eyes and see in - to your heart

let him find you and watch what hap - pens.

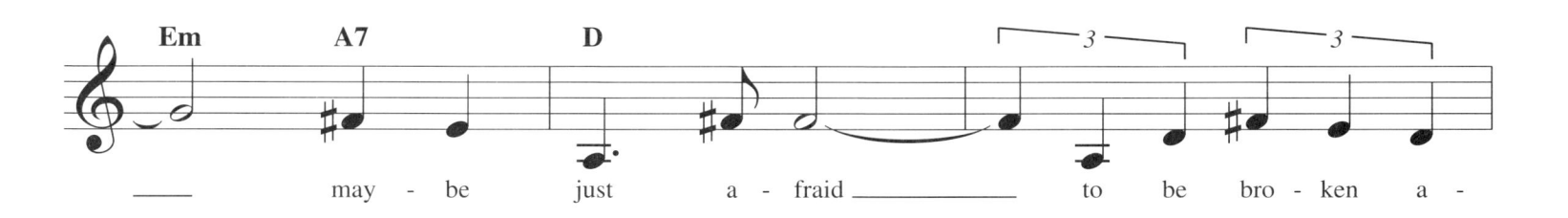

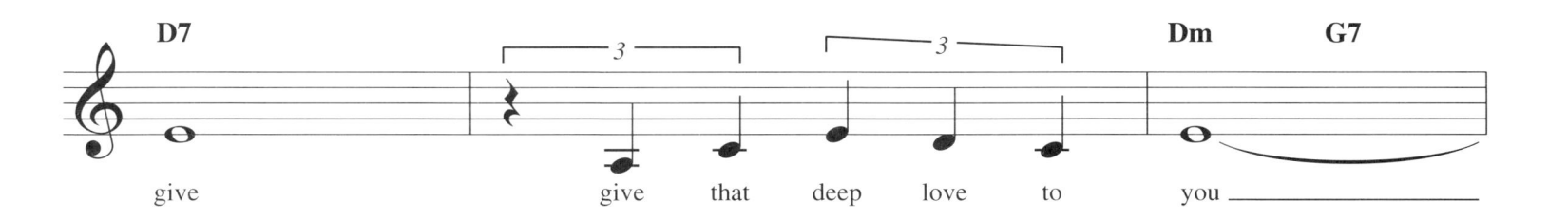

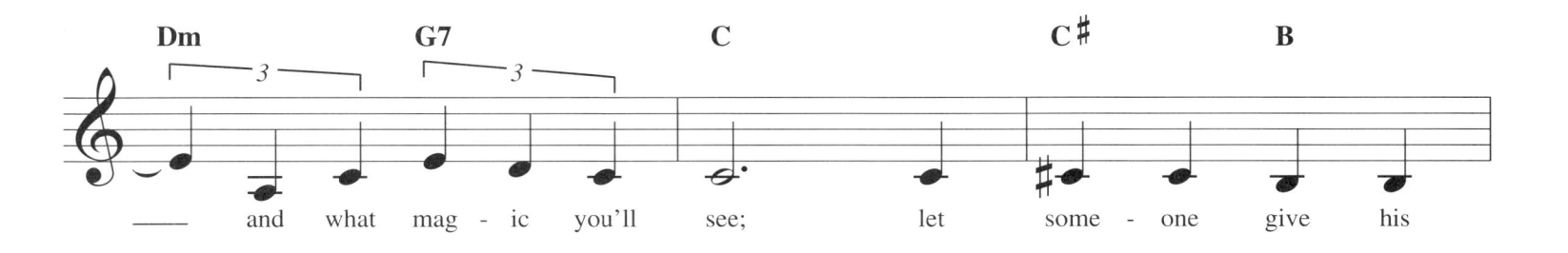

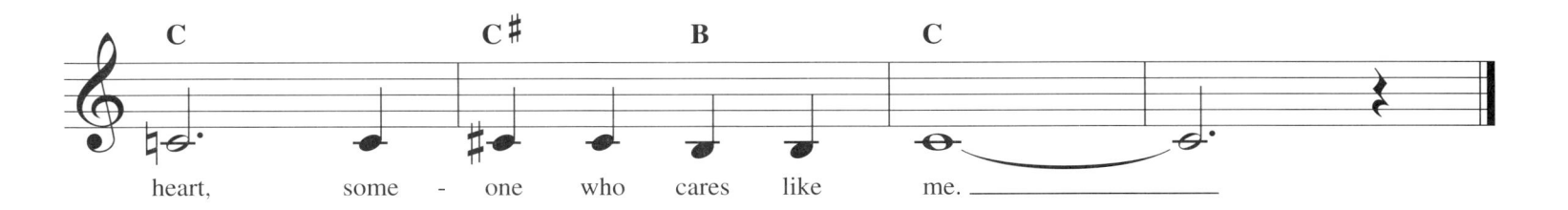

Cold, no I won't be-lieve your heart is cold maybe just a-fraid to be bro-ken a-gain. Let some-one with a deep love to give give that deep love to you and what mag-ic you'll see; let some-one give his heart, some-one who cares like me.

WAVE

Words and Music by
ANTONIO CARLOS JOBIM

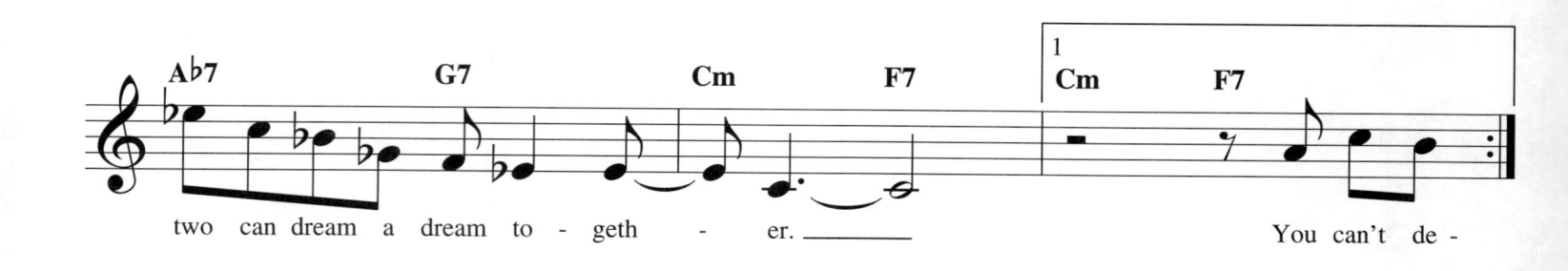

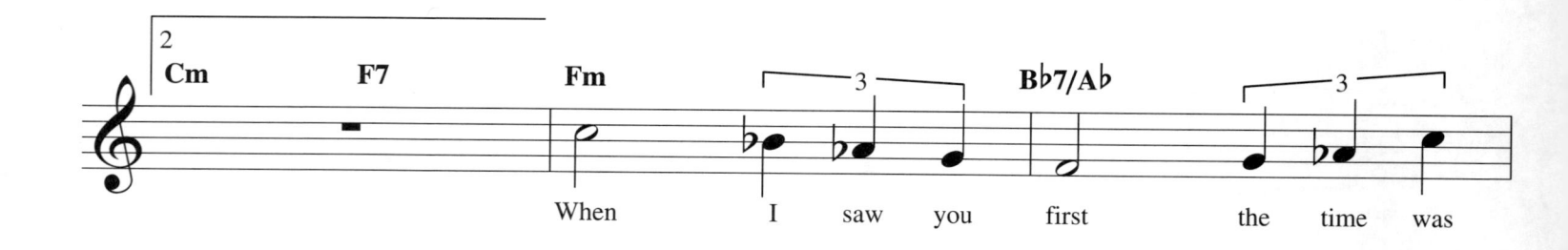

Copyright © 1967, 1968 Antonio Carlos Jobim
Copyright Renewed
Published by Corcovado Music Corp.
International Copyright Secured   All Rights Reserved

Medium Bossa Nova

So close your eyes, _____ for that's a lovely way to be. _____
ny, _____ don't try to fight the rising sea. _____

A-ware _____ of things _____ your heart a-lone _____ was meant _____ to see.
Don't fight _____ the moon, _____ the stars a-bove _____ and don't _____ fight me.

The fun-da-men-tal lone - li-ness goes _____ when-ev-er

two can dream a dream to-geth - er. _____ You can't de-

When I saw you first the time was

[Gm] half past three, [Ab7] when your eyes met

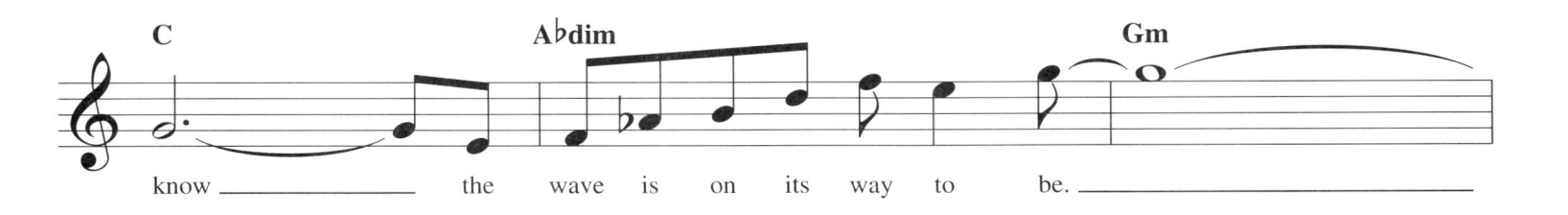

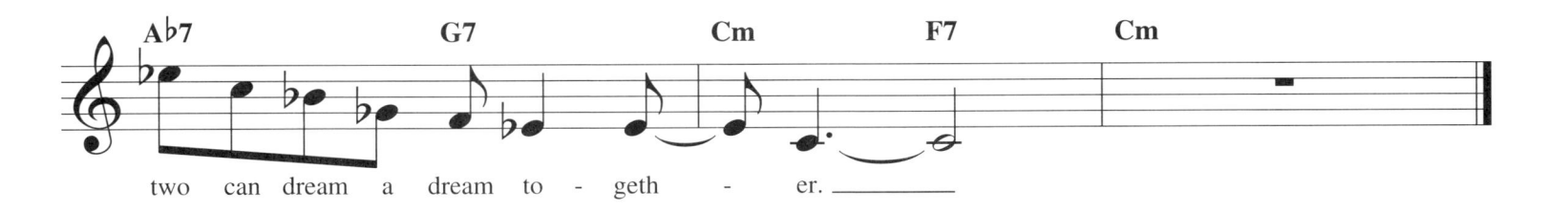

[Ab7/Gb] mine it was e-ter-ni-ty. [Fm] [G7] By now we

[C] know the wave is on its way to be. [Abdim] [Gm]

[C7] Just catch the wave, [F] don't be a-fraid [Fm] of lov-ing me.

[E7] [A7] The fun-da-men-tal lone-li-ness goes when-ev-er [D7]

[Ab7] two can dream a [G7] dream to-[Cm]geth - [F7] er. [Cm]

YELLOW DAYS

English Lyric by ALAN BERNSTEIN
Music and Spanish Lyric by ALVARO CARRILLO

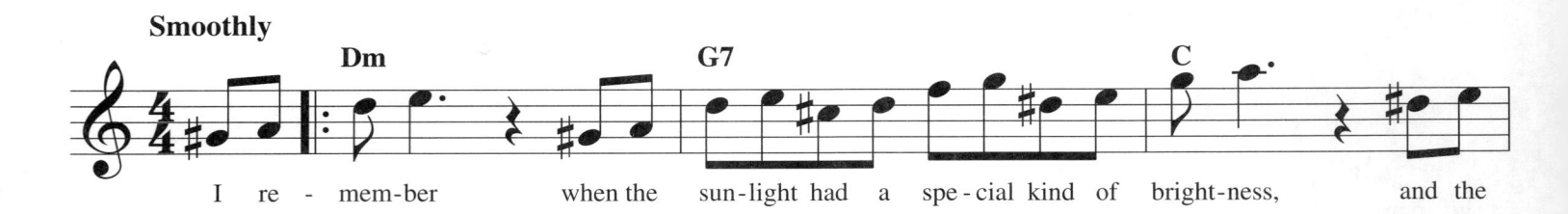

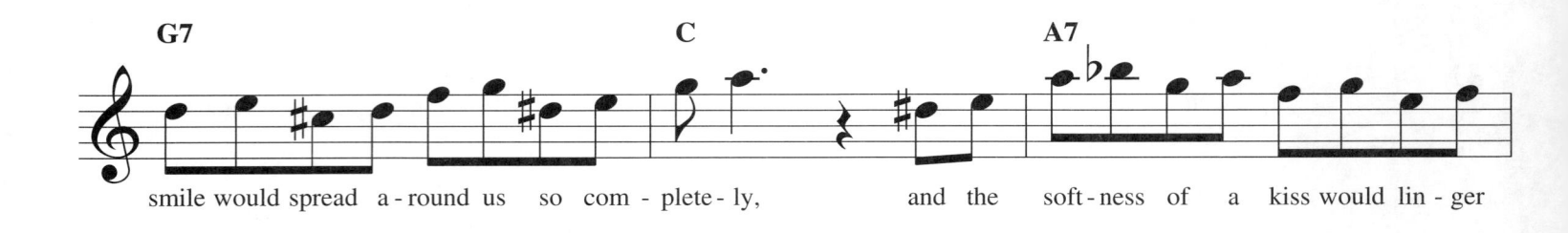

Smoothly

I re-mem-ber when the sun-light had a spe-cial kind of bright-ness, and the laugh-ter held a lov-er's kind of light-ness, yel-low days, yel-low days. She would hold me and a smile would spread a-round us so com-plete-ly, and the soft-ness of a kiss would lin-ger sweet-ly, yel-low days, yel-low days. But then came thun-der and I heard her say good-bye through tears of won - der; now I'm all a - lone and my heart wants to know, yel - low days, where'd you go? _____ Life is emp - ty and the sun - light seems so harsh in - stead of ten - der, and the laugh - ter's just an ech - o I re - mem - ber from yel - low days, yel - low

1. days. I re-
2. days.

Life is emp - ty and the sun - light seems so harsh in - stead of ten - der, and the laugh - ter's just an ech - o I re - mem - ber from yel - low days, yel - low days. _____

YOU BELONG TO MY HEART
(Solamente Una Vez)

Music and Spanish Words by AGUSTIN LARA
English Words by RAY GILBERT

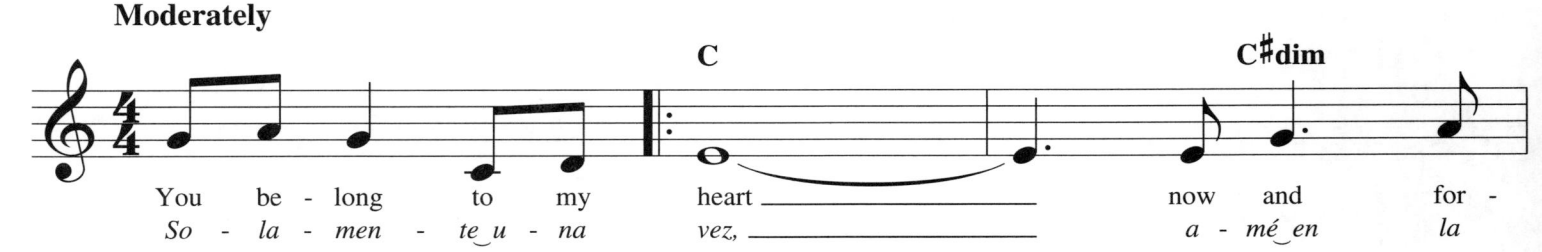

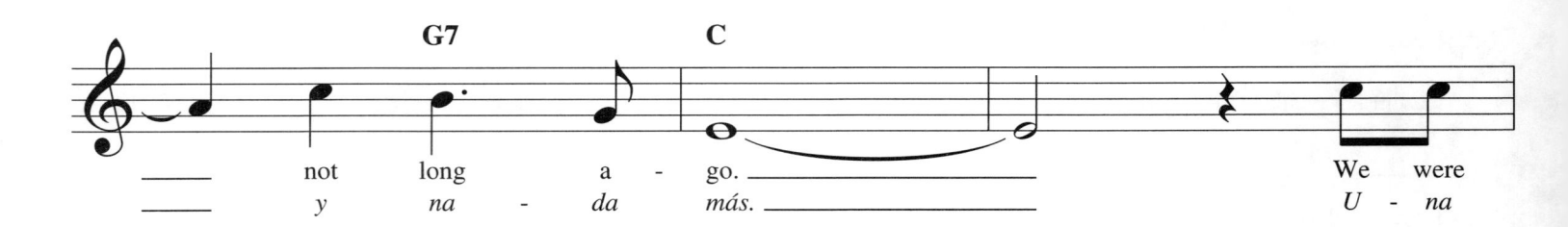

Moderately

You be-long to my heart ____ now and for-ev-er, and our love had its start ____ not long a-go. ____ We were gath-er-ing stars while a mil-lion gui-tars played our love song. ____ When I said, "I love you," ev-'ry beat of my heart said it too. 'Twas a mo-ment like

So- la- men- te u- na vez, ____ a- mé en la vi- da, so- la- men- te u- na vez, ____ y na- da más. ____ U- na vez na- da más en mi huer- to bri- lló la es- pe- ran- za, ____ la es- pe- ran- za que a- lum- bra el ca- mi- no de mi so- le- dad. U- na vez na- da

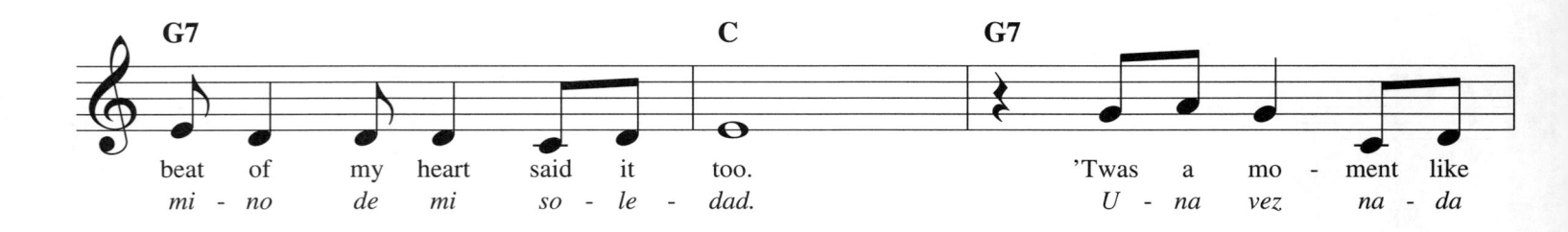

this, do you re - mem - ber?
más se en - tre - ga el al - ma,

And your eyes threw a kiss when they met
con la dul - ce y to - tal re - nun - cia -

mine. Now we own all the stars and a
ción. Y cuan - do e - se mi - la - gro rea -

mil - lion gui - tars are still play - ing. Dar - ling,
li - za el pro - di - gio de a - mar - se, Hay cam -

1.
you are the song and you'll al - ways be - long to my
pa - nas de fies - ta que can - tan en el co - ra -

heart. You be - long to my
zón. So - la - men - te u - na

2.
you are the song and you'll al - ways be - long to my heart.
pa - nas de fies - ta que can - tan en el co - ra - zón.

CHORD SPELLER

C chords	
C	C–E–G
Cm	C–E♭–G
C7	C–E–G–B♭
Cdim	C–E♭–G♭
C+	C–E–G♯

C♯ or D♭ chords	
C♯	C♯–F–G♯
C♯m	C♯–E–G♯
C♯7	C♯–F–G♯–B
C♯dim	C♯–E–G
C♯+	C♯–F–A

D chords	
D	D–F♯–A
Dm	D–F–A
D7	D–F♯–A–C
Ddim	D–F–A♭
D+	D–F♯–A♯

E♭ chords	
E♭	E♭–G–B♭
E♭m	E♭–G♭–B♭
E♭7	E♭–G–B♭–D♭
E♭dim	E♭–G♭–A
E♭+	E♭–G–B

E chords	
E	E–G♯–B
Em	E–G–B
E7	E–G♯–B–D
Edim	E–G–B♭
E+	E–G♯–C

F chords	
F	F–A–C
Fm	F–A♭–C
F7	F–A–C–E♭
Fdim	F–A♭–B
F+	F–A–C♯

F♯ or G♭ chords	
F♯	F♯–A♯–C♯
F♯m	F♯–A–C♯
F♯7	F♯–A♯–C♯–E
F♯dim	F♯–A–C
F♯+	F♯–A♯–D

G chords	
G	G–B–D
Gm	G–B♭–D
G7	G–B–D–F
Gdim	G–B♭–D♭
G+	G–B–D♯

G♯ or A♭ chords	
A♭	A♭–C–E♭
A♭m	A♭–B–E♭
A♭7	A♭–C–E♭–G♭
A♭dim	A♭–B–D
A♭+	A♭–C–E

A chords	
A	A–C♯–E
Am	A–C–E
A7	A–C♯–E–G
Adim	A–C–E♭
A+	A–C♯–F

B♭ chords	
B♭	B♭–D–F
B♭m	B♭–D♭–F
B♭7	B♭–D–F–A♭
B♭dim	B♭–D♭–E
B♭+	B♭–D–F♯

B chords	
B	B–D♯–F♯
Bm	B–D–F♯
B7	B–D♯–F♯–A
Bdim	B–D–F
B+	B–D♯–G

Important Note: A slash chord (C/E, G/B) tells you that a certain bass note is to be played under a particular harmony. In the case of C/E, the chord is C and the bass note is E.

HAL LEONARD PRESENTS
FAKE BOOKS FOR BEGINNERS!

Entry-level fake books! These books feature larger-than-most fake book notation with simplified harmonies and melodies – and all songs are in the key of C. An introduction addresses basic instruction in playing from a fake book.

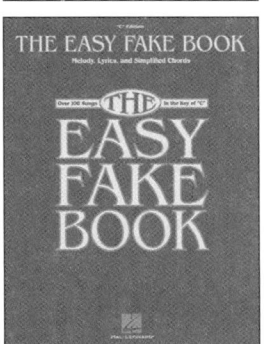

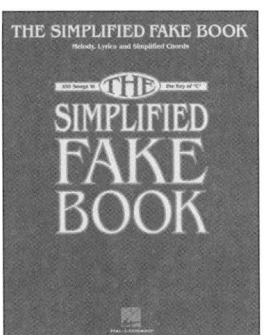

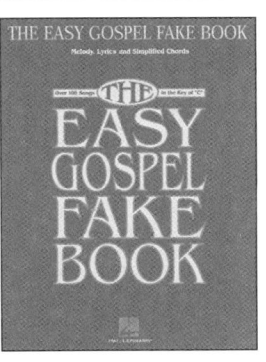

YOUR FIRST FAKE BOOK
00240112.................$19.95

THE EASY FAKE BOOK
00240144.................$19.95

THE SIMPLIFIED FAKE BOOK
00240168.................$19.95

THE BEATLES EASY FAKE BOOK
00240309.................$19.95

THE EASY BROADWAY FAKE BOOK
00240180.................$19.95

THE EASY CHRISTMAS FAKE BOOK – 2ND EDITION
00240209.................$19.95

THE EASY CLASSICAL FAKE BOOK
00240262.................$19.95

THE EASY CONTEMPORARY CHRISTIAN FAKE BOOK
00240328.................$19.95

THE EASY GOSPEL FAKE BOOK
00240169.................$19.95

THE EASY HYMN FAKE BOOK
00240207.................$19.95

THE EASY MOVIE FAKE BOOK
00240295.................$19.95

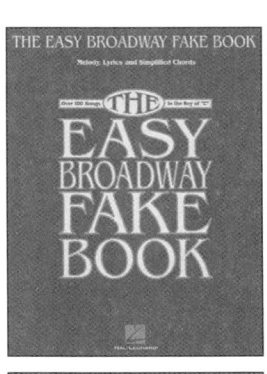

THE EASY SHOW TUNES FAKE BOOK
00240297.................$19.95

THE EASY STANDARDS FAKE BOOK
00240294.................$19.95

THE EASY WORSHIP FAKE BOOK
00240265.................$19.95

THE EASY FORTIES FAKE BOOK
00240252.................$19.95

MORE OF THE EASY FORTIES FAKE BOOK
00240287.................$19.95

THE EASY FIFTIES FAKE BOOK
00240255.................$19.95

MORE OF THE EASY FIFTIES FAKE BOOK
00240288.................$19.95

THE EASY SIXTIES FAKE BOOK
00240253.................$19.95

MORE OF THE EASY SIXTIES FAKE BOOK
00240289.................$19.95

THE EASY SEVENTIES FAKE BOOK
00240256.................$19.95

MORE OF THE EASY SEVENTIES FAKE BOOK
00240290.................$19.95

Prices, contents and availability subject to change without notice.

FOR MORE INFORMATION, SEE YOUR LOCAL MUSIC DEALER, OR WRITE TO:

HAL•LEONARD® CORPORATION
7777 W. BLUEMOUND RD. P.O. BOX 13819 MILWAUKEE, WI 53213

www.halleonard.com

THE ULTIMATE COLLECTION OF FAKE BOOKS

The Real Book – Sixth Edition
Hal Leonard proudly presents the first legitimate and legal editions of these books ever produced. These bestselling titles are mandatory for anyone who plays jazz! Over 400 songs, including: All By Myself • Dream a Little Dream of Me • God Bless the Child • Like Someone in Love • When I Fall in Love • and more.

00240221	Volume 1, C Edition	$29.95
00240224	Volume 1, B♭ Edition	$29.95
00240225	Volume 1, E♭ Edition	$29.95
00240226	Volume 1, BC Edition	$29.95
00240222	Volume 2, C Edition	$29.95
00240227	Volume 2, B♭ Edition	$29.95
00240228	Volume 2, E♭ Edition	$29.95

Best Fake Book Ever – 3rd Edition
More than 1,000 songs from all styles of music, including: All My Loving • At the Hop • Cabaret • Dust in the Wind • Fever • From a Distance • Hello, Dolly! • Hey Jude • King of the Road • Longer • Misty • Route 66 • Sentimental Journey • Somebody • Song Sung Blue • Spinning Wheel • Unchained Melody • We Will Rock You • What a Wonderful World • Wooly Bully • Y.M.C.A. • and more.
00290239 C Edition $49.95
00240083 B♭ Edition $49.95
00240084 E♭ Edition $49.95

Classic Rock Fake Book – 2nd Edition
This fake book is a great compilation of more than 250 terrific songs of the rock era, arranged for piano, voice, guitar and all C instruments. Includes: All Right Now • American Woman • Birthday • Honesty • I Shot the Sheriff • I Want You to Want Me • Imagine • It's Still Rock and Roll to Me • Lay Down Sally • Layla • My Generation • Rock and Roll All Nite • Spinning Wheel • White Room • We Will Rock You • lots more!
00240108 $29.95

Classical Fake Book – 2nd Edition
This unprecedented, amazingly comprehensive reference includes over 850 classical themes and melodies for all classical music lovers. Includes everything from Renaissance music to Vivaldi and Mozart to Mendelssohn. Lyrics in the original language are included when appropriate.
00240044 $34.95

The Disney Fake Book – 2nd Edition
Over 200 of the most beloved songs of all time, including: Be Our Guest • Can You Feel the Love Tonight • Colors of the Wind • Cruella De Vil • Friend Like Me • Heigh-Ho • It's a Small World • Mickey Mouse March • Supercalifragilisticexpialidocious • Under the Sea • When You Wish upon a Star • A Whole New World • Zip-A-Dee-Doo-Dah • and more!
00240039 $27.95

(Disney characters and artwork © Disney Enterprises, Inc.)

The Folksong Fake Book
Over 1,000 folksongs perfect for performers, school teachers, and hobbyists. Includes: Bury Me Not on the Lone Prairie • Clementine • Danny Boy • The Erie Canal • Go, Tell It on the Mountain • Home on the Range • Kumbaya • Michael Row the Boat Ashore • Shenandoah • Simple Gifts • Swing Low, Sweet Chariot • When Johnny Comes Marching Home • Yankee Doodle • and many more.
00240151 $24.95

The Hymn Fake Book
Nearly 1,000 multi-denominational hymns perfect for church musicians or hobbyists: Amazing Grace • Christ the Lord Is Risen Today • For the Beauty of the Earth • It Is Well with My Soul • A Mighty Fortress Is Our God • O for a Thousand Tongues to Sing • Praise to the Lord, the Almighty • Take My Life and Let It Be • What a Friend We Have in Jesus • and hundreds more!
00240145 $24.95

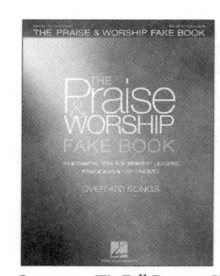

The Praise & Worship Fake Book
400 songs: As the Deer • Better Is One Day • Come, Now Is the Time to Worship • Firm Foundation • Glorify Thy Name • Here I Am to Worship • I Could Sing of Your Love Forever • Lord, I Lift Your Name on High • More Precious Than Silver • Open the Eyes of My Heart • The Power of Your Love • Shine, Jesus, Shine • Trading My Sorrows • We Fall Down • You Are My All in All • and more.
00240234 $34.95

The R&B Fake Book – 2nd Edition
This terrific fake book features 375 classic R&B hits: Baby Love • Best of My Love • Dancing in the Street • Easy • Get Ready • Heatwave • Here and Now • Just Once • Let's Get It On • The Loco-Motion • (You Make Me Feel Like) A Natural Woman • One Sweet Day • Papa Was a Rollin' Stone • Save the Best for Last • September • Sexual Healing • Shop Around • Still • Tell It Like It Is • Up on the Roof • Walk on By • What's Going On • more!
00240107 C Edition $29.95

Ultimate Broadway Fake Book – 4th Edition
More than 700 show-stoppers from over 200 shows! Includes: Ain't Misbehavin' • All I Ask of You • Bewitched • Camelot • Don't Cry for Me Argentina • Edelweiss • I Dreamed a Dream • If I Were a Rich Man • Memory • Oklahoma • Send in the Clowns • What I Did for Love • more.
00240046 $47.50

FOR MORE INFORMATION, SEE YOUR LOCAL MUSIC DEALER, OR WRITE TO:

HAL•LEONARD® CORPORATION
7777 W. BLUEMOUND RD. P.O. BOX 13819 MILWAUKEE, WI 53213

Complete songlists available online at
www.halleonard.com

Prices, contents and availabilty subject to change without notice.

The Ultimate Christmas Fake Book – 5th Edition
This updated edition includes 275 traditional and contemporary Christmas songs: Away in a Manger • The Christmas Song • Deck the Hall • Frosty the Snow Man • A Holly Jolly Christmas • I Heard the Bells on Christmas Day • Jingle Bells • Little Saint Nick • Merry Christmas, Darling • Nuttin' for Christmas • Rudolph the Red-Nosed Reindeer • Silent Night • What Child Is This? • more.
00240045 $24.95

The Ultimate Country Fake Book – 5th Edition
This book includes over 700 of your favorite country hits: Always on My Mind • Boot Scootin' Boogie • Crazy • Down at the Twist and Shout • Forever and Ever, Amen • Friends in Low Places • The Gambler • Jambalaya • King of the Road • Sixteen Tons • There's a Tear in My Beer • Your Cheatin' Heart • and hundreds more.
00240049 $39.95

The Ultimate Fake Book – 4th Edition
Includes over 1,200 hits: Blue Skies • Body and Soul • Endless Love • A Foggy Day • Isn't It Romantic? • Memory • Mona Lisa • Moon River • Operator • Piano Man • Roxanne • Satin Doll • Shout • Small World • Speak Softly, Love • Strawberry Fields Forever • Tears in Heaven • Unforgettable • hundreds more!
00240024 C Edition $49.95
00240026 B♭ Edition $49.95
00240025 E♭ Edition $49.95

The Ultimate Pop/Rock Fake Book – 4th Edition
Over 600 pop standards and contemporary hits, including: All Shook Up • Another One Bites the Dust • Crying • Don't Know Much • Dust in the Wind • Earth Angel • Every Breath You Take • Hero • Hey Jude • Hold My Hand • Imagine • Layla • The Loco-Motion • Oh, Pretty Woman • On Broadway • Spinning Wheel • Stand by Me • Stayin' Alive • Tears in Heaven • True Colors • The Twist • Vision of Love • A Whole New World • Wild Thing • Wooly Bully • Yesterday • more!
00240099 $39.95

Fake Book of the World's Favorite Songs – 4th Edition
Over 700 favorites, including: America the Beautiful • Anchors Aweigh • Battle Hymn of the Republic • Bill Bailey, Won't You Please Come Home • Chopsticks • Für Elise • His Eye Is on the Sparrow • I Wonder Who's Kissing Her Now • Jesu, Joy of Man's Desiring • My Old Kentucky Home • Sidewalks of New York • Take Me Out to the Ball Game • When the Saints Go Marching In • and hundreds more!
00240072 $22.95

0409